PROMOTING THE RULE OF LAW IN POST-CONFLICT STATES

In most post-conflict states, a strong level of legal pluralism is the norm, particularly in regions of Africa and Asia where between 80 and 90 per cent of disputes are resolved through non-state legal mechanisms. The international community, in particular the United Nations, persistently drives the re-establishment of the rule of law in war-torn areas where, traditionally, customary law is prevalent. Laura Grenfell traces the international community's evolving understanding of the rule of law in such regions, and explores the implications of strong legal pluralism for the rule-of-law enterprise. Using the comparative examples of two unique case studies, South Africa and Timor-Leste, *Promoting the Rule of Law* provides insight into the relationship between the rule of law and legal pluralism. Alongside these studies, the book offers a comprehensive introduction to the conceptual framework of the rule of law in the context of approaches taken by the international community.

LAURA GRENFELL is a senior lecturer in law at the University of Adelaide, Australia, where she teaches transitional justice, human rights, comparative constitutional law and public law.

PROMOTING THE RULE OF LAW IN POST-CONFLICT STATES

LAURA GRENFELL

CAMBRIDGE
UNIVERSITY PRESS

CAMBRIDGE
UNIVERSITY PRESS

University Printing House, Cambridge CB2 8BS, United Kingdom

Published in the United States of America by Cambridge University Press, New York

Cambridge University Press is part of the University of Cambridge.

It furthers the University's mission by disseminating knowledge in the pursuit of education, learning and research at the highest international levels of excellence.

www.cambridge.org
Information on this title: www.cambridge.org/9781107026193

First published 2013

Printed by CPI Group (UK) Ltd, Croydon CR0 4YY

A catalogue record for this publication is available from the British Library

Library of Congress Cataloging-in-Publication Data

Grenfell, Laura, 1974–
Promoting the rule of law in post-conflict states / Laura Grenfell.
p. cm.
Includes bibliographical references.
ISBN 978-1-107-02619-3 (Hardback)
1. Rule of law. 2. Legal polycentricity. 3. Postwar reconstruction. I. Title.
K3171.G76 2013
340′.11–dc23
2012044905

ISBN 978-1-107-02619-3 Hardback

Additional resources for this publication at www.cambridge.org/9781107026193

CONTENTS

ACKNOWLEDGMENTS

The genesis of this book lies in my time at Human Rights Watch in September 2001 when I was first inspired to consider the position of Afghan women in attempting to gain access to justice under the complex web of legal systems operating in Afghanistan. This led me to research how other post-conflict, transitional states are promoting the rule of law where there is a situation of strong legal pluralism.

Since that time I have had the privilege of having the doctoral supervision of Professor Hilary Charlesworth at the Regulatory Institutions Network's Centre for International Governance and Justice at the Australian National University and engaging with other members of that Centre, including Professor John Braithwaite, Dr Jeremy Farrall, Dr Gabrielle Simm, Dr Susan Harris Rimmer, Dr Bu Wilson, Aderito Soares and many others. I would also like to thank Professor Kim Rubenstein and Anthony Regan from the Australian National University for their assistance.

During my research in South Africa I gained much from engaging with members of the Faculty of Law at the University of Cape Town, particularly Professors Tom Bennett, Christina Murray, Chuma Himonga, Hugh Corder and Rashida Manjoo. For my research on Timor-Leste I am grateful to those NGOs and UN staff who have given me their valuable time, in particular the staff at the JSMP, The Asia Foundation, Fokupers, Avocats Sans Frontières, and UNDP, as well as the global community of scholars on Timor-Leste.

I would also like to thank my colleagues at the Adelaide Law School. In particular I thank Professors Judith Gardam, Ngaire Naffine and John Williams as well as Margaret Castles, Anne Hewitt and Cornelia Koch. I also thank Bethany Hender and Trang Phan for their editing assistance. I am grateful for the financial support of the Fay Gale Centre for Research on Gender at the University of Adelaide. Thanks also to Professors Martin Krygier and Ann Stewart for their insights in reading an earlier version of this book and to the anonymous reviewers.

Finally I would like to thank my family, particularly Brendan Grigg and Katarina Grenfell, for all their support.

PART I

1

Introduction

While it was at the end of the nineteenth century that English scholar A. V. Dicey proposed his definition of the rule of law,[1] the modern concept of the rule of law only came into fashion in the late twentieth century. Dicey's definition has had much influence on the concept even into the twenty-first century despite criticism that it is little more than a description of English constitutional law as it was at the time.[2] Dicey was adamant that the rule of law could not be found in the French legal system and, in his haste to demonstrate this, misdescribed some core aspects of the French system.[3] Thus, from its beginnings, an edge of Anglo parochialism has marked thinking on the rule of law. Despite this parochialism, the rule of law has enjoyed a meteoric rise in the last decade of the twentieth century and the first decades of the twenty-first; in this period it developed into one of the key concepts promoted by global institutions such as the United Nations (UN) and the World Bank and by development agencies in the West. Although there is recognition that the rule of law is vague and elastic as a concept, it is nevertheless advocated by the international community as a universal good because it conveys a host of principles, such as constitutionalism, that are considered to have been instrumental in strengthening the developed world and its state institutions.

The rule of law has, in particular, become a mantra used by the international community to address the myriad problems facing countries that are labelled 'post-conflict' and 'transitional', terms that will be

[1] Dicey, *An Introduction to the Study*. See Chapter 3, section 2.2 for a brief discussion of Dicey's definition.

[2] Shklar, 'Political Theory and the Rule of Law', 5–6.

[3] Robson, *Justice and Administrative Law*, 345. Robson also criticised Dicey for misinterpreting the English legal system: 343. See also Jennings, *The Law and the Constitution*, 54–60.

used interchangeably in this book.[4] Those states in which the rule of law is dominant, mostly Western states, are at the forefront of arguing that the rule of law must be established in post-conflict and transitional states. They cast the absence of the rule of law as the source of a host of ills, including political and social instability and international human rights violations, and pour large amounts of funding into aid programmes purporting to assist such states build the rule of law.

The modern concept of the rule of law is based on two assumptions: first, the existence of a modern state and, second, that within this modern state paradigm the state is sufficiently strong and organised to enjoy a monopoly of law. In this sense the rule of law is shorthand for the rule of state law; it does not refer to a situation where there is more than one system of law operating and where state law must compete with other forms of law. In regard to these two assumptions, it is safe to assume in the twenty-first century that every geographical region of the world is covered by a modern state in that there are few, if any, people who are not nominally subject to some form of state. However, it is another thing to assume that the prevalence of the modern state paradigm means that every state is successfully able to assert its law over other forms of law that have either preceded the modern state or that, for cultural or religious reasons, enjoy greater observance than state law. In these situations of competing non-state law, it is difficult to discern the rule of state law. This is the case in many post-conflict and transitional countries where the rule of state law is emergent and frail.

The promotion of the rule of state law by the international community has overlooked the fact that in most states there are multiple structures of law and power that operate in parallel with the state. These parallel structures operate to a small degree in many Western states such as Australia where a large number of Aboriginal people continue to observe a system of elders and social norms regardless of whether they live in

[4] In this context 'transitional' refers to countries undergoing a transition to democracy, liberalisation and the rule of law from a period when these ideals were absent or seriously undermined. See section 5 of Chapter 2. The interchangeable use of the two terms is not to imply that all transitional states are post-conflict. Indeed, those states emerging from authoritarianism have many different priorities. South Africa is primarily understood as a transitional state but the term 'post-conflict' is not inapt as conflict between the security forces of the apartheid state and the armed wings of the liberation movements did take place, albeit largely outside of South Africa. While the term 'post-conflict' will be used in this book, it is acknowledged that the term is problematic in characterising many situations, as transitions from conflict to peace are rarely clear-cut.

urban or regional areas.[5] In transitional and post-conflict states where, for various reasons, the state is weak and has limited reach, these parallel power structures are more marked. Both these cases are examples of 'legal pluralism', with a number of legal systems operating in the same geographical space.

Legal pluralism is a description that, unlike the rule of law, is rarely promoted as an ideal. During the height of decolonisation, the concept was marginalised partly because many scholars projected that, in the modern state paradigm, forms of non-state law, such as customary law, would wither and die.[6] Similarly, early literature in the field of 'transitional justice', sometimes labelled 'post-conflict justice', paid scant attention to the existence of non-state forms of law. In the past, scholars and practitioners in this field have generally neglected legal pluralism and overlooked the need to consider the process by which international and state norms are translated into, and reconciled with, norms at the local level.[7] Early transitional justice scholars failed to notice the fact that non-state law is often the type of law with which people are likely to have first and frequent contact, particularly in regions where the modern state paradigm struggles to take hold. Similarly, in the past, international organisations such as the UN and the World Bank have given little consideration to legal pluralism, preferring to focus their rule-of-law efforts on formal, state institutions and state legal systems.

In many regions of the world this sidelining of legal pluralism has been a problem in that it has meant that the experiences of large swathes of the global population have been ignored. The UK's Department for International Development observes that, 'in many developing countries, traditional or customary legal systems account for 80 per cent of total cases'.[8] This means that a sizeable proportion of the world's population relies on non-state law. For example, according to Abdullahi Ahmed An-Na'im, customary law is the most important source of law for the majority of Africans.[9] While there is consensus among legal anthropologists that customary law may not function in post-colonial states in the same way as it did before colonisation, it cannot be said that it has disappeared.[10]

5 Blagg, *Crime, Aboriginality and the Decolonisation of Justice*, 153–8.
6 Könz, 'Legal Development in Developing Countries', 96.
7 Teitel, *Transitional Justice*.
8 UK Department for International Development, *Safety, Security and Accessible Justice*, 58.
9 This statement is based on a survey of 15 African countries undertaken in 1997: An-Na'im, 'Protecting Human Rights in Plural Legal Systems of Africa', 47.
10 Mamdani, *Citizen and Subject*; Chanock, 'The Law Market' 279.

Indeed, in many parts of Africa, customary law is arguably enjoying a resurgence,[11] serving up to 90 per cent of the population.[12] In one post-conflict state, Afghanistan, the Government acknowledges that the official court system is able to resolve only approximately 10 per cent of cases.[13] In another post-conflict state, Timor-Leste, the Government concedes that 'a very substantial proportion of conflicts are addressed through traditional justice mechanisms'.[14] This means that in these regions and post-conflict states, as much as 90 per cent of disputes are resolved either through customary law and other forms of non-state law or are left unresolved.[15] For populations in these regions, their lived experience is one of 'justice in many rooms'.[16] These figures show that legal pluralism is a factor that cannot be ignored by those actors involved in promoting the rule of law.

In 2002 Rama Mani observed that, in the context of rule-of-law reform, customary law had received inadequate consideration.[17] The sheer scale of legal pluralism in parts of Asia and Africa indicates that Mani diagnosed a serious problem. Since the beginning of the twenty-first century a number of organisations have been grappling to understand how legal pluralism interrelates with efforts to establish the rule of law in these regions.[18] In this time practitioners in the field of transitional

[11] Barbara Oomen's observation that there has been a revival in traditional leadership in Africa points to the possibility that customary law is experiencing a resurgence: Oomen, *Chiefs in South Africa*, 27. For greater explanation, see Chapter 5 below.

[12] Chirayath et al., *Customary Law*, 3.

[13] Government of the Islamic Republic of Afghanistan (Ministry of Justice), *Justice for All*, 12.

[14] Democratic Republic of Timor-Leste, *Justice Sector Strategic Plan*, 10.

[15] The calculation of these percentages by international development agencies and the Afghan state assumes that if state institutions were stronger they might be able to resolve a greater percentage of cases. Marc Galanter contests this idea in regard to Western states such as the US: 'Justice in Many Rooms', 1.

[16] Galanter, 'Justice in Many Rooms'. This is not to say that the prevalence of legal pluralism and informal justice mechanisms necessarily reflects popular satisfaction with the ability of these mechanisms to achieve justice.

[17] Mani, *Beyond Retribution*, 80.

[18] From 2004 onwards the United Nations Development Programme (UNDP) has been working on programmes to improve access to justice while in 2002 the World Bank began its Justice for the Poor programme; both programmes have partly focused on customary law because it is the avenue taken by those people who are unable or unwilling to access the formal state legal system. Other organisations have been working more specifically on the interface between customary justice and the rule of law, including the Centre for Humanitarian Dialogue (HD Centre), the US Institute of Peace (USIP) and the International Development Legal Organisation (IDLO): see, e.g., Dexter and Ntahombaye, *The Role of Informal Justice Systems*; Thorne, *Rule of Law through Imperfect Bodies*; Ranheim, *Legal Pluralism in East Timor*; Isser, *Customary Justice*

justice have begun to see the benefits of harnessing legal pluralism to prevent a state relapsing into conflict.[19] In 2011 the UN finally recognised the 'potential of informal mechanisms in strengthening the rule of law' in post-conflict states.[20] At the same time the World Bank, in its *World Development Report 2011: Conflict, Security and Development* (*WDR 2011*), recommended that post-conflict states consider harnessing traditional justice institutions so as to supplement formal justice institutions.[21] On this basis these international organisations have started assisting post-conflict states to build linkages between such informal justice mechanisms and the state legal system so as to give formal recognition of the fact of 'justice in many rooms'. This gradual reconceptualisation of the rule-of-law enterprise is spreading to the field of development more broadly[22] where hybridity in both political and legal orders is also becoming understood as the norm.[23]

This book argues that a significant shift is taking place whereby practitioners and policymakers who promote the rule of law through national initiatives and international programmes in post-conflict and transitional countries are giving some serious consideration to legal pluralism by engaging with its dynamics. It is becoming accepted that policies and programmes that aim to advance the rule of law with insufficient consideration of legal pluralism can have a limited impact in the short term, particularly where large parts of the population have little contact with the state and its institutions. No longer is it the orthodox view that customary law will disappear. International organisations, governments and development agencies are slowly coming to realise that they cannot continue to sidestep customary law if the rule of law is to be established. Furthermore, they are beginning to encourage and support post-conflict states to formally engage with legal pluralism as part of the state-building process.

This book focuses on the state-building process in which post-conflict states draft new constitutions in their aspiration to establish or strengthen the rule of law. Post-conflict states hope that these

and the Rule of Law; Harper, *Customary Justice*; Harper, *Working with Customary Justice Systems*; Ubink and McInerney, *Customary Justice*.

[19] Huyse and Salter, *Traditional Justice and Reconciliation*.

[20] UN Doc S/2011/634 (12 October 2011) Report of the Secretary General on the Rule of Law and Transitional Justice in Conflict and Post-Conflict Societies, [39].

[21] World Bank, *World Development Report 2011*, 155, 257.

[22] See, e.g., Sage et al., *Legal Pluralism and Development*.

[23] Baker and Scheye, 'Multi-layered Justice'.

constitutions will assist in reconciling groups, providing stability and avenues of redress and in avoiding a relapse into conflict. In this context, post-conflict constitutions are seen as tools that can both reflect the post-conflict consensus and also aim to transform it.[24] This book argues that, in situations where legal pluralism is strong, it is critical for post-conflict constitutions to enjoy legitimacy with those parts of the population that live outside the state's reach. One means of achieving this legitimacy is for a post-conflict constitution to articulate the state's relationship with non-state institutions and authorities. Giving constitutional attention to non-state actors can affect the state's efforts to establish the rule of law. Ideally a post-conflict constitution needs to set out guidelines and non-violent spaces through which any tensions between the rule of law and legal pluralism can be incrementally debated and reconciled. Through highlighting the multifaceted interplay between the rule of law and legal pluralism in constitutional contexts, this book aims to promote a stronger understanding of the relationship between the two concepts in post-conflict situations.

In order to reveal the complexity of the relationship between the rule of law and legal pluralism, this book turns its lens on two countries, South Africa and Timor-Leste, known prior to its independence in May 2002 as East Timor. Both states have inscribed the rule of law as a guiding constitutional value for their transitions. Critically, legal pluralism has a strong presence in both countries: large parts of the population of South Africa and Timor-Leste either reject state law or find it inaccessible and rely instead on non-state law that operates in parallel to state law. This non-state, informal law takes many forms and derives from many sources; these are variously described as 'traditional', 'customary', 'indigenous', 'living' or 'local' law and are at times used interchangeably.[25]

South Africa and Timor-Leste are sometimes linked because they are post-colonial states that are undergoing dramatic transitions. Both countries were chosen by the World Bank to feature as models of post-conflict states in its *WDR 2011* because 'these societies have achieved considerable successes in preventing violence from escalating or recovering from

[24] Teitel, 'Transitional Jurisprudence', 2075.

[25] While this book uses a range of these terms, it does acknowledge the debates as to their appropriateness in certain contexts. In common, these terms denote that these forms of law are distinct from state law but the two forms of law are inevitably interconnected to varying degrees.

its aftermath'.[26] In the course of their transitions both states have experimented with similar transitional justice mechanisms, such as truth commissions, and have drafted new constitutions. In 2010 the President of Timor-Leste described to the UN Human Rights Council how South Africa provided a model to his nation in regard to transitional justice and the need to 'compromise on justice'.[27] He said:

> South Africa is a … recent inspiring example of how national leaders and our societies address the complex legacies of the past in creative and dignified ways that do justice to the victims, reconcile the divided communities, heal the wounds, and move on. We are not doing differently in Timor-Leste … moving small steps at a time in building democracy and the rule of law, and a durable peace.[28]

In both states it is possible to argue that the rule of law was lacking prior to their transitions. For example, South Africa's Truth and Reconciliation Commission found that the rule of law was absent in the apartheid state, from 1948 to 1994, and that one of the reasons for the longevity of the apartheid regime was the ruling National Party's superficial adherence to 'rule *by* law', a debased version of the rule of law.[29] Similarly, Indonesia's occupation of East Timor from 1975 to 1999 was the subject of widespread international criticism focusing partly on the regime's lack of respect for the rule of law, in the sense that there were no means of checking the abuse of state power.[30] Thus, in their current transitions, both countries are attempting to establish a new legal order by drafting constitutions and entrenching the rule of law as a guiding norm.

These two countries provide an interesting contrast. They are very different in terms of population, economy, state legal culture and infrastructure. South Africa has a population of about fifty million people, eleven official languages, and it describes itself as a 'rainbow nation' because of its many ethnicities. It is not a typical transitional country in Africa because, in contrast to most of its neighbours, it has a relatively robust economy and long-established state institutions, most of which

[26] They are two of the eleven post-conflict states chosen by the World Bank: *WDR 2011*, 11.

[27] Ramos-Horta, 'Timor-Leste: The Decade of Peace and Prosperity'.

[28] Ibid.

[29] South African Truth and Reconciliation Commission, *Final Report* (1998), Vol 4, Ch. 4, [18, 32].

[30] International Commission of Jurists and the Netherlands Institute of Human Rights, *Indonesia and the Rule of Law*, 61ff; International Commission of Jurists, *Ruler's Law*, 42–50; Amnesty International, *East Timor* (2001) 13.

have continued to play a role in the post-apartheid era.[31] In this respect, South Africa's transition is similar to those of Latin American states from the 1980s onwards. Timor-Leste has a population of just over one million people, with over seventeen languages spoken across the country's thirteen districts. As one of the poorest countries in Asia with nascent and fragile state institutions, it sits at the opposite end of the spectrum of transitional countries to South Africa.[32]

In their other key differences, South Africa and Timor-Leste are useful in examining the relationship between the rule of law and legal pluralism. For example, South Africa had very little outside assistance in executing the stages of its post-apartheid constitutional transformation while Timor-Leste's transition to independence was largely ushered in under UN administration. Critically, South Africa's Constitution recognises legal pluralism and traditional leaders, which means that its state institutions are active in protecting aspects of customary law, while the Constitution of Timor-Leste sidesteps the issue of legal pluralism and Timorese institutions have had a limited formal relationship with non-state forms of law.

This book focuses particularly on one important commonality between South Africa and Timor-Leste in their promotion of the rule of law: they are both currently attempting to enhance access to justice by developing institutional links between informal customary mechanisms and state law though introducing laws to link the two systems. In South Africa such linkage laws have a long colonial history and today the process of transforming existing linkage laws is being guided by South Africa's Constitution whereas in Timor-Leste the first ever linkage law is being produced through UN assistance. This book shows that for both post-conflict states, these linkage laws pose a myriad of challenges and cannot be considered a quick fix. The geographical and institutional differences and commonalities between South Africa and Timor-Leste provide a window into the different dynamics produced by the relationship between the rule of law and legal pluralism in transitional and post-conflict countries.

The book is divided into three parts. Part I examines the globalised and conceptual relationship between the rule of law and legal pluralism and it

[31] For a recent survey of South Africa's economy, see Organisation of Economic Cooperation and Development, *Economic Assessment of South Africa 2008.*

[32] Timor-Leste is the third lowest ranked country in the East-Asia and Pacific region according to the UNDP Human Development Index 2011.

sets the stage for the analysis that follows in Parts II and III. This chapter has introduced the two concepts of the rule of law and legal pluralism. It has briefly outlined the rise of the concept of the rule of law, sketched the neglect and scale of legal pluralism and observed a shift in international understanding of the two concepts. Chapter 2 traces how the two concepts have been understood in the key historical periods that have shaped the post-Cold War era and the contemporary international system. It focuses particularly on discourses that have dominated international institutions such as the UN and the World Bank in the 1990s. In this, it looks at how and why these institutions are promoting the rule of law while legal pluralism has been largely sidelined. It examines what interests are served by the promotion of the rule of law and questions the role played by the rule of law in the lives of the poor and vulnerable sections of society. Chapter 3 examines the relationship between the two concepts in order to gain a deeper understanding of their points of intersection. It sets out the main tenets of each concept and maps how they come into contact in transitional and post-conflict states. It argues that aspects that make the two concepts appear otherwise incompatible are transformed when they are placed alongside each other in post-conflict constitutional frameworks.

Parts II and III explore the concrete dynamics of the relationship between the rule of law and legal pluralism within the context of post-conflict state constitutions. Part II outlines these dynamics in relation to South Africa's constitutional transition from apartheid while Part III analyses this relationship in relation to Timor-Leste and its independence Constitution. Both parts follow two lines of inquiry: first, how the two concepts were negotiated in the periods leading up to, and during, the constitution-drafting process; and, second, the practical implications of these constitutional arrangements for the linkage laws being introduced by the Governments of South Africa and Timor-Leste.

Part II examines South Africa's constitutional negotiations in the 1990s. It argues that South Africa inscribed the rule of law into its Constitution, despite the concept's historical baggage, partly out of a desire to establish the legitimacy of the post-apartheid legal order within the international community. At the same time, it shows that the constitutional entrenchment of legal pluralism resulted from an attempt to secure internal legitimacy for the new legal order by negotiating with traditional leaders.

Part II then analyses the practical implications of these constitutional arrangements in South Africa, which is attempting to introduce a linkage law that will transform customary courts in line with the Constitution. It explores whether these constitutional arrangements that protect customary law and guarantee the continuing operation of customary courts are producing a patchwork rule of law. It argues that South Africa's legal institutions are actively compromising the rule of law in order to protect legal pluralism, to insulate customary law from Western values and to create cheap justice. In particular it traces how these developments affect the most vulnerable sections of society including women who live and work mostly in the private sphere outside the reach of the rule of law.

Part III explores what influences were brought to bear on the drafting of Timor-Leste's first ever Constitution which repeatedly invokes the rule of law. The constitutional drafting process was stymied by the dominance of one political party whose leaders spent their time in exile in lusophone states. These leaders were uninterested in either negotiating a political compromise with other actors or conducting proper consultations with the population. Drawing largely on lusophone constitutions as well as the *Universal Declaration of Human Rights*, the Constitution is replete with international norms and largely devoid of norms drawing from local customary law despite the fact that such law addresses a substantial proportion of conflicts. This disparate nature of the Constitution and the lived experience of the population have led to the questioning of the Constitution's social and moral legitimacy in setting the ground rules of the state.

Part III then considers the implications of such a Constitution for the state in its endeavour to establish Timor-Leste's legal framework and its formal rule-of-law institutions. It argues that the result during the state's first decade of independence has been that these institutions are fragile in times of crisis: they fail to fulfil their aims of providing a control on the Executive's use of power and offering a non-violent space in which any tensions can be resolved. The chapter surveys the divergent government policies in this first decade in relation to the rule of law and legal pluralism. The initial absence of a state policy on legal pluralism in the first half of the decade meant that mostly local NGOs were left to find ways to improve access to justice for vulnerable groups. While this allowed for the emergence of some grass roots initiatives, it has also led to a fragmented approach. The successor Government adopted a state policy of recognising legal pluralism but it has struggled to translate this policy into law despite considerable assistance from the international community. Chapter 8 contains concluding remarks.

I do not aim in this book to undermine programmes that seek to promote the rule of law or to assert that they represent the wrong path for transitional and post-conflict states. Although I am critical of those state-centric approaches to the rule of law that have dismissed legal pluralism as either a distraction or a needless obstruction, my focus is undeniably state-centric in itself as I examine how constitutional frameworks can assist in, or detract from, building the rule of law where legal pluralism is strong. Where they are successful, constitutional frameworks can operate both to reflect and construct a state's worldview, culture, and identity, much in the same way that legal systems do, whether they be customary, religious or secular legal systems. Post-conflict states entrench the rule of law into their constitutional frameworks in the hope of shoring up international legitimacy but also in the hope of building a culture that respects the rule of law, and, over time, becomes fused with other prevailing and compatible local legal cultures. This book investigates the complex relationship between legal pluralism and the rule of law within this constitutional context.

2

A globalised view of the rule of law and legal pluralism

This book contends that the benefits and drawbacks of promoting the rule of law in post-conflict states become more apparent upon consideration of the relationship between the rule of law and legal pluralism at a global level. This relationship has varied in marked ways through the major global historical shifts in modern times: the rise of the modern Westphalian state, colonialism and dispossession, decolonisation and development, the Cold War and post-Cold War transformations. In all these shifts the rule of law has, from one angle, endured as a beacon, variously symbolising civilisation, development, capitalism and Western democracy. At the same time, legal pluralism has presented a challenge to those institutions that promote a rule-of-law orthodoxy because its existence contests the idea that the state has a monopoly over law. At the ground level, legal pluralism has throughout these shifts played an important role in enabling access to justice and dispute resolution.

Most transitional, post-conflict states are in the process of decolonisation as well as post-Cold War transformation and, almost without exception, they need economic development to lift their populations out of poverty. Indeed, colonialism, underdevelopment and Cold War machinations have been major contributors to the causes of conflict and they have made transitional states vulnerable to a host of global pressures. In this post-conflict equation, the rule of law is perceived as an important norm; for example, the UN invokes it as something of a panacea for post-conflict states. In contrast, legal pluralism is characterised in ambivalent terms by those states and international organisations that enjoy global hegemony. This perception of legal pluralism is now shifting, as the past decade has shown that the concept is becoming more relevant to the work of the UN and international financial institutions (IFIs), as well as other key players, in the context of developing and post-conflict countries.

This chapter argues that in the twenty-first century the rule of law is the dominant paradigm for state governance in the international arena and that for certain sections of society this dominance has resulted in limitations and trade-offs in accessing justice. However, the dynamics of the relationship between the rule of law and legal pluralism are in constant flux as more attention is being given to the existence of legal pluralism in post-conflict states such as Timor-Leste and South Africa.

This chapter traces the international community's evolving understanding of the rule of law, legal pluralism and the post-conflict context through highlighting some of the paradigmatic shifts undergone by leading actors in the field of post-conflict development. This provides a lens through which we can examine the promotion of the rule of law in South Africa and Timor-Leste later in this book.

1. Colonialism and the rise of international law

While the rule of law did not figure overtly as part of the colonial project in the nineteenth century, legal pluralism played a major role, particularly in British colonies such as South Africa.[1] For example, in British Africa, legal pluralism was manifested in the form of official parallel legal systems of African customary law and imported law.[2] Chanock observes: 'The claim to have brought a civilizing law and order has been an important part of the justification of colonialism.'[3] The imported 'civilising law' constituted one part of the dual mandate, which comprised civilisation and commerce. Customary law was subjected to the test of Western civilised values through repugnancy clauses, worded variously in British colonies as imposing limits based on 'natural justice', 'good conscience', or 'civilisation'.[4] Practices such as polygamy and slavery were characterised as 'uncivilised' and therefore unacceptable. Thus,

[1] Van Niekerk, 'Legal Pluralism', Ch. 1; Bennett, *Customary Law in South Africa*, 34–41; Hahlo and Kahn, *The Union of South Africa*, 319–34.

[2] For a broad analysis of legal pluralism as a colonial project, see Benton, *Law and Colonial Cultures*.

[3] Chanock, 'The Law Market', 280.

[4] Hooker, *Legal Pluralism*, 130. In French colonies, customary law could not be applied if it was repugnant to 'public order and morality'; similarly in Portuguese colonies in Africa custom was applied to indigenous people so long as it was not 'contrary to public order, that is, the principles of humanity, the fundamental principles of morality or to free exercise of sovereignty'. See respectively Verhelst, *Safeguarding African Customary Law*, iii–iv; Moreira, 'Portuguese Territories in Africa', 229–30. See also Harvey, *The Legal System in East Africa*, 522–4.

while the British colonial policy of legal pluralism formally allowed parts of customary law to continue, customary law was always subservient to imported law and both its substance and procedure could be declared repugnant to those vague Western moral standards supposedly representing civilisation.[5] Furthermore, in some British colonies, customary law was subjected to codification so as to mould customary law into a Western conception of rule-centred law.[6]

In this context, law was used to secure state goals and exercise state power but there were few mechanisms by which citizens could use law in defence of their rights.[7] Below the highest courts, the administration of justice in British Africa required no separation of powers between the executive and the judiciary.[8] In sum, Chanock writes, the colonial period can be characterised as 'bureaucratisation without the rule of law'.[9] Rule *by* law is more apt a description than rule of law, as law provided few means to limit the abuse of state power.

While the rule of law was not a concept much deployed in the colonial era, the concept of civilisation marked legal thought and language at the height of colonialism in the nineteenth century. As a concept, civilisation was used particularly by positivists as a means of distinguishing between European and non-European states, especially in regard to law and sovereignty.[10] The argument was that only unique and civilised institutions created law, and for a state to be a member of international society and to enjoy and assert sovereignty, it was necessary that it possess such institutions.[11] The positivist strategy was to declare that there was no law in certain non-European regions in the sense of law which flowed from sovereign command in written form. Indeed, even today, customary law is still characterised by some as not being law because it does not have the same qualities as 'modern law'.[12] John Austin, a legal philosopher at the forefront of nineteenth

[5] Note that some contemporary African scholars discuss the repugnancy clause as an example of the rule of law: Okoye, 'Sociopolitical Dynamics in Africa', 76. This is possibly because the concept of 'natural justice' purports to be universal.

[6] See, e.g., the *Natal Code, Law 19 of 1891.*

[7] Chanock, 'The Law Market', 304.

[8] Morris and Read, *Indirect Rule and the Search for Justice*, 295ff.

[9] Chanock, 'The Law Market', 305.

[10] Anghie, *The Making of International Law*, Ch. 2. See also Koskenniemi, *The Gentle Civilizer of Nations*, Ch. 2.

[11] Anghie, *The Making of International Law*, 56.

[12] See Explanation of Australia's vote against the UN General Assembly adoption of the *UN Declaration on the Rights on Indigenous Peoples* by the Hon. Robert Hill Ambassador and

century positivism, argued that customary law was not a proper source of law and described it as 'merely a rule of positive morality'.[13] Indirectly this gave legitimacy to the colonial project, justifying European assertions of sovereignty over the 'uncivilised' non-European world. Through positivism, law came to be conceived as deriving its authority from the state.

The positivist emphasis on law as that flowing from sovereign command posed a conundrum for the proponents of international law in this era: it had to be defended from arguments that it was not law at all because it flowed from custom between states. Thus, much effort was put into refashioning international law as a doctrinal project that embodied the laws of civilised society and civilised states. As Martti Koskenniemi argues, international law arose in the late nineteenth century 'to map the breakdown of the traditional world ... into Sovereign states'.[14] In other words, its mission was to cement a connection between civilisation and a particular political form, Western statehood, sometimes referred to as the Westphalian state.

In the twenty-first century, the language of civilised states continues to be used in international law and diplomacy. For example, Article 38(1) of the *Statute of the International Court of Justice* provides that the International Court of Justice can be guided by general principles of law that are recognised by 'civilised nations'. In 1991 Nelson Mandela described apartheid as 'the antithesis of civilised values' and observed that international human rights standards 'provided the legal and moral inspiration for the [anti-apartheid] struggle'.[15] The same language also figures in the sphere of diplomacy. For example, in 2003 the Dutch Foreign Minister stated: 'If a civilised society wants to remain civilised, it has no alternative but to try and uphold the rule of law and other general human rights principles.'[16] Thus we see the link between the nineteenth-century concept of civilisation with the concept of the rule of law, which came to the fore in the twentieth century. Both concepts attempt to invoke

Permanent Representative of Australia to the United Nations, UN Doc A/61/PV.107 (13 September 2007), discussed in section 5.2 of this chapter.

13 Austin, *The Province of Jurisprudence Determined*, 31.

14 Koskenniemi, 'The Fate of Public International Law', 24.

15 Quoted in Klug, 'Hybrid(ity) Rules', 297–8.

16 Minister of Foreign Affairs of the Kingdom of the Netherlands, 'Human Rights and Terrorism' (speech delivered at the Seminar on Human Rights and Terrorism, The Hague, 18 September 2003).

something that transcends all culture; they are projected as representing (legal) rationality, the sovereign Westphalian state, and the antithesis of the 'positive morality' of custom.

2. Law and development during decolonisation and the Cold War era

After World War II, the relationship between the rule of law and legal pluralism was placed under new pressure by the waves of political, economic, social and cultural change produced by decolonisation, development and the Cold War. The Cold War gave birth to a rhetoric from the West that centred largely on the rule of law. The process of decolonisation highlighted the challenge of legal pluralism but the movements for modernisation and development attempted to negate legal pluralism by pushing for uniform and predictable laws. This section traces the dynamics of these factors in this period, which stretches from 1945 until the fall of the Berlin Wall in 1989.

During the early days of the Cold War, the United States' elite and policy makers identified the rule of law as a feature that distinguished the capitalist West from the Communist states. In this framework the rule of law was portrayed by the US administration as securing the legal structures and institutions that protected individual rights and freedoms from state intervention. In its Cold War campaign the US linked the rule of law to democracy and attempted to export its legal institutions to the developing world, particularly in Latin America, under the rubric of the rule of law. Members of the legal profession often carried out the export of the rule of law with missionary zeal. Take for example the speech of Ross Malone, a President of the American Bar Association, delivered in the late 1950s:

> The rule of law is a concept which has existed since Moses received the Ten Commandments upon Mount Sinai. It has survived autocracy, anarchy, tyranny and demagoguery and has come to its highest state of development in the democracy of the twentieth century. And what is the role of lawyers in the Rule of Law? Lawyers are the handmaidens of justice ... the technicians of democracy.[17]

Lawyers were at the forefront of this mission as attempts were made to reform legal education and the legal profession in Latin America as well

[17] Malone, 'Promoting the Rule of Law', 4.

as Asia and Africa.[18] These lawyers hoped that legal reforms would filter down to create a cultural shift towards a respect for state institutions and state law.

The rule of law was criticised by the Communist East as buttressing capitalism and serving class exploitation by the property-owning bourgeoisie.[19] The response of the West was that the Communist bloc took an instrumentalist approach to law whereby the law was employed as an instrument of the state and, in particular, the ruling party. However, the US rhetoric of the rule of law did not account for the complexity of American legal thought at the time, which, since the 1930s, was in the thrall of legal realism and a form of instrumentalism. American legal realism was a response to legal formalism in that it emphasised the gap between 'law on the books' and 'law in action' and it introduced sociological elements focusing on the process of law. Legal realism tended to shift the focus from legal rules to legal process. According to James Gardner, this legal realism bred a 'rule-sceptical approach', where scepticism was shown toward formal rules of law. Law was portrayed as 'an instrument for achieving policy and social engineering ends' and hence, in his view, it was unsurprising when dictators in Latin America used the law in a pragmatic and instrumental fashion to serve their own ends.[20] In Gardner's opinion, this 'rule-sceptical approach' undermined the entire US mission of exporting the rule of law and other legal institutions to Latin America.

While the focus of the US' rule of law efforts lay primarily in Latin America, other Western states, such as Britain, took the lead in Africa to assist decolonising states to establish the rule of law in the Westphalian state. In Africa, however, the urgent question was the role of law and moreover, the question of *which law?* Legal pluralism was at the forefront of this question as leaders of newly independent countries negotiated a panoply of challenges: the need for legitimate authority, the call for modernisation and development, the desire for centralised power, and the gap between 'law on the books' and 'law in action'. The two sides of the Cold War vied with each other to influence this

[18] Gardner, *Legal Imperialism and Foreign Aid in Latin America*, 6–8. An example of such legal reform work in Africa is in the following: Judicial Advisers' Conference, Uganda 1953, *Native Courts and Native Customary Law in Africa.*

[19] Krygier, 'Marxism and the Rule of Law', 633–63.

[20] Gardner, *Legal Imperialism and Foreign Aid in Latin America*, 15.

time of transition in Africa and legal practitioners were the vanguard of the cultural aspects of this war.[21]

Under the rubric of the 'law and development movement' (LADM), a group of mostly Western scholars attempted to respond to, and theorise, the challenges faced by the decolonising and developing world. Members of the movement received substantial financial support from the Ford Foundation and the US Agency for International Development (USAID) for projects that aimed to assist Third World countries to establish legal institutions considered essential to developing a modern nation.[22] In its crudest form, this assistance meant exporting US statutes to replace colonial or indigenous law, all in the name of development.

The LADM was influenced by the cross-disciplinary work of Max Weber on legitimate authority and the development of markets.[23] Weber identified three types of legitimate authority: (1) legal authority; (2) traditional authority; and (3) charismatic authority. He characterised the first type as 'rational' because it is based on an impersonal order of formal legality where there is a consistent system of abstract, precise and universal rules and the possibility of appeal. Administrative decisions and rules are formulated in writing: this means that bureaucracy plays a 'crucial role ... Indeed, without it capitalistic production could not continue.'[24] The second type, traditional authority, is based on personal loyalty. While it is hinged on precedent (i.e. tradition), it lacks formal principles and it privileges 'principles of substantive ethical common sense'.[25] Overall, Weber characterised this type of authority as non-rational, arbitrary, nepotistic, particularistic and prone to corruption. Moreover, he argued that it obstructs the 'development of markets ...

[21] The politicisation of the rule of law can be seen in the conference reports and declarations of the International Commission of Jurists (ICJ). During the early years of the Cold War, the ICJ wanted to promote the rule of law at the international level by establishing a universal formulation of the concept. For this purpose, from 1955 to 1965 the ICJ held conferences in every region of the world. To a very formal, sparse and Western formulation of the rule of law in the *Act of Athens* (1955), the *Declaration of Delhi* (1959) added the need to 'advance the civil and political rights of the individual ... [and] establish social, economic, educational and cultural conditions'. In 1961 the *Law of Lagos* added that: 'all Governments should adhere to the principle of democratic representation in their Legislatures'. The development of the ICJ's formulations shows the dynamics of global and regional politics. See, e.g., ICJ, *African Conference on the Rule of Law, A Report*.

[22] See Merryman, 'Comparative Law and Social Change', 457–9.

[23] Weber, *The Theory of Social and Economic Organization*. See Trubek, 'Toward a Theory of Law', 1; Trubek, 'Max Weber on Law and the Rise of Capitalism', 720; Galanter, 'The Modernization of Law', Ch. 11.

[24] Weber, *The Theory of Social and Economic Organization*, 338. [25] Ibid., 342.

and capitalism'.[26] The third type, charismatic authority, is revolutionary in nature and lacks even the minimal predictability offered by traditional authority. This authority relies neither on formal principles, such as a constitution or statutes, nor on a traditional position derived by ancestry. Weber writes: '[f]rom the point of view of rational economic activity, charisma is a typical anti-economic force'.[27]

The first type of authority in Weber's work, 'legal authority', can be identified as the rule of law. For Weber, 'legal authority' plays a crucial role in economic growth and political development. This is because procedurally the system is highly predictable and substantively it allows freedom of contract. The other two types of authority, which figured among the rank of African leaders in the 1960s, are portrayed as obstructive to the goal of development. Traditional and charismatic authority impliedly cause and reflect underdevelopment. Whereas the US Cold War rhetoric on the rule of law may have smacked of propaganda to scholars, Weber's work provided an apparently objective sociological and economic foundation on which to support the project of promoting the rule of law and, in particular, the modernisation of legal systems. Thus the LADM broadly advocated the modernisation of law and impliedly encouraged and relied on the centralisation of state power in the developing world, otherwise known as the Westphalian state.[28] The transplantation of legal institutions from the Western world was believed to hasten the process of development in the developing world.[29]

The LADM's promotion of the rule of law in the developing world usually came at the expense of legal pluralism, in particular, local, traditional and indigenous legal systems, which faced erosion and abolition by the state. This is because uniform laws are generally unable to accommodate a diversity of local norms and local forms of accountability. To some scholars, the demise of indigenous legal systems was inevitable and no great loss.[30] In the late 1960s, only a few LADM scholars, such as Marc Galanter, were ambivalent about the notion that moving

[26] Ibid., 354. [27] Ibid., 362.

[28] This faith in the state and rule of law was brought together with legal realism's aggressive approach of social engineering and was dubbed 'liberal legalism': Trubek, 'Law and Development', 8443.

[29] A direct response to modernisation theory was dependency theory, which was sceptical regarding the potency of law reform and emphasised the complexity of relationships between developing and developed countries on an economic, social and political level: see Davis and Trebilcock, 'Legal Reforms and Development', 21–36.

[30] Könz, 'Legal Development in Developing Countries', 96.

towards modern legal systems was 'necessarily a good thing per se'.[31] Galanter noted that the process would not enrich indigenous law as 'modern law includes techniques for eroding away and suppressing local law by official law ... [i]t tolerates no rivals'.[32] He believed that the problem with modernising the law was that it could make law unresponsive to the concerns and interests of diverse groups at the local level. At the same time, however, Galanter articulated a belief, which can be read between the lines of Weber's work, that the modernisation process was an 'irreversible' tide that would sweep societies world-wide.[33] Mohan Gopalan Gopal observes that the assumptions about the evolutionary processes of development of legal systems inherent in Weber's work 'reinforced the erosion of traditional legal systems' and significantly contributed to 'the crisis of law in developing countries as countries and societies were induced to move from traditional to rational legal systems'.[34]

In Africa the process of modernising the law had begun under colonial rule but this intensified in the 1950s with the project of restating customary laws, spearheaded by London University's School of Oriental and African Studies. Decolonisation and the pressures for development gave urgency to the question of how newly independent African governments could re-organise their legal systems in order to modernise and to shake off the discriminatory laws imposed by colonial regimes. During British colonial rule, for example, legal pluralism had been used to impose different laws through a system of parallel laws that applied on the basis of race and ethnicity. By the mid 1950s there was some consensus among former British African colonies that both common law and customary law should continue but it was debated whether they should be integrated into a single system so as to apply to all equally.[35] Given the rupture of colonialism, it was asserted by some that customary law could not be seen as a simple continuation of pre-colonial law but was in fact a debased version.[36] An argument made in favour of integration was that

[31] Galanter, 'The Modernization of Law', 164. [32] Ibid., 163–4. [33] Ibid., 163.

[34] Gopal, 'Law and Development', 236. Gopal argues that for law and development to move forward, it needs a new vision that is essentially pluralistic and 'resists a universalist analytical framework': 237.

[35] Judicial Advisers' Conference, Uganda 1953, *Native Courts and Native Customary Law in Africa*. Note that there were many degrees of integration: see Mamdani, *Citizen and Subject*, Ch. 4.

[36] See Mamdani, *Citizen and Subject*, 128. See also Chanock, 'The Law Market'.

the development of 'native law' could be guided in the direction of English law.[37] Many of the other arguments made for integration related to the rule of law: the need for consistency and legal certainty, the right of appeal, and a separation of powers. Legal pluralism in Africa posed a raft of technical quandaries as well as the danger of encouraging tribalism, which ran counter to the interests of the nation-state. Thus the response to legal pluralism in post-independence Africa veered towards attempting to subordinate indigenous law and abolish legal pluralism in the name of the rule of law. Indeed, Manfred Hinz observes the historical continuity in this Western attitude to legal pluralism when he comments on the 'generations of missionaries, anthropologists and lawyers, whose first interest was to force African customary law into the Procrustean bed of either the bible, civilisation or a western paradigm of Rule of Law'.[38]

In the mid 1970s the LADM lost steam: financial support for the US legal assistance programmes waned after David Trubek and Marc Galanter published a strong critique of the LADM, arguing that it had failed to assist developing countries. They attributed this failure partly to the fact that LADM programmes and literature had stressed the centrality of the state and placed the state as 'the primary agent of social control and change'.[39] In particular, the movement had paid insufficient attention to legal pluralism: '[the LADM] showed little interest in nonstate forms of legal or other social ordering; indeed, one detects a subtle bias against informal legal systems and customary law'.[40] Trubek and Galanter argued that liberal legalism's model of law was ethnocentric in that it overlooked the fact that in the developing world the grip of local law is far stronger than the law of the state.[41] It appears from this that the demise of the LADM can be traced partly to its failure to examine or understand the dynamics of the relationship between legal pluralism and the rule of law in the developing world. However, coming little more than a decade after the beginning of LADM, this critique was arguably hasty and it shows that at that time Trubek and Galanter may have had a limited understanding of the *long-term* nature of the project of building the rule of law.

[37] See, e.g., Mamdani, *Citizen and Subject*, 118; Chanock, 'The Law Market'; Snyder, 'Colonialism and Legal Form', 49.

[38] Hinz quoted in Menski, *Comparative Law in a Global Context*, 391.

[39] Trubek and Galanter, 'Scholars in Self-Estrangement', 1079. [40] Ibid.

[41] Ibid., 1080.

The demise of the modernisation paradigm led to a renewed interest in legal pluralism in the late 1970s and 1980s, and, in particular, legal anthropologists championed 'deep legal pluralism', the situation where the state does not recognise customary law.[42] According to Brian Tamanaha, the attitude among many scholars of this period was the mantra of 'folk law good' and 'state law bad'.[43] However, throughout this period legal pluralism remained located on the sidelines of mainstream legal thought.

Parallel to this in the 1970s and 1980s was the rise in popularity of alternative dispute resolution (ADR) in the US, which was part of a larger movement interested in the reform of national legal systems in order to enhance access to justice for the poor and vulnerable sections of society. Access to justice was usually equated with access to courts; ADR showed that formal courts were not always necessary for the resolution of disputes. In many developing and post-conflict states in Asia and Africa, some convergence presumably took place between traditional, indigenous dispute resolution and ADR given that conciliatory solutions have long been considered part of the traditions in these regions.[44]

3. Law and development in the post-Cold War era

The end of the Cold War in 1989 heralded a host of transitions and a revived interest in the rule of law as a tool of development. In this era the main focus was the transition of former Communist states to democracy and the free market. The rule of law was portrayed as capable of facilitating these two types of transition; it was 'advanced in the name of both principles and profits'.[45] Trubek has dubbed the 1990s as 'the R[ule]O[f]L[aw] era', a time when the rule of law 'really became big business'.[46] In this period the World Bank reportedly supported 330 rule-of-law projects[47] at a cost, according to Trubek, of about three billion US dollars.[48] Thus from the early 1990s when South Africa began its transition, to the early 2000s, when East Timor's transition began, the rule of

42 For an elaboration of what is meant by the term 'deep legal pluralism', see Chapter 3, section 1.1.
43 Tamanaha, 'The Lessons of Law-and-Development Studies', 481.
44 South African Law Commission, *Alternative Dispute Resolution*, 15.
45 Carothers, 'The Rule of Law Revival', 95.
46 Trubek, 'The Rule of Law in Development Assistance', 81–2.
47 The World Bank, *Legal Vice Presidency, Legal and Judicial Reform Observations*, 14.
48 Trubek, 'The Rule of Law in Development Assistance', 74.

law lay at the centre of promoting democracy and the free market. During this time of fervour, legal pluralism still figured as a marginal consideration, as the following sections show.

3.1 *Profit: the free market and development*

While IFIs such as the World Bank were uninterested in the work of the LADM in the 1960s, they became some of the main drivers of the movement's new manifestation. This interest in the rule of law comes from the twin beliefs that the rule of law has a 'universal quality' that makes it stand apart 'as a nonideological, even technical, solution'[49] and that the free market needs modern state legal institutions in order to encourage investment and economic development. The World Bank was influenced by the 'New Institutional Economics' of economists such as Douglass North, which focuses on legal institutions that are conducive to economic growth.[50] Drawing on this economic analysis, the World Bank supported programmes designed to boost and reform formal systems of contract law and private property, regimes for bankruptcy, capital investment and taxation, as well as functioning criminal justice systems to ensure law and order and to attract foreign investment. Thus the law promoted by this neo-liberal understanding of the rule of law is chiefly private law, which is depicted as neutral and devoid of any distributional effect. This private law is also represented as universally applicable and hence IFIs have pushed for the harmonisation of national laws based on international 'best practice'.[51]

Essential to this formalist conception of the rule of law is an independent judiciary capable of protecting property and enforcing contracts.[52] Legal predictability and enforceability are foremost so as to create a stable legal environment for the free market.[53] In this era the World Bank's

[49] Carothers, 'The Rule of Law Revival', 99.

[50] North, *Institutions*. Note that from around 1997, IFIs and the development community generally began to use the term 'good governance' to refer to a number of aspirations for the functioning of governing including transparency, accountability, participation and the rule of law. For a sophisticated analysis of the World Bank's shift to using the rule of law in the field of development, see Pahuja, *Decolonising International Law*, Ch. 5.

[51] Pistor, 'The Standardisation of Law', 97. For a critique of attempts to impose legal uniformity, see Glenn, 'Sustainable Diversity in Law'.

[52] Shihata, *The World Bank in a Changing World*, 225–30; The World Bank, *Legal Vice Presidency, Legal and Judicial Reform Observations*, 5.

[53] The World Bank, *Legal Vice Presidency, Legal and Judicial Reform Observations*, 19.

formulation of the rule of law is state-centric in nature and top-down. While constitutions are depicted as drivers of development, non-state actors such as civil society organisations are only considered relevant to the development agenda in relation to their potential impact on state institutions, such as the judicial system.[54]

Legal pluralism figures on the margins of this neo-liberal framework. Most frequently, international development bodies working within this framework have neglected customary legal systems. For example, while the World Bank was active in promoting the reform of legal systems in the 1990s, its programme did not involve explicit consideration of the dynamics of customary law even in countries where such law is predominant. In 2005 Leila Chirayath et al. observed:

> Of the 78 assessments of legal and justice systems undertaken by the [World] Bank since 1994, many mention the prevalence of traditional justice in the countries looked at, but *none* explore the systems in detail or examine links between local level systems and state regimes.[55]

Following a Weberian logic, IFIs and international development agencies (IDAs) have often considered customary legal systems in negative terms, as inefficient, 'backward' and lacking in rationality and legal authority. Customary legal systems are portrayed as overly complex, inaccessible to foreigners, discriminatory towards women and outsiders, and as hindering the project of 'greater integration into the world economy'. In this regard, Thomas Carothers argues that rule-of-law aid providers are responsible for a form of Western imperialism. He asserts:

> They do not have much interest in non-Western forms of law, in traditional systems of justice, or, in the case of some American rule-of-law experts, even in civil law. ... Aid providers know what endpoint they would like to help countries achieve – the Western-style, rule-oriented systems they know from their own countries.[56]

The turn of the twenty-first century shows a shift in this approach. The failure of neo-liberal policies to deliver promised growth has led to what David Kennedy has labelled 'chastened neoliberalism'.[57] This is illustrated by the inclusion in the World Bank's programmes of measures to limit market excess, incorporate social aspects such as social, economic

[54] Ibid., 39. [55] Chirayath et al., *Customary Law and Policy Reform*, 3.
[56] Carothers, 'The Problem of Knowledge', 15, 19, 21.
[57] Kennedy, 'The "Rule of Law"', 150.

and cultural rights, and to provide direct relief to the poor.[58] The concept of the rule of law remains central to this new approach despite the fact that some leading scholars question the causal link between the rule of law and development, citing the cases of China and Japan where rapid economic development has taken place without Western-style rule of law.[59] However, the World Bank's understanding of the concept appears to have changed from one of formalism towards a more substantive understanding.[60] This shift is seen in the following World Bank statement:

> It is asserted that *formalist* rule of law, which stresses institutionalised legal mechanisms and absolute autonomy from politics, is a necessity for economic development. But attempts to transplant *formalist* rule of law to developing and/or democratising countries could actually be counter-productive for economic, institutional, and political development, especially when *informal mechanisms* would be more effective and efficient.[61]

This statement indicates the World Bank's newfound interest in the role of informal norms and mechanisms in improving economic efficiency and growth.

From 2002 onwards the World Bank has recognised that in some contexts it may be beneficial for informal norms and mechanisms to supplement, and sometimes supplant, formal law.[62] For example, the

[58] Trubek and Santos, 'Emergence of a New Critical Approach', 8. This change has been heralded by the World Bank's Comprehensive Development Framework which was initiated by Wolfensohn, *A Comprehensive Development Framework.*

[59] Carothers, 'The Problem of Knowledge', Ch. 2; Upham, 'Mythmaking in the Rule-of-Law Orthodoxy', 75. See also Davis, 'What Can the Rule of Law Variable Tell?', 141. See generally Kennedy, 'Laws and Developments', 17.

[60] Santos describes the World Bank's formulation of the rule of law as currently something of a 'hodge-podge' because some parts of the Bank are continuing to espouse formalist understandings of the rule of law while other parts are using more substantive approaches to the rule of law based on the work of Amartya Sen. Santos points out that the World Bank is not a monolithic institution and hence it is difficult to pin down one single approach. Santos, 'The World Bank's Uses of the "Rule of Law"', 253.

[61] World Bank, Legal Institutions of a Global Economy Homepage cited in Trubek, 'The Rule of Law in Development Assistance', 91 (emphasis added).

[62] In 2002 the World Bank began its Justice for the Poor (J4P) programme in Indonesia, followed by programmes in Cambodia, Sierra Leone, Kenya, Rwanda and in mid 2008 in Vanuatu and Timor-Leste. The J4P programme is based on the link between development, accessible legal institutions and the need to understand complex local legal systems. In Timor-Leste the programme focuses on two areas: unresolved land claims involving the state and state officials, and service delivery at the local level. See also Rittich, 'The Future of Law and Development', 199–243.

World Bank's 2003 land review report showed that the Bank was questioning the previous economic orthodoxy that the recognition of customary land rights constrained economic development and that individualisation and privatisation were essential to encourage development.[63] The report acknowledged that in certain circumstances the security of customary tenure was more effective and less expensive than that provided by state institutions. It observed that only 2–10 per cent of the total land area in Africa is covered by 'modern' forms of land tenure which means that more than 90 per cent of land in Africa is regulated outside state legal systems.[64] The report states: 'the failure to formally recognise customary and other traditional institutions has effectively excluded the majority of land and the population using it from the rule of law, with potentially far-reaching implications for governance'.[65] This comment then endorses a policy in Africa of 'state law pluralism', where the state formally recognises customary land tenure, on the grounds of promoting the rule of law.[66]

A shift towards legal pluralism can also be seen among some leading IDAs. For example, since 2000 the policy of the United Kingdom Department for International Development (DFID) appears to be taking the fact of legal pluralism seriously and moving away from a purely state-centric approach to development. DFID has been developing 'safety, security and access to justice' (SSAJ) programmes in Africa that focus on how poor people experience insecurity and injustice[67] and recognise the importance of customary legal systems and other non-state legal systems in providing justice to the poor. For DFID, improving access to justice requires a focus on both state and non-state legal systems and

63 World Bank, *Land Policies for Growth*.

64 Ibid., xxiii, 62. This dichotomy between modern and traditional is used in the previous report of the World Bank on this subject, entitled *Land Reform: Sector Policy Paper*, 5.

65 Ibid., 62. World Bank, *Land Reform: Sector Policy Paper* focused almost exclusively on formal title. It briefly discusses the 'communal system' in terms that imply that customary tenure has a finite life: 19.

66 However, the report points out while state recognition in relation to customary tenure has been introduced in many parts of Africa, such recognition 'without actual institutions for enforcement' can lead to insecurity and conflict: 65.

67 UK DFID, *Justice and Poverty Reduction*; UK DFID, *Safety, Security and Accessible Justice*; UK DFID, *Non-State Justice and Security Systems*. For an overview of the operation of such programmes in Africa, see Piron, 'Time to Learn, Time to Act in Africa', Ch. 11.

ensuring that they work justly and equitably.[68] South Africa has been the subject of one of the SSAJ programmes and there is some indication that the SSAJ policy is partly influenced by South Africa's approach to legal pluralism.[69] The concept of the rule of law is relatively tangential to the programme; overall, DFID appears to be more restrained in its promotion of the rule of law than the World Bank and the USAID.[70]

Like DFID, the Danish International Development Assistance (Danida) has also taken a critical eye to its assistance programmes in transitional and developing countries such as South Africa during the 1990s. An evaluation of these programmes concluded that most of its support had been to the formal legal systems of these states; this assistance was premised on the assumption that 'a well functioning, formal legal system is a pre-requisite for establishing a "modern" society' and some of Danida's assistance involved 'systems export' whereby the Danish legal system was used as a model.[71] The 2000 evaluation found that this support for the formal legal system had 'important limitations and trade-offs' given that the majority of the population finds this system 'distant in many respects' and, for their access to justice, relies on the functioning of informal systems.[72] In other words, the evaluation implied that Danida had been giving excessive attention to state-centric strategies associated with the rule of law in countries where legal pluralism is strong and statehood is nascent and fragile. Furthermore, the evaluation noted that external efforts to strengthen the formal legal system benefit mainly professional and commercial groups rather than the poor or rural inhabitants.[73] Thus it recommended that Danida support both formal and informal systems.[74]

[68] UK DFID, *Justice and Poverty Reduction*, 22. See also Golub, 'A House Without a Foundation', 105 where he argues that in DFID's SSAJ programmes informal systems 'remain programmatic stepchildren to the judiciary and other official institutions': 119; Golub, 'The Rule of Law and the UN Peacebuilding Commission', 47. Another expert has commented that there is 'little evidence of its [SSAJ's] operationalisation' in Africa: Nyamu-Musembi, 'Ruling out Gender-Equality?', 1199.

[69] One of the authors of the SSAJ Policy document, Scharf, was at the time South Africa's leading expert on non-state justice.

[70] See USAID, *At Freedom's Frontiers*; USAID and US Department of State, *Strategic Plan: Fiscal Years 2007–2012.*

[71] Danish Ministry for Foreign Affairs and Danida, *Evaluation*, vi–vii.

[72] Ibid., vi. This point has also been articulated by Golub, 'A House Without a Foundation', 105.

[73] Ibid., 45.

[74] Danida has since shifted its approach to focus on informal justice systems as a means of access to justice for the poor and marginalised: see *How to Note: Informal Justice Systems* (June 2010).

Germany's Gesellschaft für Technische Zusammenarbeit (GTZ) appears to be taking a similar approach. The shift from 2000 onwards may have been spurred by the strategies suggested by the International Council on Human Rights Policy in 2000 which included ensuring access to justice and institutions of redress, recognising indigenous systems and empowering women and minorities.[75]

A shift is also discernible in the approach taken by USAID. Since at least 1998, USAID has shown an interest in understanding the relationship between the rule of law and ADR, which includes traditional, indigenous dispute resolution.[76] In its guide for ADR practitioners, USAID acknowledges that ADR can increase access to justice for women and other socially disadvantaged groups and can support rule-of-law objectives.

USAID's rule-of-law strategy has shifted more dramatically during the Obama administration: in 2010 it initiated a programme in Afghanistan which focuses entirely on the development of the rule of law in the *informal* justice sector, alternatively called the traditional justice system.[77] The 2011 assessment of this programme touts it as 'one of the first' such programmes among international donors in Afghanistan, possibly because most other donors look at the informal justice sector only in relation to the state legal system and not as having a direct impact in itself on the rule of law.[78] This programme signals that the international community is heading into waters that pose their own challenges. The 2011 assessment explains that in contrast to the formal justice system which is based on retributive justice principles, the informal justice sector in Afghanistan relies on 'processes that accentuate restorative justice principles with results seeking to promote social harmony within the community'.[79] While the main goal of this particular USAID programme is to decrease instability in rural areas, it also aims

[75] *Local Perspectives: Foreign Aid to the Justice Sector*, 57–66.

[76] The relationship is discussed in USAID, *Alternative Dispute Resolution*. The report broadly comments: 'ADR programs are instruments for the application of equity, rather than the rule of law' (3). The guide represents ADR as potentially unpredictable in contrast to the rule of law, which is portrayed as stable and more capable of redressing power imbalances between parties (ibid.). Since this 1998 report, USAID has commissioned a number of reports on the relationship between the rule of law and ADR in developing and transitional countries.

[77] US Department of State, *Afghanistan and Pakistan Regional Stabilization Strategy*, 12.

[78] USAID, *Afghanistan Rule of Law Stabilization (Informal Component) Assessment*, 10.

[79] Ibid., 12.

to create links between the informal justice sector and the state system and to enhance access to justice.[80]

Thus, since 1998 USAID's approach to the rule of law has moved from promoting ADR for resolving civil disputes in developing and transitional states to supporting a restorative justice approach to crime, an approach that was showcased by South Africa's Truth and Reconciliation Commission in the 1990s. Indeed, dispute resolution based on restorative justice is increasingly becoming accepted by the international community as part of what is meant by access to justice.[81] As we see in Part II of this book, this connection between access to justice and restorative justice is being developed by South Africa's Government in transforming customary courts but this entails certain compromises to the rule of law.

USAID's approach may be influencing that of the World Bank and vice versa. In 2002 the Legal Vice-Presidency of the World Bank proposed that one of the four conditions for the rule of law is that 'justice is accessible to all' and asserted that it promoted ADR and customary forums.[82] Since 2002 the World Bank has adopted a differentiated strategy for 'fragile states' which includes post-conflict countries with weak or dysfunctional institutions such as Timor-Leste. This strategy promotes the rule of law despite reports that rule-of-law assistance programmes have had limited impact on the ultimate social goals associated with the rule of law in post-conflict states.[83] A 2006 paper written for the World Bank on this problem recommends that the World Bank adopt new strategies to take advantage of the informal structures that exist in countries such as Timor-Leste, where it can take close to twenty years to establish formal institutions.[84] These suggestions appear to have some support with other arms of the Bank: six months before this paper was published, the World Bank issued a report on Timor-Leste which noted the limited access to the formal justice system and recommended to the Government of Timor-Leste that it establish a legal framework for linking customary practice to the formal justice system.[85]

[80] Ibid., 13–14.

[81] For example, Penal Reform International defines 'access to justice' to encompass, *inter alia*, 'access to formal courts and, if preferred in any particular case, a dispute resolution form based on restorative justice': *Access to Justice in Sub-Saharan Africa*, 10. For a definition of restorative justice as a process and outcome, see the *UN Basic Principles on the Use of Restorative Justice Programmes in Criminal Matters* (ECOSOC Resolution 2002/12).

[82] The World Bank, *Legal Vice Presidency, Legal and Judicial Reform Observations*, 1–2, 6.

[83] Samuels, *Rule of Law Reform in Post-Conflict Countries.*

[84] Ibid., 17–18.

[85] World Bank, *Strengthening the Institutions of Governance in Timor-Leste*, [60].

The World Bank's broader approach to addressing conflict, security and development is articulated in its report known as the *WDR 2011*. In the report, the World Bank maintains its view that weak institutions are a major cause of regional instability through post-conflict states relapsing into conflict but it is careful to emphasise that legitimate institutions should not be equated with Western institutions.[86] The *WDR 2011* recommends that post-conflict states consider 'supplementing formal justice with traditional community systems'.[87] It argues that the process of recognition and reform of such systems can be used to '"pull" them gradually in the direction of respect for equity and international norms'.[88] As its example, it discusses Timor-Leste's experience of parallel legal systems,[89] showing that Timor-Leste has had some influence on the World Bank's approach in regard to post-conflict justice systems. In regard to the rule of law, the report does not explicitly articulate the Bank's view that post-conflict states need to establish the rule of law. However, the *WDR 2011* offers a sobering table of data that estimates the number of years it takes for a country to 'achieve' the rule of law (41 years for the group of 'fastest 20' countries)[90] but it omits the data specific to fragile states, possibly because this data offers the term 'infinity'.[91]

At least on paper, IDAs and IFIs are beginning to pay more attention to the fact of legal pluralism; no longer is legal pluralism being rejected as impeding economic growth and development. The concept of the rule of law continues to be a powerful rhetoric that lends credibility to IFIs in their promotion of particular economic policies and programmes of institutional development in developing and fragile states.[92] This close relationship between IFIs and the concept of the rule of law has resulted in a top-down and state-centric approach to development that has neglected the legal mechanisms relied on by those at the ground level. Given the formidable estimates of the *WDR 2011* in relation to the time needed to achieve the rule of law, it remains to be seen whether IFIs will continue to champion the rule of law as a useful concept in the field of post-conflict justice and development.

86 World Bank, *World Development Report 2011*, 8, 84–92.

87 Ibid., 155, 257. A similar approach was recommended by the OECD in 2007: *Enhancing the Delivery of Justice and Security*.

88 Ibid., 156. 89 Ibid. 90 Ibid., 11, 109.

91 Pritchett and Weijer, *Fragile States*, 12. The authors explain: '[i]n this indicator the time to reach the threshold at either the fragile states' rate of progress or that of the average non-fragile country is infinity as, on average, there has been zero progress' (11).

92 Santos, 'The World Bank's Uses of the "Rule of Law"', 255.

3.2 *Principles: human rights and democracy*

The rule of law is also believed to be a precondition to establishing principles such as human rights and democracy.[93] The simultaneous rise of the modern human rights movement and the concept of the rule of law in the 1990s is illustrated by the *Declaration and Programme of Action of the 1993 Vienna World Conference on Human Rights* which mentions the rule of law and human rights side by side.[94] In this international context the rule of law is understood in abstract and universalising terms as requiring the observance of democratic and international human rights standards. It is seen as part of a global approach to social justice driven mainly by the human rights movement. In this sense, the rule of law is framed by the international human rights movement as having a normative content and as sharing a commitment to emancipation, thus ignoring the rule of law's conservative and ambivalent nature.[95]

To help crystallise this reframing of the rule of law, the human rights movement has pushed an agenda of constitutionalism across the world in the belief that a legal framework of constitutional guarantees of judicial review, judicial independence and separation of powers will aid the protection of international human rights standards and the rule of law.[96] In a sense, this is a natural meeting point as constitutionalism, the rule of law and international human rights law are all focused on the state as their principal subject. While the three concepts allow space to criticise the state, they rely upon the state for their fulfilment and thus reinforce the power of the state and promote it as the centre of 'emancipatory promise'.[97] However, they differ in that international human rights law overtly promotes universal norms and is more focused on the rights of individuals. This push for constitutionalism synchronises with the agenda of IFIs, for

[93] For an insightful analysis of the relationship between the rule of law and human rights, see Rajagopal, 'Invoking the Rule of Law in Post-Conflict Rebuilding', 1359–62.

[94] For example, it recommended, amongst other things, that the UN establish a comprehensive programme in order 'to help States in the task of building and strengthening adequate national structures which have a direct impact on the overall observance of human rights and the maintenance of the rule of law': UN Doc A/CONF.157/24 (12 July 1993) Vienna Declaration and Programme of Action [69].

[95] For an analysis of the ambivalent nature of the rule of law, see Chapter 3.

[96] Henkin, 'A New Birth of Constitutionalism', 547.

[97] On human rights law, see Kennedy, 'The International Human Rights Movement', 113.

whom constitutions offer an emphasis on state institution-building and a means of security of economic investment.

At the international level, international human rights law and legal pluralism are arguably incompatible because the element of universalism in the former leaves little space for diversity and local norms which may not be consistent with those promoted by international human rights law. In this sense international human rights law has a veneer of imperialism, arguably shared by the rule of law,[98] as it pushes a particular set of norms as 'universal values'. According to Kennedy, these norms are projected as civilised, rational and modern norms in contrast to any other 'particular' and backward norms. He argues:

> The human rights movement contributes to the framing of political choices in the third world as oppositions between 'local/traditional' and 'international/modern' forms of government and modes of life. This effect is strengthened by the presentation of human rights as belonging to the modern world, but coming from some place outside of political choice, from the universal, the rational, the civilised.[99]

This positioning of human rights means that it is understood as a rational mode in opposition to the sphere of the traditional and customary. Sally Engle Merry states that '[l]ike colonialism, human rights discourse contains implicit assumptions about the nature of civilized and backward societies often glossed over as modern and traditional'.[100] In contrast, legal pluralism contains no such assumptions because it is devoid of any substantive criteria or standards. This means it gives equal weight to every set of norms, including local norms and those norms lacking legal rationality, without making any claims of transcendence or universality for any set of norms.

Few of the many UN bodies mandated to promote and protect human rights pay attention to legal pluralism in their work.[101] One exception is found in the work of the UN Human Rights Committee (HRC). In its General Comment 32, the HRC outlines that where a state recognises courts based on customary law, Article 14 of the *International Covenant*

98 See Brooks, 'The New Imperialism', 2275.

99 Kennedy, 'The International Human Rights Movement', 116.

100 Merry, *Human Rights and Gender Violence*, 226.

101 A change of approach may be signalled by the joint 2012 UN Women/UNICEF/UNDP report *Informal Justice Systems* and UN Women report, *Progress of the World's Women 2011–2012.*

on Civil and Political Rights (ICCPR) on the right to fair trial is relevant. It states that the judgments of these courts cannot be considered binding

> unless proceedings before such courts are limited to minor civil and criminal matters, meet the basic requirements of fair trial and other relevant guarantees of the Covenant, and their judgments are validated by State courts in light of the guarantees set out in the Covenant and can be challenged by the parties concerned in a procedure meeting the requirements of article 14 of the Covenant.[102]

Furthermore, according to the HRC, states have a general obligation to protect the rights of those persons affected by the operation of these courts; presumably this obligation is regardless of whether these courts have received state recognition. This Comment highlights the concern of the human rights movement that legal pluralism in the form of customary courts has the potential to dilute and undermine core human rights standards.

The tension between legal pluralism and international human rights standards is particularly apparent in the sphere of women's human rights where some state actors seek to explain their non-compliance with human rights treaties by citing the prevalence of local customs or traditions whose power exceeds that of the state.[103] The response of many actors in the human rights movement has tended to brand customs and traditions as negative and harmful and to conflate them with culture in the developing world.[104] This often leads to calls for the wholesale abolition of traditions and customs.[105] For example, in 2002 the UN Committee on the Elimination of Discrimination Against Women (CEDAW) recommended to Fiji the complete abolition of the restorative justice practice of *bulubulu* on the basis that it is sometimes used to resolve rape offences, even though in some contexts it may be useful.[106] In August 2009 the

[102] UN Doc CCPR/C/GC/32 (23 August 2007) General Comment 32 – Article 14: Right to Equality before Courts and Tribunals and to a Fair Trial, [24]. In the 1999 Dakar Declaration the African Commission on Human and Peoples' Rights confirmed that traditional courts are not exempt from the provisions of the African Charter relating to fair trial. See also African Commission on Human and Peoples' Rights, *Principles and Guidelines on the Right to a Fair Trial and Legal Assistance in Africa* (2001).

[103] Ibid., Ch. 4. On this tension, see generally International Council on Human Rights Policy, *When Legal Worlds Overlap*.

[104] This is observed by Merry, *Human Rights and Gender Violence*, 12–13.

[105] The South African Rural Women's Movement and South African National Civics Organisation (SANCO) both oppose engagement with local law.

[106] Merry, *Human Rights and Gender Violence*, Ch. 4. Merry explains that this practice, which is used in relation to a range of offences, requires the offender to apologise, offer a

conclusions of CEDAW in regard to Timor-Leste stated that the 'persistence of traditional justice systems' poses an impediment for women in accessing justice.[107] The word 'persistence' implies a desire for customary law to disappear altogether and a belief that it can be simply repealed by the state like a piece of legislation. A more nuanced approach is shown by the work of Celestine Nyamu-Musembi whose work on customary law in Africa highlights that customs and traditions provide positive openings and opportunities for gender equality as well as barriers.[108] She encourages scholars and human rights activists to study legal pluralism as a means to identifying the positive aspects of custom and tradition for women.[109]

The need to understand legal pluralism has been automatic for many human rights activists working at the local level. In Timor-Leste, for instance, some local activists and women's groups have been involved in attempting to modify local customary law in line with international human rights standards by organising local education campaigns in villages on issues such as rape and domestic violence.[110] For example, some groups advocate for compensation paid under informal processes in relation to domestic violence and rape to be paid directly to the victim rather than to the victim's family as custom dictates.[111] These actions make clear that formal Western-style law is not regarded as a panacea; instead a modified form of customary law is considered an ongoing and viable means of community dispute resolution. These groups recognise that ignoring customary law is not a practical option in a post-conflict state where the state legal system is struggling to operate even in the capital, let alone in more rural areas. To ignore customary law may deny the possibility of access to justice and dispute resolution for the poor and most marginal.

whale's tooth and gift and ask for forgiveness while the victim is placed under some pressure to accept the apology and make peace. Merry relates the view that, for some offences, this practice is a useful form of dispute resolution at the village level. Under 2 (f) of the Convention on Eliminating All Forms of Discrimination against Women the CEDAW Committee is empowered to comment on whether state parties need to modify or abolish customs that constitute discrimination against women.

107 See UN Doc CEDAW/C/TLS/CO/1 (7 August 2009) Concluding Observations of the Committee on the Elimination of Discrimination against Women – Timor Leste, [21–2].

108 Nyamu-Musembi, 'Cultural Legitimization of Gender Hierarchy in Developing Countries', 381. See also Nyamu-Musembi, 'Fences or Pathways?', 126.

109 See also Harrington and Chopra, *Arguing Traditions*.

110 See Hohe and Nixon, *Reconciling Justice*.

111 Ibid.

Few commentators analyse the relationship between legal pluralism and democracy despite the fact that many states embrace forms of both concepts.[112] In the post-conflict context, one exception is Rachel Seider who argues that constitutional recognition of indigenous norms and practices strengthens democracy because it 'is an essential part of democratizing the legal structures of the pluri-cultural state'.[113] While the recognition of legal pluralism can bolster democracy as it shows respect for cultural diversity, conversely, legal pluralism is strengthened by democracy in that legal and political structures from the local level to the national level must be participatory. Furthermore she asserts in the context of post-conflict Guatemala, that such legal pluralism is a '*component* of the rule of law, not an alternative to it'.[114]

Much has been written on the relationship between the rule of law and democracy,[115] with many commentators and organisations asserting a causal link between the two. For example, Hans Corell, the former Legal Counsel of the UN, asserts with little deliberation that democracy is a 'requirement for the rule of law'.[116] USAID's approach asserts that the rule of law 'establishes the foundation for certain conditions on which democracy depends' such as equal rights and social order and it ties both the rule of law and democracy to economic development.[117] In contrast, Carothers, the director of the Democracy and Rule-of-Law Project at the Carnegie Endowment, questions the direct causal connection between the rule of law and democracy and describes it as opaque.[118] In his view, '[d]emocracy often, in fact usually, co-exists with substantial shortcomings in the rule of law'.[119]

The connection between democracy and the rule of law appears to be largely aspirational and political.[120] For example, the Final Report of the South African Truth and Reconciliation Commission claims that

[112] A burgeoning literature is appearing on constitutional pluralism. See, e.g., Tully, *Strange Multiplicity*; Walker, 'Constitutional Pluralism', 317; Anderson, *Constitutional Rights After Globalization*; Sweet, 'Constitutionalism, Legal Pluralism'. One scholar, Berman, argues that various forms of compromise between the two concepts exist in a number of national and supranational systems where different communities live under one system, whether federal or otherwise: Berman, 'Global Legal Pluralism', 1155.

[113] Seider, 'Rethinking Democratisation', 114. [114] Ibid.

[115] See, e.g., Rosenfeld, 'The Rule of Law', 1307; Carothers, 'The Rule of Law Revival', 96–7.

[116] Corell, 'Developing the Rule of Law', 393. [117] USAID, *Guide to Rule of Law* 7.

[118] Carothers, 'The Problem of Knowledge', 15. [119] Ibid., 18.

[120] See, e.g., the CSCE's 1990 declaration that 'democracy is an inherent element of the rule of law': Conference on Security and Cooperation in Europe, *Document of the Copenhagen Meeting*.

democracy is encompassed within the concept of the rule of law. The Report states: 'As argued so impressively by Dicey more than a century ago, parliamentary sovereignty and the rule of law work hand in hand and are premised on a political system that is fundamentally representative of all the people subject to that Parliament.'[121] Given that England did not have universal suffrage at the time Dicey propounded his theory of the rule of law, this interpretation is a little stretched. The motivation for this claim is clear, however, given that the apartheid Government asserted its adherence to the rule of law in the absence of universal suffrage.

Thus, in the post-Cold War era, the rule of law has been strenuously promoted in the name of both principle and profit. In the twenty-first century, IFIs and IDAs are gradually recognising that legal pluralism is not necessarily an obstacle to development but may be a link to certain sections of society. Indeed, these organisations are encouraging post-conflict states to develop formal linkages with informal justice mechanisms which were previously characterised as obsolete and backward.

4. Transitional justice

In the field of transitional justice, the rule of law is once again at the forefront due to the heavy influence of the human rights movement. Legal pluralism has hovered mostly on the field's margins but experiences in Rwanda and Timor-Leste have highlighted its role in assisting to achieve some measure of accountability and redress for victims in post-conflict states.

Transitional justice began life as a study of justice mechanisms used by countries in transition from conflict and authoritarianism to democracy and 'liberalisation'.[122] Transitional justice mechanisms are temporary processes that aim to give a once-off injection of principles and capacity to a state legal system so as to kick-start the establishment of the rule of law in a post-conflict environment. These mechanisms, which include criminal trials, truth commissions, lustration processes, reparations, conditional amnesty and constitution-making, are mostly retrospective and short term in nature[123] and

[121] (1998) Vol. 4, Ch. 4, [41]. [122] See, e.g., Kritz (ed.) *Transitional Justice*.

[123] Constitution-making is clearly the exception here although the International Criminal Court is also exceptional in that it is a permanent institution.

understand 'justice' in terms of accountability for past human rights abuses. While the human rights movement has been particularly vocal in calling for criminal prosecutions as providing the path to accountability for human rights abuses, it has been critical of truth commissions, a restorative justice mechanism used across the world and most prominently by South Africa in the 1990s as a means to bypass expensive and lengthy prosecutions.

At the national level, transitional justice mechanisms were embraced particularly in the first waves of transition, such as those in Eastern Europe and Southern Africa, where there was some semblance of key state institutions still in existence, such as judicial systems, which were capable of activating transitional justice mechanisms.[124] However, in some later transitions from conflict, such as Rwanda and Timor-Leste, the solutions were less clear-cut because there was little state infrastructure and capacity remaining.

According to Ruti Teitel, early transitional justice literature was marked by aspirations toward idealised conceptions of justice and the rule of law and the belief that transitional justice mechanisms would help transform countries into democratic states that observe international human rights standards.[125] However, today one of the main concerns of transitional justice is the project of state-building, which has shifted transitional justice to a more sustainable, partial conception of justice and a thin and compromised conception of the rule of law. This shift is presumably partly the result of the state-building exercises not only in Timor-Leste but also in Iraq and Afghanistan. There is tension in transitional justice's desire to balance the universalising drive of human rights discourse with the localising drive of state-building projects. Ultimately both of these concerns leave little room for the consideration of non-state norms. At its core, the field of transitional justice has been focused on the state:[126] it strives to understand how the state can be strengthened on a liberal and democratic basis and how prosecutions can shore up the state's stability and legitimacy. Access to justice and dispute resolution for ordinary people through state and community-based justice systems have largely been an afterthought in transitional justice literature.

[124] Lutz, 'Transitional Justice', 326. [125] Teitel, 'Transitional Justice Genealogy', 69.

[126] McEvoy argues that the 'state centric and "top-down"' nature of transitional justice can be traced to the fact that it is over dominated by legalism: McEvoy, 'Letting Go of Legalism', 25.

Much like the rule-of-law promotion field, in the past, transitional justice overlooked or attempted to ignore legal pluralism: it rarely examined non-state legal norms operating at the local level, even in situations where local legal systems are predominant. For example, in her book *Transitional Justice*, Teitel discusses the concept of constitutionalism in the transitional context by drawing on various cases studies, including from her native South America, such as Colombia.[127] However, Teitel does not examine how constitutions are made meaningful at the local level, that is, how they engage with, and translate into, local norms. Her work on constitutional norms presupposes that they automatically have some meaning in transitional countries and assumes the existence of state power, even when looking at the constitutions of countries such as Colombia where the state is very weak and limited, both geographically and normatively. This oversight is representative of much of the early transitional justice literature in that it fails to investigate the operation of norms at the local level and their engagement with national and international norms.

One transitional justice mechanism that has drawn considerable global attention is South Africa's Truth and Reconciliation Commission, which was aimed at achieving reconciliation at the local level, based on a restorative justice approach and the African norm of 'ubuntu'.[128] The Commission neither claimed any role in reinforcing the rule of law in South Africa nor did it, in practical terms, directly use any aspects of customary law in its procedures.[129] However, its counterpart in Timor-Leste, the Commission for Reception, Truth and Reconciliation (known by the Portuguese acronym, CAVR), incorporated aspects of customary law into its reconciliation programme and subsequently it claimed that its programme 'reinforced' the rule of law.[130] The CAVR was initiated by the recognition that the state's nascent court system would not be able to

[127] Teitel, *Transitional Justice*, Ch. 6.

[128] *Ubuntu* is a Zulu word sometimes translated as humaneness and human dignity. It implies unity and interconnectedness. See, e.g., English, '*Ubuntu*', 641.

[129] While s. 11(g) of the *Promotion of National Unity and Reconciliation Act 34 of 1995* (South Africa) provided that customary law and practice could be applied by the Truth and Reconciliation Commission where facilitating reconciliation and redress for victims, there is no evidence that the Commission took this approach.

[130] *Chega!, Report of the Commission for Reception, Truth and Reconciliation*, Part 9, [164]. For an elaboration on this claim and on the work of the CAVR, see section 4.4 of Chapter 7.

address the minor crimes that took place during the Indonesian occupation and withdrawal, as the hybrid court established by the UN was designed to hear only serious crimes.[131] This transitional justice mechanism, the CAVR, was Timor-Leste's first formal experiment with egal pluralism.

The turning point for transitional justice in its understanding of legal pluralism was Rwanda's decision to establish *gacaca* courts to hear cases against the approximately 100,000 prisoners who, more than five years after the 1994 genocide, were still languishing in prisons without trial. The Rwandan Government estimated that it could take two centuries for the UN international tribunal and the national courts to hear all the cases.[132] Thus, desiring full accountability, the Government created another level of special courts, this time at the local level, claiming to draw on aspects of traditional dispute resolution indigenous to Rwandan society, that were used in pre-colonial days to resolve family and neighbourhood disputes. Known as *gacaca* (literally 'small grass') courts, these new state courts represent a compromise between the local indigenous system and Western legal standards and practices.[133] An aspect of the former is the popular participation and adjudication by respected community elders while an aspect of the latter is the fact that the state was involved in organising the election of the *gacaca* judges, and in this process encouraged the selection of women.[134] Furthermore, the state formally organised these courts and promulgated a code of court rules. The state-run *gacaca* courts have been heralded as 'an impressive innovation in the area of transitional justice'[135] possibly because of their grassroots nature as well as the fact that they form the lowest level of the pyramid of multilayered-transitional justice mechanisms operating simultaneously in Rwanda. However, these courts produced a storm of

[131] This court, the Special Panel for Serious Crimes, was hybrid only in that it was an arm of the Dili District Court and local and foreign judges constituted the bench. The law applied by the SPSC was not a mixture of international law and customary law.

[132] The Government of Rwanda, *Genocide and Justice.*

[133] Longman, 'Justice at the Grassroots?', 210. See also Fierens, '*Gacaca* Courts', 912–13. Fierens argues that the process 'endeavours to legitimise a hereto unheard-of attempt at people's justice'. He points out that the hybridisation of the process mutes its traditional aspects and therefore there is little that could be traditional about the process. See also Waldorf, 'Posthumous Justice in Post-Genocide Rwanda', 183.

[134] Longman, 'Justice at the Grassroots?', 206, 211.

[135] Honeyman et al., *Gacaca Jurisdictions*, 6. Tondini argues that traditional justice institutions have been 'successfully employed' in Rwanda: 'Restoring Justice Systems', 241.

debate as to whether, as a transitional justice mechanism, the *gacaca* system serves the rule of law.[136]

In 2002, Amnesty International expressed concern that the rule of law would not prevail in Rwanda if the *gacaca* system did not strictly adhere to international human rights standards, in particular guarantees of due process articulated in Article 14 of the *ICCPR*.[137] It argued that the *gacaca* system fails to guarantee impartiality, equality of arms between the parties to the proceedings, full appeal rights and judicial competency. It read Article 14 as guaranteeing 'the right to equal access to court',[138] by which it understood a Western-style court. Rwanda's Supreme Court responded by stating that the authors of the Amnesty International report were ignorant of the traditional system of *gacaca*, 'which is normal since it is different from the systems they are used to'.[139] The Court argued that this transitional justice mechanism places respect for human value and dignity at the forefront rather than blindly following international texts.[140] The intention of the *gacaca* system was to reconcile people and rehabilitate Rwandan society, and, given the massive scale of the violence and the limited resources of Rwanda, the system was an appropriate means to achieving full accountability.[141] At its heart, Rwanda's decision to establish the *gacaca* system was motivated by a concern that victims receive some form of redress and that all prisoners have 'access to justice' within a reasonable time period; unlike Amnesty International, Rwanda did not understand 'access to justice' narrowly to mean 'access to Western-style courts'. For many international NGOs

[136] Amnesty International, *Rwanda: The Troubled Course of Justice*; Amnesty International, 'Rwanda: Gacaca – Gambling with Justice'; Amnesty International, *Rwanda: Gacaca: A Question of Justice*; Human Rights Watch, 'Elections May Speed Genocide Trials'.

[137] *Rwanda – Gacaca: A Question of Justice*, 5. Note that as of November 2007, Amnesty International was still expressing concerns about the *gacaca* process and encouraging states to use universal jurisdiction to prosecute perpetrators of the Rwandan massacre: see Amnesty International, *Rwanda: Suspects must not be transferred to Rwandan courts for trial until it is demonstrated that trials will comply with international standards of justice*. The *gacaca* courts were wound up at the end of 2007. For a similar and more detailed argument, see Gahima, 'Alternatives to Prosecution', Ch. 10.

[138] Amnesty International, *Rwanda: Gacaca: A Question of Justice*, 31.

[139] République du Rwanda, Cour Suprême, *Mise au Point au Sujet du Rapport et Différentes Correspondances d'Amnesty International*, 2.

[140] Ibid., 2.

[141] Ibid., 6. See also Ingelaere, 'The Gacaca Courts in Rwanda' in Huyse and Salter, *Traditional Justice and Reconciliation after Violent Conflict*.

such as Amnesty International, the problem was the failure of *gacaca* courts to conform to dominant understandings of the rule of law.[142]

This dialogue between one of the leading international human rights NGOs and one of the poorest post-conflict states in the world brings to the fore the tension in transitional justice in relation to the rule of law and legal pluralism in the form of customary law. On the one hand, the use of these hybrid local courts represents an affirmation of local norms of dispute resolution; it also assists Rwanda in building a legal culture and encouraging large-scale participation in a state institution, both important aspects of the rule of law. On the other hand, the *gacaca* system potentially violates international legal standards, which, at a more abstract level, are considered closely connected to dominant understandings of the rule of law. In its response, the Rwandan Supreme Court did not deny the importance of these international legal standards; instead it argued that these international standards needed to be translated and adapted to the situation on the ground. No doubt the Court saw the international human rights movement as using the rule of law as a stick to enforce the values of 'civilising nations'.[143]

On the whole, the field of transitional justice is shifting towards greater acceptance of the Rwandan 'innovation', with the UN's Office of the High Commissioner for Human Rights (OHCHR) describing the innovation as a 'hopeful model'.[144] Despite the concerns of some human rights groups, legal pluralism is playing an increasingly larger role in transitional justice mechanisms. For example, in Northern Uganda, the promotion of traditional justice has become the 'current vogue' as an alternative to the International Criminal Court.[145] According to Huyse, the Rwandan innovation has given birth to 'hype' for tradition-based approaches in transitional justice.[146] This shift can be attributed to a greater focus on state-building, rather than international mechanisms, as well as on local norms and participation, and community-based justice

[142] Drumbl, 'Law and Atrocity: Settling Accounts in Rwanda', 57–8.

[143] Bell and O'Rourke describe this as 'a sinister side to transitional justice as liberalising justice': Bell and O'Rourke, 'Does Feminism Need a Theory of Transitional Justice?', 38.

[144] OHCHR, *Rule of Law Tools for Post-Conflict States: Mapping the Justice Sector*, 15.

[145] Allen, 'Ritual (Ab)Use?', 47. For the comments made in 2005 by the Chief Prosecutor of the International Criminal Court on the role of traditional justice in relation to the ICC, see 'Statements by ICC Chief Prosecutor and the Visiting Delegation of Acholi Leaders from Northern Uganda'. See also Huyse and Salter, *Justice and Reconciliation after Violent Conflict*.

[146] Huyse and Salter, *Justice and Reconciliation after Violent Conflict*, 1.

mechanisms. It is also partly a result of studies conducted in the post-conflict states of Rwanda and Bosnia-Herzegovina which have found that the international *ad hoc* courts set up for these two states by the international community have had limited impact on, and legitimacy with, local populations.[147]

In 2009 Fletcher, Weinstein and Rowen conducted a qualitative analysis of seven transitional states and came to the view that while prosecutions and truth commissions 'share symbolic celebration of rule of law principles', they do not 'perform the work of building the rule of law culture and its supporting institutions'.[148] They concluded that 'legitimacy of domestic legal systems is critical to the success of transitional justice',[149] thus implying that direct efforts to strengthen long-term institutions, such as the state legal system, may be more important to building a rule of law culture than short-term transitional justice mechanisms. The study of Fletcher et al. does not go further to investigate whether or not the legitimacy of these state legal systems may depend in part on a state harnessing, and building upon, community-based justice systems by developing linkage laws to give formal recognition to legal pluralism.

After two decades, transitional justice literature largely fashions itself as a reflection on the 'lessons learned'. However, this teleological understanding of the field was disturbed by the manifest failure of the US to learn many of these lessons and to put them into practice in its occupation of Iraq.[150] According to one commentator, a critical mistake made by the US was to ignore local interests in Iraq,[151] which affected the legitimacy of the occupation. One example is that those US officials tasked with working to reform Iraq's legal system had little background in either Iraq's legal system or even civil law systems generally.[152] Since the invasion of Iraq, state-building literature generally emphasises that more attention has to be paid to local politics and social needs, to the grass roots level, otherwise the introduction of new laws will have no connection to the people. For example, in their 2006 book entitled *Can Might Make Rights?*, Stromseth, Wippman and Brooks exhort military interveners such as the US and the UN to design rule-of-law programmes

[147] See Longman et al., 'Connecting Justice to Human Experience', 213–15; Fletcher and Weinstein, *An Interview of Bosnian Judges and Prosecutors.*

[148] Fletcher et al., 'Context, Timing and the Dynamics of Transitional Justice', 220.

[149] Ibid. [150] Stover et al., 'Bremer's "Gordian Knot"', 830.

[151] Lutz, 'Transitional Justice', 333. [152] Stromseth et al., *Can Might Make Rights?*, 322.

that 'build on pre-existing informal dispute resolution mechanisms'.[153] They reason that: 'rule of law efforts should not ignore the role of traditional and informal dispute settlement mechanisms, because these may command substantial loyalty and may offer useful models for more formal institutions'.[154] As shown by the current programmes of IDAs, it is now widely recognised that the top-down imposition of the rule of law is unlikely to generate a culture of the rule of law.[155]

In 2010 Shaw, Waldorf and Hazan observed that transitional justice practitioners are giving 'unprecedented attention' to customary law and other forms of local justice.[156] They attributed this 'surge of enthusiasm for adding customary law to the transitional justice "toolkit"' to 'the length and expense of internationalized criminal trials ... [and] a new-found pragmatism and a concern with local ownership'.[157] Transitional justice has developed into a field that is more pragmatic, contextualised and nuanced than the universalised and abstract discourse of international human rights law. The shift in the conceptualisation of the rule of law has mirrored this development. More than anything, this divergence from international human rights law is driven by necessity in the post-conflict state; in the cases of Timor-Leste and Rwanda, necessity led the state to harness legal pluralism in the form of customary law in order to achieve some accountability and redress for the victims. In moving towards pragmatism, transitional justice has lost some of the law and development movement's idealism regarding law's power to transform society. A group of leading transitional justice scholars observe: 'The question of law's capacity to deliver (or hinder) meaningful change in transitional societies is an open one.'[158]

5. The United Nations

The UN claims to provide rule of law assistance in over 150 member states through its agencies such as the UN Development Programme (UNDP) under the coordination of the UN's Rule of Law Coordination and Resource Group.[159] In 2012 eight UN peace operations were

[153] Ibid., 315 and 334–9. [154] Ibid., 336. [155] Chandler, *Empire in Denial*, 166ff.

[156] Shaw et al., *Localising Transitional Justice*, 4. [157] Ibid., 15.

[158] Bell et al., 'Foreword – Transitional Justice', 83.

[159] UN Doc A/66/133 (8 August 2011) *Report of the Secretary General, Strengthening and Coordinating United Nations Rule of Law Activities*, [2]. In 2006 the UN established a Rule of Law Assistance Unit. The Unit's Rule of Law Coordination and Resource Group has, since 2007, had responsibility for the overall coordination and coherence of rule of

mandated to provide rule of law assistance to post-conflict states. Despite the wide scale of the UN's rule-of-law activities, its embrace of the rule of law is relatively recent.[160] The year 2004 represents a turning point in the UN's promotion of the rule of law, for after this date the UN's approach to the concept of the rule of law shifted from one of caution to open and frequent invocation of the concept as something of a cure-all, particularly for post-conflict states. In UN reports, the rule of law has been paired not only with human rights and international justice but also with democracy, investment, development and poverty alleviation.[161] In this context the UN rarely invokes the concept of legal pluralism and has yet to develop a comprehensive understanding of legal pluralism in the form of local customary law.[162] This is confirmed by a 2003 review of four UN peace operations conducted by King's College London, which observes the UN's 'consistent lack of acknowledgment of the role of traditional justice systems'.[163] That an understanding of traditional justice is developing at all can perhaps be partly traced to its near-decade-long presence and experience in Timor-Leste.[164]

At the 2005 World Summit, the UN General Assembly adopted a resolution recognising 'the need for universal adherence to and implementation of the rule of law'.[165] The resolution states that the rule of law

law within the United Nations system: it is the focal point for providing doctrinal guidance and 'lessons learnt' regarding UN rule-of-law assistance.

160 In contrast, human rights have been incorporated into the mandate of UN peace operations since the early 1990s: Kondoch, 'Human Rights Law'.

161 UNDP, in conjunction with the Commission on Legal Empowerment of the Poor, claims that there is a direct connection between poverty and the absence of protections provided by the rule of law: Commission on Legal Empowerment of the Poor and UNDP, *Making the Law Work for Everyone: Volume 1*, 2. The Report claims 'most studies find that the rule of law makes a significant contribution to growth and poverty reduction' (19).

162 The UN's understanding of legal pluralism has been considerably advanced by the joint 2012 UN Women/UNICEF/UNDP report *Informal Justice Systems* which identifies strategies by which engagement with these systems can take place in a manner that abides by human rights standards.

163 King's College London, *A Review of Peace Operations*, Overall Introduction, 34.

164 Apart from its peace operations in post-conflict states, the UN's understanding of traditional justice is informed by the work of UNDP as well as the UN Special Rapporteur on the situation of human rights and fundamental freedoms of indigenous peoples – see, e.g., UN Doc E/CN.4/2006/78 (15 December 2005) *Report of the Special Rapporteur on the situation of human rights and fundamental freedoms of indigenous people.*

165 GA Res. 60/1 (24 October 2005) 2005 World Summit Outcome, [134]. The rule of law has been on the GA's agenda since 1992. See also GA Res. 61/39 (18 December 2006)

is 'essential' for a host of universal goods, including 'sustained economic growth, sustainable development, and the eradication of poverty and hunger'.[166] In 2006 the UN Secretary-General stated that the rule of law was central to the work of the UN.[167] While the *Charter of the United Nations* (UN Charter) does not make any reference to the concept,[168] it is mentioned only obliquely in the preamble of the *Universal Declaration on Human Rights* when it states that: 'human rights should be protected by the rule of law'. Since the signing of the *UN Charter* in June 1945, the concept of the rule of law has come a long way. However, its progress was stalled for almost forty-five years,[169] as the concept was a political football, manipulated by both sides of the Cold War. In the new millennium the UN's embrace of the concept has been intense: it is pushing the rule of law to the forefront of transitional justice, and to a lesser degree in the field of peacekeeping.[170] At the same time it has shown some ambivalence towards engaging with the dynamics of legal pluralism in these two fields. This section considers official UN views on the relationship between the rule of law and legal pluralism in relation to: (i) UN peace operations and its strategy for transitional justice; (ii) the policies of UN member states; and (iii) structural aspects of the UN.

5.1 UN peace operations and transitional justice

The need to strengthen rule-of-law institutions and respect for human rights in the post-conflict environment is recommended as a goal for UN

The Rule of Law at the National and International Levels and GA Res 62/70 (8 January 2008) The Rule of Law at the National and International Levels. Both resolutions add that the rule of law is essential to 'the protection of all human rights and fundamental freedoms'.

166 GA Res. 60/1 (24 October 2005) 2005 World Summit Outcome, [11].

167 UN Doc A/61/636-S/2006/980 (14 December 2006) *Uniting Our Strengths: Enhancing United Nations Support for the Rule of Law, Report of the UN Secretary General*, 1. See also [24] of the UN Millennium Declaration passed by the UN General Assembly which states 'We will spare no effort to promote democracy and strengthen the rule of law': UN Doc A/RES/55/2 (18 September 2000).

168 However, note that references to the peaceful resolution of disputes in conformity with international law are made in the preamble as well as paragraphs 1 and 3 of Article 1.

169 According to Farrall, only one UN Security Council Resolution referred to the rule of law between 1945 and 1989: *United Nations Sanctions and The Rule of Law*, 465–7.

170 The UN acknowledges that the role of the rule of law in peacekeeping has not yet received universal recognition: see UN Doc A/61/636-S/2006/980 (14 December 2006) *Uniting Our Strengths: Enhancing United Nations Support for the Rule of Law, Report of the UN Secretary General*, [7].

peace operations by the 2000 *Report of the Panel on UN Peace Operations* (the Brahimi Report) which reflects on the decade of UN peace-building and peace-keeping since the end of the Cold War.[171] This report also considers the role of legal pluralism in UN peace operations. Written ten months after the UN began its administration of East Timor in October 1999, the Brahimi Report addresses the novel challenges presented in attempting to set and enforce the law in Kosovo and East Timor. One major obstacle in establishing some semblance of the rule of law was the choice of applicable law. The difficulties in achieving consensus and clarity on the local legal code, and the differences in 'language, culture, custom and experience', led Brahimi to recommend the development of an interim criminal code based on international standards for use by UN operations.[172] To bolster the case for a uniform code, which could include regional adaptations, Brahimi cited the problem of a mission's justice team having to learn the law and procedures of the particular country.[173] This attitude towards local law can be characterised as dismissive, but it is not apparent in the 2006 Primer put out by the UN Department of Peacekeeping Operations (UNDPKO).[174] The Primer directs that upon arrival a justice team must quickly move to identify, collect and organise the applicable local law and then map and assess the judicial and legal system. It goes further and includes in these steps the mapping of non-judicial dispute resolution and the assessment of informal structures that impact on the operation of the legal system.[175] These documents show that in the past decade the UN has made an important pragmatic shift not only towards respecting local law in post-conflict states but also towards awareness of the dynamics of legal pluralism.

[171] UN Doc A/55/305-S/2000/809 (21 August 2000) *Report of the Panel on United Nations Peace Operations*, [47b]. From 1989 to 1999 the UN deployed fourteen major peace operations.

[172] Ibid., [80, 83]. See O'Connor and Rausch, *Model Codes for Post-Conflict Criminal Justice Volume I.* On whether such a model legal code would have resolved the problems faced by the UN in East Timor, see Harper, *(Re)Constructing a Legal System in East Timor.*

[173] Ibid., [80].

[174] UNDPKO, *United Nations Primer for Justice Components.*

[175] Ibid., 19–20. In terms of strengthening the national legal framework, it states that there must be 'appropriate balance between international expertise and local legal traditions, values and culture, and the participation of the community': 29. This is more clearly spelt out by the UN Secretary General, who identifies 'customary, traditional and community-based justice and dispute resolution mechanisms' as additional priority areas for UN activities that focus on the rule of law in the context of long-term development: UN Doc A/61/636-S/2006/980 (14 December 2006) *Uniting Our Strengths: Enhancing United Nations Support for the Rule of Law, Report of the UN Secretary General*, [42]. See also [15] and [17].

Since the end of the Cold War, few mandates of the UN's peace operations have addressed transitional justice and rule-of-law activities.[176] According to the 2004 UN Report on *The Rule of Law and Transitional Justice in Conflict and Post-Conflict Societies*, this is a problem because, in the UN's diagnosis, most post-conflict societies suffer a 'rule of law vacuum'.[177] The Report further finds that where the international community is providing rule-of-law assistance, it is not always appropriate to the country context because of the tendency to impose foreign models without sufficient assessment and consultation with local stakeholders.[178] While the Report argues that 'sustainable justice' requires respect and support for local ownership and leadership as well as a local constituency,[179] there is no recognition in the Report that the concept of the rule of law may itself be a foreign model where it has little extant local tradition in the post-conflict state.

The 2004 Report usefully offers a definition of the concept so as to enable a 'common language' in the United Nations. It states that the concept is:

> a principle of governance in which all persons, institutions and entities, public and private, including the State itself, are accountable to laws that are publicly promulgated, equally enforced and independently adjudicated, and which are consistent with international human rights norms and standards. It requires, as well, measures to ensure adherence to the principles of supremacy of law, equality before the law, accountability to the law, fairness in the application of the law, separation of powers, participation in decision-making, legal certainty, avoidance of arbitrariness and procedural and legal transparency.[180]

The extensive number of principles that the concept of the rule of law subsumes according to this definition explains why the UN is pushing this concept to the forefront. The rule of law appears to be useful shorthand for a panoply of values deriving mainly from Western liberal traditions. It includes values such as 'separation of powers' and 'legal certainty' that may not be given equal weight in non-liberal traditions, such as customary traditions in South Africa, where norms regarding

[176] UN Doc S/2004/616 (23 August 2004) *Report of the Secretary General on the Rule of Law and Transitional Justice in Conflict and Post-Conflict Societies*, [11]. This is despite the fact that the UN has been the instigator of many transitional justice mechanisms. For an overview of the role of the rule of law in UN peace operations, see Hurwitz, 'Civil War and the Rule of Law', Ch. 1.

[177] Ibid., [1] and [27]. [178] Ibid., [15]. [179] Ibid., [17]. [180] Ibid., [6].

substantive justice in the context of the group as a whole outweigh legal certainty.[181] Critically, the UN definition also includes international human rights norms: these norms are central to the UN's understanding of the rule of law.[182] Thus, the rule of *law* refers *not* to any law enacted by a state but state law that is consistent with these standards. This definition is controversial, but arguably the Report only offers this definition for the purposes of the work of the UN as an organisation and does not purport to impose this definition on all its member states.[183] Nevertheless, the omnibus nature of this definition makes it more of an ideal and aspiration to strive towards, for few states in the world, if any, could be said to realise all these listed principles in their legal systems.

The 2004 Report gives legal pluralism limited recognition in relation to transitional justice. It states that 'justice' includes traditional dispute resolution *mechanisms*[184] and attention must be given to informal processes and non-official institutions.[185] Notably it does not extend this to non-state *law*.[186] The Report qualifies that this recognition of non-state processes is subject to international standards. It states:

> due regard must be given to indigenous and informal traditions for administering justice or settling disputes, to help them to continue their often vital role and to do so in conformity with both international standards and local tradition.[187]

[181] See Chapter 5.

[182] UN Doc S/2004/616 (23 August 2004) *Report of the Secretary General on the Rule of Law and Transitional Justice in Conflict and Post-Conflict Societies*, [10]. The report identifies the normative foundation for the UN's advancement of the rule of law as the four pillars of the modern international legal system: international human rights law, international humanitarian law, international criminal law and international refugee law.

[183] Note that in debates in the Sixth Committee that took place on 25 October 2007 Singapore pointed out that there was no universally agreed definition of the rule of law: UN Doc GA/L/3326 (25 October 2007) As Legal Committee Begins Debate on Rule of Law, Delegates Discuss Difference in National, International Implications. Its own definition does not appear to include international human rights norms and standards. This position might be representative of a broader Asian view, as few Asian states have ratified the International Covenant on Civil and Political Rights.

[184] UN Doc S/2004/616 (23 August 2004) *Report of the Secretary General on the Rule of Law and Transitional Justice in Conflict and Post-Conflict Societies*, [8].

[185] Ibid., [35].

[186] The report expresses concern that 'if there are no modern laws to be applied', various rule of law actors such as the police may not be effective: ibid., [30]. This suggests the UN has an ambivalent attitude to 'traditional' law and its role in peace-building.

[187] UN Doc S/2004/616 (23 August 2004) *Report of the Secretary General on the Rule of Law and Transitional Justice in Conflict and Post-Conflict Societies*, [36].

The Report acknowledges that where such traditions 'are ignored or overridden, the result can be the exclusion of large sectors of society from *accessible justice*'.[188] Here the Report links legal pluralism to accessible justice, but it is noteworthy that even though the Report asserts that UN programmes 'must support access to justice',[189] accessible justice is not included in the UN's lengthy definition of the rule of law quoted above. As Parts II and III of this book illustrate, there is tension between the rule of law and accessible justice in both South Africa and Timor-Leste where the majority of the populations have serious difficulties in accessing the state legal system.

A similar approach is taken by the OHCHR in its 2006 guide for UN field missions and transitional administrations, entitled *Rule of Law Tools for Post-Conflict States*, which emphasises that despite the 'great legitimacy' enjoyed by customary law, field officers should not blindly endorse it.[190] The guide advises that field officers can assist national reformers by setting out which elements are consistent with international human rights norms and which elements present problems. However, it acknowledges that this task 'can be a delicate undertaking with varying degrees of risk'.[191] Consistent with other UN documents, the guide's advice distinguishes the substantive aspects of customary law from the procedural by recommending the use of the 'local traditional justice mechanism or mediation model'.[192] From this we can conclude that the UN does not consider the procedural aspects of customary law and traditional justice to be inconsistent with the concept of the rule of law. Rather, it raises concern that the substance of such law is framed as potentially incompatible with international human rights law and, by implication, with the rule of law.[193]

While the 2004 UNSG's report recognised the vital role played by 'indigenous and informal traditions' in offering accessible justice, it did not directly comment on their connection with the rule of law. This connection is articulated in the 2011 follow-on report of the UNSG on *The Rule of Law and Transitional Justice in Conflict and Post-Conflict Societies* (2011 Report):

188 Ibid., [36].
189 Ibid. See UNDP, *Access to Justice – Practice Note*; UNDP, *Programming for Justice.*
190 OHCHR, *Rule of Law Tools for Post-Conflict States: Mapping the Justice Sector*, 14.
191 Ibid. 192 Ibid., 15.
193 See also *Guidance Note of the Secretary-General: United Nations Approach to Rule of Law Assistance* (April 2008) 7, 3.

> In many post-conflict settings, informal justice mechanisms are the only available recourse to serve the public's justice needs. *Recognizing the potential of informal mechanisms in strengthening the rule of law*, the Organization has increased its understanding of informal justice systems. While providing timely and enforceable decisions, the Organization is aware of their uneven compliance with international norms and standards, and pervasive gender bias. ... The potential role of informal justice practices to enhance peace and security through traditional mediation techniques has been recognized.[194]

This recognition of the role that informal justice mechanisms can play in strengthening the rule of law as well as peace and security is a turning point in the UN's approach to the rule of law which previously focused exclusively on formal justice mechanisms.[195] This partly reflects the work of the UN Development Programme (UNDP) which, since 2004, has been examining the role that informal justice mechanisms play in providing access to justice that is 'timely and enforceable'.[196] As the 2011 Report makes clear, the UN continues to express concern regarding the compliance of these mechanisms with human rights standards, particularly those relating to women. Despite this, through UNDP, the UN's current approach has been to assist post-conflict states in building linkages between informal and formal systems, for example in Afghanistan, Liberia, Nepal, Somalia, South Sudan and Timor-Leste,[197] presumably in a bid to strengthen the rule of law in these states.[198]

194 UN Doc S/2011/634 (12 October 2011) *Report of the Secretary General on the Rule of Law and Transitional Justice in Conflict and Post-Conflict Societies*, [39] (emphasis added). The 2011 UN Women report *Progress of the World's Women 2011–2012* also addresses the issue of legal pluralism: it highlights the issue of legal pluralism and justice for women, arguing that it is not sufficient to look at the institutional barriers that women face in pursuing justice within the formal state system but it is imperative to also address the barriers posed by customary law, for example, that operate in plural legal systems.

195 The shift is also demonstrated by the fact that UNDP now claims to embrace Dag Hammarskjold's broad definition of the rule of law which states that it 'includes not only the written law, but also the whole pattern of established rule of action and behaviour': UNDP, *Strengthening the Rule of Law in Conflict and Post-Conflict Situations.*

196 See Wojkowska, *Doing Justice.*

197 UN Doc S/2011/634 (12 October 2011) *Report of the Secretary General on the Rule of Law and Transitional Justice in Conflict and Post-Conflict Societies*, [39].

198 The nature of these linkages has differed from state to state. The UN explains that in Uganda and South Sudan, UNDP has been involved in the codification of customary laws while in Darfur, Indonesia and Afghanistan, UNDP has focused on raising awareness of informal justice leaders regarding women's rights. In Somalia UNDP has been involved in a referral system by which sexual and gender-based violence cases can be

The trajectory of the UN's shifting policy towards the rule of law and its relationship with legal pluralism can be seen in its approach to the administration of Timor-Leste. Express reference to the rule of law is noticeably absent from the initial UN Security Council mandate for the UN's transitional administration of East Timor in 1999. The rule of law has only been mentioned since 2003 with regard to the mandate of UN Missions in Timor-Leste.[199] The UN responded to the 2006 crisis in Timor-Leste by appointing a Deputy Special Representative to focus on 'Security Sector Support and the Rule of Law'.[200] In regard to legal pluralism, it appears that at the beginning of the UN's administration of East Timor the UN had little awareness of the local population's extensive reliance on customary law. However, since 1999 the UN has shown constant concern about the population's limited access to state justice. In January 2008, the Secretary-General's Report on the UN Integrated Mission in Timor-Leste (UNMIT) once again emphasised 'the need for increased access to justice'.[201] However, the Report revealed that Timor-Leste's Ministry of Justice had 'requested UNMIT assistance in drafting a legal framework to formalise traditional justice mechanisms'.[202] This followed recommendations made by the World Bank, as well as UNMIT's Human Rights and Transitional Justice Section, to formally incorporate aspects of traditional justice, specifically traditional 'mechanisms', into the formal legal system so that they operate in a more transparent and human rights-abiding way.[203] In response, UNDP has assisted Timor-Leste to draft a 'linkage' law to link these traditional mechanisms to the formal legal system.[204]

5.2 *UN member states*

To date the UN has not expressed a general position on legal pluralism. This may be in part due to the fact that the status of customary law is

referred to the formal courts. See UN Doc A/66/133 (8 August 2011) *Strengthening and Coordinating United Nations Rule of Law Activities*, [27].

199 SC Res. 1473 (4 April 2003), [1(iii)]. See also SC Res 1599 (28 April 2005), [3].

200 This position lapsed after eighteen months. On the 2006 crisis in Timor-Leste, see Chapter 7, section 1.1.

201 UN Doc S/2008/26 (17 January 2008) *Report of the Secretary-General on the United Nations Integrated Mission in Timor-Leste (for the period from 21 August 2007 to 7 January 2008)*, [24].

202 Ibid., [36].

203 Recommendation made by UNMIT's Human Rights and Transitional Justice Section, *Report on Human Rights Developments in Timor-Leste* (2007), 29.

204 See Chapter 7, section 4.5 for an explanation of this UN assistance.

controversial for a number of member states. The fault lines regarding customary law became apparent in 2007 during debates in the General Assembly on the adoption of the *UN Declaration on the Rights of Indigenous Peoples* (UNDRIP).[205] The resolution had particularly strong support from Latin American states, many of which have given constitutional recognition to indigenous justice institutions and indigenous laws.[206] Four Western states, Australia, the US, Canada and New Zealand, were alone in voting against the adoption of UNDRIP, partly out of concern that this non-binding instrument introduced a form of legal pluralism via Article 34. This article provides that indigenous peoples have the 'right to promote, develop and maintain their … juridical systems or customs, in accordance with international human rights standards'. The concern was that this recognition of customary law 'placed Indigenous customary law in a superior position to national law' and hence customary law could potentially override national law.[207] Given the fact that the Declaration is non-binding and any recognition of customary law is subject to international human rights law, this concern was largely misplaced. Despite this, the concern indicates a high level of anxiety and aversion to legal pluralism on the part of some leading Western states with sizeable indigenous populations.

During the debates on UNDRIP, Australia asserted: 'Customary law is not "law" in the sense that modern democracies use the term; it is based on culture and tradition.'[208] This projection of 'modern' law being acultural and ahistorical coincides with the UN's conception of the rule of law as a universal value that transcends culture and tradition. Following changes in governments, these four Western states later reversed their positions and expressed their support for the Declaration.

[205] The Declaration (UN Doc A/RES/61/295 (2 October 2007)) was approved on 13 September 2007 by 143 member states, with 11 abstentions, 4 votes against and 34 absences. Similar concerns are set out in the Convention concerning Indigenous and Tribal Peoples in Independent Countries (ILO No. 169), Art 8 and 9.

[206] For the UN GA voting record and statements, see UN Doc GA/10612 (13 September 2007) General Assembly Adopts Declaration on Rights of Indigenous Peoples; 'Major Step Forward' Towards Human Rights for All, says President. On Latin American constitutions and legal pluralism, see UN Doc E/CN.4/2006/78 (26 January 2006) *Report of the UN Special Rapporteur*, [8–9]; Seider and Sierra, *Indigenous Women's Access*, 4–9; Fajardo, 'Legal Pluralism, Indigenous Law'.

[207] Explanation of Australia's vote against the UN GA adoption of the *UNDRIP* by the Hon. Robert Hill, Ambassador and Permanent Representative of Australia to the UN: UN Doc A/61/PV.107 (13 September 2007), 11.

[208] Ibid.

Nevertheless, Australia's comments are telling: they arguably articulate an unspoken view about customary law held among those Western democracies with significant indigenous populations.

The UN's political organs have not made any statements which endorse customary law as law *per se*. There are some hurdles to the UN shifting its current approach to legal pluralism: first, the UN is a leading promoter of international law, which means that at the international level it is already involved in promoting a particular form of legal pluralism (the convergence of international and national law) and a further layer of legal pluralism could distract from this programme. Second, a strong invocation of a third level of law would be structurally inconsistent with the principle of state sovereignty, the basis of the UN system. Thus the UN is unlikely to go any further in its advocacy of the local as it is already walking a tightrope between legal pluralism and state centralism. Overall, given that the UN system is based on nation-states, it is surprising that the UN pays any attention to legal pluralism at the national level. In the post-conflict context, this attention can be put down to the UN's concern that the Westphalian model of the state is failing in some regions such as Africa, Asia and the Pacific where non-state custom and tradition still command more reliance than centralised administration.

5.3 *Structural aspects of the UN and the World Bank*

It is important to remember that the UN system has not been set up as a model for the rule of law in the domestic setting. For example, the horizontal, decentralised and consensual nature of the international system does not oblige all states to accept the compulsory jurisdiction of the International Court of Justice or the International Criminal Court. Compliance with international law cannot be easily enforced. While breaches of international law may be followed by political sanctions by other states, the system embodies few checks and balances.[209] Although the *Charter of the United Nations* states that one of the purposes of the United Nations is to

[209] See Chesterman, 'An International Rule of Law?', 351–4; Rajagopal, 'Invoking the Rule of Law in Post-Conflict Rebuilding', 1373–4. In regard to the UN Security Council, see Chesterman, *The UN Security Council and the Rule of Law*; Security Council Report, *Cross-Cutting Report on the Rule of Law* (2011). For discussion of the lack of transparency and formal review in regard to individuals listed for UN targeted sanctions, see Chesterman, 'The Spy Who Came in From the Cold War', 1109–20. See the 2006 UN Security Council debates on the rule of law in the international sphere: UN Doc S/PV.5474 (22 June 2006) Security Council's 5474th meeting, New York.

promote and encourage 'respect for human rights', and that the United Nations 'shall promote universal respect for, and observance of, human rights', the scope of these obligations is unclear when applied to the Organization as an actor.[210] Indeed, there is uncertainty as to whether, and to what extent, the UN, as an international organisation, is subject to international human rights law. As the United Nations is not party to the core UN human rights treaties, which technically can only bind nation-states, it is not formally bound by their provisions, though it is arguable that it is bound by customary international human rights law.[211]

Similarly, IFIs are not structured along a domestic rule-of-law model. As Antony Anghie points out, the World Bank lacks a process of independent judicial review of executive actions.[212] He asserts that these institutions are not only 'fundamentally undemocratic' but they 'appear not to be subject to any external scrutiny as to their adherence to the rule of law'.[213]

Despite the fact that these international organisations do not model the domestic rule of law, they are leading international efforts to promote the rule of law in post-conflict states such as Timor-Leste. As Roland Paris observes, peacebuilders such as the UN have been actively involved in the transmission of standards to the periphery.[214] These include the liberal norms of international human rights law. The transmission of these liberal norms need not involve their imposition by an external actor such as the UN or the IFIs. South Africa embraced these norms without any obvious external imposition while Timor-Leste also voluntarily embraced these norms in its Constitution, with little overt UN influence. While these standards are defined as acceptable behaviour by 'the centre', the UN, they are not necessarily always upheld by it. This is shown during the UN's transitional administration of Timor-Leste where in response to the *Alves* case the UN attempted to use retroactive legislation to validate a period of pre-trial detention contrary to Articles 9 and 14 of the *International Covenant on Civil and Political Rights*.[215] Arguably the

210 Articles 1(3) and 55(c).

211 See Chesterman, 'An International Rule of Law?', 352; Devereux, 'Searching for Clarity', 298–9; White and Klaasen, *Post-Conflict Situations*, Ch. 19.

212 Anghie, 'Time Present and Time Past', 263–72.

213 Ibid., 270, 271.

214 Paris, 'The "Mission Civilisatrice"', 638.

215 See section 3.1 of Chapter 6. For similar examples in Kosovo, see Ombudsman Institution in Kosovo, *Second Annual Report (2001–2002)* 1, 5. See also Trenkov-Wermuth, *United Nations Justice*, Chs 3 and 4. On the accountability deficit in international organisations involved in post-conflict states, see Caplan, *International Governance*, Ch. 9.

contemporary promotion of the rule of law by bodies such as the UN may be viewed as a modern rendering of the *mission civilisatrice*, in that it demonstrates that there is still a belief that a state with functioning rule-of-law institutions is superior to all others.

Finally, we need to consider why, since the end of the Cold War, international organisations such as the UN and the World Bank promote a rule-of-law orthodoxy directed primarily toward working with state institutions[216] and prefer the rule of law to other concepts such as 'legal empowerment' and 'access to justice'.[217] This choice to promote the rule of law is surprising given three factors: first, the LADM's poor track record of establishing the rule of law in various regions prior to the 1990s; second, the scant empirical evidence that the concept operates to meet its goal of protecting the most vulnerable members of society[218]; and third, the fact that the rule of *customary* law is prevalent in many developing and post-conflict countries in Africa and the Asia-Pacific region.[219] The answer lies partly in the structural biases of the UN and IFIs. For the UN it seems that the top-down nature of the rule of law, its focus on the state institutional level rather than the grass-roots level, is well suited to an organisation that is a creature of treaty and is based on state membership. Indeed, it is precisely its top-down nature that makes the rule of law the preferred concept for the UN. For IFIs such as the World Bank it is simply easier to organise loan schemes targeting state institutions rather than the grass-roots level. The emphasis on the rule of law and good governance means that IFI loans can be aimed at inducing state institutions to act in a way that is conducive to the dual mandate of democracy and the market.

6. Conclusion

Since the era of colonialism, there have been a number of important shifts in the understanding of the rule of law and legal pluralism, culminating in the rule of law becoming the dominant paradigm. The concept has been linked with civilisation, the modern state, capitalist

216 Golub, 'A House Without a Foundation', 131.

217 This question is posed by Golub in regard to the UN: Golub, 'The Rule of Law'.

218 Kavanagh and Jones, *Shaky Foundations*, [22]–[24]. In *Making the Law Work for Everyone: Volume 1*, the Commission on Legal Empowerment of the Poor (in conjunction with UNDP) claims that 'most studies find that the rule of law makes a significant contribution to growth and poverty reduction' (19) but the Report does not specify which studies this claim is based on.

219 See statistics cited in Chapter 1.

investment, human rights and democracy, and it has been transformed into a cure-all for post-conflict states. This is despite the widespread recognition that most rule-of-law programmes have been playing a marginal and ambiguous role in relation to the lives of the poor and vulnerable sections of society because they have focused almost exclusively on strengthening the formal state legal system. It is broadly acknowledged that the rule of law's focus on strengthening institutions of the Westphalian state has served the interests of capitalism and the state-based system. Since the beginning of the twenty-first century, however, there have been signs that this approach is changing, as there is increased attention on access to justice and dispute resolution. Customary law is no longer ignored as anachronistic, backward and uncivilised. Legal pluralism is becoming the subject of a more nuanced understanding among key actors in the international community. The limitations and trade-offs of a rule-of-law approach are increasingly apparent. International NGOs, IDAs and international organisations are beginning to engage with this non-state sphere as they recognise the role of legal pluralism in the lives of the poor and vulnerable, particularly in regard to access to justice and dispute resolution. It is arguable that post-conflict states such as Timor-Leste have influenced this shift of the international community toward legal pluralism as a result of the failure of state-based rule-of-law programmes to deliver access to justice in such states.

The impact of this globalised relationship between the rule of law and legal pluralism on post-conflict states can be seen in their willingness to sign up to the rule of law. This is the case even where other concepts may be more useful to such states given their particular circumstances. This willingness relates not only to the dominance of the rule of law as a norm in the global arena but also to its elastic nature. However, while post-conflict states embrace the rule of law on the international stage, their internal negotiation of the concept alongside legal pluralism is much more complex. The next chapter investigates the conceptual relationship between the rule of law and legal pluralism in order to illuminate their intersection in the post-conflict context.

3

The conceptual relationship between legal pluralism and the rule of law in post-conflict states

This book emphasises that actors involved in promoting the rule of law in post-conflict states should be equipped with a nuanced understanding of the relationship between the rule of law and legal pluralism at both a global and conceptual level. In regard to the latter, one leading legal scholar has asserted that while legal pluralism is a 'fact', the rule of law, as a form of legal centralism, is a 'myth'.[1] To what extent is this true? How do these two concepts intersect and come into contact in post-conflict and transitional states? While in the context of the Western state the two concepts may often appear incompatible, this book argues that the relationship between the two concepts is often transformed in the context of the particular dynamics of those post-conflict and transitional states with strong legal pluralism.

This chapter sets out how these two concepts are understood in theory and practice. As a prelude to Parts II and III of this book, this chapter briefly traces how the two concepts intersect in the context of post-conflict Afghanistan where there is discussion of linking state law with informal systems of law so as to enhance both the legitimacy of the state and access to justice outside the capital, Kabul.

1. Legal pluralism

Legal pluralism is considered both a fact and a programme. In these forms it has been largely marginalised in global debates on justice. William Twining speculates that the reason for this is the domination of Western legal theory by:

> conceptions of law that tend to be monist (one internally coherent legal system), statist (the state has a monopoly of law within its own territory), and positivist (what is not created or recognised as law by the state is not law).[2]

1 Griffiths, 'What is Legal Pluralism?', 38.

2 Twining, *Globalisation and Legal Theory*, 232.

This statement highlights the tension in the relationship between the rule of law and legal pluralism. As a programme, legal pluralism is the assertion that the state does not have a monopoly over law. It recognises the fact of legal pluralism, that there are plural sources of law, and it gives these sources equal status. The idea that there are plural sources of law in society challenges the central assumptions made by liberal adherents of the rule of law. Advocates of the rule of law assume that there is a single, coherent body of norms that derive from one clear source, the state. Rule-of-law approaches predominantly identify law solely with the state; they are mostly blind to non-state law. This assumption is called state centralism or state-centrism.

As both a fact and a programme, legal pluralism offers a broader understanding of the law, one that is not limited to state coercive power in the public sphere. Legal pluralism opens law to the understanding of other forms of power, such as regulatory power, and how law cuts across both public and private spheres.[3] It embraces civil society as a source of law and regulation and in this it turns its focus equally on the private sphere and on the public sphere. In this sense it incorporates a 'bottom-up' approach. At a general level, legal pluralism understands all laws as equal; unlike state centralism it does not presuppose one law to be superior to another. There is no particular formula for the relationship between these different spheres of law that constitute legal pluralism: they can exist in a symbiotic or complementary relationship or they can be antagonistic and hegemonial in nature.[4]

In Africa and the Asia-Pacific region, the question of legal pluralism arises constantly. For example, in Timor-Leste, apart from customary laws in each district and the national laws passed by the Government and Parliament of Timor-Leste, the individual must also contend with the ambiguity surrounding the applicability of the laws of Portugal, its former coloniser, Indonesia, its former occupier, the Regulations issued by the UN, its former administrator, and international laws incorporated through constitutional provisions. In South Africa the matter becomes more complex as the individual must navigate an even greater plurality of laws: Roman-Dutch common law, apartheid laws, post-apartheid laws, religious laws of Islam, Judaism and Hinduism, international law, 'people's law' and customary law, both official and 'living' versions.[5]

[3] Davies, 'The Ethos of Pluralism', 103.
[4] Baxi, 'Discipline, Repression and Legal Pluralism', 52.
[5] For an overview, see van Niekerk, 'Legal Pluralism', Ch. 1.

The above form of inquiry into legal pluralism in former colonial societies is that of 'classic legal pluralism'[6] which has been the mainstay of legal anthropologists and legal sociologists since the early twentieth century. Its focus on former colonies has meant that legal pluralism became characterised as something particular only to such states. This 'particularism' has allowed legal pluralism to be easily sidelined by mainstream legal theorists.

Since the 1970s, however, the lens of legal pluralism has been turned back onto the West: 'new legal pluralism' asserts the plurality of laws in *all* societies, regardless of whether they were colonised. It finds plural normative orders in all modern societies but it focuses particularly on modern Western societies.[7] New legal pluralism emphasises the universality of legal pluralism: for example, John Griffiths argues that legal pluralism is a 'universal feature of social organisation'.[8] Merry observes that there is 'general agreement that pluralism does not describe a type of society but is a condition found to a greater or lesser extent in most societies'.[9] This has led Griffiths to make the above-quoted claim that: 'Legal pluralism is the fact. Legal centralism is a myth, an ideal, a claim, an illusion.'[10]

1.1 State law pluralism and deep legal pluralism

Legal pluralism has two forms: (1) *state law pluralism* is where the state has incorporated parts of non-state law, such as customary law, into its legal hierarchy. This can happen through various means[11] such as the annexation of non-state courts or through the codification or restatement of aspects

[6] This term as well as 'new legal pluralism' is used by Merry, 'Legal Pluralism', 872.

[7] New legal pluralism rejects the narrow preoccupation of classic legal pluralism with state-recognised law. Legal plurality is seen broadly, as operating in institutions such as universities, trade unions, companies and factories where the dominance of the state legal system is less apparent.

[8] Griffiths, 'What is Legal Pluralism?', 38. Merry is more guarded in asserting that: 'virtually every society is legally plural': Merry, 'Legal Pluralism', 871.

[9] Merry, 'Legal Pluralism', 879. Unlike deep legal pluralism, which can be described as an incontrovertible 'fact', state law pluralism is a choice made by states to engage formally with other forms of law. States can, of course, choose to attempt to abolish other forms of law but this inevitably relegates that form of law to the sphere of deep legal pluralism, as states rarely have the power to control other forms of law to the point of total abolition. However, groups can also make a conscious choice as to whether to use state law or to use an alternative form of law. Hence, like state law pluralism, deep legal pluralism is more than a fact; it is also a matter of ideology but it is not a fixed ideology.

[10] Griffiths, 'What is Legal Pluralism?', 4.

[11] For an insightful analysis of the various options open to states, see Toomey, 'Building Complementary'.

of indigenous law such as native title law in Australia; (2) *deep legal pluralism* is where there is no hierarchy of legal systems – state law and non-state law exist without any formal relationship. Like many Western states, Australia also has deep legal pluralism because many indigenous groups have continued to observe their own laws, which, with few exceptions, such as native title, are not recognised or regulated by the state.[12] Kosovo also has deep legal pluralism as Kosovo Serbs continue to operate parallel courts that answer to Belgrade rather than Pristina.[13]

The balance between these forms of legal pluralism is not static in any particular region. According to Lauren Benton, deep legal pluralism was dominant in the West from the fourteenth century until the late eighteenth century, at the time when Portugal was colonising parts of Asia and the Dutch were colonising the southern tip of Africa.[14] Early modern Europe enjoyed deep legal pluralism, as secular law and canon law both operated outside a single hierarchy, often alongside a form of Germanic customary law that influenced many parts of Europe.[15] By the mid-nineteenth century, state law pluralism became the dominant policy in European states as well as their colonies in Asia and Africa.[16] This change was possibly related to the rise of legal positivism and the notion of the Westphalian state in Europe. Benton argues that this historical shift shows that state law pluralism is not timeless but 'historically recent and contingent'.[17] In other words, there is a long history of legal pluralism in the West.

The 1970s shift away from studying state law pluralism is illustrated by the work of Griffiths, who argues that in order to escape from state centrism, legal pluralism should be discussed outside a hierarchical framework of law.[18] For Griffiths, one of the problems with state law pluralism is the tendency of many of its adherents to assume that it is a means to the harmonisation and unification of two or more legal systems. In this framework, legal pluralism is not seen as an end in itself.

[12] Australian Law Reform Commission, *Aboriginal Customary Laws*; Law Reform Commission of Western Australia, *Aboriginal Customary Laws*.

[13] Baylis, 'Parallel Courts'; Trenkov-Wermuth, *United Nations Justice*, 82. A form of customary law, known as Leke Dukagjini, also operates.

[14] Benton, *Law and Colonial Cultures*, 5.

[15] Tamanaha, *On the Rule of Law*, 23–5.

[16] Benton, *Law and Colonial Cultures*, 6.

[17] Ibid., 30.

[18] In other words, Griffiths views state law pluralism as consistent with the ideology of state-centrism because it uses a hierarchical approach and hence he dismisses it as a false form of legal pluralism. Thus, true legal pluralism is an attribute of a social field rather than of a legal system: Griffiths, 'What is Legal Pluralism?', 8, 38.

The framework shows a teleological and linear view of law and transition that can be seen in Weber's work. The assumption here is that legal pluralism is not a durable solution: it is considered a temporary, stop-gap solution until traditional communities have 'integrated' with the modern, Western-influenced legal system in the name of 'development'. This approach was taken by a number of newly independent countries in Africa and the Asia-Pacific region in the second half of the twentieth century. Efforts were made not only to unify different court systems and the various local forms of customary law into one law but some countries, such as Ghana and Senegal, went so far as to try to integrate customary law with modern colonial law, thus attempting to do away with legal pluralism entirely.[19]

Some post-colonial countries, such as Mozambique and Ethiopia, did not integrate customary law but endeavoured to abolish it. According to Gordon Woodman, state law pluralism is to be preferred over abolition because it is not possible for a state to abolish customary law entirely. He disputes Griffiths' rejection of state law pluralism as irrelevant to the study of legal pluralism.[20] Woodman believes that Griffiths has assumed that state law is a coherent body of norms and that when non-state law is incorporated into state law it becomes part of a totality, a unified structure of norms, practices and institutions.[21] This account of state law fails to recognise its inconsistencies and inner plurality. In other words, legal pluralism exists both outside and *inside* the state legal system.[22] When customary law is incorporated into state law, through the unification of court systems, communities may remain the source of the law and hence there are multiple sources of validity, some of which are independent of the state. The transfer of the application and enforcement of customary law to state institutions does not mean that coherence and consistency is automatically produced within state law. Indeed, state law becomes a more highly contested terrain. This contestation can be seen in South Africa's post-apartheid negotiation of state law pluralism. It is partly the contested nature of state law pluralism that leads Woodman to plead that it not be ignored by the field of legal pluralism.

[19] Mamdani, *Citizen and Subject*, 129.

[20] Woodman, 'Legal Pluralism', 152. His approach is less abstract in that he considers legal pluralism from the perspective of the subject: from this standpoint he argues that, 'in the search for justice', state law pluralism is preferable to deep legal pluralism because it creates greater certainty for the subject.

[21] Ibid., 158. [22] Davies, 'The Ethos of Pluralism', 103.

1.2 The benefits and limitations of legal pluralism

Legal pluralism can be used in many ways: while some governments and groups have attempted to use legal pluralism as a programme by which to achieve equality, others have used it for the purposes of domination and subordination. This explains why legal pluralism is at times romanticised by scholars such as Griffiths, and sometimes deplored.

Legal pluralism is often understood as a means of increasing access to justice and dispute resolution in developing countries and transitional states. Where access to the state justice system is limited, legal pluralism is beneficial in enabling other paths to accessing justice and dispute resolution. In this regard legal pluralism assists in the critical job of maintaining law and order because the state is often incapable of providing these basic services. By allowing people to use law that is embedded in local values, as opposed to potentially alien national values, legal pluralism can facilitate a sense of community, cultural accommodation and equality. Indirectly, this can be a step towards justice for minorities, and reconciliation between various groups. For example, the recognition of customary law by the 1996 South African Constitution symbolises the equal status of the African groups that observe such law.[23] However, where the state is hostile to the law of such groups, deep legal pluralism can be an avenue of resistance to oppressive state law. This was the case in apartheid South Africa where 'people's courts' developed a form of non-state law that was observed in urban areas, particularly in the 1980s, as a reaction to the lack of legitimacy of the apartheid legal order.[24]

At a more abstract level, legal pluralism ensures interaction between the law and its social context and hence it is a 'bottom up' approach to law. Legal anthropologists such as Sally Falk Moore remind us that spheres of law, such as state law, do not operate in an autonomous or isolated fashion. They can never be abstracted from the social context or from other spheres of law, whether they are local or international, because to do so is to miss half the picture. Moore calls these legal fields and orders 'semi-autonomous social fields' because they are porous and fluid. She observes that innovative legislation and other attempts to direct

[23] See s. 211(3), discussed in Chapter 5, section 3.2.

[24] People's courts began appearing in black townships in 1960s and 1970s and they were particularly prevalent in the last decade of apartheid as a form of resistance to the apartheid legal system. In 1985 police reports estimated there were 400 people's courts in operation. Association with mob violence tainted some of these courts when leadership fell to unsupervised youths. See Chapter 5, section 1.

change, such as those of the LADM and the World Bank, often fail to meet their intended purposes, or they produce unplanned consequences because social arrangements with binding obligations may already exist in the same field, and these arrangements may be stronger than the new legislation.[25] She concludes that: 'Law and the social context in which it operates must be inspected together.'[26]

On the other hand, legal pluralism as a programme has been criticised as being 'quite reactionary'.[27] One leading social theorist, Boaventura de Sousa Santos, asserts: 'there is nothing inherently good, progressive or emancipatory about legal pluralism'.[28] Legal pluralism has been used for the domination, control and subordination of various groups. The apartheid era in South Africa illustrates the 'pathological'[29] side of legal pluralism as it was used not only for the purposes of law and order but also to segregate and subordinate Africans on tribal and racial grounds through the court system. As a programme, legal pluralism can also be used to condone and encourage different standards of justice. At independence, most former colonies in Africa and the Asia-Pacific region chose not to preserve legal pluralism because they wanted equal justice for all.[30] Today the problem of different standards of justice being applied on the basis of urban-rural and class divides is particularly fraught in developing countries such as India[31] and transitional countries such as South Africa. While forum shopping can assist the vulnerable sections of society in enjoying a choice between forums, more generally it

[25] Moore, *Law as Process*, 58.

[26] Ibid., 55. Moore's work argues that legal analysis has been too legocentric in nature. In this she follows a long line of thinkers such as Friedrich Carl von Savigny, Henry Maine, Eugen Ehrlich and Bronislaw Malinowski who emphasise the cultural and social nature of law. Moore's approach has proved to be useful particularly for the study of women's engagement with the law in Africa: see Bentzon et al., *Pursuing Grounded Theory*, 46.

[27] Santos, *Law, Globalization and Emancipation*, 89.

[28] Ibid. Santos prefers to speak of a plurality of legal orders.

[29] Chanock, 'The South African Native Administration Act', 295.

[30] In 1945 in newly independent Indonesia, for example, the government chose to discard local law because there was a belief that having two legal systems bred inequality, discrimination and confusion as different laws were for different people. Previously in colonial Dutch Indonesia, European law governed the legal rights of Europeans, Chinese and Arabs and others classified as 'foreign orientals' while locals were subject to local laws. However, a local who commenced a legal action in one region would be judged differently from a local in another region because of the variance in local laws. The new national government sought to impose uniformity on the laws.

[31] Galanter and Krishnan, 'Debased Informalism', 109; Whitson, 'Neither Fish, nor Flesh', 391.

advantages the wealthy and politically savvy, who have both the knowledge and resources to take advantage of the situation. In this sense legal pluralism can reinforce social and economic inequalities, which can have a particular impact on women.[32]

Apart from problems relating to equality, legal pluralism is the subject of other criticisms. Deep legal pluralism can subject individuals to conflicting duties, place defendants in danger of double jeopardy and generally increase unpredictability in the law. At an abstract level, deep legal pluralism makes it difficult to distinguish law from culture:[33] the boundaries between law, legal culture and societal traditions are left unclear. This challenges the coherence of the law but it also dulls the lustre of legal pluralism as a useful concept. Tamanaha's practical suggestion here is that law should be understood as 'whatever people identify and treat through their social practices as "law"'.[34] On a more abstract plane, legal pluralism as a programme can be criticised for strengthening relativism, in that it is not possible to judge particular practices,[35] and for demoting the superior position of international law, because legal pluralism holds all spheres of law to be of equal status.

The main problem with legal pluralism is that as a programme it fails to say anything about justice: it does not set out a path by which it is best for plural systems of law to interact in order to best achieve justice. Many theorists suggest that the core study of legal pluralism is to examine the *interactions* between legal systems but they do not prescribe any particular strategy by which this interaction could most benefit the most vulnerable.[36] In this sense it is no more than a description of a fact. Overall, legal pluralism says little about the nature of justice except that it flows from multiple sources. It provides no criteria by which to assess which source of law provides justice to the most vulnerable sections of society.

[32] International Council on Human Rights Policy, *When Legal Worlds Overlap*, 82–4. For examples in South Africa and Timor-Leste, see Chapters 5 and 7.

[33] For example, two proponents of legal pluralism, Malinowski and Ehrlich, respectively assert that all binding obligations should be considered law and that: 'the law is an ordering': Malinowski, *Crime and Custom*, 14; Ehrlich, *Sociology of Law*, 24. This was a response to ethnocentric claims that identified law with civilisation and asserted that 'primitive' societies did not have law.

[34] Tamanaha, *A General Jurisprudence*, 193–4. For a critical reading of this approach, see Roberts, 'After Government?' 21.

[35] But see Selznick, who argues that a pluralist would admit that there are objective moral principles but each practice must be scrutinised and assessed in light of the particular circumstances: Selznick, *The Moral Commonwealth*, 115.

[36] See, e.g., Chiba, 'Introduction'; Santos, *Toward a New Common Sense*.

As a programme, legal pluralism provides guidance neither in relation to procedural justice nor to substantive justice. As Koskenniemi observes, apart from highlighting diversity and freedom, legal pluralism 'cannot sustain a project of law in its own right'.[37]

2. The rule of law

In contrast, the concept of the rule of law is often spoken of in the same breath as justice and even sometimes substituted for it. E.P. Thompson famously praised the rule of law as 'an unqualified human good', despite the fact that laws themselves can often be unjust.[38] On the other hand, Joseph Raz has advised that we should be 'wary of disqualifying the legal pursuit of major social goals in the name of the rule of law'.[39] Far from being characterised as a 'fact', the rule of law has been called 'the white myth of transition' because it is an aspiration of states undergoing transition during the post-Cold War era.[40]

While in Germany the comparable notion to the rule of law is *Rechtsstaat* or 'constitutional state' and in the US it is 'due process of law', all these notions can be characterised alongside the rule of law as state-centric: at their heart they make the assumption that the state has a monopoly on law. Rarely do the many proponents or even critics of the rule of law examine this assumption in much depth. The following exposition of some of the main tenets of the key approaches to the rule of law shows that these approaches take for granted the existence of a strong state in the Westphalian model. I argue that these approaches have given little consideration to the rule of law in the context where legal pluralism is strong.

Krygier describes the rule of law as 'an interconnected cluster of values'.[41] The two key approaches to this cluster of values are variously explained as thin or thick, formal/procedural or substantive, and rule-book or rights-based. The first approach advocates the following procedural values: (1) legal predictability and certainty; (2) government bound by law; (3) equality before the law; and (4) law and order.[42] The second

37 Koskenniemi, 'The Fate of Public International Law', 24.

38 Thompson, *Whigs and Hunters,* 266.

39 Raz, 'The Rule of Law', 228–9.

40 Krastev, 'Corruption, Anti-Corruption Sentiments', 323.

41 Krygier, 'The Rule of Law', 13404.

42 These values are identified by Kleinfeld as the end goals of the rule of law: 'Competing Definitions', 31.

of these approaches generally upholds all the same four values as the first but adds substantive values based on human rights or moral dignity. In certain circumstances, this second approach holds that the added fifth, substantive, value can trump those four values more highly cherished by the first approach. As we saw in the previous chapter, all five values are advocated by the international human rights movement as well as by both the UN and recent World Bank policy, but the mode in which they are promoted is often inconsistent and elastic, depending on the particular arm or agency of these two large international institutions. Within the group advocating this thick approach, there is debate as to precisely which rights should be included; whether they should be confined to civil and political rights or extended to socio-economic rights.[43] I now explore the manner in which the first three of the procedural values have been theorised in order to underline the degree to which they can be fairly characterised as state-centric and to illustrate how the post-conflict context poses a different set of challenges and dynamics than those generally considered by Western scholars.

2.1 *Legal predictability and certainty*

Like Max Weber, the English philosopher Friedrich Hayek, an influential proponent of a formal approach and a conservative liberal, argues that predictability is the primary value of the rule of law. He asserts that this predictability promotes individual liberty: it enables individual autonomy to flourish in that people are able to plan their affairs. He defines the rule of law thus:

> Stripped of all technicalities, this means that *government in all its actions is bound by rules fixed and announced before-hand* – rules which make it possible to foresee with fair certainty *how the authority will use its coercive powers* in given circumstances and to plan one's individual affairs on the basis of this knowledge.[44]

[43] For the inclusion of only civil and political rights in post-conflict and development rule-of-law programmes, see Stromseth et al., *Can Might Make Rights?* and Trebilcock and Daniels, *Rule of Law Reform*. For the inclusion of socio-economic rights, see Charlesworth, 'Human Rights and the Rule of Law After Conflict'. More broadly, Lord Bingham's increasingly influential conception of the rule of law includes 'such human rights as, within that society, are seen as fundamental'. In discussing the British context he doubts that the rule of law addresses the full range of civil and political rights protected by the European Convention on Human Rights: 'The Rule of Law', 77, 76.

[44] Hayek, *Road to Serfdom*, 54 (emphasis added).

Hayek emphasises that for predictability, 'the laws must be general, equal and certain'.[45] By 'general' he means that the laws are not aimed at any individual or action; they are abstract. He argues that 'a true law should not name any particulars, … it should not single out any specific persons or group of persons'.[46]

Hayek's understanding of predictable laws clearly assumes that these laws are state laws. While deep legal pluralism would, to Hayek, provide insufficient predictability, state law pluralism would amount to particular laws for particular people and hence offend his understanding of equality.

Joseph Raz agrees with Hayek that one of the important goals of the rule of law is for the law to be predictable. He articulates the underlying doctrine of the rule of law as requiring the law to 'be capable of guiding the behaviour of its subjects'.[47] From this idea he draws the following list of elements of the rule of law: the law must be prospective, open, clear, public, certain and relatively stable. The making of particularised laws should be guided by rules that are open, stable, clear and general. To realise and support these elements, the following mechanisms are necessary: independence of the judiciary, open and fair hearings, accessible courts, a limited form of legislative and administrative review and a limit on police and prosecution discretion.[48] For law to be predictable, certain and stable, it is important, according to these two leading theorists, that judges adjudicate as closely as possible according to the rules set out publicly and clearly by the legislature, and presumably the constitution. A separation of powers is presupposed by the formal approaches: the judiciary must be separate from legislative and executive interference in order to adjudicate on general laws in a predictable manner. Raz and Hayek agree that judges should not depart from pre-determined rules so as to achieve substantive justice except in exceptional circumstances, if at all. Thus predictability and procedural law are generally more important than any other consideration.

Hayek's influence on approaches to the rule of law has been felt widely.[49] For example, courts in some transitional countries have

[45] Hayek, *The Political Ideal of the Rule of Law*, 34.

[46] Hayek, *The Constitution of Liberty*, 153–4.

[47] Raz, 'The Rule of Law', 214.

[48] Ibid., 214–18.

[49] Hayek's belief that predictability is pivotal to the rule of law is shared by many but debate exists as to whether universal, general laws are essential to achieve predictability. Hayek's view that particularised laws threaten predictability and the rule of law is followed by Australian scholar Suri Ratnapala who reasons that general laws have an advantage over

emphasised predictability as the determinative value of the rule of law.[50] In the 1990s, the World Bank based much of its policy and its programmes on this aspect of Hayek's work.[51] Ibrahim Shihata, the World Bank's General Counsel in the 1990s, wrote that for the rule of law it is necessary to have 'a set of rules which are known in advance' as well as 'known procedures for amending the rules when they no longer serve their purpose'.[52] In the 1990s, the concept of the supremacy of law, in the form of constitutional supremacy, was incorporated into almost every single post-Cold War constitution, including South Africa's 1996 Constitution and Timor-Leste's 2002 Constitution.

One of the appeals of this approach to the rule of law is that it appears to be politically neutral and devoid of content, substance or moral criterion, a claim often made for the formal approach to the rule of law. This attracted Shihata, as he believed it was compatible with a variety of different legal systems and traditions,[53] and hence suitable for World Bank policy. This line continues to be promoted by Randall Peerenboom who argues that this formal approach provides 'a bridge across the various fault lines': it is endorsed across religions, regions, regimes and ideologies.[54] Even though he recognises the liberal roots of the rule of law, Peerenboom concludes that the 'thin rule of law is universally … valued'.[55] Heralding the universality of the rule of law he asserts that: '[c]ommunitarians and liberals alike can find much to value in rule of law'.[56]

One of the assumptions made by Peerenboom and Hayek is that legal certainty and predictability, and hence formal legality, are of primary importance to all cultures, and are more important than substantive justice. However, it appears that this may be a Western assumption: many systems in the world determine law on a case-by-case basis with sensitivity to the particular context of the matter. In other words, they do not hold it necessary to be bound by rules and treat 'like cases alike'.[57]

specialised laws because they correlate with greater efficiency of the market: Ratmapala, *Australian Constitutional Law*, 10–11.

50 See, e.g., *Retroactive Criminal Legislation Case*, Hungarian Constitutional Court, decision 11/1992 (III.10.) AB hat.

51 Santos, 'The World Bank's Uses of the "Rule of Law"', 272–3; Kleinfeld, 'Competing Definitions', 31, 43.

52 Shihata, *The World Bank*, 85.

53 Santos, 'The World Bank's Uses of the "Rule of Law"', 270.

54 Peerenboom, 'What's the Relationship?', 824–5.

55 Ibid., 825. Here he makes the exception of the Critical Legal Studies Movement.

56 Ibid., 824.

57 See, e.g., Penal Reform International, *Access to Justice in Sub-Saharan Africa*, 36.

This is especially true in non-liberal, communitarian societies where the law is seen as a tool for compromise and reconciliation between the parties, who must continue to live side by side. A strictly procedural approach to justice may affront and alienate people who adhere to different notions of justice. The application of predictable and general rules and a process of adjudication that results in losers and winners may not always accord with the community's interest, which may focus on reconciliation and communal harmony. Tamanaha observes that rule by rules is culturally particular. He writes:

> Contemporary Asian and African societies, in particular, notwithstanding penetration by Western ideas and practices, continue to have significant communitarian cultural strains which may in various ways and in various contexts clash with aspects of formal legality.[58]

An emphasis on formal legality may be at odds with local values and norms.[59] Japanese scholar Onuma Yasuaki confirms that this is the case in some Asian cultures:

> Legalistic behaviour has been, and still is, regarded as indecent, as it destroys the harmonious and mutually respectful relationship among society members. Resorting to legalistic measures is often regarded as signifying a lack of virtues.[60]

Another difficulty with formal legality is that it has limited application to the private sphere and the realm of community activity.[61] One of the serious limits of the concept of the rule of law is that it provides protection only in the areas in which the state legislates, which means that full protection of the rule of law is only available in the public sphere.[62] This is because the rule of law is premised on the liberal idea that the law should refrain from interfering in the private sphere so as to ensure individuals remain free to 'regulate their own personal lives ... according to their full personal conceptions of how life should be lived'.[63] However, a majority of women and other vulnerable groups spend most of their lives in the non-state, private sphere where they face most abuse and violence. The state often leaves customary or religious law to operate in this sphere and such law has elements of discrimination against

58 Tamanaha, *On the Rule of Law*, 121. 59 Ibid., 140.
60 Yasuaki, 'In Quest of Intercivilizational Human Rights', 60.
61 Tamanaha, *On the Rule of Law*, 140. 62 Coomaraswamy, 'Broken Glass', 143.
63 Nagel, 'Moral Conflicts and Political Legitimacy', 238–9; Aolain and Hamilton, 'Gender and the Rule of Law'.

women.[64] This is particularly the case in post-conflict states such as South Africa and Timor-Leste. Thus, at a practical level the rule of law provides limited protection for women and other vulnerable sections of society. The 2011 UN Women report states: 'for millions of women and girls, the reality is that the rule of law means little in practice'.[65]

In his later writing, Raz acknowledges the cultural and institutional assumptions that underpin the end goal of predictability, sometimes referred to as 'formal legality' or as 'bureaucratic justice'.[66] Predictability serves a society in the process of rapid change, in terms of geographical and social mobility, and constant workplace and technological transformation. In this society the rule of law 'concerns the conduct of bureaucratic institutions in their relations with *isolated* individuals'.[67] Such a society requires bureaucratic institutions that are impersonal and impartial and that have elaborate and well-policed procedures and machinery so that they can function no matter who controls them or uses them. Raz explains that this approach to the rule of law is particularly pertinent to pluralistic societies, which are divided along religious, ethnic, or economic lines, because the impartiality of the bureaucratic institutions and their procedures operates to remedy the lack of common values and practices in that society. In other words, this approach is apt for a modern industrialised society.[68] In the context of an industrialised and liberal pluralistic society the rule of law can be used as a tool for reaching a level of fairness in state–individual relations.

Raz acknowledges that the formal approach to the rule of law raises serious problems for communitarian societies that are based on communal law. Indeed, he believes these problems 'refute any claim that the rule of law is a universal standard of justice'.[69] He writes: 'The ideal of communal law is a valid ideal for some societies. In those societies the rule of law, far from being a requirement of justice, does more harm than good.'[70] Hence Raz believes that the rule of law is a valuable concept only for certain types of society. He warns that the concept may be harmful for

64 UN Women, *Progress of the World's Women 2011–2012*, 69. 65 Ibid., 11.

66 Raz uses the term 'bureaucratic justice': *Ethics in the Public Domain*, 355.

67 Ibid. (emphasis added).

68 Ibid., 355–7. This appears to be a 'free market' society of the kind assumed by Hayek. Raz, however, does not use this description.

69 Ibid., 356. Krygier agrees, stating that: 'a universal, institution-based definition of the rule of law is implausible'. He argues that the 'rule of law is a very good thing … at least in conditions of modernity': 'The Rule of Law: An Abuser's Guide', 129.

70 Raz, *Ethics in the Public Domain*, 356.

those types of societies that do not meet the 'cultural and institutional presuppositions for the rule of law' on which the concept relies for its success.[71] David and Brierly agree that the rule of law may cause social damage to non-liberal societies. They write:

> By wishing to install prematurely the rule of law, such as it is understood in the West, we have upset the old order of societies which were not ready to receive western legal ideas. African civilisation was founded on certain values: a sense of community, ... Unconsciously, perhaps, we have thus contributed to the breaking-up of the ties of family and clan, and we have been incapable of replacing them with a sense of solidarity extending to African society as a whole.[72]

The growth of a specially trained legal profession required by the rule of law has a number of drawbacks according to Raz in that justice becomes expensive and legal issues become technical. Raz points out that: 'The law becomes financially inaccessible and conceptually remote and alienating. It serves the business community, but is unresponsive and unavailable to serve the people.'[73] In his view formal legality can create 'a gulf between the law and the people'.[74]

Clearly the relevance of predictable laws depends on the nature of the society. Many aspects of South African and East Timorese society are communitarian. While the overall makeup of the two nation-states is pluralistic in terms of ethnicity, many of their communities are close-knit and homogeneous groups. People rely on their neighbours for social and economic cooperation and predominantly observe and identify with local laws rather than state laws.

The importance of these distinctions between industrialised and communitarian societies is identified by the comparative legal scholar Ugo Mattei, through his proposed taxonomy of world legal systems into three families based on whether the primary sources of social norms and order are based on law, politics, or philosophical and religious traditions.[75] The first family is a rule of (professional) law system where state law is promoted as the main mechanism for resolving disputes. The second family Mattei puts forward is intended as a description of transitional countries wherein legal institutions are weak and the law is often not perceived as separate from politics.[76] The third family encompasses legal systems where there is no separation between the individual's internal

[71] Ibid., 354. [72] David and Brierly, *Major Legal Systems in the World*, 520.
[73] Raz, *Ethics in the Public Domain*, 356. [74] Ibid., 355.
[75] Mattei, 'Three Patterns of Law', 17. [76] Ibid., 28, 30.

dimension and the societal dimension.[77] This covers communitarian societies where traditional law prioritises harmony and the family or kinship group as the main unit, and, importantly, invokes the supernatural rather than the rule of law as a main source of legitimacy. This third family is less legocentric than the first family; it is difficult to characterise it as a law-based order as it does not set out 'legal' mechanisms as the only path to resolving disputes.[78]

South Africa and Timor-Leste have elements of all three families; they are transitional states with strong systems of customary law and through their constitutions they aspire to the rule of law – in other words, they are mixed systems.[79] Mattei's taxonomy is not presented in an evolutionary strain; unlike many who have used Weber's work, he does not imply that the legal systems falling into the last two families should be encouraged to move towards the first group or that such a shift is inevitable. His taxonomy connects with the work of legal anthropologists who underline that each family of legal systems has a distinct logic, social structure and form of social control that cannot be easily transplanted from one to the other. For example, to simply insert a formal concept of the rule of law into a kin-oriented society is likely to have little effect unless the nature of that society changes.[80]

2.2 *Government bound by law*

Underlying the understanding of the rule of law as 'government bound by law' is the belief that the rule of law via the state is better than the rule of man. This was a sentiment expressed by Aristotle many centuries before the birth of the Westphalian state. Aristotle implied that the problem with the rule of man is that it is unchecked power, which can act on an individual's desire, passion or anger.[81] But to prefer the rule of

77 Ibid., 36.

78 Non-legal mechanisms such as fighting, shaming, the withholding of social contact and the unilateral withdrawal of economic cooperation are common sanctions in traditional law. See Roberts, *Order and Dispute*, 26–7.

79 Mattei's theory recognises that all legal systems are mixed, but their family classification depends on which elements are hegemonic in a system. The existence of two legal systems operating in parallel within the one country, a state known as legal pluralism, thus fits within his theory. States where informal, local legal systems are hegemonic fall into the third family: Mattei, 'Three Patterns of Law', 21.

80 See, e.g., Lawrence, 'The State versus Stateless Society', 34.

81 Aristotle, *The Politics*, Book III, Ch. xvi. But note that in the previous chapter Aristotle states that rule of the best man may be better than the rule of the best laws because in

law to the rule of man is not a simple case of the state using the law to conduct its affairs: this constitutes rule *by* law, a very thin conception of the formal approach to the rule of law. The rule *of* law requires the supremacy of law, sometimes also discussed as supremacy of the constitution. This means that no one is above the law and, moreover, the law binds the state.

It is here that we can observe how formal approaches to the rule of law understand the state. For Hayek and Raz (in his early work), the state is the focal point of law and power, but both liberal scholars conceptualise the state in a negative framework. While Hayek believes that the state has crucial functions to perform, he worries that state power can be 'coercive' and argues that the rule of law 'means that government in all its actions is bound by rules fixed and announced before-hand'.[82] He reasons that if the state were bound by fixed rules, then a person could plan his or her affairs in order to avoid this intervention and minimise their fear of the state. In his early work, Raz expresses fear of the arbitrary power of the state, its law and its institutions. Dicey, another Western scholar, fears the possibility of discretionary power being wielded by the state in the form of retroactive legislation against the defenceless individual.[83] Fear of the state is a central motif of the formal approach, whether it is fear of state violence, fear of state abuse, or fear of state arbitrariness. In common, these theorists understand the rule of law as a *shield* against state power and the possibility of its abuse. The shield is designed to minimise the citizen's fear of the state and its power in the public sphere.

Hayek, Raz and Dicey understand the rule of law in relation to the potential strength of the state and its institutions. This nexus between the rule of law and the state can be also seen in the 'thick' and 'substantive' approach to the rule of law, which incorporates a moral criterion through the inclusion of moral dignity and human rights. However, in this

individual cases a man will give sounder counsel than the law. But he adds that rulers cannot do without the general principles enunciated by the law. In *On Rhetoric* Aristotle says that it is best to settle as many matters as possible by general rules set out in advance: 31, Bk 1, Ch. ii, 1354a.

[82] Hayek, *Road to Serfdom*, 54 (emphasis added).

[83] In *An Introduction to the Study of the Law of the Constitution,* Dicey sets out the first of his three principles as 'no man is punishable or can lawfully be made to suffer in body or goods excepts for a distinct breach of law established in the ordinary legal manner before the ordinary courts of the land. In this sense the rule of law is contrasted with every system of government based on the exercise by persons in authority of wide, arbitrary, or discretionary powers of constraint': 188.

framework, state institutions such as the judiciary are considered not only as powerful but also as benevolent. The courts are able to force the state to refrain from acting, so as to protect individual negative rights such as those relating to due process, and to force the state to act, so as to fulfil positive rights. Ronald Dworkin's work is a good example of this approach as it is premised on the idea that judges have both the skills and inclination to use their discretion to interpret the law and its principles in the morally best light.[84] This assumes that state institutions have power and capacity *and* are considered legitimate and relevant by the general populace.

Most of the promoters of the two key approaches to the rule of law do not consider whether the rule of law is apt for societies where the state is so weak or fragile that the population neither fears it nor relies on it, but instead turns to non-state, and possibly non-legal, mechanisms to resolve disputes. These two approaches do not address the relevance of the rule of law in the context of a society where 80–90 per cent of the population prefers to use informal mechanisms.

One point that is widely recognised is that the rule of law is a political ideal that needs political, social and cultural support to have any meaning. Hayek observes:

> It will be effective only in so far as the legislator feels bound by it. In a democracy this means that it will not prevail unless it forms part of the moral tradition of the community, a common ideal shared and unquestioningly accepted by the majority.[85]

In other words, the rule of law must become part of the culture of a society or community for it to have any meaning. Rosa Ehrenreich Brooks takes this point further by arguing that:

> the rule of law is most fundamentally an issue of norm creation. The rule of law is not something that exists 'beyond culture' and that can be somehow added to an existing culture by the simple expedient of creating formal structures and rewriting constitutions and statutes. In its substantive sense, the rule of law is a culture.[86]

However, Brooks believes that for the rule of law to be relevant and effective there must be a broader culture that values *formal* law.[87] As we saw earlier in this chapter, it cannot be assumed that all cultures value

[84] Dworkin, 'Political Judges', 262. [85] Hayek, *The Constitution of Liberty*, 206.
[86] Brooks, 'The New Imperialism', 2285. [87] Ibid., 2314.

formal state law: legal pluralism demonstrates that there can be multiple sources of law valued by society that compete with formal state law. For example, some states such as China have a history of holding formal law in low regard and avoiding its use in favour of informal means of resolving disputes.[88] While Peerenboom acknowledges this, like Weber he observes it through an evolutionary framework, implying that a shift to formal law is not only desirable and possible but, for states such as China, also inevitable.[89]

2.3 Equality

Inequality is a prime problem in post-conflict states. Among Western scholars there is much debate as to whether the rule of law requires formal equality or substantive equality.[90] For example, Hayek is adamant that substantive equality and distributive justice are incompatible with the rule of law[91] and this view strongly influenced the World Bank's approach to the rule of law in the 1990s. However, there is no set form of equality for the rule of law, which makes the concept of the rule of law attractive to many governments, and empty to critics.

One of the main questions in the post-conflict context is whether equality means 'equal access to justice' or 'equal standards of justice for all', both of which are aspects of formal equality. As explained above, legal pluralism assists in the former by highlighting a diversity of justice forums while it has no input in regard to the latter except in that it holds each standard as equal. In 2002 the World Bank expressed equality as 'every person in society is treated equally under the law' and added the further condition that 'justice is accessible to all'.[92] In contrast, the UN takes a slightly more substantive approach, at least on paper, in that the UNDP's 'access to justice' programme is styled as a 'human rights-based

[88] Pereenboom, 'Varieties of Rule of Law', 44–5.

[89] Peerenboom points to the shift to highly law-based orders made by Singapore, South Korea and Hong Kong to support his view that such change is possible, inevitable and desirable for other Asian countries: ibid.

[90] For example, many scholars have attempted to decipher whether Dicey intended his formulation of equality to be limited to formal equality: see Craig, 'An Analytical Framework', 470–4; Allan, *Constitutional Justice*, 17–21.

[91] Hayek, *The Constitution of Liberty; Road to Serfdom*, Ch. 6.

[92] The World Bank, *Legal Vice Presidency, Experiences and Approach of the Legal Vice Presidency*, 1.

approach to access to justice'.[93] The distinction is the UN's focus on the standard of justice that is to be equally accessed and applied.

Rachel Kleinfeld comments on the global proliferation of access-to-justice programmes 'as a means of helping to create de facto equality before the law'.[94] *De jure* equality in regard to justice simply requires the state to open up courthouses and to pass general legislation that does not distinguish between people. Equality is *de jure*, and not *de facto*, where groups in society, such as women and children, are not able to access the state legal system due to prevailing cultural norms or, for example, because domestic violence legislation is not enforced or properly adjudicated by state institutions.[95] To produce *de facto* equality, access-to-justice programmes need to have a strong understanding of the barriers facing people in accessing justice.

To understand equality in the post-conflict and transitional context it is necessary to consider the role of informal, non-state justice mechanisms such as customary law, otherwise one is looking at only a small part of the overall picture. Since about 2002, both the UN and World Bank have formally acknowledged that such mechanisms have a role in providing access to justice. The pertinent question is how the recognition or non-recognition of such mechanisms affects equality in the post-conflict state. Regardless of state recognition, these mechanisms often constitute the main paths to justice by poor and vulnerable sections of society, such as female victims of domestic violence, who turn to these mechanisms when weak state institutions do not properly enforce state law or when state institutions alienate them. The past reluctance of international organisations to embrace and support these non-state justice mechanisms has been partly a result of concerns regarding the risk of institutionalising low quality justice for the vulnerable and poor sections of society that access them and hence entrenching two different standards

93 See UNDP, *Access to Justice – Practice Note* (2004); UNDP, *Programming for Justice: Justice For All*. The latter document defines 'access to justice' as 'the ability to seek and obtain a remedy through formal and informal institutions of justice, and in conformity with human rights standards': 5. Note that UNDP does not invoke equality as a basis of its programme but instead it states its mandate 'to reduce poverty and strengthen democratic governance'. Some idea of the proportionate support UNDP has given to the formal and informal parts of the justice sector prior to 2006 can be gauged from Wojkowska, *Doing Justice*, 11.

94 Kleinfeld, 'Competing Definitions', 39.

95 Similarly, equality is only *de jure* and not *de facto* where there is inconsistent enforcement, prosecution and adjudication of laws in that the more powerful groups in society are able to evade the law through bribery and corruption or the threat of violence.

of justice, such as was the case during British colonialism and apartheid. For example, local customary systems in Timor-Leste are perceived as discriminatory and biased against women and they are generally run entirely by men.[96] Furthermore, these systems do not hold it necessary to treat 'like cases alike'. For these reasons, these systems are unlikely to be directly embraced as rule-of-law institutions even though they arguably contribute to the rule of law by assisting in the provision of equal access to justice. However, the flipside is that the decision to ignore these systems may have a greater impact on equality in that some 80 per cent of the population is accessing systems to which no international support or attention, in the form of monitoring, is being given. Furthermore, in some post-conflict contexts, this attitude may be discriminatory as it fails to recognise the collective right to normative and institutional autonomy of indigenous peoples.[97]

As the question of equality illustrates, the rule of law and legal pluralism intersect particularly in the post-conflict context. This shows that it is useful to examine the particularities of this context. According to Krygier, a mix of the particular and the universal is essential for the rule of law.[98] However, this dichotomy between the particular and the universal is not always useful. For example, while Hayek puts forward predictability as a universal and Dworkin's substantive definition proposes human rights, both these 'universals' appear to be 'particulars', because they are formulated for states with strong state institutions, where formal law matters. The particulars/universals proposed by these leading Western scholars may not be apt for countries in Africa and the Asia-Pacific region where legal pluralism is prevalent and state institutions are frail.

3. Points of intersection and contact

Customary law is seldom paired with the rule of law. It is negatively characterised as particular. At the international level, there has been an unspoken assumption that customary law is inimical to the rule of law because many customary norms sit in tension with international norms,

96 Swaine, *Traditional Justice*, 2–4, 27–33.

97 See Convention concerning Indigenous and Tribal Peoples in Independent Countries (ILO No. 169), Arts 8 and 9; UN Doc A/Res/61/295 (2 October 2007) UN Declaration on the Rights of Indigenous Peoples, Art 34; Wojkowska, *Doing Justice*, 13.

98 Krygier, 'The Rule of Law: An Abuser's Guide', 146.

in particular international human rights standards. There are a number of factors that underpin this assumption about the relationship between customary law and the rule of law. One is that customary law does not emanate from the state but from the people and hence its control does not lie within the state domain. A related second factor is that customary law empowers actors who are unelected and non-accountable, at least to the state and the wider community. Third, it competes with state law. A fourth factor is that customary law appears unpredictable, and hence inaccessible, to outsiders because it is generally not written. A fifth factor is that customary law is generally not uniform across the state: for example, in Timor-Leste it is localised to the extent that it is difficult for legal anthropologists to discern many commonalities across the array of its local legal systems.[99] A sixth factor is that customary law generally has few mechanisms of scrutiny because it is designed to guide small and generally insular communities as to appropriate behaviour. A final factor is that customary legal norms are at times inconsistent with 'universal' international human rights norms and this mainly affects the most vulnerable including women.[100]

One exception to this trend in thinking about customary law is Mark Plunkett who argues, ahead of time, that customary law systems can be 'micro ROL [rule of law] systems'.[101] He reasons that people living according to customary law 'follow a sophisticated ROL system derived from ancient legal systems that regulate the distribution of all resources – material, human, and spiritual'.[102] To make this argument, Plunkett uses a very broad definition of the rule of law: 'where both the ruler and the ruled respect the legal rules that govern the relationships'.[103] This definition appears to stretch even to 'ROL systems offered by warlords'.[104] Plunkett posits that in the process of building the rule of law, these micro ROL systems are as important as the institutional model for the rule of law put forward by Hayek, and thus they need to be harmonised in the post-conflict context.[105] He is effectively arguing that all informal legal systems *per se* can be considered to be rule-of-law systems and that there is a need in the post-conflict context to reconcile this paradigm of customary law with the state legal system. However, Plunkett's definition of the rule of law fails to include mechanisms to ensure that the ruler

99 Mearns, *Looking Both Ways*, 31; Hohe and Nixon, *Reconciling Justice*, 13.
100 See, e.g., Amnesty International, *East Timor*, 40ff.
101 Plunkett, 'Re-establishing the Rule of Law', 78. 102 Ibid., 79. 103 Ibid., 76.
104 Ibid., 80. 105 Ibid., 78–9.

respects the same legal rules as the ruled (i.e. government bound by law) and hence the definition appears to impose few criteria on what constitutes a rule-of-law system.

A more sustained illustration of the intersection between the rule of law and legal pluralism can be seen in a definition of the rule of law proposed in 2007 for Afghanistan, a post-conflict state where 80–90 per cent of cases are settled through traditional justice bodies while the state legal system deals only with 10–20 per cent, at most, of all disputes.[106] The definition put forward by the *Afghanistan Human Development Report 2007*[107] ('the Afghan report') classifies customary law systems and other non-state justice institutions as rule-of-law systems. It states:

> the rule of law refers to **all** those state and *non-state* institutions that promote justice and human development through the application of public rules that are deemed fair, applied independently, enforced equally, and consistent with human rights principles.[108]

The four main dimensions of this definition (independence of rule of law institutions, public and fair laws, equal enforcement, and consistency with human rights principles) have been impliedly identified as 'universals' by the authors of the Afghan report. The four dimensions can be recognised as similar to those values conventionally proposed by Western scholars and international institutions even though predictability and government bound by law are notably absent. However, this definition is distinguished by the fact that it includes 'non-state institutions' as 'rule of law institutions' where they observe the four listed dimensions.

[106] See Afghanistan Human Development Report 2007. These statistics come from annual surveys conducted by the Asia Foundation (see, e.g., *Afghanistan in 2006: A Survey of the Afghan People,* 59) and a survey conducted by the Afghan Ministry for Justice entitled *Justice for All – A Comprehensive Needs Analysis* (2005).

[107] Human Development Reports are commissioned by the UNDP. They are independently written and researched. The concept of human development is influenced by Amartya Sen's concept of human development being measurable by 'capabilities'. The 'capabilities' approach takes into account an individual's social context in relation to their ability *to do or to be* and it aims to get people above a threshold level of each capability. In this framework, law must enhance people's capabilities to enjoy rights and entitlements. See generally Sen, *Development as Freedom; Inequality Re-examined.*

[108] *Afghanistan Human Development Report 2007*, 43 (emphasis in bold original, emphasis in italics added). In June 2008 the Afghan Supreme Court issued a warning against the citation and distribution of the report. According to Sukhre and Boorchgrevink, critics of the report fear it may lead donors to prioritise informal justice and decrease funding to the formal legal sector: 'Negotiating Justice', 22.

The Afghan report's proposed definition of 'rule of law institutions' embraces legal pluralism in the form of three major legal traditions: Western positive law, Islamic Sharia law and customary law. According to its authors, during consultations, people described the rule of law negatively but emphasised the importance of customary law and traditional institutions of dispute settlement for the rule of law.[109] Indeed, one senior judge pointed out that these institutions were able to enforce their decisions more effectively than state courts, and, unlike the courts, they could achieve reconciliation between parties through using various forms of alternative dispute resolution.[110] Overall, these traditional institutions are perceived as more effective, less corrupt and more legitimate than state institutions despite the fact that *jirgas* and *shuras* do not conform to international human rights standards either in their composition or in some of their norms.[111] In Afghanistan, legal pluralism is clearly a dominant paradigm. Alongside the rule of law, legal pluralism is put forward by the Afghan report as a means to 'human development'.

For many Western scholars and practitioners, this proposed definition of the rule of law was perhaps initially controversial because the rule-of-law orthodoxy promoted by the UN and IFIs has been geared towards working with state institutions.[112] Conventionally, rule-of-law institutions are understood as the familiar triad of state courts, police and prisons and not *non*-state institutions. Consideration of non-state institutions has often been limited in post-conflict literature to the work of non-governmental organisations (NGOs) in civil society[113] and, as Chapter 2 shows, only very gradually has this been extended to traditional justice mechanisms.

For the Afghan community, the most controversial aspect of the proposed definition appears to be the inclusion of human rights: the Afghans consulted for the Afghan report stated that the fairness

[109] Ibid., 42–3. [110] Ibid., 43.

[111] Women are generally excluded from participation in *jirgas* and *shuras* and have difficulty in accessing them without the assistance of a male relative. The practice that is of most concern to IDAs and human rights advocates is that of *bad*, explained in the notes below.

[112] Golub, 'A House Without a Foundation', 131. See Chapter 2.

[113] See, e.g., Tolbert and Solomon, 'United Nations Reform', 54–6. It should be noted, however, that while the reference to 'non-state institutions' in the Afghanistan Human Development Report 2007 covers dispute resolution forums, it excludes non-state prisons and non-state police: *Afghanistan Human Development Report 2007*, 97.

of the law could only be judged in relation to Islamic principles.[114] Few considered human rights as an important dimension of the rule of law.[115] This is consistent with an earlier study that concluded that fairness in Afghanistan is measured according to local norms.[116] The Afghan report acknowledges that the inclusion of human rights as a dimension of the definition is imposed: it 'largely represents the demands of the international community and donor countries'.[117]

The proposed definition of the rule of law is pragmatic in that it recognises that the Afghan state does not have a monopoly of law, and that the reach and legitimacy of the state legal system is unlikely to improve dramatically for a number of decades. Thus the Afghan report recommends a hybrid system with horizontal forms of accountability whereby a unit of the Afghan Independent Human Rights Commission (AIHRC) is given the responsibility for monitoring and supervising these traditional institutions in each district in order to ensure that human rights standards are upheld.[118] Decisions that are deemed compatible with human rights standards and Afghan law would be endorsed by the AIHRC as legally binding on other justice institutions.[119]

In this picture, tension is palpable between access to justice, enabled by legal pluralism, and the rule of law, which here includes human rights and denotes a particular standard of justice. The Afghan report sets out 'access to justice and the rule of law' as separate concepts and separate paths to human development.[120] In relation to the unequal treatment of women by non-state institutions, the two concepts appear to collide.

[114] *Afghanistan Human Development Report 2007*, 44. [115] Ibid., 46.

[116] USAID, *Afghanistan Rule of Law Project*, 9.

[117] *Afghanistan Human Development Report 2007*, 46. The report notes that while the 2004 Afghan Constitution as well as new and amended legislation is generally consistent with human rights principles, there remains tension between national legislation and these principles: 46–7.

[118] The *Afghanistan Human Development Report 2007* asserts that existing vertical accountability mechanisms in Afghanistan, such as the judicial system's internal appeals process, are 'outdated and generally unused': 100. For a critical view of justice reform in Afghanistan, see Tondini, 'Restoring Justice Systems'; Tondini, *Statebuilding and Justice Reform*; Senier, 'Rebuilding the Judicial Sector'.

[119] It is not clear whether making non-state decisions binding would be a sufficient carrot for non-state actors to comply with 'international' rather than local standards of fairness.

[120] *Afghanistan Human Development Report 2007*, 6, 34, 58. This compartmentalisation is also apparent in UNDP, *Programming for Justice: Justice for All*, 84. In this context 'access to justice' denotes access to dispute resolution which satisfies dominant local standards of fairness.

Most reports on Afghanistan's legal system[121] express grave concerns regarding the violation of women's human rights at the hands of non-state justice mechanisms in relation to practices such as *bad*.[122] However, what is striking is that these concerns appear to be overridden by the emerging consensus among many NGOs and IDAs that non-state law must be recognised and engaged with in Afghanistan at a formal level so as to ensure greater access to justice for the population.[123] Most of the reports of these organisations consistently prioritise access to justice over the rule of law in that they agree that state law pluralism is the only viable path for justice in Afghanistan, at least in the short term. The Afghan report undergirds its position of prioritising legal pluralism by pointing out that certain features of *jirgas* and *shuras* are 'consistent with values and principles of the restorative justice paradigm that is now increasingly prominent internationally'.[124] In a context where conflict and violence have been the norm for decades, access to justice and non-violent means of dispute resolution are understood as a necessity while the rule of law is cast as a longer-term aspiration.

The rule of law is a concept that government heads across the globe have endorsed and none have defiantly rejected,[125] even when the concept holds little currency at the local level. As the dominant paradigm in the global arena, the international norm provides a badge of legitimacy for governments at the international level. Regardless of the fact that the rule of law is an aspiration that may be unrealisable in Afghanistan's short-term future, the Afghan state is keen to invoke the concept and

[121] *Afghanistan Human Development Report 2007*, 6, 34, 58; Barfield et al., *The Clash of Two Goods*; USAID, *Afghanistan Rule of Law Project.*

[122] *Bad is* where a dispute is settled by the offer of a woman for marriage from the offender's family to the victim's family without the consent of the woman. This practice is part of *Pashtunwali*, principles that apply specifically to Pashtuns who comprise approximately 40 per cent of the population. It is prohibited by both state positive law and *sharia*. While the *Afghanistan Human Development Report 2007* arguably downplays this practice as more an exception than a norm (126), the USAID report highlights the practice as prevalent in rural and remote communities: USAID, *Afghanistan Rule of Law Project*, 49.

[123] *Afghanistan Human Development Report 2007*; USAID, *Legal Empowerment and Access of Women to Justice Assessment*, 67–74. This is not the case with the report of the International Commission of Jurists: Lau, *Afghanistan's Legal System and its Compatibility with International Human Rights Standards, Final Report* (2003). The title of this report indicates its orthodox approach to the rule of law.

[124] *Afghanistan Human Development Report 2007*, 94. The authors appear to use this 'international prominence' as a hook to international legitimacy.

[125] Tamanaha, *On the Rule of Law*, 2.

institute it as a central pillar and goal of its *Afghanistan National Development Strategy* (ANDS), a document which sets out for the international community the Afghan state's development agenda.[126] The legitimacy conferred by the concept is recognised by ANDS, which states: 'The rule of law is the foundation of legitimate government.'[127] Thus, the 'myth' of the rule of law is a flag that countries fly to signal their legitimacy and sovereignty to the international community.

For post-conflict states where former resistance leaders are now heading governments, such as South Africa and Timor-Leste, the rule of law carries additional value as it provides a point of distinction from the past regime, in respect of which it can be claimed that the rule of law was absent, and places the present governments in a morally superior position. Thus there is acute pressure on governments of post-conflict states to assert this legitimacy through invoking the rule of law before the international community. This generally involves the rule of law being proclaimed in a state document such as a National Development Strategy. Most commonly, though, it is found in the constitutions of post-conflict states, often in the constitutional preamble, as is the case with Afghanistan's Constitution, or in the 'state's objectives' and 'founding values', as seen in the constitutions of Timor-Leste and South Africa.[128] The preamble of Afghanistan's Constitution speaks of 'regaining Afghanistan's deserving place in the international community', and similarly the South African constitutional preamble talks of South Africa 'tak[ing] its rightful place as a sovereign state in the family of nations'.[129] These preambles highlight the fact that drafters of post-conflict constitutions invariably consider the international community as an important part of the readership.

Constitutional frameworks are one of the main means by which post-conflict states assert their sovereignty within the international

[126] The rule of law forms part of Pillar 2 of the *Afghanistan National Development Strategy 2008–2013 (ANDS),* prepared by the Government of the Islamic Republic of Afghanistan (Presidential Oversight Committee).

[127] Ibid., Ch. 7.3.

[128] See s. 1 of South Africa's 1996 Constitution; ss. 1(1) and 6(b) of Timor-Leste's 2002 Constitution as well as its preamble which states: 'Fully conscious of the need to build a democratic and institutional culture proper appropriate to a State based on the rule of law where respect for the Constitution, for the laws and for democratically elected institutions constitute its unquestionable foundation'.

[129] The Constitution of Timor-Leste devotes a whole section, s. 8, to aspirational statements about 'international relations'.

community. The device has emerged as part of the current Westphalian model of the state. According to J. Samuel Barkin, '[s]ince the emergence of the state system, sovereignty has always been seen by the society of states to require a certain constitutional structure'.[130] In other words, to enjoy sovereignty, states believe that they are required to proclaim and establish a certain relationship between the state and its population. Over the centuries, since the Treaty of Westphalia, the nature of this relationship has changed but in the post-Cold War twenty-first century it appears that the dominant norm in this regard involves the limitation of state power by the rule of law.

Effectively this means that the process of constitution-making is not merely a matter of establishing internal legitimacy, but is also a matter of external legitimacy. Thus, even though most actors in the international community recognise that it is inadvisable that the international community has direct involvement in a state's 'national sovereign process',[131] indirect influence comes through the need for states to make a constitutional commitment to the rule of law in order to establish their external legitimacy.[132]

Barkin observes that 'states' need for certain institutional structures to legitimate themselves [on the international stage] can act as a significant constraint on states' final authority over their internal affairs'.[133] He reasons that:

> States that do not honour dominant constitutional norms, and that as a result are not seen as fully legitimate by the community of states, are likely to be excluded to some degree from regular patterns of discourse within this community.[134]

While Barkin is referring more narrowly to international human rights norms, he could just as easily be referring to rule of law norms. He notes that to many, 'the international normative structure ... may look like a form of cultural imperialism, the imposition of Western values internationally'.[135] However, Barkin observes that '*all international normative*

[130] Barkin, 'The Evolution', 230.

[131] *Guidance Note of the Secretary-General: United Nations Assistance to Constitution-Making Processes* (April 2009) 4.

[132] Apart from Constitutions and Strategic Development Plans, states also use speeches in international forums to articulate and affirm their commitment to the rule of law. This is because the assertion of state legitimacy and sovereignty is a 'continuous' process. See Zaum, *The Sovereignty Paradox*, 35, 40.

[133] Barkin, 'The Evolution', 232 [134] Ibid., 235. [135] Ibid., 249

structures can be interpreted as having a strong culturally imperialist element'.[136]

The application of Barkin's theory to constitution-making helps to explain that in drafting and adopting constitutions, states are partly acting to shore up their external legitimacy within the international community. A constitution that invokes the rule of law can signal a break with the state's past, it can ease admission into regional bodies such as the European Union,[137] it can facilitate trade relations and aid, and it can flag to foreign investors and international financial organisations that the state is modern and suitable for investment. Barkin's theory underlines the constitutional conformity that is implicitly required by the international community. It also shows us that it is difficult to draw a clear line between 'external' and 'internal' since, in the context of post-conflict transitions and particularly international administrations, the boundaries between 'the international' and 'domestic' are increasingly fluid.

Within the post-conflict state, the constitutional concept of the rule of law must be balanced and reconciled with dominant paradigms operating within the state and thus the concept becomes more muted at this national level. The characterisation of traditional dispute resolution forums as possible 'rule of law institutions' in Afghanistan is an example of this attempt at balancing because it aims to realign those aspects of these forums which would, at least in the eyes of most Western scholars, disqualify such a characterisation. This realignment or balancing is now evident in the approach taken by the UN and US to the relationship between the rule of law and informal justice systems. As discussed in the previous chapter, the US' current strategy in Afghanistan involves a focus on the informal justice sector while in 2011 the UN recognised the potential of informal justice systems to strengthen the rule of law. Arguably these approaches have been influenced by the 2007 Afghan report.[138]

[136] Ibid., 250 (emphasis added).

[137] Articles 6 and 49 of the European Union Treaty govern the entry of new states to the EU and set out respect for the rule of law as part of the criteria, known as the Copenhagen criteria. It is also mentioned in the preamble to the European Convention on Human Rights. The rule of law is articulated as a core value in the constitutive instruments of most regional bodies: OSCE, ASEAN, the Commonwealth, the African Union and the Organisation of the Islamic Conference. It is not included in the 1945 constitutive act of the Arab League.

[138] See Chapter 2, section 5.1.

For post-conflict states, this balancing and reconciling of the two seemingly antithetical concepts should ideally take place within a state's constitutional framework. Constitutions set out the ground rules by which a state should be governed. They can open non-violent spaces in which tensions and divisions can be debated, filtered and reconciled and in which an appropriate compromise is sought at the state level. Barkin's work shows us that post-conflict constitutions can be understood as a 'double compact': between the governed and the government and between the government and the international community.[139] Through the constitution-drafting process post-conflict states attempt to shore up both their internal and external legitimacy. Given the international community's interest in maintaining regional stability, asserting a commitment to the rule of law, due to the concept's association with predictability and constitutionalism, is a conventional means by which a post-conflict state can assert and strengthen its membership and sovereignty within the international community. Equally, though, recognising legal pluralism and the role of non-state authorities through the state's constitutional framework is a means of seeking a degree of internal legitimacy for the state where legal pluralism is strong and the state has limited reach. The constitutional embrace of legal pluralism, dubbed 'pluralist constitutionalism' or 'plurinational constitutionalism', has marked transitions in many regions of the world; for example, the Latin American transitions that took place in the 1990s and 2000s.[140] However, constitutional commitment to the rule of law and legal pluralism can also carry negative implications: for example, a constitutional commitment to the rule of law may be problematic where the concept is widely considered alien or even an instrument of Western cultural imperialism, while the constitutional recognition of legal pluralism can signal potential unpredictability and backwardness to parts of the international community, particularly foreign investors.

The constitution-making processes in South Africa and Timor-Leste illustrate how the rule of law and legal pluralism are negotiated and, in some cases, balanced and reconciled in particular post-conflict states in a bid to satisfy the various parties to the double compact. South Africa and Timor-Leste are useful examples as they have constitutions that invoke the rule of law and have large sections of the population that use non-

[139] See also Ghani and Lockhart, *Fixing Failed States*, 193.

[140] See UN Doc E/CN.4/2006/78 (18 January 2006) *Report of the UN Special Rapporteur* [8–9]; Sieder and Sierra, *Indigenous Women's Access*, 4–9.

state law and institutions as a means of resolving disputes. The two post-conflict states offer a contrast: South Africa represents a strong post-conflict state where state institutions continued operating after the end of apartheid while Timor-Leste represents a fragile post-conflict state where state institutions collapsed upon the withdrawal of Indonesian forces and international assistance was required.

4. Conclusion

The relationship between the rule of law and legal pluralism is highly dependent on context. On the one hand, Western scholars have purported to formulate abstract and universal formulations of the 'myth' of the rule of law while on the other hand, some legal anthropologists have romanticised the 'fact' of legal pluralism. Neither formulation of these concepts appears particularly useful or relevant to the post-conflict context where the nature and power of each concept depends on whether the state is attempting to use the concepts to shore up its *external* legitimacy or its *internal* legitimacy, or both. As I show in the following parts of this book, this double act of legitimacy in post-conflict states is a complex process. Both Part II on South Africa and Part III on Timor-Leste begin with the constitutional moment of recognising legal pluralism and the international norm of the rule of law and the two parts then trace how the two concepts are practically negotiated and transformed at ground level through the development of linkage laws to link state law with informal law. Each part aims to understand the manner in which vulnerable groups in these post-conflict states experience legal pluralism and the rule of law and whether 'fact' and 'myth' are adequate descriptions of this experience.

PART II

4

'One law for one nation': how the rule of law and legal pluralism figure in South Africa's constitutional dispensation

The slogan "One Law for One Nation" became the chorus line for South Africa's constitutional song, the by-line for newspaper advertisements for the new constitutional dispensation, and it is the banner under which the text of the 1996 Constitution, known as the Final Constitution, sits. While 'one law' accords with the concept of the rule of law and constitutionalism, it sits uncomfortably with the concept of legal pluralism, where two or more legal systems operate. However, for post-colonial and post-conflict states emerging from significant periods of oppression, aspects of which involved the legal regime subjecting people to different legal systems or standards according to their race, ethnicity or citizenship, the concept of one law for all may be a revolutionary and liberating one. The tension between, on the one hand, the rule of law and constitutionalism and, on the other hand, legal pluralism is a reason why actors involved in promoting the rule of law in post-conflict states need a firm understanding of the relationship between these two concepts. Post-apartheid South Africa offers a lens by which this relationship can be analysed as its transition has been held up as a model by many in the international community.

While 'one law' accords with the concept of the rule of law and constitutionalism, it sits uncomfortably with the concept of legal pluralism, where two or more legal systems operate. South Africa's 1996 Constitution was designed to revolutionise its legal system from one based on racial segregation and oppression to a system founded on equality and human dignity. Like most constitutions drafted in the 1990s, it is a cocktail of values drawing heavily from the international order, with some added local, home-grown values.[1] In this respect, the rule of law and legal pluralism, in the form of customary law, can be characterised to represent respectively the global and the local. This chapter examines South Africa's

[1] Klug, 'Constitution-making in South Africa', 152. Klug argues that while many of the principles listed were clearly influenced by international norms, they were nevertheless locally formulated and approved.

constitutional dispensation in the 1990s in order to understand the relationship between the rule of law and legal pluralism in this period.

This chapter shows that both the invocation of the rule of law as a constitutional founding value and the constitutional entrenchment of legal pluralism can be traced to a host of pressures applied by external and internal forces. The negotiating parties to the South African constitutional dispensation responded to these pressures believing the two concepts would promote the legitimacy of the state's new constitutional framework on a number of fronts. Thus, the parties embraced the rule of law and legal pluralism on the assumption that they might assist the post-apartheid state to establish its legitimacy both at the international level and the rural, local level. However, before this could happen, the stains of the past, namely apartheid, had to be removed from both concepts so as to transform them.

The chapter begins by setting out the historical context in which the two concepts operated and by exploring the role of constitutions in the post-Cold War era in shoring up international legitimacy. It traces the inclusion of the rule of law as a constitutional founding value and it then examines the internal negotiations that led to the constitutional recognition of legal pluralism. It observes that, in the case of the former, international organisations may have been instrumental in influencing the decision to entrench explicitly the rule of law as a founding value of the 1996 Constitution. In terms of the latter, the African National Congress (ANC) allowed traditional leaders to drive the agenda of legal pluralism in the belief that they could provide a much-needed connection to the rural population. Overall, it argues that pragmatism played a large role in South Africa's constitutional negotiations and hence it is possible that the main actors gave insufficient consideration to the relationship between the rule of law and legal pluralism and its future operation within the constitutional framework.

1. Context

To understand the relationship between the rule of law and legal pluralism in South Africa it is necessary at first to consider aspects of the history of both South Africa's legal system and the ANC's relationship with law.

Of apartheid, John Dugard writes: 'The apartheid order was a legal order. Most of the injustices perpetrated by successive apartheid governments between 1948 and 1990 were committed in the name of the law.'[2] During apartheid, the governing National Party used the law and legality as a substitute for legitimacy. Thus, one of the ANC's main opposition strategies

[2] Dugard, 'Retrospective Justice', 270.

was to undermine the state legal system. It rejected the legitimacy of state law as well as state judges, whom it generally saw as conniving with the apartheid regime.[3] In the mid-1980s the ANC and its political allies, such as the United Democratic Front, went so far as to encourage people to take law into their own hands. They aimed to make the country 'ungovernable' for the state and promoted the establishment of people's courts in opposition to the apartheid state's local councils.[4] This strategy contributed to a strong level of deep legal pluralism in South Africa, which is still prevalent today.

During the decades of its opposition to apartheid rule, the ANC looked to international legal standards as a vehicle by which to establish its own legitimacy. The ANC recognised international law not just as a tool of justice and political transformation but also as a 'passport to international acceptability'.[5] The apartheid regime, in contrast, saw international law as 'an alien and hostile legal order' and 'a threat to the state'.[6] On the whole, South African courts and lawyers largely ignored public international law during apartheid.

The ANC's concerted efforts to gain support from the international community and to influence international law can be seen having effect after 1960, when the UN Security Council passed a resolution condemning the South African Government for the Sharpeville massacre which left sixty-nine black protesters dead.[7] The UN General Assembly played a significant role in championing the ANC: in 1962 it attempted to impose sanctions on South Africa and in each of the three decades until 1990, it passed resolutions condemning apartheid as an international crime,[8] culminating in the drafting of the 1973 *UN Convention on the Suppression and Punishment of the Crime of Apartheid*.[9] In 1974 the

[3] See, e.g., ANC, 'Mass Action for People's Power', 4. In some situations, state law was used as a means of resistance. Abel analyses some of the legal victories against apartheid during the 1980s and concludes that they 'strengthened the commitment of the anti-apartheid movement to legality – and also, perhaps that of the post-apartheid polity': Abel, *Politics by Other Means,* 549.

[4] MacKinnon, *The Making of South Africa,* 255ff.

[5] Klug, *Constitutional Democracy,* 48.

[6] Dugard, 'International Law', 77; Dugard, 'The South African Judiciary', 110.

[7] SC Res. 134 (1 April 1960).

[8] See GA Res. 1761 (6 November 1962) The Policies of Apartheid of the Government of the Republic of South Africa (sanctions); GA Res. 2202A (XXI) (17 November 1966) The Policies of Apartheid of the Government of the Republic of South Africa; GA Res. 2627 (XXV) (24 October 1970) Declaration on the Occasion of the Twenty-fifth Anniversary of the United Nations; GA Res 39/72A (13 December 1984) Policies of Apartheid of the Government of the Republic of South Africa.

[9] By the end of apartheid in 1990, the Convention had been ratified by 89 states. During this period, apartheid was declared a crime in other international instruments such as the 1968

President of the General Assembly rejected the credentials of the South African delegation and the state subsequently withdrew from other UN organs and specialised agencies such as the International Labour Organisation (ILO).[10] In 1975 the UN gave observer status to the ANC and in 1976 it invited Oliver Tambo, the President of the ANC, to address the General Assembly. The ANC also formed a close relationship with specialised international agencies: for example, in the 1980s its trade union members received training from the ILO and in 1980 it became a signatory to the *1948 Geneva Conventions* as well as their *First Additional Protocol 1977* which was directed at protection of actors involved in internal conflict, such as the situation in South Africa. In the ANC's view, apartheid was contrary to the UN Charter and it used international law as far as possible to isolate the apartheid government in the international community. In 1991 ANC leader Nelson Mandela argued:

> By characterizing apartheid as a crime, by protecting our combatants, by describing certain aspects of apartheid as genocide, *international rules have validated our struggle* ... We have been cut off from full membership of the international community through South Africa's refusal to adhere to the basic international texts governing human rights.[11]

The ANC also built relations at the regional level, effectively influencing the agenda of the Organisation of African Unity (OAU), now the African Union. In 1989 the ANC was at the forefront of the OAU's *Harare Declaration*, which set out a list of principles such as democracy and equality and called for an 'internationally acceptable solution' so that South Africa could take its 'rightful place' in the international community.[12] The Declaration included guidelines for the process of negotiation, which focused squarely on a new constitution as a means of establishing a new order. The UN General Assembly subsequently upheld the

Convention on the Non-Applicability of Statutory Limitations to War Crimes and Crimes against Humanity and the 1977 First Additional Protocol to the Geneva Conventions.

[10] Note that despite this, South Africa did retain its membership of the UN so it could assert its status as a sovereign state and prevent a black government in exile from taking its place.

[11] Quoted in Klug, 'Hybrid(ity) Rules', 298. As South Africa's Truth and Reconciliation Commission states, the effect of international law's designation of apartheid as a crime against humanity was 'to render as just the moral, political and legal status of the struggle against apartheid': *Truth and Reconciliation Commission of South Africa Report*, Vol 6, Section 5, Ch. 1, [28–9].

[12] Declaration of the OAU Ad Hoc Committee on Southern Africa on the Question of South Africa, 21 August 1989, [17].

principles of the *Harare Declaration* but emphasised that a new constitutional order should be based on the *UN Charter* and the *Universal Declaration of Human Rights*.[13] The ANC understood that, in the struggle for South Africa, it was largely in the international arena that the struggle would be won.[14]

Thus, while encouraging people to flout apartheid state law within South Africa, the ANC was also active in participating in, and influencing, circles of international law, and preparing to set up a new legal order at the state level. During the transition, which involved a series of political negotiations between the major players behind closed doors, international law continued to play an important role for the ANC. When negotiations broke down in mid-1992, the ANC successfully appealed to the UN to send a mediation team.[15] The UN Observer Mission in South Africa was active in attempting to prevent the escalation of violence and in monitoring the 1994 elections.[16] International involvement displeased the cabinet of the governing National Party, which was determined to limit international involvement to observation and analysis.[17]

Hence there is much complexity in the ANC's relationship with the law and the concept of the rule of law during apartheid. While the ANC considered the rule of law to exist only at the international level, it was equivocal in relation to the rule of customary law in rural areas and gave it only marginal consideration.[18] Upon the collapse of the apartheid regime at the end of the Cold War, the ANC had to restore the legitimacy of state legal institutions and begin promoting the rule of law in relation to state law. This was a challenge, given that it had encouraged the people to subvert the state and had led by example. To transform the state legal order and restore the legitimacy of state institutions after apartheid, the ANC used the entrenchment of international norms. Thus, international

[13] UN Doc A/RES/S-16/1 (14 December 1989) Declaration on Apartheid and its Destructive Consequences in Southern Africa. South Africa's Foreign Minister responded by calling the GA's statement a 'flagrant contravention' of the *UN Charter* because of its interference with the state's internal affairs: Gutteridge, 'South Africa: Apartheid's Endgame', 174.

[14] Ellis and Sechaba, *Comrades Against Apartheid*, 203.

[15] See SC Res. 765 (16 July 1992) and SC Res. 772 (17 August 1992).

[16] On the role of the UN in South Africa, see The United Nations and Boutros-Ghali, *The United Nations and Apartheid*, 105–26.

[17] Schreuder, 'The Commonwealth and Peacemaking in South Africa', 95.

[18] Ntsebeza, *Democracy Compromised*, 258–66.

norms came to enjoy an important position in the constitutional dispensation: the Final Constitution embodies a number of mechanisms to ensure that the new legal order evolves in accordance with international law,[19] and great care was taken in the drafting to ensure that the Final Constitution's extensive bill of rights complies with international human rights standards.[20]

The legacy of South Africa's isolation by the international community is illustrated in the eagerness of the post-apartheid state to show the international community its credentials. This can be seen in the 1995 case of *S* v. *Makwanyane*[21] where the newly established Constitutional Court ignored national sentiment at the time, which favoured the death penalty, in unanimously ruling that the death penalty was not constitutional under the Interim Constitution. The Court was acutely aware that the world's eyes were upon it as this was its first hearing and its first important case of adjudicating the values of the new legal order. Furthermore, the case was decided at a time when the world was watching the drafting of the Final Constitution. The judges in *Makwanyane* made extensive reference to both international law and comparative law: for example, a third of the main judgment by Chaskalson P was spent exploring cases from UN bodies as well as the decisions of some of the world's leading courts including those of the US, India and Canada. The judgment of Mokgoro J explained that the 'interpretation clause [section 35] prescribes that courts seek guidance in international norms and foreign judicial precedent … thereby promoting *the ideal and internationally accepted values* in the cultivation of a human rights jurisprudence for South Africa'.[22] No member of the Court disputed the role of international and foreign norms in aiding constitutional interpretation. The Court appeared to heed the warning 'that the state which disclaims the authority of international law places herself outside the circles of civilized nations'.[23]

Many members of the Court referred to the concept of 'civilisation' as representing a benchmark for the new legal order. The judgment of Kentridge AJ framed the issues in terms of the 'evolving standards of

[19] See ss 39, 231–3 of the Final Constitution. For example, s. 233 provides that preference shall be given to any reasonable interpretation of legislation that is consistent with international law over any alternative interpretation that is inconsistent with international law.

[20] Dugard, 'International Law', 77, 84.

[21] 1995 (3) SA 391 (CC).

[22] Ibid., [304] (emphasis added).

[23] This warning was made by Maine, as quoted by Chief Justice Kotze in *CC Maynard et alii* v. *The Field Cornet of Pretoria* (1894) 1 SAR 214, 223.

civilisation' which he held demonstrated 'the unacceptability of the death penalty in countries which are or aspire to be free and democratic societies'.[24] He affirmed the view that 'the State is (or should be) "institutionalised civilisation"' and held that statement to be apt for South Africa's new constitutional order.[25] Similarly, Madala J questioned the existence of the death penalty in a 'civilised society'.[26] Mahomed J referred to the international community as the 'civilised community' and called the ethos of the Constitution 'universalistic'.[27] The inference in these judgments is that for the new legal order to be recognised as 'civilised', it needed to take note of the standards observed by the 'civilised' international community.[28]

However, there is some tension in the case in relation to the role of 'indigenous' norms in constitutional interpretation. This is made apparent in the judgment of Mokgoro J. While Mokgoro J acknowledged that section 35 requires consideration of international norms, she stated: 'However, I am of the view that our own (ideal) indigenous value systems are a premise from which we need to proceed and are not wholly unrelated to our goal of a society based on freedom and equality.' She urged that the courts 'should recognise that indigenous South African values are not always irrelevant nor unrelated' to the task of constitutional interpretation. In common with Langa, Madala, and Mahomed JJ, Mokgoro J singled out the concept of '*ubuntu*', often translated as humaneness or human dignity, which was included in the post-amble to the Interim Constitution.[29] The judges held that this African concept was a shared value, running 'across cultural lines', and was one that should be promoted when interpreting the Interim Constitution's Bill of Rights.[30]

[24] 1995 (3) SA 391 [199]. [25] Ibid. [26] Ibid., [239]. [27] Ibid., [278, 262].

[28] Didcott J also uses this terminology when writing of 'the civilised, humane and compassionate society to which the nation aspires and has constitutionally pledged itself': ibid., [190]. The strategy of measuring the values of South Africa's new legal order against those of the 'civilised world' is also apparent in *S* v. *Williams* 1995 (3) SA 632 (CC), which considers the constitutionality of corporal punishment.

[29] The Constitutional Postamble relates to 'National Unity and Reconciliation'. There is much literature on *ubuntu*. See, e.g., English, '*Ubuntu*', 641. See also Cornell and Van Marle, 'Exploring *Ubuntu*', 195.

[30] See 1995 (3) SA 391 [307–9]. *Ubuntu* was articulated in the post-amble to the Interim Constitution but not in the Final Constitution. Sachs J limited the scope of traditional African jurisprudence to the practices of various tribes in South Africa. Madala J opened up the scope of African jurisprudence much wider than his fellow judges by stating that there is a 'need to bring in the traditional African jurisprudence to these matters, to the extent that such is applicable, and [I] would not confine such research to South Africa only, but to Africa in general': [258].

Sachs J agreed that the consideration of indigenous norms was a necessary aspect of interpreting the provisions of the Interim Constitution's Bill of Rights. He held:

> In my view, s.35 requires this Court not only to have regard to public international law and foreign case law, but also to all the dimensions of the evolution of South African law which may help us in our task of promoting freedom and equality. *This would require reference not only to what in legal discourse is referred to as 'our common law', but also to traditional African jurisprudence.*[31]

Sachs J stated that constitutional interpretation requires the giving of 'long overdue recognition to African law and legal thinking as a source of legal ideas, values and practice'.[32] He pointed out that legal texts and reports gave little coverage to such law but '[t]hat is no reason for this Court to continue to ignore the legal institutions and values of a very large part of the population'.[33] In this statement he clearly intended to rebuke certain members of the Court for failing to consider such law and to stress that the new legal order needed to engage with 'all sections of society',[34] in particular the 'very large part of the population', in order to enjoy legitimacy.

Makwanyane can be read as an early attempt by some members of the Constitutional Court to transform legal pluralism from a tool of state oppression and subordination into a vehicle to promote a renaissance in African identity and legal tradition. Mokgoro J and some of her brother judges attempted to cast the new legal order as one that embraced its 'rainbow' legal heritage and gave equal consideration to 'the traditions, beliefs and values of all sectors of South African society'.[35] Using this approach, they tried to strike a balance between establishing legitimacy in the eyes of the majority black population and earning support from the international community. The case also illustrates the strong acceptance of international norms both within the Court and in the text of the Interim Constitution. In 1995 the Court gave significant detailed consideration to international law in its judgments,[36] manifesting the willingness of the new legal order to engage with the values of 'civilised' community.

[31] Ibid., [373] (emphasis added). [32] Ibid., [365]. [33] Ibid., [371].
[34] Ibid., [370]. See also [361]. [35] Ibid., [361] per Sachs J.
[36] In 1995 the Constitutional Court gave detailed consideration to international law in more than a third of cases dealing with the Bill of Rights. In 2004 the Court gave such consideration in only one in five cases. See Williams and Hovell, 'A Tale of Two Systems', 116.

Constitutions lie at the national–international interface in that they aim to shore up the state's internal and external legitimacy. As Chapter 3 explained, at the international level, a constitution represents a state's 'mission statement' articulating for the international community the state's guiding values so as to establish its position in the community of civilised states. Indeed, many constitutions appear to have been written with an international audience in mind, composed mainly of IFIs, the UN and states like the US. For example, in the cases of Iraq, Afghanistan, Bosnia and Timor-Leste, Feldman observes the 'substantial intervention and pressure imposed from outside to produce constitutional outcomes preferred by international actors, including NATO, the United Nations, and international NGOs, as well as foreign states like the United States and Germany'.[37] At the national level, constitutions are aimed at guiding both state institutions and the people. Moreover, they are aimed at achieving internal legitimacy for the new state or government and thus it is essential that they connect with the people. In relation to Iraq, Feldman relates the general consensus among Iraq's political elites that if the new Iraqi Constitution did not recognise Islam as the official state religion, the new government would have had little chance at all of 'achieving the smallest measure of legitimacy'.[38]

While South Africa's Constitution was not the product of such 'imposed constitutionalism', it nevertheless shows a complex, self-imposed process of negotiation between global norms such as the rule of law and more local norms such as legal pluralism, in the form of customary law. In the 1990s, the ANC was keen to maintain its relationships within the international community but it was also vulnerable to pressure from international organisations such as the World Bank and IMF to turn to neo-liberal economic policies.[39] While the ANC had previously been aligned with the Soviet Union, its manifesto for the 1994 elections integrated elements of neo-liberalism and social democracy. The shift of the ANC Government towards neo-liberalism was illustrated by the introduction in 1996 of a conservative economic policy entitled Growth, Employment and Redistribution (GEAR),[40] an initiative of the World Bank.[41]

The 1990s also saw a general re-emergence of traditional leaders in Sub-Saharan Africa,[42] which Barbara Oomen sees as governed by two

[37] Feldman, 'Imposed Constitutionalism', 858–9. [38] Ibid., 877.
[39] Gumede, *Thabo Mbeki*, 77. [40] MacKinnon, *The Making of South Africa*, 284–6.
[41] Bond, *Against Global Apartheid*, 69.
[42] Oomen, *Chiefs in South Africa*, 11. See also Ntsebeza, *Democracy Compromised*, 272.

scenarios: the collapse of state institutions in weak states and the desire of relatively strong states to attain extra legitimacy.[43] South Africa fits neatly into the second scenario as the ANC wanted to broaden its support base on the home front and promote the legitimacy of the Constitution with rural inhabitants by keeping traditional leaders on side. This meant that local 'African' norms and African identity were embraced in constitutional debates and often offset against 'foreign' Western values. The following two sections trace these dynamics and examine how the rule of law and legal pluralism were negotiated in South Africa's constitutional dispensation in the 1990s.

2. The rule of law

In state-building and transitional justice literature, the rule of law is understood as pivotal to constitutions and the principle of constitutionalism. For example, Simon Chesterman opines: 'the most basic purpose of a constitution [is] to provide for the peaceful exercise of power in accordance with the rule of law'.[44] According to Stanley Katz, constitutionalism is a process within society by which the 'community commits itself to the rule of law'.[45] For post-apartheid South Africa, the process of drafting the constitution and the constitutional text itself were both important symbols of the new legal order and its legitimacy. Thus the South African constitutional preamble talks of South Africa 'tak[ing] its rightful place as a sovereign state in the family of nations'. In this section I argue that the recognition of the rule of law as a founding principle of South Africa's supreme law was also designed to establish the state's place in the international community of 'civilised nations'.

2.1 The interim Constitution and section 1(c) of the Final Constitution

The rule of law did not explicitly figure as an issue during the first rounds of political negotiations, which led to the drafting of the 1993 Interim Constitution and the formulation of the 34 Constitutional Principles

[43] Oomen, *Chiefs in South Africa*, 11. See also 104, where Oomen discusses the forced resurgence of traditional leaders in Angola and Zimbabwe.
[44] Chesterman, 'Imposed Constitutions, Imposed Constitutionalism and Ownership', 949; Rosenfeld, *Constitutionalism, Identity*, 3.
[45] Katz, *Constitutionalism in East Central Europe*, 14.

('CPs') that bound the drafters of the 1996 Final Constitution.[46] Most of the 34 CPs are broadly stated and draw on internationally recognised norms. For example, CP IV provides: 'The Constitution shall be the supreme law of the land. It shall be binding on all organs of state at all levels of government.' This principle arguably captures the rule of law, as it is understood by dominant Western approaches. Other principles, such as separation of powers (CP VI) and judicial review (CP VII) also relate to Western approaches to the rule of law but none of the principles make any express reference to the concept.[47] The absence of an explicit reference to the rule of law in the 1993 Interim Constitution[48] can be explained by the fact that, as a provisional document, it was more focused on the mechanics of transforming the social order than on what could be construed as a question of symbolism, language and style.

The 1993 Interim Constitution was a substantive revolution in that it shifted South Africa from a system of parliamentary supremacy to a system of constitutional supremacy. It was the first time a national constitution of South Africa had entrusted courts with the function of reviewing the constitutionality of legislation to ensure compliance with constitutional values and principles. Furthermore, it was the first time that the courts were given the role of protecting human rights through the Constitution. In the new Bill of Rights, found in Chapter Three of the 1993 Interim Constitution, a guarantee of equal rights was placed first in order. By undertaking the process of drafting a constitution, and enshrining values such as equality, the negotiating parties indicated their commitment to the rule of law.

The rule of law was finally introduced explicitly into the constitutional dispensation in the 1996 Final Constitution's list of 'founding values' in section 1, which provides:

[46] For a history of how the Constitutional Principles were negotiated, see Spitz and Chaskalson, *The Politics of Transition*, 77ff. Note that the Constitutional Principles also influenced the drafting of the Interim Constitution.

[47] The omission of the rule of law is slightly surprising given that many of the transitional constitutions drafted in the 1990s make some express reference to the rule of law. See, e.g., Article 1(1) of the 1990 Constitution of Namibia which provides: 'The Republic of Namibia is hereby established as a sovereign, secular, democratic and unitary State founded upon the principles of democracy, the rule of law and justice for all.'

[48] Note that the preamble to the Interim Constitution refers to the 'constitutional state' which is understood by some commentators as a translation of the German word *Rechtsstaat*: Currie and de Waal, *The Bill of Rights Handbook*, 11. See also Blau, 'The *Rechtsstaat*', 90.

> The Republic of South Africa is one sovereign democratic state founded on the following values:
>
> (a) Human dignity, the achievement of equality and the advancement of human rights and freedoms.
> (b) Non-racialism and non-sexism.
> (c) Supremacy of the constitution and *the rule of law*.
> (d) Universal adult suffrage, a national common voters' roll, regular elections and a multi-party system of democratic government, to ensure accountability, responsiveness and openness. (emphasis added)

In section 1 the rule of law is placed alongside other central values of the new social order such as 'the achievement of equality'. The rule of law is connected to these other values, but it is particularly tied with 'supremacy of the constitution', which is reiterated more extensively in section 2.[49] The order of these two provisions is clearly meant to signal that the values set out in section 1 will be enforced according to section 2. Notably, most of the values in section 1 are liberal values; only human dignity could be construed as a value common both to Western liberal value systems and traditional African systems.[50]

It is widely accepted that the main international influences on the drafting of South Africa's Final Constitution are the Constitutions of Canada, Namibia, Germany and the US[51] but only the first two of these Constitutions make any express reference to 'the rule of law'.[52] Given the agreement that the influence of foreign experts was to be minimised,[53] it can be surmised that the reference in section 1 to the rule of law is largely a result of the state's desire to bolster its legitimacy on the international

[49] Section 2 provides: 'This Constitution is the supreme law of the Republic; law or conduct inconsistent with it is invalid, and the obligations imposed by it must be fulfilled.'

[50] Human dignity is partly captured by the African concept of *ubuntu* which was included in the Postamble to the Interim Constitution: see English, '*Ubuntu*', 641; Cornell and Van Marle, 'Exploring *Ubuntu*', 195.

[51] See Davis, 'Constitutional Borrowing', 181; Du Bois, 'The Influence of Foreign Law', 625ff; Sarkin, 'The Effect of Constitutional Borrowings', 176.

[52] See the Preamble to the 1982 Canadian *Charter of Fundamental Rights and Freedoms*. However, in all of these Constitutions, the rule of law is woven into ideas of constitutionalism. Klug asserts that 'it is uncontroversial to state that South Africa's new constitutional order was shaped by and reflects the post-cold war hegemony of an American-style constitutionalism': Klug, *Constitutional Democracy*, 132. Although the ANC initially embraced socialist models, it also had its own rights-based tradition, as demonstrated by its *Freedom Charter* of 1955, and this 'facilitated the [ANC's and South Africa's] transition towards constitutionalism': 131.

[53] Klug, *Constitutional Democracy*, 69.

front. As set out in Chapter 2, by the early 1990s, the concept of the rule of law was fast becoming the dominant global paradigm. For example, in 1989 the World Bank stressed that Africa was suffering a crisis of governance and that development needed the establishment of the rule of law.[54] At the time of the drafting of the Final Constitution, the World Bank had become very influential in South Africa, particularly among the top ranks of the ANC leadership; many ANC officials were sent to Washington DC for a familiarisation course at the World Bank and in 1996 the World Bank was important in steering South Africa towards adopting the conservative economic policy, GEAR.[55] The World Bank was giving policy advice to the ANC Government in a number of areas[56] and the Government was keen to do all it could to attract foreign direct investment.[57] Given the nexus between investment and the rule of law promoted by the World Bank in the 1990s, it is possible that this could have had an impact on the drafters of South Africa's Final Constitution and their decision to include the rule of law as a founding value of the new legal order.

2.2 *The rule of law during apartheid*

It is apparent that South Africans did not rush into embracing the concept of the rule of law as the 'magic bullet' to their problems during the constitutional dispensation. Indeed, Yvonne Burns wryly comments: 'It is an interesting exercise to consider why the drafters of the Constitution thought fit to include this doctrine in the Constitution, given [the rule of law's] former rather dismal performance in protecting human rights.'[58] G. E. Devenish explains that during apartheid the concept of the rule of law was 'savagely mutilated' because it was unable to restrain the

[54] The World Bank, *Sub-Saharan Africa*, 192. Note that this report did not cover either South Africa or Namibia.

[55] Taylor, *Stuck in Middle GEAR*, 63–5. There is also some indication of influence by USAID, which asserts that it has 'a long tradition of supporting the rule of law in South Africa': *Independent Evaluation of SDC's Human Rights and Rule of Law Guidance Documents*, 113.

[56] Bond, *Against Global Apartheid*, 69.

[57] See the speech made by Mbeki in mid-2001 quoted in Bond, ibid., 127–8.

[58] Burns, *Administrative Law*, 70. Interestingly, most South African writers in this area discuss Dicey's approach to the rule of law as having founded the modern conception of it: Burns, *Administrative Law*, 70; Currie and de Waal, *The New Constitutionalism*, Vol 1; and Devenish, *The South African Constitution*.

power of the legislature which was strengthened by the doctrine of parliamentary sovereignty. She explains:

> South Africa's lamentable history in relation to ferocious and draconian security laws was such that the rule of law provided little or no inhibition as far as these were concerned. ... in apartheid South Africa it proved singularly and tragically ineffectual.[59]

During apartheid, the concept of the rule of law was not widely embraced because Afrikaners in the legal profession identified it with foreign English traditions.[60] Indeed, the courts avoided referring to the concept during this era.[61] Furthermore, the legal profession was dominated at the time by the doctrine of legal positivism as articulated by John Austin.[62] Through the lens of strict legal positivism, the rule of law was rejected as a legal value or political standard rather than a juridical concept.[63] According to this view, the rule of law simply required that laws be properly enacted and enforced. Liberal critics of apartheid, such as Dugard, also rejected the idea of the rule of law as a useful concept because of the vagueness of the concept and the uncertainty as to its content.[64] This vagueness and uncertainty meant the concept was often equated with its narrowest end goal, the maintenance of law and order, and hence was more rule *by* law than the rule of law. The vagueness associated with the concept also lent it too easily to manipulation, as demonstrated by a booklet published in 1968 by the South African Government entitled *South Africa and the Rule of Law*.[65] The booklet offered its own definition of the rule of law, stating that 'it requires that a person on trial be accused in open court; be given an opportunity of denying the charge and of defending himself and that he be given the choice of a counsel'.[66] The booklet went on to assert that South Africa's

[59] Devenish, *The South African Constitution*, 11. [60] Dugard, *Human Rights*, 41.

[61] Currie and de Waal, *The New Constitutionalism*, Vol 1, 76. [62] See Chapter 2 at n. 13.

[63] Austin, *The Province of Jurisprudence Determined*, 44–5. See, e.g., Venter, 'The Withering', 69. Venter asserts that the rule of law is incompatible with the political philosophy of 'humanism' articulated in South Africa's 1961 Constitution. He further argues that the rule of law is an 'ethical doctrine' which cannot properly be called a 'juridical concept'. He states: 'The conclusion must therefore be that the Rule of Law doctrine *withers* as soon as it is subjected to jurisprudential analysis': 88 (emphasis original). For a general overview, see Abel, *Politics by Other Means*, Ch. 2.

[64] Dugard, *Human Rights*, Ch. 3.

[65] See also Schreiner, *The Contribution of English Law*; Snyman, *South Africa and the Rule of Law*.

[66] Department of Foreign Affairs of the Republic of South Africa, *South Africa and the Rule of Law*, 47.

court system fulfilled all these requirements of the rule of law. This very thin and distorted approach to the rule of law fails to mention the function of the rule of law in regard to curtailing arbitrary government action or guaranteeing equality before the law.[67] But to most South African lawyers at the time, the problems of arbitrary and discriminatory legislation were political problems that could not be remedied by the legal concept of the rule of law.[68]

On the international front, reports of the International Commission of Jurists (ICJ) refuted the assertions of the apartheid Government, such as those found in the 1968 booklet, arguing that the mere performance of legal formalities did not satisfy the rule of law.[69] The ICJ's position was that the rule of law had been eroded in South Africa because the rule of law was not fulfilling its main function of limiting state power.[70] It argued that in apartheid South Africa, parliamentary supremacy and political interference with the judiciary meant that the courts were unable to fulfil this function of checking the limits of state power.[71] However, the breadth of the ICJ's definition of the rule of law, encompassing respect for a wide range of human rights, including social and economic rights, meant that even proponents of the rule of law sidelined its work.[72] Given the perceived weaknesses of the rule of law, critics such as Dugard preferred to advocate for a Bill of Rights rather than the rule of law as a more direct means of addressing the inequalities produced by the apartheid system.

Despite this negative perception of the rule of law among many quarters, the concept was placed alongside equality as a founding value in section one of the Final Constitution, which is super-entrenched.[73] Unlike equality, it does not receive any explicit elaboration in the body of the Constitution although it is clearly tied to provisions, such as the separation of powers and access to courts, that underlie the rule of law. Given the poor perception of the rule of law during apartheid, it has

[67] Dugard, *Human Rights*, 42. To charges of racial discrimination South Africa held up its 'separate but equal' policy and the concept of self-determination in the different homelands.

[68] Ibid., 45.

[69] International Commission of Jurists, *South Africa and the Rule of Law*, 144. [70] Ibid.

[71] International Commission of Jurists, *Erosion of the Rule of Law in South Africa*, iv.

[72] Mathews, *Dilemmas of the Apartheid Society*, Ch. 3.

[73] See s. 74 (1) of the Final Constitution which requires that amendments of s. 1 be passed by higher majorities than any other constitutional amendment: 75 per cent majority of the National Assembly and two-thirds majority in the National Council of Provinces.

needed to undergo a significant transformation, from a weak concept denoting vagueness, uncertain content and possible complicity to a strong and credible concept that can stave off future abuses, in order to play the role of a founding value. However, it is arguable that, at a technical level, the rule of law is also somewhat superfluous in South African constitutional jurisprudence on three grounds elucidated below.

2.3 *The vague role of the rule of law in South Africa's Final Constitution*

One reason why explicit constitutional entrenchment of the concept of the rule of law could be considered jurisprudentially superfluous is that the concept and its import were implied in constitutional jurisprudence relating to matters that took place before the enactment of the Final Constitution. This is apparent when looking at cases dealing with the principle of legality, which is understood to be an integral part of the rule of law.[74] In the 1999 case of *Fedsure Life Assurance Ltd* v. *Greater Johannesburg Transitional Metropolitan Council*[75] ('*Fedsure*') the Constitutional Court looked at the applicable Interim Constitution and held that the principle of legality is a 'fundamental' part of the rule of law. Given that the Interim Constitution is devoid of any textual reference to the rule of law, it seems that the principle of legality does not need an express articulation of the 'rule of law' for its operation. The Court held that 'the principle of legality is implied within the terms of the interim Constitution' and it stated that: 'fundamental to the interim Constitution is a principle of legality'.[76] Unfortunately the Court did not identify which part of the Interim Constitution was relevant in this respect; it stated vaguely that the rule of law was a 'fundamental principle of constitutional law' but to support this proposition it was forced to refer to the 1996 Final Constitution as well as the constitutional jurisprudence

[74] Hoexter defines the principle of legality as 'a convenient way of requiring all exercises of public power – including non-administrative action – to conform to certain accepted minimum standards': Hoexter, 'The Principle of Legality', 184.

[75] 1999 (1) SA 374 (CC). The constitutional principle of legality holds that all legislative and executive organs of state are limited to exercising only those powers conferred on them. In administrative law, the principle as a ground of review is articulated in s. 6 of the *Promotion of Administrative Justice Act 3 of 2000*. This Act is connected to s. 33 of the Constitution, which requires administrators to act lawfully, reasonably and procedurally fairly and to give reasons in certain circumstances.

[76] Ibid., [58].

of Canada and Germany. The Court's invocation of the principle of legality in *Fedsure* has caused some concern: this is partly because the principle was used (and abused) as a common law constitutional principle during the apartheid era and today some critics believe the principle should derive from the text of the post-apartheid constitutions and not from outside the 'one law'.[77]

Fedsure demonstrates that enshrining the rule of law as a founding principle in section 1(c) of the Final Constitution did not introduce the principle of legality into South African jurisprudence because the principle pre-exists the Final Constitution.[78] However, the explicit articulation of the rule of law meant that the principle of legality, and other principles deriving from the rule of law, became firmly rooted in the Final Constitution and no longer needed to be implied into the Constitution. Constitutional recognition of the rule of law bolstered the concept and its principles, as well as corollary principles such as constitutionalism, which is not explicitly articulated in the Constitution.

A second reason for the possible superfluity of the explicit constitutional articulation of the rule of law is the rule of interpretation that norms of greater specificity should be exhausted before norms of generality and abstraction, such as the rule of law, should be applied. This is apparent in the case of *Pharmaceutical Manufacturers Association of SA: In re: ex parte President of the Republic of South Africa*[79] where the Constitutional Court articulated a 'definitive statement'[80] on the requirement rising from the rule of law that all law and state conduct must have a rational relation to a legitimate government purpose. Here the Court held:

> It is a requirement of the rule of law that the exercise of public power by the executive and other functionaries should not be arbitrary. Decisions must be rationally related to the purpose for which the power was given, otherwise they are in effect arbitrary and inconsistent with this requirement. It follows that in order to pass constitutional scrutiny, the exercise of power by the executive and other functionaries, must, at the least, comply with this requirement.[81]

[77] See, e.g., Michelman, 'The Rule of Law', 11–1.

[78] Indeed, the principle of legality was part of South Africa's pre-transitional constitutional law. See Michelman, 'The Rule of Law', 11–1.

[79] 2000 (2) SA 674 (CC).

[80] Currie and de Waal, *The Bill of Rights Handbook*, 12.

[81] 2000 (2) SA 674 (CC) [85]. The Court found that despite the fact that the President had acted in good faith in making the decision to bring certain legislation into force, there was no rational connection, objectively viewed, between this decision and a legitimate

Before the Court could consider this requirement, it had to decide whether the relevant conduct was administrative action and subject to some specific rights in the Bill of Rights. Generally, however, any consideration of the constraints placed on public power by the rule of law is preceded by an examination as to whether another form of constraint on public power is operative, which is that arising from the Bill of Rights. This constraint requires that rights are only limited by laws of general application if they satisfy the conditions set out in the Final Constitution's limitation clause, section 36. Because it is more specific, the limitation clause is perhaps the primary constraint, and it is operative in almost every case because of the extensive nature of the Bill of Rights. This leaves very little scope for the rule of law to operate, possibly explaining why it has been invoked in a noteworthy way in so few cases.

A third reason is that the rule of law underpins doctrines that already appear to be self-standing. For example, the Constitutional Court has found that the concept of the rule of law underpins the doctrine of vagueness, which requires that laws must be written in a clear and accessible manner: there must be reasonable certainty.[82] In *President of the Republic of South Africa* v. *Hugo*,[83] Mokgoro J said:

> The need for accessibility, precision and general application flow from the concept of the rule of law. A person should be able to know of the law, and be able to conform his or her conduct to the law. Further, laws should apply generally, rather than targeting specific individuals.[84]

Here Mokgoro J states one of the key principles of Hayek's approach to the rule of law, which is that laws should apply generally and never specifically. However, it is unclear from Mokgoro J's judgment whether the doctrine of vagueness requires the explicit constitutional recognition of the rule of law.

A related example is an aspect of the rule of law that is more relevant to transitional countries where the state legal system is not at full strength. In the case of *Chief Lesapo* v. *North West Agricultural Bank*,[85] the Constitutional Court held that 'self-help', in the sense of vigilantism

government purpose because the schedules relating to the relevant legislation were not yet in operation.

[82] *Affordable Medicines Trust and Others* v. *Minister of Health and Another* 2006 (3) SA 247 (CC) [108]. See also *Minister of Health and Another* v. *New Clicks South Africa (Pty) Ltd and Others In re: Application for Declaratory Relief* 2005 (3) SA 238 (CC) [246].

[83] 1997 (4) SA 1 (CC). [84] Ibid., [102]. [85] 2000 (1) SA 409 (CC).

and taking the law into one's own hands, is inimical to a rule-of-law society.[86] Writing for the Court, Mokgoro J stated:

> *The right of access to court* is indeed foundational to the stability of an orderly society. It ensures the peaceful, regulated and institutionalised mechanisms to resolve disputes, without resorting to self-help. *The right of access to court* is a bulwark against vigilantism ... Construed in this context of the rule of law and the principle against self-help in particular, access to court is indeed of cardinal importance.[87]

Thus the concept of the rule of law is connected to the right to access to court, set out in section 34 of the Final Constitution, which provides: 'Everyone has the right to have any dispute that can be resolved by the application of law decided in a fair public hearing before a court or, where appropriate, another *independent and impartial tribunal or forum.*'[88] This provision means that, for the state to satisfy the rule of law, it is not necessary that it provide access to a court so long as the alternative is a 'tribunal or forum' that is 'independent and impartial'. Presumably, however, the principle against self-help is strengthened by the rule of law but not necessarily founded by it, for in *Makwanyane* the Constitutional Court located the principle operating in the Interim Constitution, but there the Court traced it to the concept of constitutionalism.[89]

The Constitutional Court also considered the relationship between the rule of law and section 34 in a case dealing with eviction orders granted by a court to a landowner against 40,000 people squatting on his land in *President of the Republic of South Africa and Another* v. *Modderklip Boerdery (Pty) Ltd.*[90] The Court emphasised the state's obligation 'to provide the necessary mechanisms for citizens to resolve disputes that arise between them'.[91] Specifically, it held that it would be inconsistent with the rule of law if the court orders for eviction were executed because it would 'cause unimaginable social chaos and misery'.[92] On the other hand, the state's failure to do anything, such as expropriate the property, breached the landowner's constitutional right to an effective remedy as

[86] Ibid., [11].

[87] Ibid., [22] (emphasis added). Here the Court held that 'any constraint upon a person or property shall be exercised by another only after recourse to a court recognised in terms of the law of the land': [16].

[88] Emphasis added. [89] 1995 (3) SA 391 (CC) [168]. [90] 2005 (5) SA 3 (CC).

[91] Ibid., [39]. The Court stated that these mechanisms were legislative, executive and judicial in nature.

[92] Ibid., [47].

required by the rule of law and section 34. Here, once again, it appears that section 34, or other provisions in the Bill of Rights,[93] would have produced the same result in the absence of section 1(c).

From the above it appears that the rule of law is purely procedural in nature in South African constitutional law, much like the thin approach to the rule of law. For example, the principle of legality existed during apartheid despite the contracted interpretations given by the apartheid regime to its requirements.[94] However, constitutional scholars maintain that the rule of law in the Final Constitution has a substantive content that 'dictates that the government must respect the individual's basic rights'.[95] While it is not clear to Iain Currie and Johan de Waal as to what kinds of rights might qualify in this regard, they argue it 'seems logical' that 'respect for human dignity, equality and freedom' 'ought also to be the rights protected by the rule of law' because they are repeatedly emphasised in the Bill of Rights.[96] While this fits in neatly with the thick approach to the rule of law, the problem is that, unlike Dworkin's scenario where the rule of law helps to fill the gaps in the rule book,[97] the concept of the rule of law does not fill any gaps: it merely bolsters existing rights in the Bill of Rights. As the Constitutional Court has clarified, the rule of law does not give rise to 'discrete and enforceable rights' in itself but it works to 'inform and give substance' to the rights provisions in the rule of law.[98] In this sense the rule of law appears somewhat superfluous to the constitutional jurisprudence of post-apartheid South Africa.[99]

If the constitutional recognition of the concept of the rule of law is superfluous, in the sense that the courts were already happy to imply it in its absence and it fails to go much further than existing constitutional provisions, then the question is why it was included given the concept's reputation for being weak, vague, manipulable, dismal and 'singularly

[93] Ibid., [51]. This case is interesting because the Court preferred to rely on the rule of law and s. 34 rather than the parties' right to private property and to housing. See Corder, 'Judicial Policy', 101.

[94] Michelman, 'The Rule of Law', 11–1.

[95] Currie and de Waal, *The Bill of Rights Handbook*, 13.

[96] Ibid., 13.

[97] See Chapter 3, section 2.2.

[98] *Minister of Home Affairs* v. *National Institute for Crime Prevention and the Reintegration of Offenders (NICRO) and Others* 2005 (3) SA 280 (CC) [21, 23]. This decision held that all the founding values in s. 1 of the Final Constitution had this effect.

[99] For an analysis of some of the rule of law problems currently facing South Africa, see Dyzenhaus, 'The Pasts and Future', 734.

and tragically ineffectual'. Perhaps an answer is that it came as part of the Bill of Rights package. Much of the debate during the apartheid era concerned whether the rule of law could have effect in the absence of a bill of rights, but this debate was swept aside by the entrenchment of an extensive Bill of Rights in the Final Constitution. However, it is not entirely clear why the Bill of Rights, which is so sweeping, should need to be bolstered by the rule of law. It is possible that the drafters of the Final Constitution were influenced by the emerging rhetoric of global institutions, hegemonic states and the international human rights movement that project the rule of law as a precondition to human rights and democracy and hence they were keen to shore up the Constitution's legitimacy on the international front. Regardless, section 1(c) reinforces the checks and balances of power in the Final Constitution and symbolises the new legal order's commitment to the rule of law. As Cora Hoexter says, it 'acts as a kind of safety net' and enables judicial review of all public power.[100]

3. Legal pluralism

Legal pluralism represents another front for establishing the legitimacy of the Constitution and the new legal order. As a means to fostering a form of internal legitimacy, the need to reinvent and transform legal pluralism was manifest given the history of its exploitation and manipulation by colonial and apartheid governments in South Africa. Since the 1927 *Black Administration Act* state law pluralism had been operating uniformly across South Africa but prior to that it had operated in different provinces at various times. Particularly during apartheid legal pluralism was viewed in negative terms.[101] The apartheid regime refashioned the 'separate but equal doctrine', first propounded in the US, in order to prop up minority white rule until the end of the Cold War. Legal pluralism was used to subject Africans to different laws and pen them into a separate court system on tribal and racial lines with arguably inferior safeguards. Thus courts such as the Commissioners Courts and the Divorce courts

[100] According to Hoexter, the rule of law fills the gaps in the judicial review of public power because it catches 'exercises of public power that do not qualify as administrative action' under s. 33 of the Final Constitution, which sets out the rights to administrative justice, and the *Promotion of Administrative Justice Act 3 of 2000*: Hoexter, 'The Principle of Legality', 183.

[101] Griffiths, *In the Shadow of Marriage*, 28.

were set up solely for 'African' and coloured people. Their association with Chiefs Courts allowed apartheid governments to argue that they were accommodating cultural differences. Thus, the state embraced state law pluralism through the recognition of fragments of customary law only to the extent that it served the interests of the apartheid regime. In 1951, for example, the nascent apartheid Government passed the *Bantu Authorities Act*, which transformed the existing tribal structures so as to include new local authorities who were responsible for the peaceful and orderly administration of their jurisdiction. The new scheme allowed the Government to appoint rulers regardless of traditional legitimacy so long as they acquiesced with government directives. This process of grafting elements of state control onto traditional structures and laws was just one of the many steps which took place in the transformation of customary law from its pre-colonial form. While these separate courts could apply customary law, this law was not considered equal to the common law applied by the ordinary courts. The repugnancy clause[102] meant that the common law had always been regarded as the 'dominant' system while customary law had been relegated to the position of 'servient' law, applying only to 'blacks'.[103] Customary law was marginalised and neglected; this was largely as a result of a policy designed to exclude Africans from fully participating in the South African legal system.[104] Legal pluralism is called by some of its detractors in South Africa 'legal dualism' because its state manifestation is founded on a racist ideology of segregation. During apartheid, state law pluralism was based on inequality. For the architects of post-apartheid South Africa, the challenge was to develop a form of state law pluralism based on the equality of legal systems.[105]

The process by which legal pluralism became recognised in the Final Constitution was complex and contested. However, it is worth exploring in some detail because of the dynamics between legal pluralism and two core constitutional values often associated with the rule of law, equality and democracy. The process shows the compromises that were made to these core values in order to secure the support of traditional leaders and

[102] Section 1(1) of the *Law of Evidence Amendment Act 45 of 1988* provides: 'Any court may take judicial notice ... of indigenous law ... [p]rovided that indigenous law shall not be opposed to the principles of public policy and natural justice'. See also Chapter 2 at n. 4.

[103] Pieterse, 'It's a Black Thing', 372. [104] Bennett, *A Sourcebook*, v.

[105] Van Niekerk, 'Succession', 486.

to promote the legitimacy of the Constitution with the 'very large part of the population' referred to by Sachs J in *Makwanyane*.

3.1 *The initial negotiations and the interim Constitution*

The process began with CP XIII, which represented the negotiated position on customary law and the role of traditional leaders. It states:

> The institution, status and role of traditional leadership, according to indigenous law, shall be recognised and protected in the Constitution. Indigenous law, like common law, shall be recognised and applied by the courts, subject to the fundamental rights contained in the Constitution and to legislation dealing specifically therewith.[106]

According to Christina Murray, this principle was intended to remedy the fact that during the apartheid regime the Government often replaced unco-operative chiefs 'with more compliant people'.[107] Thus, this principle was designed to protect the traditional roles of chiefs and headmen and to transform their future.[108] As is clear, this principle also recognises indigenous law (here used interchangeably with 'customary law' by the drafters of both the Interim Constitution and the Final Constitution) and it requires that courts apply such law to the extent that it is consistent with both the Constitution and legislation. Effectively, this principle appears to place customary law on an equal footing with the common law of South Africa.[109] This was a symbolic and momentous event as it was the first constitutional

[106] Section 2 of Act 3 of 1994 inserted this second part to Principle XIII on 25 April 2004. Note that two days before the first democratic national elections were held in April 1994, an amendment was added to CP XIII via a second sub-principle:

> Provisions in a provincial constitution relating to the institution, role, authority and status of a traditional monarch shall be recognised and protected in the Constitution.

This amendment to the Constitutional Principles recognised the constitutional status of the king of the Zulus at the provincial level. Its aim was to persuade the Inkatha Freedom Party (IFP) to reverse its decision to boycott the national and provincial elections, and in this the amendment was successful. See Du Plessis and Corder, *South Africa's Transitional Bill of Rights*, 11. However, as a whole the amended Principle sits uncomfortably with CP XVII's requirement of democratic representation at all levels. It states: 'At each level of government there shall be democratic representation. This principle shall not derogate from the provisions of Principle XIII.' This non-derogation proviso is curious and it later led to some contention before the Constitutional Court during the certification hearings. However, these Constitutional Principles illustrate the highly negotiated nature of the constitution-making process.

[107] Murray, 'Negotiating Beyond Deadlock', 105. [108] Ibid.

[109] The question of whether customary law operates on an equal footing with the common law in South Africa is addressed in Chapter 5.

articulation of legal pluralism. This constitutional recognition of customary law would have most impact on South Africa's rural population, who number approximately 20 million, or 40 per cent of the population. It is this part of the population to which customary law is most likely to apply.

CP XIII was translated into Chapter 11 of the Interim Constitution. Section 181 differed from CP XIII in the fact that it gave recognition to 'indigenous law' 'subject to regulation by law', possibly making customary law subject, not only to legislation, but also to the common law. Three sections of Chapter 11 also operated to include traditional leaders in all three tiers of government: local, provincial and national government.[110] At the top two tiers, this inclusion in government was in the form of a body of traditional leaders, which was empowered to advise the elected governments on matters relating to traditional leadership and customary law and to delay relevant legislation for thirty days. At the local level, traditional leaders were guaranteed seats in local government without the need of election. These provisions were a response to the demand for inclusion by traditional leaders; they argued that a majority of South Africans owed them allegiance and that to ignore their role would ensure resistance to a new government.[111] Although their representativeness as a lobby group had not been proven, the nature of the negotiating process allowed traditional leaders even to lobby for 30 per cent of the seats in the Senate.[112] At this point their demands were rebuffed, as it was apparent that this option would have had a disproportionate impact on the principle of democracy in shielding traditional leaders from the electoral process.

Chapter 11 of the Interim Constitution was a huge success for the negotiators representing traditional leaders, especially given that they were accepted in the negotiating process only late in the negotiating process.[113] Up until this point in the negotiations, little consideration

[110] Sections 182–4. The effect of s. 184 is similar to that of CP XIII in that it gives recognition to the continuation of traditional authority and its 'powers and functions', as well as giving recognition to 'indigenous law', but only subject to regulation by law.

[111] Atkinson, 'Principle Born of Pragmatism?', Ch. 4, 115–16. According to Atkinson, the ANC, through Cyril Ramaphosa, initially responded to these demands by proposing a 'sub-council on local and regional government be responsible for paying traditional leaders'. This did not satisfy the demand of traditional leaders that councils be established at all three levels.

[112] Ibid., 116. Atkinson notes that the Pan African Congress, a minor party, supported these demands that traditional leaders be given seats in the Senate.

[113] Traditional leaders and their representatives were initially excluded from the 1991 Convention for a Democratic South Africa (CODESA), but, some, such as Chief Nonkonyama, attended as part of a homeland delegation. Following CODESA, four

had been given to the question of customary law and traditional leadership.[114] On the other hand, the initial concern of traditional leaders was to secure a guarantee that their existing salaries, status and powers would be maintained under the new constitutional order.[115] The question of customary law appears to have been a secondary consideration for traditional leaders.

For traditional leaders, it was disappointing that customary law was made subject to the Interim Constitution, its Chapter 3 Bill of Rights, and specifically its guarantees of equality. They demanded that customary law be insulated from the Constitution's guarantees of equality.[116] This was not without constitutional precedent in Africa. To support their case, traditional leaders could draw on the constitutional arrangements found in other jurisdictions in Southern Africa such as Zimbabwe,[117] Zambia,[118] Swaziland[119] and Botswana,[120] as well as many other jurisdictions in Africa and the Asia-Pacific region.[121] The Constitutions of these countries in Southern Africa and elsewhere include provisions whereby customary law is shielded from the application of norms of equality and/or non-discrimination.[122]

delegations of traditional leaders (each with eight members) were invited to participate in the Multi-Party Negotiation Process that began in 1993 and was responsible for drafting the Interim Constitution.

114 Bennett, *Human Rights*, 21. 115 Currie, 'The Future of Customary Law', 149.

116 Albertyn, 'Women and the Transition', 57ff; Nhlapo, 'Indigenous Law', 61.

117 *Zimbabwe Constitution* (Order 1600 of 1979), subss. 23(3)(a), 23(2)(b).

118 *Constitution of Zambia* (Act 1 of 1999), subs. 23(4)(d).

119 *Swaziland Constitution* (1377 of 1968), subs. 15(4)(b); note that this constitution has been superseded by a 2005 Constitution.

120 See, e.g., *Botswana Constitution* (Independence Order 1171 of 1966), subs. 15(4)(d), which provides:

15. Protection from discrimination on the grounds of race, etc.

Subject to the provisions of subss. (4), (5) and (7) of this section, no law shall make any provision that is discriminatory either of itself or in its effect.

...

(4) Subs. (1) of this section shall not apply to any law so far as that law makes provision –

(c) with respect to adoption, marriage, divorce, burial, devolution of property on death or other matters of personal law;

(d) for the application in the case of members of a particular race, community or tribe of customary law with respect to any matter whether to the exclusion of any law in respect to that matter which is applicable in the case of other persons or not...

121 Some constitutions which allow customary law to override anti-discrimination provisions in the Pacific region are as follows: the *Constitution of Fiji Islands*, s. 38 (8)–(10); *Constitution of Tuvalu*, s. 27(3)(d); and *Constitution of Solomon Islands*, s. 15 (c).

122 Bennett, *Human Rights*, 28.

The relationship between the right to gender equality and the status of customary law became the site of a battle between women and traditional leaders. At the heart of the question lay the legality of the customary system of patrilineal succession,[123] which traditional leaders felt had to be protected against the gender equality clause.[124] One delegate, Chief Nonkonyana, objected to the equality provisions in the Bill of Rights, stating that as a traditional leader, he did not support equality for women.[125] The notion of equality, he asserted, 'is foreign to us': 'We are in Africa and we remain in Africa. We are not prepared to sacrifice our Africanism.'[126] In his view, the Bill of Rights would 'inflict irreparable harm on the entrenched cultural values of indigenous people of South Africa'.[127] In short, he demanded that customary law be excluded from the operation of the Bill of Rights.[128] Various clauses on customary law were drafted for inclusion in Chapter 3 in order to reach a compromise with traditional leaders. For example, one compromise, Clause 32, gave people the right to opt in and out of customary law by voluntary association with a community that observed such law or chose its application to their personal relationships. These compromise clauses were removed when the position of the traditional leaders kept shifting and following strong lobbying by women's groups,[129] many representing rural women whose lives are most affected by these issues. The concession made to traditional leaders was in the form of Chapter 11, discussed above. Thus, to keep the traditional leaders on side, the two main negotiating parties, the ANC and National Party, had to compromise the principle of democracy but they were successful in protecting the Bill of Rights, specifically the equality guarantees, from any similar compromise.

[123] Bennett argues that as a result of this particular concern for patrilineal succession, the traditional leaders 'almost inadvertently … emerged as the champions of customary law': ibid., 21.

[124] For a detailed history of the battle between women's groups and traditional leaders on the question of gender equality in the Interim Constitution, see Spitz and Chaskalson, *The Politics of Transition*, Ch. 19.

[125] Rickard, 'Equality for Women?'.

[126] Quoted in Oomen, *Chiefs in South Africa*, 48.

[127] Ibid., 79.

[128] Albertyn, 'Women and the Transition', 57. In response, women's groups, such as the Women's National Coalition representing over ninety women's groups, argued that to shield customary law from the Bill of Rights would be to deny human rights protection to a third of the population, black women. Such a denial would defeat the purpose of the Bill of Rights, which was to provide everyone with equal protection of the law.

[129] See Spitz and Chaskalson, *The Politics of Transition*, 385–90.

3.2 *The Final Constitution*

Elections were held in 1994 for the Constitutional Assembly that was to draft the Final Constitution. The ANC gained a sizeable majority of the seats in the Constitutional Assembly but not the two-thirds required for the adoption of the Final Constitution. The elections meant that the drafting of the Final Constitution was underpinned by democratic legitimacy and there was an emphasis on popular consultation and participation in order to secure greater legitimacy for the final product.[130] This process was responsible for transforming the thirty-four CPs into enduring constitutional principles.

In May 1995, the Congress of Traditional Leaders of South Africa (CONTRALESA), an organisation with some 2,000 members, forwarded a resolution to the Constitutional Assembly putting its case for strengthening the institution of traditional leadership in the Constitution:

> The constitution … should be a mirror of the soul of the nation – it must include all aspirations, beliefs and values. The constitution will not be successful if it relies only on foreign concepts and institutions. The institution and role of traditional leaders, which have been in existence as long as – if not longer than – liberal democracy in the West, have to be treated with respect and accordingly be integrated within the structures of national, provincial and local government.[131]

In this statement, CONTRALESA appears to cast itself as 'the soul of the nation'. The statement shows its desire to manipulate the tension between the inclusion of international norms and local norms in the Constitution so as to promote its own interests.

Traditional leaders were concerned about two aspects of the Final Constitution. First, they were upset about the demotion of the constitutional status of the bodies of traditional leaders, provided for in the Interim Constitution, to an enabling clause in Chapter 12 of the Final

[130] The process undertaken by the Constitutional Assembly comprised two elements: a public participation programme, and a political programme. The public participation programme invited ordinary South Africans to engage with the process by making submissions to the CA, either by writing or via a telephone talk-line. The programme lasted about three and a half months, between 1 January and 17 April 1996. It succeeded in attracting over two million submissions, mostly in the form of petitions, and the media provided significant coverage of the process, reportedly reaching about 73 per cent of the adult population. The aim of the public participation programme was to engender local ownership of the Constitution and to ensure that the Constitution reflected local realities: Murray, 'Negotiating Beyond Deadlock', 106.

[131] Constitutional Assembly, *Traditional Authorities, Block 4* (May 30, 1995) 36.

Constitution which allowed national and provincial legislatures to provide for such bodies.[132] While provisions dealing with the constitutional status of traditional leaders were demoted in the Final Constitution, traditional leaders would have noticed that guarantees of equality were promoted and upgraded.[133] These changes made apparent the position of equality as one of the primary guarantees in the Final Constitution.[134] Arguably these constitutional guarantees of equality were strengthened in the face of the demands of traditional leaders, thus making the tension between international and local norms apparent. Thus, traditional leaders continued to protest their second concern, that neither customary law nor traditional leadership were shielded from the Final Constitution and legislation.[135] In regard to customary law, the relevant provision of the Final Constitution was section 211(3) in Chapter 12, which provides: 'The courts *must* apply customary law when that law is applicable, subject to the Constitution and any legislation that specifically deals with customary law.'[136] Traditional leaders desired the entrenchment of

[132] Klug, 'Constitution-making in South Africa', 152. For traditional leaders, this may have felt like a step backwards as previously the Interim Constitution had guaranteed the establishment of these councils whereas under s. 212 of the Final Constitution they would need to lobby the government in the future to act. Section 212 provides: '(1) National legislation may provide for a role for traditional leadership as an institution at local level on matters affecting local communities. (2) To deal with matters relating to traditional leadership, the role of traditional leaders, customary law and the customs of communities observing a system of customary law (a) national or provincial legislation may provide for the establishment of houses of traditional leaders; and (b) national legislation may establish a council of traditional leaders.'

[133] For example, the limitation clause of the Final Constitution, s. 36, no longer referred specifically to customary law (subs. 33(3) of the Interim Constitution) but was drafted more broadly. Section 36(1) provides: 'The rights in the Bill of Rights may be limited only in terms of law of general application to the extent that the limitation is reasonable and justifiable in an open and democratic society *based on human dignity, equality and freedom*, taking into account all relevant factors' (emphasis added). Note that subs. 33(3) of the Interim Constitution became part of the Interpretation clause of the Final Constitution, subs. 39(3). Equality was also incorporated into the interpretation clause of the Final Constitution, s. 39 and under s. 37 it was listed as a non-derogable right in times of emergency.

[134] Note that s. 9 of the Final Constitution is the Constitution's main guarantee of equality.

[135] The relevant provision for traditional leadership was subs. 211(1) which provides: 'The institution, status and role of traditional leadership, according to customary law, are recognised, subject to the Constitution.'

[136] Emphasis added. After the enactment of the Interim Constitution, traditional leaders still held hope for a final constitution in which customary law would operate outside of the constitution, despite the fact that CP XIII had been entrenched to the contrary. Furthermore, Nhlapo suggests in his writing at the time that it is possible to read the

customary law rather than its mere recognition. Thandabantu Nhlapo implies that women's groups were collectively advocating for a third option, the abolition of customary law, but there is little evidence for this at a broad level.[137]

Traditional leaders had a final opportunity to press their concerns before the Constitutional Court, whose role was to certify the Final Constitution as the concluding step in South Africa's constitutional dispensation.[138] The main group of 'objectors', which included CONTRALESA,[139] complained to the Court about the 'destructive confrontation' between the Bill of Rights and legislation on the one side and indigenous law on the other,[140] and asserted that traditional authority is the reality of government for millions of people living in rural South Africa. They complained that sections 211 and 212 of Chapter 12 failed to comply with CP XIII on three main grounds. First, the sections failed to *protect* the 'institution, status and role' of traditional leadership; the sections merely *recognised* it but failed to extend to 'protect[ion]'.[141] A second ground related to the recognition of traditional courts. Here the objectors argued that the Final Constitution failed to comply with CP

Constitutional Principles as requiring the entrenchment of customary law in the Constitution, a position which would place customary law beyond the reach of legislation. Nhlapo, 'Indigenous Law', 52, 61.

137 Nhlapo, 'Indigenous Law', 52, n 19. In early 1994 the Women's National Coalition, comprising approximately ninety women's groups, agreed on a *Women's Charter* and presented it to the President. The document aimed to influence the drafting of the Final Constitution. The Charter does not call for the abolition of customary law. While Article 9 notes that customary practice often subordinates and excludes women, it merely calls for 'Custom, culture and religion … [to] be subject to the equality clause in the Bill of Rights.' Note, however, that the Rural Women's Movement did call for the total abolition of customary courts.

138 This process provided an opportunity for minority parties and individuals to challenge certain provisions that they had reluctantly agreed to in order to meet the drafting deadline, or, in the case of the Inkatha Freedom Party, to which they had not agreed at all.

139 The objectors to Chapter 12 also included the Traditional Authorities Research Group and Professor A. J. Kerr. It should be noted that various organisations voiced support for Chapter 12: the Legal Resources Centre, the Centre for Applied Legal Studies and the Community Law Centre at the University of the Western Cape.

140 *Certification of the Constitution of the Republic of South Africa* 1996 (4) SA 744 (CC) [202].

141 A related argument was that the words 'institution', 'status' and, in particular, 'role', envisage a constitutionally entrenched function. The underlying purpose of CP XIII was to guarantee, not simply enable, a role for traditional forms of government in the constitutional structure: *Certification of the Constitution of the Republic of South Africa* 1996 (4) SA 744 (CC) fn 14[0].

XIII because it did not specifically mention these courts. The third related argument was that the horizontal application of the Bill of Rights would effectively undermine traditional leadership and thus nullify the Constitution's protection of customary law.

The Court dismissed the first argument, holding that Chapter 12 of the Final Constitution did comply with CP XIII(1), in that the 'institution, status and role of traditional leadership' were recognised and protected in the Final Constitution. It identified that CP XIII sought to acknowledge the existence of three elements of traditional African society: traditional leadership, customary law and, at the provincial level, traditional monarchy.[142] Chapter 12 gave an express guarantee of the continued existence of the first two elements. The Court stressed that without this express guarantee being given to customary law, the principle of equality in CP VI would have led to a presumption against legal pluralism in the constitutional framework.[143] Traditional leadership was guaranteed under section 211(2).[144] The Court argued that the fact that the three elements of traditional African society are declared to be subject to the Final Constitution highlights the point 'that in a constitutional state, no-one exercises power or authority outside of the constitution'.[145] In effect the Court was articulating the concept of constitutionalism, whereby the constitution aims to provide a check on all forms of power. Hence the 'one law' referred to in the constitutional slogan is the law of the Constitution.

[142] *Certification of the Constitution of the Republic of South Africa* 1996 (4) SA 744 (CC) [195].

[143] Ibid., [195].

[144] The Court held that s. 212(1) should be read as complementing s. 211 rather than diminishing it. On the drafting of s. 212 the Court opined: 'The CA cannot be constitutionally faulted for leaving the complicated, varied and ever-developing specifics of how such leadership should function in the wider democratic society, and how customary law should develop and be interpreted, to future social evolution, legislative deliberation and judicial interpretation': [197]. The Court implied that it was not necessary to read s. 211 (2) in light of s. 212(1) in that the reference to 'applicable legislation' in s. 211(2) did not necessarily relate to s. 212: [192]. In response to an argument that a reduction of powers was made in relation to customary law, the Court noted that whereas the power to establish a provincial House of Traditional Leaders had previously been an exclusive provincial power, s. 212(2) transformed this into a concurrent power. However, this was a case of a small reduction in provincial power rather than a case of non-compliance with CP XIII(1): [409]. Another argument related to the ability of the national government to set the salaries of traditional leaders at the provincial level. The impact of these two matters was raised in the Second Certification Case: see *Certification of the Amended Text of the Constitution of the Republic of South Africa* 1997 (2) SA 97 [176–8].

[145] Ibid., [194].

The Court also dismissed the second argument, pointing out that traditional courts, which numbered about 1,500 at the time, were recognised in section 166 of the Final Constitution, subsection (e) of which refers to 'any other court established or recognised by an Act of Parliament'.[146] Its response to the third argument, relating to the horizontal application of the Bill of Rights and its effect on customary law, was that the objection concerned not the Final Constitution but the Constitutional Principles, upon which it could not comment.[147] With this, the Court closed down all attempts to alter the position of legal pluralism and customary law in the Final Constitution.

3.3 *Pragmatism*

The approach to legal pluralism by the drafters of the Interim Constitution appears to have been largely pragmatic. During its struggle against apartheid, the ANC's policies on traditional leadership were vague and ambivalent.[148] For example, in 1988, the ANC had stated its position on traditional leadership in its Constitutional Guidelines: 'The institution of hereditary rules and chiefs shall be transformed to serve the interests of the people as a whole in conformity with the democratic principles embodied in the constitution.'[149] These guidelines make it clear that the ANC preferred democracy to traditionalism. However, during the negotiations in 1992–1993, this principle was tested as the ANC backflipped in order to embrace traditional leaders. Spitz and Chaskalson argue that '[t]his was one area where the ANC and the NP/government were particularly alive to electoral considerations'.[150] Once it became plain to the two parties that traditional leaders might still possess the power to sway a large part of the population, the parties began to include them in negotiations in order to broaden their support base. In particular, in 1992 the ANC was intent on preventing the leader of the Inkatha Freedom Party, Chief Buthelezi, from manipulating traditional leaders so as to stall or undermine the negotiations. Hence, from mid 1992, it

[146] Ibid., [199]. The Court also points to Sched. 6, s. 16(1) which provides: 'Every Court, including courts of traditional leaders … continues to function.'

[147] CP XIII (quoted in full above in the text) set out that customary law would be 'subject to the fundamental rights contained in the Constitution and to legislation dealing specifically therewith'.

[148] Ntsebeza, *Democracy Compromised*, 258.

[149] Principle (c) of the *Constitutional Guidelines for a Democratic South Africa*, 130.

[150] Spitz and Chaskalson, *The Politics of Transition*, 380.

campaigned for the inclusion of traditional leaders in all levels of government.[151] However, many members of the ANC only really envisaged traditional leaders as performing ceremonial and advisory roles. This is shown in the policy guidelines formulated by the ANC in 1992:

> The institution of chieftainship has played an important role in the history of our country and chiefs will continue to *play an important role in unifying our people and performing ceremonial and other functions* allocated to them by law. The powers of chiefs shall always be exercised subject to the provisions of the constitution and other laws. Provision will be made for an appropriate structure consisting of traditional leaders to be created by law, *in order to advise parliament* – on matters relevant to customary law and other matters relating to the powers and functions of chiefs.[152]

In terms of rural governance members of the ANC believed that traditional leaders would play a subordinate role to that of elected representatives and would not have the power to control the allocation of land in rural areas as they did in the days of apartheid.[153] Both the ANC and National Party wanted to make a deal with the traditional leaders but there were deep divisions within each party as to the acceptable cost of such a deal.[154] Traditional leaders rejected the ANC's view that their functions would be limited to ceremonial and advisory roles. For the ANC, the cost flowing from the negotiations of the 1993 Interim Constitution was the compromise to the principle of democracy at the local level as traditional leaders were effectively guaranteed *ex officio* membership of local government. Meanwhile, the principle of gender equality was left intact as a result of lobbying by women's groups, particularly within the ANC.

As the ANC consolidated its domination of the sphere of parliamentary politics, it was concerned to prevent power bases outside this sphere from developing and flourishing.[155] Given that the ANC had used legal pluralism in the past in order to encourage resistance to the state and its legal system, it presumably understood the potential of deep legal pluralism to divide and fragment the state and make it ungovernable if legal pluralism went unchecked and unsupervised by the state. Thus it was considered

[151] Maloka and Gordon, 'Chieftainship', 45.
[152] Quoted in Ntsebeza, *Democracy Compromised*, 266 (emphasis added).
[153] Ntsebeza, *Democracy Compromised*, 267.
[154] Spitz and Chaskalson, *The Politics of Transition*, 381.
[155] MacKinnon, *The Making of South Africa*, 282.

safer to bring traditional leaders within the constitutional framework, under state control, than to have them outside fomenting resistance to state power, even at the cost of compromising democracy.[156]

Despite this, the drafters of the Final Constitution recognised traditional leadership as a non-democratic institution. An effort was therefore made to wind back and limit the scope of these powers by using vague and discretionary language in Chapter 12 so as to lessen the damage wrought by the Interim Constitution in compromising democracy. Traditional leaders used all means to block these limits by lobbying the Constitutional Assembly, boycotting local government elections, protesting on the streets[157] and submitting objections to the Constitutional Court. However, in the end, traditional leaders managed to retain much of their power. First, they succeeded in winning a role at the local level,[158] despite the fact that they are unelected and unaccountable in a liberal democratic sense. Second, they retained their role in presiding over customary law courts, subject to the Constitution's rights protections, without people being given the choice of accessing the court system of their preference by opting in or out of customary law in communities where traditional leaders still function. While this book focuses on customary law and not on local government, scholars of traditional leadership have argued that traditional leaders derive most of their authority from their position at the local level of government and specifically, their control of the land allocation process.[159] This not only

[156] In addition, the ANC no doubt realised the potential of traditional leaders to be key players in addressing law enforcement problems in rural areas. Crime reached a peak during the drafting of the Interim Constitution and crime rates continued to soar after the 1994 election: Leggett, 'Just Another Miracle', 583.

[157] In late 1995, some traditional leaders from both the ANC and the Inkatha Freedom Party protested in Pretoria on the grounds that they were not adequately represented despite the broad public participation programme: Klug, 'Constitution-making in South Africa', 151. In 1995, traditional leaders threatened to boycott the local government elections.

[158] Bennett and Murray point out that s. 212(2) refers to 'local level' rather than the 'local sphere of government' or 'local government', which technically means that traditional leaders do not have a constitutionally guaranteed role in local government. They argue that the position of Chapter 12, separated from other chapters dealing with the main institutions of government, implies that the role of traditional leadership may not be governmental. Despite this, a framework of national and provincial laws is setting up traditional leaders as organs of state with governmental responsibilities: 'Traditional Leaders', 26–20, 26–25.

[159] Ntsebeza, *Democracy Compromised*, 22. The system of communal land tenure in rural areas is currently being reformed under the *Traditional Leadership and Governance Framework Act 41 of 2003* (TLGFA). One part of this package, the *Communal Land*

puts traditional leaders into conflict with elected councillors at the local level but it also places pressure on people in rural areas to obey the decisions of traditional leaders relating to customary law. Moreover, the dual function of traditional leaders raises separation of powers issues, which are examined in the following chapter.

Overall, debate on the constitutional role of customary law and legal pluralism in South Africa was largely sidelined in both the negotiations and constitution-drafting process because attention was focused on the future role of traditional leaders. The ANC gave customary law little consideration and, in this respect, traditional leaders were mainly interested in the issue of the principle of male primogeniture, which later became a constitutional issue, as explained in the following chapter. Tom Bennett argues that the ANC had no intention of suppressing customary law,[160] but it is noteworthy that the ANC did not mention the role of customary law in any of its bills of rights preceding the constitution, such as the 1955 *Freedom Charter*, and did not initially include it as a point of discussion during the negotiations.[161]

Penelope Andrews suggests a number of reasons as to why the ANC may have initially overlooked the issue of customary law. First, she asserts that the ANC was mainly dominated by urban elites who often neglected the concerns of rural communities.[162] Its ally, the United Democratic Front, was urban-oriented and poorly organised in rural areas.[163] Second, traditional leaders were often seen as 'puppets of the apartheid government' because of the way in which they had been

Rights Act 11 of 2004 (CLARA), was held to be constitutionally invalid in 2010 by the Constitutional Court in *Tongoane* v. *Minister for Agriculture and Land Affairs and Ors* 2010 (6) SA 214 (CC). The TLGFA deems existing traditional authorities to be traditional councils, subject to composition requirements, while the CLARA recognises traditional councils as land administration committees with the power to represent a community owning communal land. Only 40 per cent of the membership of these councils are elected while 30 per cent of the membership is reserved for women. For a critical analysis of the impact of these land reforms on power and gender relations, see Claasens and Ngubane, 'Women, Land and Power', 154. See also s. 10(2)(i) of the Traditional Courts Bill 2012 which effectively enables a customary court to deprive a person of their land rights.

160 Bennett, *Human Rights*, 21.

161 As above. See, e.g., Constitutional Committee of the ANC, 'A Bill of Rights for a Democratic South Africa: Working Draft', 64.

162 Andrews, 'The Stepchild of National Liberation', 333.

163 Ntsebeza, *Democracy Compromised*, 260. Ntsebeza describes the UDF as 'largely regarded as an internal above ground wing of the then banned ANC': ibid.

manipulated to serve the apartheid administration.[164] Third, much of the solidarity among black South Africans had been undermined by apartheid policies of separate development, which tended to exaggerate cultural and ethnic differences.[165] To these three reasons, two factors can be added. The first is that the ANC desired to bring unity to a nation of highly diverse ethnicities, dubbed a 'rainbow nation', and may have believed that customary law would bring division between various ethnic groups and cultures. For example, the Inkatha Freedom Party was endeavouring to divide the nation by playing on the link between custom and ethnicity; the ANC countered this by attempting to redefine custom and traditional leadership through emphasising their African and nationalist character.[166] The second additional factor is the fact that the recognition of customary law may be seen as the continuation of apartheid, as well as the segregationist politics and racism that underpinned the preservation of customary law in that system. As explored in the following chapter, the critical question here is, what law was it that the drafters were intending to recognise as customary law – was it the apartheid and colonial version of customary law or the law being practised by communities?

It is doubtful that the ANC promoted the constitutional entrenchment of customary law solely as a means of affirming the legitimacy of customary law. It appears to have been a vehicle to establish the legitimacy of the ANC, the Constitution and state governance among rural inhabitants. The ANC assumed traditional leaders enjoyed high popular legitimacy in rural areas despite the fact that there was ongoing conflict in many areas between traditional leaders and grass roots organisations.[167] On the related topic of community justice, a 1995 memorandum to the Constitutional Assembly illustrates the logic being used by some of the Assembly's advisers. It points out that 'recognition [of community justice mechanisms] will provide the state with a certain amount of

164 Andrews, 'Women's Rights', xi.

165 Andrews, 'The Stepchild of National Liberation', 333.

166 Oomen, *Chiefs in South Africa*, 92–3.

167 Ntsebeza, *Democracy Compromised*, 274. Ntsebeza argues that traditional leaders 'were unpopular and/or feared' in many areas and that the ANC failed to understand the realities on the ground: 294–5. See also Oomen, *Chiefs in South Africa*, 60, 98, 44. Oomen points out that in 1994 the South African National Civics Organisation had the constituency and political clout to compete with CONTRALESA but it lost traction because CONTRALESA was more adept and experienced in participating in official politics and international NGOs were keen to support traditional leadership: 99.

legitimacy, which is needed in this crucial period of transformation if the rule of law is to prevail'.[168] This memorandum shows that at least some advisers understood the critical nexus between legal pluralism and the rule of law, in that law operating outside the state has the potential to undermine the state and its attempt to centralise power. However, on the whole, the drafters of the Final Constitution gave little consideration to the relationship between the rule of law and legal pluralism. In particular, there is no evidence that they understood the challenge of fitting customary courts within a constitutional rule-of-law framework which emphasises equal justice, due process, separation of powers and 'independent and impartial' forums.

The end result of South Africa's constitutional negotiations was that constitutional recognition was given to legal pluralism: section 211(3) of the Final Constitution gives equal status to customary law and the common law by stating that the courts 'must' apply customary law where it is applicable. Officially, neither system is inferior or superior: in line with the rule of law, both are equally subject to the 'one law', the Constitution and its Bill of Rights. The constitutional dispensation transformed legal pluralism by elevating customary law and by requiring that it conform to the Bill of Rights. It did not fully transform the position of traditional leaders, as they resisted attempts to curtail the powers they enjoyed under apartheid. However, when presiding in customary courts, traditional leaders are constitutionally bound to promote the 'spirit, purport and objects of the Bill of Rights'.[169] The following chapter examines the extent to which this can be observed.

4. Conclusion

Much has been written about the process of drafting South Africa's transformative Constitution. In many respects, it is regarded as a model mainly because the dispensation involved a proper process of public participation but also because it involved much political negotiation. Both of these factors have led to a broad sense of ownership of

[168] The memo continues: 'The question of state recognition at this stage means the possibility of gaining legitimacy at the bottom of the social structure. But fundamentally, this process will facilitate the consolidation of the rule of law.' Memorandum addressed to 'Members of the Theme Committee #5 of the Constitutional Assembly' from Kobese et al., Re Community Courts, 9 February 1995, 2.

[169] See s. 39 of the Final Constitution as well as the horizontality clause, s. 8(2), which applies to traditional leaders as 'organs of state'.

the Constitution within South Africa and hence the legitimacy of the Constitution has rarely been the subject of serious questioning.

During this inclusive process the main players in South Africa's constitutional negotiations gave little consideration to the practical relationship between the rule of law and legal pluralism within the new constitutional framework. They looked to both the international level and the local level in order to shore up the legitimacy of the state and its new legal order. The rule of law provided a signal to the international community, particularly foreign investors, while the negotiation of legal pluralism appeased traditional leaders, at least in the short term, and attempted to forge a connection between the Constitution and the very large part of the population that apparently lives under customary law. However, the rule of law is a concept with a close association with common law principles in South Africa's legal system while legal pluralism remains tied to the political pressures exerted by traditional leaders in the post-conflict context. In entrenching the rule of law as a constitutional founding value, South Africa's constitutional drafters took a gamble that it would be possible to transform this concept from its Western common law roots but, in their optimism, they may not have fully considered the pressures borne by the constitutional programme of legal pluralism and its advocates.

The following chapter explores the complexity of the practical relationship between the rule of law and legal pluralism. Its windows into this relationship are twofold: first, the Government's attempt to introduce a linkage law, the Traditional Courts Bill, to transform South Africa's customary courts in line with constitutional values; and second, the approaches taken by South Africa's courts in balancing the constitutional protection of the rights of vulnerable groups with the Constitution's programme of legal pluralism.

5

Can the rule of law and legal pluralism assist 'the most vulnerable groups' in South Africa?

South Africa's Constitution aims to be transformative. Given that South Africa's state institutions were structured around the goal of enforcing racial segregation in the form of apartheid until 1994, transforming these institutions in line with the constitutional values of democracy, equality and the rule of law is an ongoing challenge.

Despite the transformative goals of the Constitution, some commentators believe that South Africa's constitutional dispensation has led to a 'patchwork democracy' because the dynamics of legal pluralism have allowed democracy to be compromised at the local level.[1] This chapter examines whether the dynamics of the dispensation has also led to a 'patchwork rule of law' in South Africa.

South Africa has a long history of both deep legal pluralism, where non-state justice operates without any nexus with state justice, and state law pluralism, which in the post-apartheid era is manifested in the Constitution's recognition of customary law. State law pluralism is understood as a means of extending the reach of the state, as well as constitutional values such as the rule of law, into communities which live predominantly by various systems of customary law. Almost two decades after the end of apartheid, South Africa's ANC Government is struggling to legislate for a constitutional programme of state law pluralism. This linkage law, the Traditional Courts Bill 2012, has been introduced in order to transform the traditional justice system 'in line with constitutional imperatives and values'.[2] Pragmatism and compromise have shaped this linkage law. This chapter argues that the Bill mutes and compromises the constitutional value of the rule of law in a bid to improve access to justice in rural areas and to appease traditional leaders and their support base. At the same time, the Bill transforms legal

[1] See, e.g., Oomen, *Chiefs in South Africa*; Ntsebeza, *Democracy Compromised.*

[2] Part of the Long Title and Preamble to the Bill.

pluralism as it changes some key features of the traditional justice system but, as this chapter shows, this transformation is not necessarily in line with constitutional values.

The chapter also analyses the way in which South Africa's courts have negotiated the constitutional demands of the rule of law and legal pluralism. In the context of deep legal pluralism, South Africa's courts show little reluctance to explicitly invoke the rule of law as a dominant norm. This is in contrast with the context of state law pluralism where the courts rarely invoke the rule of law despite the fact that it is a founding constitutional value that is super-entrenched. The nature of this particular relationship between the rule of law and legal pluralism in South Africa's new legal order is illuminated by five cases emanating from different levels of the court system. At first sight it appears that the rule of law is not registering on the radar of these courts but a closer look reveals that the concept is forced to play a muted and compromised role in relation to state law pluralism because of its continuing close association with common law principles and its Western roots.[3] The courts appear to be insulating legal pluralism from various constitutional principles relating to the rule of law as a means of elevating the concept of legal pluralism. To a certain extent this mirrors and furthers the attempts made by traditional leaders during the constitutional negotiations to have customary law insulated from the Bill of Rights, but the approach of the courts is careful not to go so far as to compromise the principle of equality.

This chapter explores the practical effect of these approaches taken by the Parliament and the courts on women and children, described by the Constitutional Court as the state's most vulnerable groups.[4] It questions whether these approaches have the potential to enhance access to justice for these groups.

1. The rule of law, legal pluralism and access to justice

Access to government services and all parts of government including justice is a strong theme of the Final Constitution.[5] This is a response to

[3] This close association with common law principles and the Western roots of the rule of law are shown in the previous chapters.

[4] *Bhe and Others* v. *The Magistrate, Khayelitsha and Others* 2005 (1) SA 580 (CC) [32].

[5] Fifteen provisions in the Final Constitution guarantee access to government services, national resources and the arms of government. Six of these provisions are found in the Bill of Rights, Ch. 2.

the apartheid regime which denied such access to the majority of the population. As the previous chapter noted, the Constitutional Court has interpreted section 34 and the rule of law as guaranteeing 'the right of access to court' and as requiring the state to provide mechanisms for dispute resolution including a legislative framework, mechanisms and institutions such as courts, and infrastructure to facilitate the execution of court orders.[6] This section briefly examines the background to section 34 in order to sketch the relationship between the rule of law and the two main forms of legal pluralism operating in South Africa, deep legal pluralism and state law pluralism. It then outlines the proposals made by the South African Law Reform Commission ('Law Commission') to address the dynamics of these two forms of legal pluralism and the problem of access to justice.

Section 34 provides: 'Everyone has the right to have any dispute that can be resolved by the application of law decided in a fair public hearing before a court or, where appropriate, another independent and impartial tribunal or forum.' Apart from creating a right of access to a court or another tribunal or forum, section 34 requires tribunals and forums other than courts to be 'independent and impartial' when they resolve civil disputes and it guarantees due process in that disputes must be resolved by fair and public hearings.[7] The provision effectively directs all civil disputes to be resolved by the state, indicating the state's ambition to monopolise dispute resolution, and to counter the phenomenon of 'self-help', which was fostered by resistance forces during apartheid. In the following paragraph from *S* v. *Makwayane*[8] the Constitutional Court commented on 'self-help' as a problem in relation to the 'constitutional state', a German notion of an aspect of the rule of law, mentioned in the preamble to the Interim Constitution:

> [I]n a constitutional State individuals agree (in principle at least) to abandon their right to self-help in the protection of their rights only because the State, in the constitutional State compact, assumes the obligation to protect these rights. If the State fails to discharge this duty

[6] See *Chief Lesapo* v. *North West Agricultural Bank* 2000 (1) SA 409 (CC) [41]; *President of the Republic of South Africa and Another* v. *Modderklip Boerdery (Pty) Ltd* 2005 (5) SA 3 (CC), discussed in Chapter 4 section 2.3.

[7] 'Due process' is the term used in Currie and De Waal, *The Bill of Rights Handbook*, 704.

[8] 1995 (3) SA 391 (CC).

> adequately, there is a danger that individuals might feel justified in using self-help to protect their rights. This is not a fanciful possibility in South Africa.[9]

One of the most serious problems facing South Africa in its endeavour to become a 'constitutional state' is that the state does not have a monopoly over dispute resolution and presently, despite its relatively robust economy, it does not have the capacity to establish such a monopoly. Inadequate access to state justice means that individuals and communities have not 'abandon[ed] their right to self help'; the problem is most acute in rural areas without traditional leaders[10] and urban communities, such as black townships and informal settlements.

The Law Commission has described the wide range of non-state justice forums operating in South Africa as 'diverse, fragmentary and tentative'.[11] These include customary courts other than those recognised by the state, urban forums in townships and informal settlements, and religious courts. In the sphere of customary law, ward heads generally run non-state recognised courts in rural areas; in 2006 there were approximately 12,000 such courts in South Africa[12] operating as courts of first instance before the dispute is referred to the state-recognised courts of traditional leaders, known as customary courts.[13] In urban areas, in townships and informal settlements where there are few traditional leaders, community dispute resolution forums operate in the form of street committees and yard, block or area committees.[14]

9 Ibid., [168].

10 Three of the nine provinces do not have traditional leaders, namely the Western Cape, Gauteng and the Northern Cape.

11 South African Law Commission [hereafter SALC], *Community Dispute Resolution Structures*, [3.3.4.5]. Note that in 2002 the SALC's name changed to the South African Law Reform Commission but to avoid confusion I will refer to it throughout as the SALC.

12 Koyana et al., 'Traditional Authority Courts', 137. Customary courts are estimated to number around 1,500: see Chapter 4, section 3.3.

13 The term 'customary court' will be used in this book to refer to state courts presided over by traditional leaders.

14 See Scharf and Nina (eds.), *The Other Law*. During apartheid, these forums were mostly used as a stop-gap to the problem of crime while some were used as a form of resistance to the state. Quality was not always assured: in the mid 1980s, 'kangaroo-type courts' (sometimes known as 'people's courts') emerged, involving reports of mob justice and brutal punishments. These courts brought discredit to unofficial community justice structures generally. While non-state urban courts are not customary courts, they are informed partly by African customary law and sometimes use aspects of customary law such as shaming and community censure.

These dispute resolution mechanisms employ non-state law, often referred to as 'people's law',[15] and are examples of self-help, which the Constitutional Court has held contravenes the rule of law and section 34 of the Final Constitution.[16] Currently all these non-state justice structures operate beyond the reaches of state control in the form of deep legal pluralism. As mentioned in Chapter 3, the prevalence of deep legal pluralism, sometimes in the form of 'mob justice', can be partly explained by the resistance strategy of undermining the apartheid state and its legal apparatus. The problem with deep legal pluralism is that there are no state controls on the quality of the justice meted out and no mechanisms to ensure conformity to constitutional guarantees. Hence, in the context of the prohibition of self-help and the right of access to state courts, the courts are willing to embrace the rule of law as a dominant and determinative norm.

There is another, deeper reason for the prevalence of deep legal pluralism in South Africa, according to the Law Commission. In 1997, the year that the Final Constitution came into force, it diagnosed South Africa's legal system as suffering from a 'legitimacy crisis' and stated: 'The essence of the legitimacy crisis lies in the historical superimposition of a foreign legal system with its concomitant Western jural postulates upon those of Africa.' [17] The Law Commission believed that black South Africans perceive the formal legal system as illegitimate, repressive and prohibitively expensive.[18] It explained:

> For many, a foreign, dominant Western legal system, is seen to be superimposed on an intuitive, indigenous legal system. It is seen as alien, inaccessible and inappropriate for dealing with conflict which most South Africans experience in their daily lives. This invariably prevents meaningful access to court … Many Black communities have actively rejected this system which has been seen as intricately linked in their oppression.[19]

The problem is that the formal legal system was created to suit the needs of only one part of the population, the white minority. The Law

[15] On people's courts, see Burman and Schärf, 'Creating People's Justice'; Seekings, 'Social Ordering'.

[16] See *Chief Lesapo* v. *North West Agricultural Bank* 2000 (1) SA 409 (CC): see discussion in Chapter 4, section 2.3.

[17] SALC, *Simplification of Criminal Procedure*, [2.3–2.4] (emphasis added).

[18] SALC, *Community Dispute Resolution Structures*. [1.2.1].

[19] Ibid.

Commission observed that Western dispute settlement procedures based on 'retributive justice' are regarded as 'not suited to solve legal problems as well as problems of social adjustment encountered by urban blacks'.[20] In contrast, informal law is related to 'restorative justice' as it attempts to promote reconciliation between parties and promote community values.[21] Thus, using the retributive/restorative justice dichotomy, the Law Commission reasoned that many South Africans have preferred the path of 'self-help' to formal state justice because the former is better adjusted to their needs than the latter.

As a state institution, the Law Commission has predictably proposed state law pluralism as a solution to the problem of 'self-help'. In a series of discussion papers and reports, the Law Commission has recommended means by which state law pluralism can be transformed from a colonial[22] and apartheid concept based on racialised inequality into one that promotes equality and serves the interests and needs of the majority of the population in accessing state justice.

The Law Commission has made proposals on two sets of projects on legal pluralism. One set is focused on dispute resolution mechanisms and their procedures: (1) the establishment and recognition of community courts by the state so as to 'meet the needs' of urban communities that suffer minimal access to state justice;[23] and (2) the transformation of customary courts so as to meet the needs of rural communities. In regard to the latter, part of the customary courts project has been to propose changes to their current operation so that they conform to the constitutional framework. A second set of projects is focused on the substance of customary law and on 'harmonising' customary law with the common law so that there is little substantial divergence resulting in the application of either system. The Law Commission's harmonisation project does not aim to unify the common law and customary law into

[20] SALC, *Simplification of Criminal Procedure*, 6.

[21] SALC, *Community Dispute Resolution Structures*, [1.2.5]. Note that CONTRALESA submitted to the Law Commission that customary courts apply a form of restorative justice: [3.3.1.11].

[22] According to van Niekerk, state law pluralism dates back to 1806 during the second British occupation of the Cape. In 1927, the *Black Administration Act* consolidated the diverse colonial legislation on customary law and entrenched state law pluralism for the country as a whole: van Niekerk, 'Legal Pluralism', 7.

[23] See, e.g., SALC, *Community Dispute Resolution Structures*. As at mid 2011, thirteen community courts have been established in urban communities in South Africa. The policy and legislative framework to establish these courts as a permanent feature of the judicial system has not been finalised.

a single system applicable to all, as this might take place at the expense of customary law. Instead, it is based on the continuing operation of customary courts.

In these two Law Commission projects to transform legal pluralism, the rule of law has received little consideration, perhaps because the concept is seen as a common law principle and to represent the dominant Western legal system.[24] As we see in the following sections, South Africa's Parliament, in common with the Law Commission as well as with the courts, is reluctant to invoke the constitutional founding value of the rule of law as a yardstick for aspects of state law pluralism.

2. The rule of law and customary courts

The post-apartheid state inherited a complex structure of courts and legislation. Under Schedule 6 to the Final Constitution, which sets out South Africa's transitional arrangements, 'every court, including courts of traditional leaders, existing when the new Constitution took effect, continues to function' subject to any new legislation as well as consistency with the new Constitution.[25] This Schedule also provides that 'as soon as is practical … all courts … be rationalised with a view to establishing a judicial system suited to the requirements of the new Constitution'.[26] These sections show the Constitution's aim of transforming South Africa's judicial system that was established under colonialism and apartheid and developed to serve the purposes of those governing during these two eras. This transformation of the judicial system was also a recommendation of South Africa's Truth and Reconciliation Commission. In regard to the courts of chiefs and headmen, the Commission's *Report* specifically recommended they 'respect the rights established by the Constitution, including the right to due process', and that 'codes of practice, including rules pertaining to written records, must be implemented'.[27]

Almost two decades after the end of apartheid, customary courts continue to derive their power from apartheid-era legislation, specifically the *Black Administration Act 38 of 1927*. Under the Act the Minister has the power to authorise a traditional leader to hear civil claims between 'Blacks' and to try more minor criminal matters where the accused is

[24] See Chapter 4, section 2.3 regarding the perception of the rule of law as a common law principle.
[25] Section 16(1). [26] Section 16(6). [27] (1998) Vol 5, Ch 8, [59].

'Black'.[28] The relevant provisions of this Act are in the process of being repealed[29]: customary courts are to be transformed and regulated by the Traditional Courts Bill 2012, once enacted, which makes no mention of race as a basis of the jurisdiction of customary courts. The Traditional Courts Bill 2012 is part of a package of laws under the *Traditional Leadership and Governance Framework Act 41 of 2003* (TLGFA) dealing with traditional leadership and authority.[30] It was drafted mainly in consultation with those traditional leaders sitting in the National House of Traditional Leaders; there is little evidence that consultation has taken place with community groups and civic organisations in rural areas.[31] The Bill was first introduced in 2008 in the National Assembly but it was deferred for two years to enable consultation before being withdrawn in 2011. Despite this lengthy period for consultation and the volume of criticism, the virtually unchanged Bill was introduced in 2012 in the National Council of Provinces, South Africa's Upper House.

The Traditional Courts Bill 2012 is partly the Government's response to the problem of self help and deep legal pluralism in rural areas. As the Law Commission notes, many rural inhabitants prefer not to use the courts operating under the race-based, apartheid-era legislation. The new Bill grants state recognition only to the courts of chiefs and headmen/women; it does not recognise the dispute resolution forums that exist in the customary system below these levels of these courts, such as the

[28] *Black Administration Act 38 of 1927*, ss. 12(1) and 20. Section 35 defined 'Black' to 'include any person who is a member of any aboriginal race or tribe of Africa'. Schedule 3 to the *Black Administration Act* limited the criminal jurisdiction of customary courts to minor matters. According to Oomen, there is no such thing as a typical customary court in South Africa: Oomen, *Chiefs in South Africa*, 202.

[29] The *Black Administration Act* has been deemed to be unconstitutional and hence is to be repealed in stages by the *Repeal of the Black Administration Act and Amendment of Certain Laws Act No 28 of 2005*. The relevant provisions of the *Black Administration Act* that are being saved until final repeal are ss. 12 and 20.

[30] Under s. 20 of the TLGFA the national government may set out a role for traditional leaders and traditional councils in regard to a number of areas including the administration of justice.

[31] This failure to consult with rural communities was a major criticism of the 2008 Bill, articulated via the right to public participation in the legislative process set out in s. 59(1) of the Constitution. In addition, two of South Africa's 'chapter 9 institutions', the South African Human Rights Commission and the Commission on Gender Equality, did not support the policy thrust of the 2008 Bill: *Memorandum on the Objects of the Traditional Courts Bill 2008* (see [3.2]–[3.3]).

unofficial courts of ward heads. This means that the Government's approach to transforming state law pluralism involves a certain degree of recognition and acceptance of the deep legal pluralism operating in rural communities.

The transformation of South Africa's customary courts is a means of integrating these courts into South Africa's new legal order. This transformation process appears to entail balancing, pragmatism and compromise. On the one hand the rule of law means that all courts need to fit within the state's court hierarchy so that they are aligned with constitutional values and can be properly supervised. On the other hand, respect for the constitutional programme of legal pluralism means that the state must take care to respect the dignity of customary courts and not subject customary courts to common law principles, as this would undermine the equal status that both forms of law enjoy under the Final Constitution.

While the Bill does not avowedly establish a hybrid system, this result is apparent from some of its features which are not, according to its critics from both NGOs as well as among traditional leaders, part of the traditional justice system. One feature of the Bill is that it sets up traditional leaders in the role of a 'presiding officer' who acts in these courts as a judge and single decision-maker. According to the Law, Race and Gender Research Unit, this effectively professionalises a non-professional institution along the lines of Magistrates' Courts,[32] contrary to customary practice where decisions are reached by consensus through a group of councillors as well as the participation of ordinary members of the community. Making decisions by consensus and with community participation are considered traditional mechanisms which operate to democratise and limit the abuse of decision-making powers at the customary level. This single decision-maker, the 'presiding officer', was not envisaged in the draft Bill submitted by the Law Commission as part of its 2003 Report on customary courts. The Law Commission's Bill sets out different levels of state-recognised customary courts and in accordance with customary law these courts are constituted by a council of members. The composition of this council would only diverge from customary law in that half, or some, of its members would be women, in line with the Constitution and relevant equality legislation.[33] The Government's

[32] Law, Race and Gender Research Unit, *Submission on the Traditional Courts Bill* 17.

[33] Three options are offered by the Law Commission's Draft Bill in regard to the gendered composition of customary courts: women being 'no less than half the members'; 'a reasonable representation of men and women'; and the inclusion of both men and women.

Traditional Courts Bill 2012 does not include either of these suggestions, rejecting the use of a council of members and the establishment of different levels of customary courts.

In order to illuminate the balancing of the relationship between the rule of law and legal pluralism, the following section examines the operation of customary courts in relation to three areas: their position within the state court hierarchy and their general compliance with the constitutional order; their level of independence and separation of powers; and their role in delivering 'equal justice'.

2.1 Supervision, appeals and compliance of customary courts

Appeals from customary courts are currently heard by Magistrates' Courts, although such appeals appear to be very infrequent.[34] Given that customary courts are not courts of record,[35] these appeals are generally heard *de novo*.[36] For the Law Commission, the problem lies in the fact that magistrates generally have little training in customary law and thus they 'are likely to reinterpret customary law in a way that undermines the whole system of customary justice'.[37] To remedy this, the Law Commission proposed the establishment of a 'Customary Court of Appeal' to hear all appeals.[38] Despite the widely consultative process conducted by the Law Commission into this issue, this has not been included in the Traditional Courts Bill 2012. Section 12 of the Bill provides for appeals to Magistrates' Courts whereby magistrates can confirm, dismiss, amend or substitute the orders of customary courts. The Government does not share the Law Commission's concerns for protecting customary law in

[34] No statistics are available but Oomen relates that between 1994 and 1999, the Sekhukhune Magistrates' Court registered only six appeals from customary courts. Furthermore, when some matters are taken directly to this court, the magistrate frequently sends them to be dealt with at first by the customary court despite the fact that plaintiffs have a choice of court: Oomen, *Chiefs in South Africa*, 205.

[35] The Law Commission has expressed the general view that 'customary courts are not equipped and are not likely to be equipped, both in material and human resources terms' to be courts of record: SALC, *Report on Traditional Courts*, [4.5]. Instead it has recommended that customary courts make more detailed records of hearings: Recommendation 7, xiii.

[36] Note that parties are not permitted to change their cause of action: Bennett, *Customary Law*, 148. See also Koyana et al., 'Traditional Authority Courts', 139–40.

[37] SALC, *Report on Traditional Courts*, 33.

[38] Alternatively the SALC proposed that this new court would hear only civil appeals, with the next tier being the High Court, or, for criminal matters, the Magistrates' Courts: *Report on Traditional Courts*, 33.

this regard: it is more concerned that a parallel system of courts of this kind would perpetuate segregation and also be a financial burden on the state. In addition, the Government claims that a separate Court of Appeal is not necessary because decisions of traditional courts are usually based on consent and involve community participation, which means that the concept of appeal is 'consequently not a feature of the traditional court system'.[39]

Customary courts currently operate without any supervision.[40] The Law Commission recommended that the position of a Registrar or a Commissioner be established to supervise customary courts so that supervision comes from within the realm of customary law and customary courts are shielded from the common law world of Magistrates' Courts.[41] It stated that the aim of the appointment of a Registrar or Commissioner would be to:

> *insulate customary law and its adjudicatory procedures from encroachment by the common law* through too much association with magistrates' courts. The commission would *preserve a strictly customary universe*, sufficient unto itself until human rights and constitutional considerations compelled referring out of a matter to the general law system.[42]

Here we see the Law Commission attempting to protect legal pluralism while simultaneously suggesting the introduction of greater uniformity and consistency in the manner in which customary courts are regulated on a national level, a concern of the rule of law.[43] Once again, this proposal has not been accepted by the Government, as the Traditional Courts Bill 2012 gives Magistrates' Courts the power of procedural review over customary courts.[44] According to its critics, the Bill fails to anchor this power to the traditional justice system and, at the same time,

[39] Department of Justice and Constitutional Development, *Policy Framework on the Traditional Justice System under the Constitution*, 36.

[40] Under the *Black Administration Act* Magistrates' Courts do not appear to have the power of supervising 'customary courts'. They are unable to guide or monitor them without the commencement of an appeal by a party: Bennett, *Customary Law*, 147.

[41] SALC, *Report on Traditional Courts*, 32.

[42] Ibid., 30 (emphasis added).

[43] The Report quoted with approval the view of Mqeke who suggests in regard to this last aspect that: 'Such an office would also strive for *uniformity* on such crucial issues as jurisdiction, the imposition of appropriate sentence', 9 (emphasis added). This emphasis on uniformity indicates that the Law Commission has some desire to balance rule of law concerns with the preservation and maintenance of legal pluralism.

[44] Traditional Courts Bill 2012, s. 14.

the power does not meet constitutional standards of review, showing that the Bill is an awkward compromise of the two systems.[45]

The failure of customary courts to comply with state regulations has also been of some concern to the state's legal institutions. For example, in 1999, the Law Commission noted that any attempt to change the powers of these courts and to circumscribe their criminal jurisdiction 'is unlikely to meet with compliance'.[46] One reason for this non-compliance lies in the fact that customary law, by its nature, does not distinguish precisely between civil and criminal matters,[47] and to require precise compliance in this regard would be to force customary law into the prism of the common law, which makes this distinction. Under the Traditional Courts Bill 2012 non-compliance is a concern because the draft legislation sharply limits the criminal jurisdiction of customary courts to theft, malicious property damage, assault excluding grievous bodily harm and crimen injuria, thus diverting all other criminal offences to the Magistrates' Courts.[48] While the Law Commission's Draft Bill explicitly listed domestic violence and rape as offences outside the jurisdiction of customary courts, this approach was not followed by the Government, leaving the matter ambiguous.[49] One problem is that the limited criminal jurisdiction conferred on customary courts by the Bill appears to operate outside of section 35 of the Constitution which gives every accused person the right to a 'fair' and 'public trial' before an 'ordinary court'.

[45] According to the Legal Resources Centre, this section subjects the orders of traditional courts to a lesser, pre-constitutional standard of review which has been rejected by the Constitutional Court: *Submissions to the Portfolio Committee* 16.

[46] SALC, *Report on Conflicts of Law*, [3.17].

[47] Ibid. See also Koyana et al., 'Traditional Authority Courts', 137, 144.

[48] See Sched. 1 of the Bill. Anecdotally, some scholars observe that in some remote regions, customary courts have been hearing all criminal matters including rape and attempted murder. In regard to rape, Bennett observes that 'customary law tends to regard it as a civil matter of adultery or illicit fornication': 'Customary Criminal Law', 383. This is similar to the approach taken by customary law mechanisms in Timor-Leste. However, Hohe and Nixon observe that in Timor-Leste the term 'rape' can sometimes be used to refer to consensual sex where the relationship is considered 'against the social order': 'Reconciling Justice', 19.

[49] The *Domestic Violence Act 116 of 1998* provides that only certain courts, not including customary courts, can hear domestic violence cases. Magistrates' Courts are the courts of first instance for these cases. In *Customary Law and Domestic Violence*, Curran and Bonthuys point out that while the benefit of the Magistrates' Courts is that there is generally no social relationship with the perpetrator, there are factors that militate against these courts such as their distance, differing procedures and their tendency to apply official customary law rather than living customary law (22). On this distinction, see section 3.2 of this chapter.

Under the Bill, customary courts are not ordinary courts: section 9(3)(a) prohibits parties from using a legal representative in court. While this level of informality is in line with customary practice, it is contrary to section 35(3)(f) of the Constitution which guarantees this right of representation to 'every accused person'. Given the social reality that appeals from these courts are rare and that compliance with state regulation is minimal, those persons subject to the limited criminal jurisdiction of customary courts under the Bill do not appear to be able to enjoy one of the main benefits of the post-apartheid era, constitutionally entrenched human rights.[50]

One example of non-compliance relates to customary marriages. Since 2000, state courts have had jurisdiction over the dissolution of such marriages under section 8 of the *Recognition of Customary Marriages Act 2000*. This is reiterated in section 5(2)(b) of the Traditional Courts Bill 2012. Previously this was a matter for customary courts. Despite this, there is evidence that customary courts continue to hear such matters, either out of ignorance of the legislation or out of disregard.[51] In this regard, where a party believes that the traditional court does not have jurisdiction over the matter, they are not empowered by the Traditional Courts Bill 2012 to request a transfer of jurisdiction. Under section 19(1) of the Bill, this power can only be exercised by a presiding officer.

Non-compliance of customary courts with state regulation stems from some practical realities. For example, most traditional leaders have no training in the implications of the Constitution;[52] thus, in the day-to-day operation of customary courts, compliance with constitutional principles, if any, is presumably sketchy. The Traditional Courts Bill 2012 requires all traditional leaders who preside over customary courts to attend

[50] But see the argument of Bennett that Magistrates' Courts and the High Court are 'notoriously slow' and hence do not fulfil the constitutional 'due process' requirement under s. 35(3)(d) that a 'trial begin and conclude without unreasonable delay'. In comparison, he observes that customary courts are 'likely to be speedier' because they leave less room for technical points to be raised: 'Customary Criminal Law', 384. Bennett argues that the Constitution's procedural guarantees seek to protect accused persons against harsh penalties and that where a customary court aims to reconcile parties in regard to a criminal matter, these procedural guarantees 'become redundant': 380.

[51] Women's Legal Centre, *Recognition of Customary Marriages*, 21.

[52] Traditional authorities come under provincial administration which, according to Bekker, has neither the means nor the will to provide such training: Bekker, 'Administration of Justice', 241. Under the Traditional Courts Bill 2012, this training will presumably be the responsibility of the national administration but according to Bennet, 'the bill fails to commit the state to definite support': 'Customary Criminal Law', 386.

training but it does not specify the nature of this training.[53] However, attempts by Parliament to structure and regulate customary courts are, according to Bekker, 'paper law. It is really much ado about nothing.'[54] His point is that despite the fact that there are state regulations[55] governing the structure, jurisdiction and general operation of these courts, '[f]ew chiefs know about these rules',[56] and if they do, they do not work by them.[57] For example, the requirement of a written record of the case[58] to be prepared and sent to the local magistrate has in practice been almost meaningless, as it was not clear whether the Magistrates' Court had review jurisdiction[59] and there was no supervision as to whether all cases were recorded. Moreover, the records that are made are reportedly 'barely intelligible' and rarely filed.[60] Under section 18 of the Traditional Courts Bill, a fairly minimal record of each case must be made by the court but the Bill does not provide any mechanism to ensure compliance in this regard.

In some instances there may be cultural reasons for non-compliance, as traditional leaders find it difficult to comply with state law where the norms of their communities greatly diverge from state norms. For example, under Schedule 3 to the *Black Administration Act*, customary courts are prohibited from hearing cases of 'pretended witchcraft'.[61] The *Witchcraft Suppression Act 3 of 1957* makes it a criminal offence for a person to impute witchcraft to another; these, and similar, offences can be heard only by Magistrates' Courts and other formal courts. However, given the strong level of belief in witchcraft prevailing in many rural communities in South Africa, in practice customary courts often resolve disputes relating to witchcraft so as to keep the peace.[62] It is in relation to witchcraft that we see a clash

[53] Section 4 of the Traditional Leaders Bill 2012 requires all traditional leaders who have been designated as presiding officers of customary courts to attend training programmes. Failure to attend within a certain time period can lead to suspension or revocation of their designation.

[54] Bekker, 'Administration of Justice', 243.

[55] See Chiefs' and Headmen's Civil Courts: Rules R2082 of 1967. For a useful compendium of rules relating to customary courts, see De Villiers, *Selected South African Legislation*.

[56] Bekker, 'Administration of Justice', 242.

[57] Ibid., 241.

[58] Chiefs' and Headmen's Civil Courts: Rules R2082 of 1967, r. 6.

[59] There is some uncertainty as to whether Magistrates' Courts have review jurisdiction: Bennett, *Customary Law*, 147.

[60] Dlamini, *The Role of Chiefs*; Oomen, *Chiefs in South Africa*, 206.

[61] See *Black Administration Act*, Sched. 3.

[62] See Ralushai Commission, *Report of the Commission of Inquiry into Witchcraft Violence and Ritual Murders in the Northern Province*. Where local disputes remain unmediated, they can escalate into killings; indeed witchcraft killings in rural areas where police

between the Western legal paradigm, which is based on a liberal rational discourse, and the customary law paradigm, which accommodates belief in the supernatural and the power of ancestors.

In regard to compliance with state law, then, the rule of state law is largely absent in the sphere of customary courts. Customary courts operate at the interface between state law pluralism and deep legal pluralism and the new attempt to regulate customary courts through the Traditional Courts Bill 2012 may end up as nothing more than 'paper law'.

2.2 *The independence and impartiality of customary courts and the principle of separation of powers*

It has generally been held that customary courts enjoy constitutional recognition because they qualify as a court under section 166(e) of the Final Constitution.[63] Inclusion in this list means that they must conform to strict standards of independence and impartiality pursuant to section 165(2).[64] Customary courts have struggled to establish the standard of independence and impartiality required by section 165(2).

A corollary is that customary courts appear to breach the principle of separation of powers that is impliedly entrenched in the 1996 Final Constitution.[65] The principle of separation of powers was explained by the Constitutional Court in the case of *South African Association of*

presence is thin account for a significant number of murders every year. The Report illuminates a schism between traditional courts and other state courts in that: '[t]raditional courts agree that witches exist, whilst the formal courts say witches do not exist': 51. The Report states that traditional courts regard the *Witchcraft Suppression Act 3 of 1957* 'as a very unjust piece of legislation, because its aim is not to punish witches but those individuals who name others as witches': 52. This refers to the fact that the Act does not provide a basis upon which witches can be prosecuted but it stipulates the prosecution of those who impute witchcraft to another. Some scholars share this criticism. Hund, for example, argues that: 'By criminalizing these traditional remedies on the ground that they were contrary to the British rule of law, ... the seeds of lawlessness were sown': Hund, 'African Witchcraft and Western Law', 9.

[63] See *Certification of the Constitution of the Republic of South Africa* 1996 (4) SA 744 (CC) [199] discussed in Chapter 4, section 3.2; Bennett, *Customary Law*, 127, n. 221.

[64] In contrast, if they were recognised as tribunals, they would only need to conform to the requirements of s. 34. This section is subject to the limitations clause in the Bill of Rights which allows 'significant deviations' from the standards imposed by s. 165(2): Currie and de Waal, *The Bill of Rights Handbook*, 731.

[65] The text is structured so as to provide separate chapters for the three arms of government. See *South African Association of Personal Injury Lawyers* v. *Heath* 2001 (1) SA 883 (CC) [19]. See also Currie and de Waal, *The New Constitutional and Administrative Law*, Vol. 1, 96.

Personal Injury Lawyers v. *Heath*[66] ('*Heath*') where the Court held that there 'can be no doubt that our Constitution provides for such a separation [of powers], and that laws inconsistent with what the Constitution requires in that regard, are invalid'.[67] The Constitutional Court made it clear that the Constitution requires a separation between the courts and the two other branches of government. Chaskalson CJ stated that this separation:

> must be upheld, otherwise the role of the courts as an independent arbiter of issues ... will be undermined. The Constitution recognises this and imposes a positive obligation on the State to ensure that this is done. It provides that courts are independent and subject only to the Constitution and the law which they must apply impartially without fear, favour or prejudice. No organ of State or other person may interfere with the functioning of the courts and all organs of State, through legislative and other measures, must assist and protect the courts *to ensure their independence, impartiality, dignity, accessibility and effectiveness.*[68]

The concluding clause of this statement places independence and impartiality alongside values that are connected to legal pluralism, namely accessibility and effectiveness. Dignity can arguably relate to courts that are respected either as impartial and independent or as administering customary law and upholding legal pluralism. It indicates that the Constitutional Court believes that these values should be balanced against each other and hence the principle of separation of powers should not be interpreted too rigidly.

The position of customary courts is illustrated by two cases from the Transkei Division Court, *Bangindawo* v. *Head of Nyanda Regional Authority*[69] ('*Bangindawo*') and *Mhlekwa and Feni* v. *Head of the Western Tembuland Regional Authority & Anor*[70] ('*Mhlekwa*'), which were decided before the *Heath* case. They provide a valuable insight into the balancing of legal pluralism and the rule of law in the lower courts. Neither of these cases dealt directly with an appeal from a customary court. In both cases the courts were asked to deal with the constitutional validity of the legislation regulating the Regional Authority Courts (RACs), which were hybrid courts as they derived some of their simplified procedural aspects from customary courts and some of their other

[66] *South African Association of Personal Injury Lawyers* v. *Heath* 2001 (1) SA 883 (CC) [19].
[67] Ibid., [22]. [68] Ibid., [26] (emphasis added). [69] 1998 (3) SA 262 (Tk).
[70] 2001 (1) SA 574 (Tk).

more technical procedural aspects from 'Western' courts. In a sense, the RACs were a legislative attempt to assimilate the procedure of customary courts with that observed by Western type courts.[71] These two judgments make *obiter dicta* on the constitutionality of customary courts and the position of traditional leaders as presiding officers.

In the first case, *Bangindawo* v. *Head of Nyanda Regional Authority*, Madlanga J heard a challenge to the constitutionality of two criminal convictions that had been made pursuant to the *Regional Authorities Courts Act 13 of 1982* ('*RAC Act*'). The applicants argued that provisions of the *RAC Act* violated the constitutional requirement that the judiciary be independent and impartial.[72] In considering this question, Madlanga J looked at the case of *R* v. *Valente*[73] in the Canadian Supreme Court, and held that, while the case's test assisted in determining the appropriate standards for courts traditionally of a *Western* origin, common law courts, the same could not be said for other courts such as the RACs which used procedures of customary courts. He asserted:

> [T]he position is different when it comes to the African customary law setting. There is a danger in a wholesale transplant of a concept suited to one legal system onto another legal system.[74]

Madlanga J distinguished these other courts on the basis that 'African customary law knows of no distinction between the executive, the judicial and the legislative arms of government'.[75] Therefore, he found:

> no reason whatsoever for the *imposition of the Western conception* of the notions of judicial impartiality and independence in the African customary setting. Any such imposition is very much akin to the subjection of matters African to 'public policy'.[76]

This last reference to 'public policy' is to the repugnancy clause and hence the reference brings in overtones of the colonial project of subordinating African customary law to Western common law. Madlanga J proceeded to hold that the impartiality of presiding officers is satisfied in the RACs, and in customary courts,[77] because the adherents of African customary law believe in the impartiality of their traditional leaders when

[71] *Mhlekwa*, ibid., [629D]. [72] See Interim Constitution, s. 96(2).

[73] [1985] 2 SCR 673.

[74] *Bangindawo* v. *Head of Nyanda Regional Authority* 1998 (3) SA 262 (Tk) [272B].

[75] Ibid., [272B]. [76] Ibid., [273B-C] (emphasis added).

[77] Ibid., [274]. Madlanga J asserts that his comments relate more to the courts of chiefs and kings than to the RACs.

they exercise their traditional authority.[78] He stated: 'The imposition of anything contrary to this outlook *would strike at the very heart of the African customary legal system*, especially the judicial facet thereof.'[79] Madlanga J based this reasoning on two provisions of the Interim Constitution, section 31 which guaranteed the right to culture[80] and section 181 (1) that gave constitutional recognition to legal pluralism.

The reasoning in Madlanga J's judgment is guided by South Africa's constitutional programme of legal pluralism. For example, his interpretation of what standard is required by the Constitution in relation to judicial impartiality and independence is coloured by legal pluralism and the need to elevate African customary law to a status equal to the common law. In the Appeal Court decision of *Mhlekwa and Feni* v. *Head of the Western Tembuland Regional Authority and Another*, which followed *Bangindawo*, the Court opined that because Madlanga J accepted that RACs do not have the independence required by the Interim Constitution, he must not have considered the level of independence required by the Constitution.[81] However, this reading seems to overlook the fact that Madlanga J did look at the Interim Constitution's requirements but was guided on this point by sections 31 and 181.

In *Mhlekwa* the Appeal Court considered the same legislation and many of the same questions but here it was determining a civil case in light of the Final Constitution and it was bound by the Constitutional Court's decision in *De Lange* v. *Smuts NO and Others* ('*De Lange*').[82] *De Lange* approved of the Canadian Supreme Court's test in *R* v. *Valente* and did not limit the application of this test to only courts of 'Western origin'. Thus the Court in *Mhlekwa* examined whether the appointment of presiding officers to the RACs complied with the 'traditional constitutional value of judicial independence'.[83] The Court considered the fact that the traditional leaders presiding in RACs were performing administrative functions, exercising powers similar to the police (such as the powers of arrest, search and seizure) and reporting to, and advising, government on various matters.[84] It concluded that there were insufficient measures to guarantee judicial independence of presiding officers in the RACs because there were no measures to prevent such officers from

[78] Ibid., [273B]. [79] Ibid., [273D]. [80] Interim Constitution, s. 31.
[81] 2001 (1) SA 574 (Tk) [612]. [82] 1998 (3) SA 785 (CC).
[83] *Mhlekwa and Feni* v. *Head of the Western Tembuland Regional Authority and Another* 2001 (1) SA 574 (Tk) [613]
[84] Ibid., [610–13].

performing non-judicial duties that might result in findings that may be the subject of public controversy.[85]

However, the Court in *Mhlekwa* observed in *obiter dicta* that its decision did not necessarily affect the position of chiefs in customary courts, thus indicating that it is not clear cut in either direction. It held:

> Section 165(2) of the Constitution does not, in my view, constitute a prohibition against the appointment of chiefs or the head of a traditional authority as a judicial officer simply by reason of the fact that they also perform other functions. ... The Constitution does not prohibit traditional leaders or laymen from being appointed presiding officers in courts of law.[86]

The relevant issues here are the lack of separation of powers in the customary law arena and the fact that traditional leaders do not necessarily have any training in the common law. The Court did not identify either issue as fatal for the appointment of traditional leaders. However, the decision was made before the *Heath* case and thus the reasoning in *Mhlekwa*, that 'there is no general or entrenched separation of powers in the Constitution'[87] and therefore no necessary problem of a lack of independence and impartiality in the courts of traditional leaders, cannot stand. Overall, the courts in *Bangindawo* and *Mhlekwa* were attempting to insulate customary courts from the 'imposition' (to use Madlanga J's word) of certain constitutional principles because some principles, like the rule of law, have a close connection with common law principles such as the principle of legality.

In the same vein the Law Commission declared in 1998:

> If courts and Parliament are sincere in their respect for African cultural traditions, they must construe application of the bill of rights in such a way that the common law does not become a dominant regime.[88]

In 1999 it conceded that there is a lack of a separation of powers in the institution of customary courts because traditional leaders have no security of tenure, and in some cases they act as both prosecutor and judge.[89] However, the Law Commission concluded that while a formal separation of powers is desirable, it is neither 'crucial' nor 'practical at

[85] Ibid., [616].

[86] Ibid., [616], citing *President of the Republic of South Africa and Others* v. *South African Rugby Football Union and Others* 2000 (1) SA 1 (CC), and [617].

[87] Ibid., [616D]. [88] SALC, *Harmonisation*, [1.7.8]. [89] Ibid., [4.2].

this juncture'.[90] The Law Commission has made no further comment on the matter, except in a puzzling footnote where it observed: 'The principle of separation of powers does not appear to apply to traditional leaders and their councillors.'[91] The Law Commission has not canvassed the various rule-of-law problems facing customary courts.[92] Its silence on the rule of law appears to endorse the view of Madlanga J in *Bangindawo* that Western norms are not relevant to the sphere of African customary law. At a broad level it appears to be attempting to shield and insulate the procedural sphere of customary law from various constitutional principles, including those relating to the rule of law, in a bid to protect the 'dignity' of customary courts and respect legal pluralism, in particular the status of African customary law. This parallels the attempt by traditional leaders during the drafting of the Interim Constitution to seek permanent insulation for customary law from the Bill of Rights.

The Law Commission's reasoning also appears to be driven by pragmatism. In 1999 it candidly acknowledged that the state cannot afford to abolish customary courts. It asserted that Magistrates' Courts 'would probably grind to a halt' if they had to hear all the disputes presently resolved by the courts of traditional leaders.[93] The Law Commission noted that traditional leaders had responded to debate on the option of abolishing customary courts by threatening to cause disruption and to withhold cooperation with the state.[94] Thus, in this context, the Law Commission gave the practicalities of 'dignity, accessibility and

[90] Ibid., [4.2].

[91] SALC, *Report on Traditional Courts*, 31 fn 76. Its approach is similar in relation to the question of community courts. In discussing community courts, the Law Commission only gives a token nod to the Constitution and does not discuss any principles: see SALC, *Community Dispute Resolution Structures*, [4.7].

[92] In its 2003 *Report on Traditional Courts* the Law Commission considered whether customary courts should continue to be recognised as 'courts' or as 'tribunals'. However, while the Law Commission explored the problems of enforcement and dignity, the Report did not discuss the constitutional requirement in s. 165(2) that all 'courts' be independent and impartial. The failure to discuss this constitutional issue implies that either that the issue was not presented or that the Law Commission did not consider it a problem and subscribed to Madlanga J's view in *Bangindawo*. Note that the Report makes no mention of this case or of *Mhlekwa*. However, in 1999, the Law Commission quotes some of the above passages cited from *Bangindawo* with approval: SALC, *Report on Traditional Courts*, [4.2].

[93] SALC, *Report on Traditional Courts*, [3.2.2].

[94] Ibid., [3.2], which details the submissions of CONTRALESA and NADETRAC (National Development and Restoration of Traditional Customs Forum).

effectiveness' much weight in balancing them against the constitutional principles of judicial 'independence and impartiality'.

In the Traditional Courts Bill 2012 the Government has attempted to clear up some of the confusion as to the applicability of the principle of separation of powers to customary courts. Section 7 of the Bill provides that customary courts 'are distinct from courts referred to in section 166 of the Constitution', meaning that the principle of separation of powers does not apply. The attempt to detach customary courts from section 166 is curious given that the Constitutional Court held in 1996 that section 166 'does indeed provide for … [the] recognition of customary courts'.[95] This decision has led to a widespread view that section 166 delineates the full extent of the judicial sphere of government. Section 7 of the Traditional Courts Bill 2012 does not spell out the precise constitutional position of these courts but it states that these courts seek to resolve disputes 'in a manner that promotes restorative justice and reconciliation and in accordance with the norms and standards reflected in the Constitution'. It appears that the Traditional Courts Bill does not intend to integrate customary courts as part of the judiciary but aims to insulate these courts from principles of separation of powers and judicial independence. This is despite the fact that under the Bill customary courts do not adhere to customary practices in many regards, as illustrated by the role given to traditional leaders as 'presiding officers' of customary courts.

The reference to restorative justice in section 7 is explained in the Objects of the Bill in Section 2 which first states that the object is to affirm the values of the traditional justice system, based on restorative justice and reconciliation and to align them with the Constitution. A second stated object is that of affirming the role of traditional leadership in 'enhancing access to justice by providing a speedier, less formal and less expensive resolution of disputes'. From this the Government's purpose of using customary courts appears to be as a means of improving access to justice through restorative justice mechanisms that are cheap, fast and efficient. The Bill's guiding principles are set out in section 3 and section 3(2)(d) in particular states that in applying the Act it should be recognised that 'the principles underlying the traditional justice system are not, in all respects, the same as in the context of *due process*, as applied or understood in the retributive justice system'.[96] Presumably

[95] *Certification of the Constitution of the Republic of South Africa* 1996 (4) SA 744 (CC) [199].

[96] Emphasis added.

'due process' here means a fair and public hearing, as it has no specific constitutional meaning. This clause can be read as directing the rule of law to be muted in the context of constitutional courts.

The Traditional Courts Bill 2012 subtly compromises the rule of law despite the fact that, unlike the approach of the Law Commission, it purports to make the Constitution and its norms central to the post-apartheid transformation of customary courts. Rather than aiming to 'restore' customary courts, the Government appears to be willing to transform aspects of customary courts but not necessarily in light of constitutional values such as the rule of law. The due process rights associated with the rule of law are compromised by the Bill's object of enhancing access to justice which prioritises a system which is informal as well inexpensive for the state to support. In contrast, the Law Commission's proposal compromises the rule of law in order to insulate from the Constitution and the dominant common law paradigm a programme of legal pluralism that seeks to preserve and protect customary law. The end result of the Government approach is a patchwork rule of law: at the lowest rung of the state court system it is the factors of speed, informality and affordability that are allowed to outweigh the constitutional value of the rule of law and the 'due process' rights entrenched in the Constitution.

One problem with this compromise is that the Bill aims to promote restorative justice while prescribing a process that is partly coercive and punitive rather than consensual, participatory and empowering for the victim. Under section 10(2) of the Bill, presiding officers have the power to impose a wide range of civil and criminal sanctions on parties, including forced labour, and for those convicted of criminal offences, the deprivation of a benefit accrued under customary law and custom which could include benefits relating to housing and land.[97] Thus, although the Bill aims to promote restorative justice as an alternative to a retributive justice system, it uses processes and sanctions which are not characteristic of restorative justice. For example, it is inconsistent with the 2002 *UN Basic Principles on the Use of Restorative Justice Programmes in Criminal Matters* which provide that restorative justice processes should apply 'fundamental procedural safeguards guaranteeing fairness' to both parties.[98] The concern is that such a punitive and coercive justice system would operate with few accountability mechanisms.

[97] Subsections 10(2)(g) and (i).

[98] Principle 13, ECOSOC Resolution 2002/12.

The strategy of invoking restorative justice in this context reveals an assumption on the part of South Africa's legislators that there is growing acceptance in the international arena that restorative justice mechanisms do not apply the same standard of the rule of law and human rights as retributive justice mechanisms *and* that they should not be forced to fit the same mould. It is not clear how this strategy fits in with South Africa's international obligations. As Chapter 2 outlined, Article 14 of the ICCPR stipulates that due process rights must be guaranteed by the state party regardless of whether the relevant court is a customary court. The UN Human Rights Committee's General Comment 32 interprets Article 14 as requiring that the basic requirements of fair trial be met for a judgment of such a court to be binding.[99] It is questionable whether customary courts under the Traditional Courts Bill would meet these basic requirements.

Furthermore, the Bill is inconsistent with the 2002 *UN Basic Principles on the Use of Restorative Justice Programmes in Criminal Matters* which provides guidelines as to the use and operation of restorative justice programmes. In particular, these Basic Principles emphasise the following: that such programmes should only be used where the parties give their 'free and voluntary consent'; that neither party should be coerced to participate; that fundamental procedural safeguards guaranteeing fairness to both parties be applied; and that, in referring a case to a restorative process, consideration be given to 'disparities leading to power imbalances' among the parties.

2.3 *Unequal justice and forum shopping*

The cases of *Bangindawo* and *Mhlekwa* also highlighted the fact that some courts enjoy concurrent jurisdiction in South Africa. This opens up the possibility of forum-shopping and unequal justice, aspects of legal pluralism that are considered antithetical to the rule of law. At the same time, in some circumstances, the lack of a choice may also be understood as 'unequal justice' and incompatible with the rule of law.

In *Bangindawo*, the applicants challenged the jurisdiction of the RAC, which enjoyed concurrent jurisdiction with the Magistrates' Courts. They pointed out that in appeals the respondent has the prerogative of choice

[99] The UN Human Rights Committee has not had an opportunity to specifically comment on this issue given that South Africa has thus far not submitted a single report to this treaty body since its ratification of the ICCPR in 1998.

and this prerogative, they argued, is arbitrary and without rational basis and hence violated the equal protection and non-discrimination clause, section 8, of the Interim Constitution. In dismissing the submission, Madlanga J observed that this situation 'occurs daily in our legal system'.[100] On the submission that the RACs' truncated procedures entailed a lower standard of justice, he stated:

> It amounts to no more than comparing apples and potatoes. The elaborate procedure the applicants emphasise can be criticised for providing fertile ground for the raising of technical points which are not infrequently upheld by the courts. On the other hand the less elaborate procedure of the regional authority courts has the advantage of leaving less room for such technicalities and of having the real substance of disputes dealt with and laid to rest. ... 'judging one court by the other is senseless'.[101]

Madlanga J implied that the procedures applied by courts of 'Western origin' are overly technical to the point of failing to reach the real substance of disputes. Thus he refused the imposition of various concerns of the rule of law as unnecessary and potentially harmful.

The Appeal Court in *Mhlekwa* examined these questions in more detail. Here the issue was articulated as one of different procedures in the two concurrent courts with one court (in this case, the RAC) providing fewer procedural rights for a fair trial, as guaranteed by section 35(3) of the Final Constitution, than the other. In circumstances where there are concurrent courts and no relevant rule, the accused person is not given a choice of forum as this prerogative is left to the complainant. Thus, two persons charged with the same offence could be treated quite differently, contrary to section 9(1) of the Final Constitution, which guarantees equality before the law. The Court examined whether the denial of rights by the RAC could be justified: was there a rational relationship in the differentiation between persons falling within the same category and a governmental purpose?

The respondents suggested that the purpose was evident in the intention of the *RAC Act*, which was to provide for a 'culturally defined legal regime' and restore some of the powers that traditional leaders had lost via legislation.[102] They submitted that the aim of the *RAC Act* was to

[100] 1998 (3) SA 262 (Tk) [278G].

[101] Ibid., [279–80], quoting Bekker at the end of the quotation.

[102] *Mhlekwa and Feni* v. *Head of the Western Tembuland Regional Authority & Anor* 2001 (1) SA 574 (Tk) [621C].

allow litigants to enjoy a style of justice with which they were familiar, and quoted the second reading speech made in Parliament concerning the Bill for the *RAC Act*, that: 'In a country where a large section of the population lives according to customary law, it would seem appropriate that certain courts are set aside for this use.'[103] Therefore, the RACs' procedures were kept simple so that they could be easily followed, low in cost, expedient and broadly in line with the procedures followed by customary courts. However, the respondents were unable to link these purposes relating to legal pluralism to the differential treatment suffered by the applicants who were afforded fewer procedural rights in the RACs than they would enjoy in the Magistrates' Court. The respondents failed to establish that the applicants were believers in, and adherents of, customary law or that the issues raised required adjudication in accordance with customary law.[104] The Court found that the manner in which the legislation allowed different standards to operate was arbitrary and had no rational relationship with a governmental purpose.[105] Regarding the constitutional right to culture, the Court held it was a matter of individual choice and freedom and it could not be used to impose a culture and its practices on a person.[106] Furthermore, reconciliation, the purported objective of customary courts, cannot be forced onto an unwilling participant.[107]

On this point of unequal justice, legal pluralism failed in *Mhlekwa* as a justification for the denial of rights and thus the Court held the RACs to be unconstitutional.[108] Pitted against legal pluralism were rule-of-law concerns regarding arbitrariness and unequal treatment but, once again, the Court chose not to invoke the rule of law and turned to tests flowing from the Bill of Rights, specifically, the constitutional guarantee of equality. Unlike the rule of law, the norm of equality is considered a relevant norm in the sphere of customary courts. Given South Africa's

103 Ibid., [623G]. 104 Ibid., [621D].

105 Ibid., [621E]. See also [623B]. The Law Commission's response was to recommend that defendants in criminal matters be given the right to opt out of the jurisdiction of a customary court in favour of any other court: SALC, *Report on Traditional Courts*, Recommendation 12, xiv.

106 *Mhlekwa* [629–30].

107 Ibid., [630A]. Overall the Court disagreed with Madlanga J in *Bangindawo* that the RACs were similar to customary courts on the ground that the RACs enjoy a wider jurisdiction to try serious offences and have the power to impose imprisonment as a penalty: [628].

108 Since the decision, the Minister of Justice has called for the RACs to cease operation.

apartheid history, it is likely that only the invocation of equality can outweigh legal pluralism.

In the Traditional Courts Bill 2012, the 'achievement of equality' is listed as one of the constitutional imperatives which guide the transformation of this part of South Africa's court system.[109] One aspect of the Bill which diminishes this goal is that it does not allow people to 'opt out' of customary courts, contrary to the decision in *Mhlekwa* and the constitutional right to culture. Under section 20(c) of the Bill it is an offence for a person, even a passerby, not to appear before the court when summoned by the presiding officer. Thus, for rural inhabitants and those passing through rural areas, the new legislative scheme means there is no choice of court unlike under the *Black Administration Act*. At the same time, the territorial jurisdictions for these customary courts are those set out under the *Black Administration Act* which means that the new Bill entrenches the jurisdictional boundaries established under the apartheid regime. In addition, traditional leaders are those leaders designated by the Government under the TLGFA but this legislative scheme protects those appointments made by the apartheid Government under the *Black Administration Act*.[110] The Bill fails to facilitate the achievement of equality as it means that those rural inhabitants accused of crimes within the jurisdiction of customary courts are unable to choose to access 'ordinary courts' where their constitutional 'due process' rights receive greater protection. In terms of customary courts operating as restorative justice programmes, the UN Basic Principles emphasise that they should be used only where parties give their 'free and voluntary consent', that neither party should be coerced to participate and that, in referring a case to a restorative justice process, consideration be given to 'disparities leading to power imbalances' among the parties.[111] Thus, international standards require that restorative justice programmes abide by a minimum level of voluntariness and ensure a degree of equality between the parties.

There is much tension in the Bill's aim to align the values of the traditional justice system with constitutional values such as equality, in particular gender equality. This tension is partly captured in section 7(b) of the Bill which states that traditional courts are to operate in accordance with a system of customary law that 'maintains harmony'. In this

[109] See ss. 3(1)(a)(ii) and 3(2)(b). [110] See s. 28(1) of the TLGFA.

[111] Principles 7, 13(c) and 9 of the *UN Basic Principles on the Use of Restorative Justice Programmes in Criminal Matters* (ECOSOC Resolution 2002/12).

vein, section 9(3)(b) of the Bill provides that a party 'may be represented by his or her wife or husband'. While this provision appears gender neutral, it reflects the practice of most African customary law where women are not allowed to represent themselves. In this sense the Bill assists to 'maintain harmony', but critics are right to point to the fact that this Bill is not intended to maintain the gender status quo in rural communities but to transform customary courts and the customary system in light of constitutional values such as equality.[112] Indeed, this aspect of the Bill has attracted international criticism: the CEDAW has expressed concern that the relevant provision 'may jeopardize women's access to justice and equality of treatment before the law', because the provision 'enables the continuing representation of women by male family members'.[113] The onus of ensuring women's full participation as litigants is placed on the presiding officer; as mentioned earlier, the Bill excludes the participation of women as part of a group of councillors in that the Bill does not provide for the presiding officer to sit with a council. As the Bill does not have a provision requiring the Government to appoint an equal number of women as presiding officers, the majority of presiding officers will be men, reflecting the small number of traditional leaders who are women.[114] Given that the presiding officer exercises both judicial and executive power, including power over land use, there are few avenues by which women can challenge the actions of this person in the case that he does not ensure their full participation as litigants. On this broader issue, CEDAW has urged South Africa to 'introduce measures to address negative customs and traditional practices, especially in rural areas, which affect full enjoyment of the right to property by women'.[115]

Thus, for women, unequal justice appears to be the likely result of the Traditional Courts Bill 2012. It is arguable that through the Bill the Government is effectively compromising the constitutional founding

[112] Legal Resources Centre, *Submissions to the Portfolio Committee on Justice and Constitutional Development* (2008) 10.

[113] UN Doc CEDAW/C/ZAF/CO/4 (4 February 2011) *Concluding Observations of the Committee on the Elimination of Discrimination against Women – South Africa*, [16].

[114] The absence of such a provision is contrary to South Africa's ratification of the *Protocol to the African Charter on Human and Peoples' Rights on the Rights of Women in Africa*, Art. 9(2) of which provides that states parties shall 'ensure increased and effective representation and participation of women at all levels of decision-making'.

[115] Ibid., [38].

values of equality and the rule of law in its attempt to appease those traditional leaders sitting in the National House of Traditional Leaders.

3. The rule of law and customary law

South Africa's legal institutions are committed to ensuring that customary law enjoys equal status with common law, even at the expense of compromising the constitutional founding value of the rule of law. These institutions have been involved in a project to 'harmonise' and 'integrate' the substance of customary law and common law, particularly in relation to marriage and succession, so that the application of either system does not produce substantially different results. However, this process of harmonisation is subject to the constitutional norm of equality and thus legislation and rules that are discriminatory are unlikely to survive constitutional review.

As we shall see, such developments are adding fuel to the belief of some scholars that the constitutional dispensation is leading to the demise of legal pluralism. These scholars continue to maintain that the substance of customary law must be completely insulated from the Constitution in order to give it equal status to common law. The proposal to insulate customary law then raises the question of which version of customary law, official or living, is recognised by the Constitution. The Constitutional Court addressed this conundrum in a trilogy of cases dealing with customary law: *Bhe and Others* v. *The Magistrate, Khayelitsha and Others* ('*Bhe*')[116] and *Shilubana and Ors* v. *Mwamitwa* ('*Shilubana*')[117] which concern the impact of customary law and state law in the sphere of succession on 'the most vulnerable groups' in society; and *Gumede* v. *President of the Republic of South Africa*,[118] which concerns the property rights of those women married under customary law.

3.1 'True legal pluralism' and the rule of law

The question of whether the two legal systems enjoy equality has produced much debate, particularly in relation to the application of the Bill of Rights to the two systems. In 1997, shortly after the Final Constitution came into force, A. J. Kerr predicted that the application of the Bill of Rights to customary law would mean that 'the whole of the present

[116] 2005 (1) SA 580 (CC). [117] 2009 (2) SA 66 (CC). [118] 2009 (3) BCLR 243 (CC).

customary law of intestate succession' would be inconsistent with the Constitution, as would be much of customary marriage law and property law.[119] He argued that the result could be a vacuum in customary law of 'considerable proportions'[120] and calculated that 85 per cent of customary law could be invalidated through inconsistency with the Bill of Rights.[121] Other scholars share this view of the potential destructive impact of the Constitution on customary law. For example, Gardiol van Niekerk commented:

> it may be argued that the Constitution is a typical western instrument which entrenches mainly western values and that by advancing the Constitution as the meta standard, indigenous law will disappear.[122]

In light of this potential impact, Kerr reasoned that the Constitutional Court should view customary law as 'exempt' from the Bill of Rights.[123] Presumably Kerr envisaged some temporary form of exemption or insulation for the substance of customary law from the Bill of Rights, which would allow it to be developed to a position of equal strength with the common law. However, this reasoning is curious given that section 8(1) of the Final Constitution provides that the Bill of Rights applies to 'all law' and, in effect, such insulation would place customary law outside the Constitution and produce a situation of deep legal pluralism.

Thomas and Tladi present a similar argument by arguing that section 211(2) of the Final Constitution (which recognises the judicial powers of traditional leaders) 'excludes the supremacy of the constitution over customary laws applied by tribal authorities'.[124] In other words, the authors argue that customary courts should be exempt from all the provisions of the Constitution while at the same time enjoying constitutional recognition. In their view, this path would allow the Constitution

119 Kerr, 'The Bill of Rights', 352. 120 Ibid., 355.

121 Kerr, 'Inheritance in Customary', 268. 122 Van Niekerk, 'Succession', 487.

123 Kerr, 'The Bill of Rights', 355. Kerr argued that there is scope for this under s. 8(2) of the Constitution, which provides that the Bill of Rights 'binds a natural or a juristic person *if, and to the extent that, it is applicable, taking into account the nature of the right and of any duty imposed by the right*' (emphasis added). Alternatively, the Constitutional Court could suspend a declaration of invalidity under s. 172 (1)(a) of the Constitution to allow either the national or provincial legislatures (who enjoy concurrent competence in this area) to legislate. Kerr reasoned that the Constitutional Court would not have certified the Constitution if it understood the Bill of Rights as being able to invalidate large sections of customary law.

124 Thomas and Tladi, 'Legal Pluralism or a New Repugnancy Clause', 363.

to create 'true legal pluralism'.[125] They argue that the dire alternatives to this interpretation of section 211(2) are for the Bill of Rights to operate either like a repugnancy clause, with the power to 'annihilate' customary law, or for it become mere 'paper law', because in practice it would apply only to a small part of South Africa where Western law is respected and enforced.[126] To Thomas and Tladi, these alternatives do not entail 'true legal pluralism', a form of legal pluralism on which they place much value. Overall, the Constitution is painted as inimical to 'true legal pluralism'.

The above two approaches to the interpretation of the Constitution's recognition of legal pluralism are effectively arguing for the substance of customary law to be on an equal footing with the common law while, at the same time, being insulated from interference by the courts. Underlying these approaches appears to be the view that customary law deserves to be shielded and accorded special treatment given the decades of its neglect and subordination during colonial and apartheid governments. Chuma Himonga and Rashida Manjoo appear to take this 'insulation' approach further, by arguing that intervention with customary law by the democratically elected legislature ought to be restricted. They warn that 'an unrestricted use of legislation will in no time unnecessarily ossify and distort customary law, and even bring it to its demise'.[127] Thus it appears that some scholars believe that legal pluralism would be best protected by divorcing it from key aspects of South Africa's new legal order: the widely heralded Final Constitution, the Constitutional Court, and the democratically elected legislature. In effect, they appear to be arguing for the removal of 'rule-of-law' checks on the substance of customary law.

3.2 Competing versions of customary law

What constitutes 'customary law' is also highly contested. Anthony Costa encapsulates a widely held view: '[C]ustomary law as it stands is corrupted, inauthentic and lacking authority. It is a foreign imposition,

[125] Ibid. [126] Ibid.

[127] Himonga and Manjoo, 'What's in a Name?', 341. Himonga and Manjoo imply that it is preferable for the development of customary law to be the domain of the courts rather than the legislature because this allows the development to take place on a case-by-case basis.

a stranger in Africa.'[128] Given that traditional leaders fought so hard for the constitutional recognition of customary law, it is necessary to examine what is meant by the term 'customary law'. Was constitutional recognition given to the law that was officially recognised by the apartheid state or to the law that communities are living and practising?

A dichotomy is commonly drawn between official customary law and living customary law, two versions of customary law. Broadly speaking, official customary law assumes that customary law can be understood as a code of rules. This assumption regarding custom has produced much debate among legal anthropologists. On the one hand, Isaac Schapera and Adam Kuper assert that rules determine behaviour and outcomes and can be distinguished from social rules.[129] On the other hand, Simon Roberts and John Comaroff challenge this approach by stressing the *process* of dispute resolution and the shifting power relations between the negotiating parties in this process.[130] The latter approach has been highly influential among legal anthropologists in the last few decades,[131] and thus customary law has come to be understood as 'processual', 'relational' and 'negotiated' rather than rule-based.[132]

'Living customary law' is the term used to describe the law that is lived and practised by people on a daily basis. However, some scholars, such as Oomen and Himonga, prefer the term 'living law' because such law is negotiated using a variety of sources that would be considered both customary and *non*-customary.[133] Oomen observes that these sources range from custom to constitutional law to developmental values, thus showing that state law, the Constitution, often forms one element of this law but it does not necessarily determine the outcome. She explains:

> The local system of dispute resolution is about mixing and matching rules that refer to culture, common sense, state regulations, the Constitution, precedent and a variety of other resources hardly considered contradictory.[134]

Oomen stresses that the 'rules' are not determinative as the varied sources can be mixed and matched in multiple ways depending on the

[128] Costa, 'The Myth of Customary Law', 534.
[129] See, e.g., Schapera, *A Handbook*; Kuper, 'The Kgalagari', 466–82.
[130] Comaroff and Roberts, *Rules and Process*.
[131] Griffiths, *In the Shadow of Marriage*, 16–17.
[132] Oomen, *Chiefs in South Africa*, 233.
[133] See Himonga and Manjoo, 'What's in a Name?'; Oomen, *Chiefs in South Africa*, Ch. 6.
[134] Oomen, *Chiefs in South Africa*, 210.

power relations between the two parties. Presumably, for this law to operate in a harmonious fashion in South Africa, *ubuntu*, the African concept of humanness and human dignity, needs to be a controlling value in this process of mixing and matching.

Official customary law includes all customary law incorporated into legislation[135] or articulated in judicial decisions, as well as all customary law that 'can be ascertained readily and with sufficient certainty',[136] as long as such law is not in conflict with the Constitution or repugnant to natural justice and public policy.[137] Under section 211(3) of the Final Constitution, customary law is exempt from legislative amendment unless Parliament does so explicitly. All courts in South Africa can apply customary law.[138] For example, a person who lives by customary law can theoretically ask a Magistrates' Court to hear their civil dispute arising out of customary law.[139] However, studies show that higher courts tend to apply official customary law while lower courts are more likely to apply living customary law, because they generally live closer to the communities they serve.[140] In this sense, lower courts are at the interface of state law pluralism and deep legal pluralism.

Proponents of living customary law argue that the constitutional right to culture[141] entails 'the right of the people to have the courts apply the law practised by them'.[142] Himonga and Craig Bosch argue, for example, that the Constitution recognises 'the law generated by the cultural communities' and they therefore reason that if the courts ignore living customary law when they are applying or developing customary law, they will be depriving individuals and communities of their rights.[143] In the same vein, living customary law is sometimes

135 In parts of South Africa, codes were drafted and enacted from the 1880s onwards: Bennett, *Customary Law*, 46.

136 *The Law of Evidence Amendment Act 45 of 1988*, s. 1(1). Note that there is no single, uniform system of customary law in South Africa: Bennett, 'The Conflict of Laws', 25.

137 *The Law of Evidence Amendment Act 45 of 1988*, s. 1(1). Although the repugnancy clause has been rarely invoked, the Law Commission has recommended its repeal: SALC, *Harmonisation*. The clause is criticised as a means of imposing Western values onto customary law. See, e.g., van Niekerk, 'Indigenous Law', 403.

138 Bennett argues that it is not clear whether the application of customary law by the courts is mandatory or permissive: Bennett, 'The Conflict of Laws', 17.

139 It is theoretical because there is evidence that in some areas, magistrates automatically direct matters to be heard at first by a customary court: Oomen, *Chiefs in South Africa*, 205.

140 SALC, *Customary Law: Succession*, [4.2.4].

141 Final Constitution, ss. 30–1.

142 Himonga and Bosch, 'The Application of African Customary Law', 331.

143 Ibid.

portrayed as a democratic form of law in that the people themselves shape it.[144] In contrast, the development of official customary law was neglected by legal institutions during the apartheid era and hence it became stagnant and out of touch with community practices.[145] This is particularly apparent in relation to the position suffered by women in official customary law: generally official customary law is seen as discriminatory towards women and as institutionalising gender inequality. This perception relates to the fact that until 1998, under official customary law, married women were considered legal minors and could not own or inherit any property or make contractual relations.[146] Thus, scholars such as Himonga argue that it is living customary law rather than official customary law that should receive constitutional recognition alongside the common law. To bolster their argument regarding living customary law, scholars point to the words of the Constitutional Court in the *Certification of the Constitution of the Republic of South Africa* to the effect that the Constitution guarantees 'the survival of an evolving customary law'.[147] In all, this is an endeavour to reinvent legal pluralism as a positive force: to transform customary law from a source of law historically oppressive to black people, particularly black women, to a source of law that is not only receptive of community mores but also driven by these evolving values. At a more abstract level, it is an attempt to draw deep legal pluralism (living customary law) and state law pluralism (state law) closer together.

In 2003, the Constitutional Court indicated the likely constitutional recognition of living customary law as customary law. In *obiter dicta* it described customary law as follows:

> It is important to note that indigenous law is not a fixed body of formally classified and easily ascertainable rules. By its very nature it evolves as the people who live by its norms change their patterns of life ... In applying indigenous law, it is important to bear in mind that, unlike common law, indigenous law is not written. It is a system of law that was known to the community, practised and passed on from generation to generation. It is a system of law that has its own values and norms.[148]

144 Hamnett, *Chieftainship*, 10.

145 Bennett, *A Sourcebook*, v; SALC, *Customary Law: Succession*, [3.1.2].

146 This inequity was remedied by the *Recognition of Customary Marriages Act 120 of 1998*.

147 1996 (4) SA 744 (CC) [197].

148 *Alexkor Ltd and Anor* v. *Richtersveld Community and Others* 2004 (5) SA 460 (CC) [52–3].

From this description it is clear that legal certainty, an aspect of the rule of law extolled by Hayek and Raz, is not a value prioritised by customary law. Instead, the value of flexibility is central to customary law. In the 2004 decision of *Bhe* and the 2008 decisions of *Shilubana* and *Gumede*, the Constitutional Court considered the question of whether the Final Constitution recognises official customary law or living customary law and how such customary law can be balanced with the value of legal certainty.

3.3 Bhe, Shilubana, *and* Gumede *and state recognition of customary law*

The cases of *Bhe*, *Shilubana* and *Gumede* are useful in giving us an insight into the relationship between the rule of law and legal pluralism in South Africa's constitutional framework. In *Bhe*, the Constitutional Court was asked to examine section 23 of the *Black Administration Act*, which provided a separate scheme for black Africans whose kin died intestate. The Act runs parallel to the *Intestate Succession Act 81 of 1987* and it enables customary law to regulate matters of succession amongst Africans. The case rolled together three cases concerning the rights of daughters and sisters to succeed a deceased male person. Parliament had attempted to deal with this question back in 1998 but the proposed Bill[149] met a hostile reaction from those traditional leaders sitting in the National House of Traditional Leaders who declared that they were 'fundamentally opposed to the Eurocentric approach which is prevalent in [our] country' and expressed concern that common law principles were replacing customary law.[150] In an attempt to avoid the repetition of such confrontation, in 2004 the Court invited the National House of Traditional Leaders to make a submission in regard to the issues raised by *Bhe* but this offer was declined.

In 2008 the Court again invited the National House of Traditional Leaders to make a submission in regard to the issues raised by *Shilubana*. The case involved a decision by a traditional community in the province of Limpopo to promote gender equality in the succession of traditional leadership through the appointment of a woman to a chieftainship position, for which she was previously disqualified on account of her

[149] *Customary Law of Succession Amendment Bill 1998.*

[150] The submission of the National House of Traditional Leaders is quoted in SALC, *Customary Law: Succession*, [1.2.2].

gender. Once again the National House of Traditional Leaders declined to make a submission but the invitation was accepted by three other public organisations: the Commission for Gender Equality, the Congress of Traditional Leaders of South Africa (CONTRALESA) and the National Movement for Rural Women. The National House of Traditional Leaders had no involvement in the 2008 case of *Gumede* although the Women's Legal Centre Trust was accepted as *amicus curiae*.

3.3.1 Bhe

Specifically, the case of *Bhe* challenged the constitutionality of section 23 of the *Black Administration Act* when read together with the relevant regulations, and the constitutionality of the customary law principle of male primogeniture. The Constitutional Court was unanimous in finding that the *Black Administration Act* and the customary rule of male primogeniture were unconstitutional in that they violated the constitutional rights to equality and human dignity[151] of women and children, described by the court as 'the most vulnerable groups in our society'.[152] This was on the basis that, in relation to the *Intestate Succession Act*, the *Black Administration Act* and the customary rule resulted in substantially different outcomes depending on which system of law was applied.

The Court was, however, not unanimous as to the remedy. The remedy posed a problem because in striking down the impugned provisions of the Act, a gap would result which would mean uncertainty for black Africans attempting to deal with intestate estates. The Court had three options: (1) to suspend its declaration of invalidity for a specified period and hence allow the impugned provisions of the Act to apply until Parliament passed legislation; (2) to develop customary law rules of succession on a case-by-case basis in line with the 'spirit, purport and objects of the Bill of Rights', as set out in section 39(2) of the Final Constitution, or; (3) to substitute the invalid provisions with a modified version of the *Intestate Succession Act*, legislation which applies to all non-black South Africans. The majority chose the last remedy and ordered that the *Intestate Succession Act* apply to most African families until Parliament passes legislation on the matter. In contrast, the minority chose the second option. It is at this point of divergence that the tension between the rule of law and legal pluralism is most acute.

[151] Sections 9 and 10 (respectively).

[152] *Bhe and Others* v. *The Magistrate, Khayelitsha and Others* 2005 (1) SA 580 (CC) [32], per Langa DCJ in the majority. See also [115, 118, 187, 236] of Ncgobo J in the minority.

On the place of customary law in South Africa's legal system, the majority made it clear that the Constitution required that customary law not merely be tolerated but also accommodated. Citing the constitutional right to culture, as well as section 211(2) and section 39 of the Final Constitution, the majority held that: 'It [customary law] is protected by and subject to the Constitution in its own right.'[153] It emphasised that customary law should no longer be seen as subordinate to the common law, as it was in the past when customary law was seen through the lens of the common law.[154]

The majority judgment, authored by Langa DCJ, extolled the positive aspects of customary law, emphasising consensus, dispute resolution and prevention, communitarian values such as *ubuntu* and family unity.[155] It also acknowledged the negative aspects of customary law. For example, Langa DCJ stated: 'Customary law has, in my view, been distorted in a manner that emphasises its patriarchal features and minimises its communitarian ones.'[156] The majority judgment attributed such negative aspects to official customary law, which it noted was 'no longer universally observed'.[157] The majority stated: 'official customary law as it exists in the text books and in the Act is generally a poor reflection, if not distortion, of true customary law'.[158] Thus the majority judgment set up a dichotomy between official customary law and living customary law, describing the latter as 'an acknowledgment of the rules that are adapted to fit in with changed circumstances'.[159] In describing living customary law as 'true customary law'[160] we see an implicit acceptance of living customary law[161] but the judgment added: 'The problem with the adaptations is that they are *ad hoc* and not uniform.'[162] Thus, while the majority appears to have made the momentous acceptance of living customary law, it simultaneously rejected it on grounds that resemble rule-of-law concerns.

These rule-of-law concerns also drive the majority's choice of remedy. This choice of remedy, whereby the common law temporarily replaces customary law, has led to fears that legal pluralism is not being upheld and respected, contrary to the Constitution. The majority rejected the

153 Ibid., [41]. 154 Ibid., [43]. 155 Ibid., [45]. 156 Ibid., [89]. 157 Ibid., [84].
158 Ibid., [86]. 159 Ibid., [87]. 160 Ibid., [86].
161 Ibid., [109]. The majority held: 'The difficulty lies not so much with the acceptance of the notion of "living" customary law, as distinct from official customary law, but in determining its content.'
162 Ibid., [87].

proposed remedy of the case-by-case approach of developing customary law on the ground of its slowness and, moreover, it rejected '[t]he lack of uniformity and the uncertainties it causes'.[163] The uncertainty the Court referred to is two-fold. First, there is the Court's own lack of certainty in developing customary law: the difficulty of determining the content of living customary law when there is 'insufficient evidence and material' to make such a determination.[164] Second, the majority appeared to be concerned that a case-by-case approach would cause greater uncertainty and confusion in the lower courts than already exists; it observed that some lower courts have been incorrectly applying the common law system to African intestate estates while others have been adhering to the official rules of customary law.[165] This 'piecemeal'[166] development of customary law was not considered sufficient to guarantee the constitutional protection of the rights of women and children in such circumstances. In the majority's view, only legislation can provide the necessary certainty and uniformity necessary to guarantee these rights.

In this judgment, it is apparent that rule-of-law concerns are given greater weight than the survival of customary law and the concept of legal pluralism. The majority refused to develop customary law according to the 'spirit, purport and objects of the Bill of Rights'.[167] In its view, the fate of customary law hangs with the democratically elected legislature.[168] However, according to the majority's own judgment, the rules of succession in customary law have not been able to keep pace with changing social conditions and values for the reason 'that they were captured in legislation'.[169] Thus the majority judgment left the future of customary law uncertain, as it appeared such law would be left to stagnate once again unless the courts recognised living customary law or Parliament legislated to the effect that the courts themselves must develop customary law on a case-by-case basis.

[163] Ibid., [112]
[164] Ibid., [109]. Himonga challenges this: Himonga, 'African Customary Law', 177.
[165] Ibid., [112]. Here the Court cites *Makholiso and Others* v. *Makholiso and Others* 1997 (4) SA 509 (Tk) as an example of the former, and *Mthembu* v. *Letsela and Another* 2000 (3) SA 867 (SCA) as an example of the latter.
[166] Ibid., [113].
[167] Final Constitution, s. 39(2).
[168] In direct response to this decision, South Africa's Parliament enacted the *Reform of Customary Law of Succession and Regulation of Related Matters Act, 2009*.
[169] *Bhe and Others* v. *The Magistrate, Khayelitsha and Others* 2005 (1) SA 580 (CC) [82].

The minority judgment held that the Court has an obligation to develop customary law in the same way it has an obligation to develop the common law, on a case-by-case basis.[170] This obligation to develop customary law is triggered in two instances: first, where it is necessary to adapt customary law to changed circumstances, and second, when customary law must be brought into line with the Bill of Rights.[171] The first instance relates to living customary law and the changing needs of the community. In the minority, Ngcobo J held that only the second instance matched the facts of *Bhe* as the issue was whether customary law complied with the Bill of Rights.

The constitutional programme of legal pluralism drives the remedy offered by Ngcobo J's minority judgment. While the judgment noted that the *Intestate Succession Act* will bring about uniformity in succession for all races, it argued that differences in family structures among the races renders this uniform application 'inadequate'.[172] It speculated that the majority's solution 'may well lead to the obliteration of indigenous [customary] law' and it pointed out that the Constitution guarantees the 'survival of an evolving customary law'[173] and the right of those people who wish to live by their law. In Ngcobo J's view, South Africa is just one of many countries that have 'a pluralist legal system in the sense of common, statutory and indigenous law' and he pointed out that other such African countries have not felt compelled to replace customary law with common law or statutory laws.[174] Ngcobo J stated his belief that:

> the answer lies ... in flexibility and willingness to examine the applicability of indigenous [customary] law in the concrete setting of social conditions presented by each particular case. It lies in accommodating different systems of law in order to ensure that the most vulnerable are treated fairly ... Indigenous [customary] law is part of our law. It must therefore be respected and accorded a place in our legal system. It must not be allowed to stagnate as in the past or disappear.[175]

170 Ibid., [212–23] per Ngcobo J who cites *Carmichele* v. *Minister of Safety and Security and Another* 2001 (4) SA 938 (CC) as authority.

171 Ibid., [216–18].

172 Ibid., [229]. One example offered is that of polygamous marriages; however, note that the majority ordered that the *Intestate Succession Act* be modified for such marriages. While the majority held that all estates (except those in the process of being wound up under customary law) are subject to the *Intestate Succession Act*, these estates are administered by the *Administration of Estates Act 66 of 1965*.

173 Ibid., [230]. The judgment cites the *Certification* case: *Certification of the Constitution of the Republic of South Africa* 1996 (4) SA 744 (CC) [197].

174 Ibid., [235].

175 Ibid., [236] (emphasis added).

Ncgobo J recommended that the 'overriding consideration must be to do that which is fair, just and equitable'.[176] In the absence of an agreement in the deceased's family, the magistracy should decide the dispute as to the choice of law according to what is fair, just and equitable in the circumstances. Unlike the majority, Ngcobo J appeared to place much trust in the skills of the lower courts and their ability to deal with the wide discretion that the choice of law rules and the values of fairness, justice and equity confer. He deemed this judicial discretion to be more useful in this context than the principles of certainty and uniformity.

In *Bhe*, we see that in balancing the rule of law and legal pluralism, the majority of South Africa's Constitutional Court gave greater weight to the concerns of the rule of law. However, as the lower court in *Mhlekwa* shows, these rule-of-law concerns are only able to outweigh the interests of legal pluralism when combined with the constitutional right to equality. In contrast, the minority judgment of Ncgobo J was prepared to forgo certainty in order to achieve equity in each case. The rule of law is not explicitly referred to in either of the judgments but, as I argue further shortly, it looms just beneath the surface as an 'imposed' Western norm that is no longer in fashion when dealing with customary law in the new legal order.

3.3.2 Shilubana

In *Shilubana* the Constitutional Court reiterated the need to balance legal certainty and the need to protect rights with the importance of respecting legal pluralism.[177] However, it illuminated a path by which the Constitution and the courts could recognise living customary law while retaining legal certainty. Specifically, in this case the Court was asked to determine whether a traditional community could change its norms and customs so that they were in line with the Constitution and the Bill of Rights. The lower courts in this case had decided that traditional leaders have only narrow discretion to develop customary law. The Constitutional Court disagreed on the basis that this would mean that no body or person could exercise the power to make constitutionally-driven changes in traditional leadership. The Court unanimously held that section 211(2) of the Constitution gives traditional communities the power to act so as to develop their customary law incrementally and

[176] Ibid., [238]. [177] 2009 (2) SA 66 (CC), [76].

bring it in line with the Constitution.[178] On the question as to the procedure that should be used to change customary law, the Court reasoned that the right to amend and repeal customary law under section 211(2) included the right to decide how to do so. The Court stated: '[C]ustomary law is living law and will in future inevitably be interpreted, applied and, when necessary, amended or developed by the community itself or by the courts.'[179] In this statement the Court clarified that section 211(2), alongside section 39(2), empowers the Court to recognise living customary law. However, the Court appears to limit this recognition to the sphere of succession and traditional leadership by distinguishing *Bhe* on a number of grounds: first, that *Shilubana* raises concerns relating to a single traditional community and hence does not affect legal certainty in other communities; second, the Court's decision does not violate vested rights; and third, the Court's decision does not deny vulnerable persons the protection of the law.[180] Thus, in this case we see the Court's growing confidence and willingness to engage with the interface between deep legal pluralism and state law pluralism inhabited by living customary law.

3.3.3 Gumede

The third case in the trilogy, *Gumede*, deals with the *Recognition of Customary Marriages Act 1998* ('RMCA') which aims to transform spousal relations in customary marriages in line with the Constitution and its values, as well as South Africa's international obligations under the ICCPR and the *Convention on the Elimination of Discrimination against Women*. Under section 7(1) and (2) of the RMCA, only those customary marriages concluded after November 2000, when the RMCA came into force, are automatically in 'community of property', meaning that they are subject to equal proprietary consequences. In contrast, those customary marriages concluded before 2000 come under customary law, which in the case of the applicant meant that her husband was the family head and the exclusive owner of all family property. The prospective nature of this law may have been decided in part to insulate customary law, albeit temporarily, from its virtual destruction, as predicted by Kerr.

The applicant, Mrs Gumede, was entitled to nothing upon the dissolution of her marriage because, during the apartheid era, provincial

[178] Ibid., [73]. It stated: 'Any other result would be contrary to s. 211(2) and would be disrespectful of the close bonds between a customary community, its leaders and its laws.'

[179] Ibid., [81]. [180] Ibid., [77].

legislation had codified customary law to this effect. This act of codifying customary law meant that official customary law had not evolved and adapted to changing circumstances along the lines of living customary law and hence, to use the words of the Constitutional Court, it 'fostered a particularly crude and gendered form of inequality, which left women and children singularly marginalised and vulnerable'.[181] The code failed to recognise the values that animated the customary law of marriage. On this point the Court quoted from the work of Nhlapo who argues that this codification 'deprived [African women] of the opportunity to manipulate the rules to their advantage through the subtle interplay of social norms, and at the same time, denied the protection of the formal legal order. Women became "outlaws".'[182] The code did not reflect the lived experience of women and children within customary marriages and moreover, it meant that 'those who were bound by customary law had no power to adapt it'.[183]

The Court rejected the Government's argument that spouses in this situation could approach the divorce courts for appropriate relief by arguing that it is just and equitable for them to be awarded part of the matrimonial property. The Court observed that it was uncertain whether divorce courts could rely on their equitable jurisdiction to adjudicate on customary marriage. In addition, such litigation is 'not always feasible or affordable'.[184] Presumably another factor was the minimal certainty of outcome promised by such litigation which would involve the hearing of considerable evidence.

The Court noted that the RMCA introduced not only equality in spousal relations for those customary marriages concluded after 2000 but also 'certainty and uniformity to the legal validity of customary marriages throughout the country'.[185] However, the Act did not extend protection to vulnerable people such as Mrs Gumede; because her customary marriage was concluded before 2000, she was not covered by the Constitution's guarantees of equality and dignity. Thus the Court unanimously declared that subsections 7(1) and (2) of the RMCA were discriminatory on the basis of gender, constitutionally inconsistent and hence invalid. In effect, this declaration rendered all customary law 'consistent with the guarantees and ethos of the Constitution'.[186]

As in *Bhe*, the Constitutional Court in *Gumede* decided that it did not need to develop the rule of living customary law in line with the

181 (3) BCLR 243 (CC) [17]. 182 Ibid. 183 Ibid., [20]. 184 Ibid., [41].
185 Ibid., [24]. 186 Ibid., [32].

Constitution because no such rule was relied upon in the proceedings.[187] However, it did refer with apparent approval both to *Bhe*'s distinction between official customary law and living customary law and to the academic research of Himonga and Bosch on the latter form of law.

3.4 *The trilogy of cases, customary law and 'the most vulnerable sections of society'*

In *Gumede* the Court prefaced its decision by observing that it 'poses intricate questions about the relative space occupied by pluralist legal systems under the umbrella of one supreme law, which lays down a common normative platform'.[188] In the decision, the values of certainty and uniformity are part of this constitutional 'platform' of protection for vulnerable people like Mrs Gumede alongside equality and dignity.

One of Himonga's concerns regarding the *Bhe* case pinpoints a key problem with the majority's reasoning in that case, which is its failure to clarify the source of the values of legal certainty and uniformity in the Final Constitution, a criticism equally applicable to *Shilubana* and *Gumede*. The confusion caused by the Constitutional Court's failure to refer to the rule of law is apparent in the following criticism from Himonga:

> It may be argued that certainty and uniformity may be admirable features of the common law, but they are not necessarily more desirable than the living customary law feature of flexibility. Neither can they be wholly justified in a constitutionally self-acclaimed multicultural and democratic society.[189]

In her view, these values of certainty and uniformity are important to the common law (in which she includes statutory law) but the courts should not assume that they are shared by all legal systems in South Africa. Himonga implies that this assumption is inappropriate in 'a society that has a constitutionally entrenched legal pluralism'.[190]

Himonga argues that customary law is by 'its very nature flexible, which predisposes it to uncertainty'[191] and she contrasts it with the certainty and uniformity of the common law. Given the Constitution's recognition of customary law, it is not apparent to her why one value is more desirable than the other. In Himonga's view, the common law

[187] Ibid., [29]. [188] Ibid., [1]. [189] Himonga and Manjoo, 'What's in a Name?', 342.
[190] Himonga, 'African Customary Law', 177–8. [191] Ibid., 178.

values of certainty and uniformity are being used to hinder and frustrate the development of living customary law, and hence it is essential that they should be subjected to constitutional scrutiny.[192] The Court's failure in *Bhe* to articulate in a transparent fashion that these values derive not from the common law but from one of the Constitution's founding values, the rule of law, has clearly led to some confusion and misunderstanding.[193] In *Gumede*, the Constitutional Court explicitly invokes the constitutional norms of equality and dignity, but it mutes any invocations of the rule of law despite the fact that certainty and uniformity are rule-of-law values. These omissions indicate the difficulty of the task of transforming the concept of the rule of law from a reviled common law concept that proved, to use Devenish's words, 'singularly and tragically ineffectual'[194] in upholding the rights of the majority of South Africans during apartheid.

As a supporter of legal pluralism, Himonga is also critical of *Bhe* because she believes it indicates a move towards the replacement of customary law by the common law or the abolition of customary law,[195] thus seriously undermining legal pluralism in South Africa. Van Niekerk is also critical in this respect and believes that the majority decision in *Bhe* fails to 'bear out a commitment to honour the status of indigenous law as entrenched in the Constitution'.[196] This is because the Court eliminated the rule of male primogeniture, which she believes is 'fundamental' to customary law,[197] rather than adapting and modifying it in such a way that would harmonise the two legal systems and ensure their equal status. In van Niekerk's view, customary law is 'yet to be accorded equal status' because 'Western law is still regarded as the dominant system and legal development is largely directed by Western values'.[198]

The view of van Niekerk is that customary law and common law are being forced to converge 'within a framework of Western values',[199] by which she presumably means the common law and the Constitution. The law of succession is a good example of this forced convergence. The official customary law of succession conflates succession to status and

[192] Himonga, 'The Advancement of African Women's Rights', 105.

[193] Note that in *Shilubana* 2009 (2) SA 66 (CC) the Court refers obliquely to the rule of law at [68].

[194] Devenish, *The South African Constitution* (1998) 11.

[195] Himonga, 'Taking Stock', 222–3.

[196] Van Niekerk, 'Succession', 487.

[197] Ibid., 486.

[198] Van Niekerk, 'Legal Pluralism', 6.

[199] Ibid., 11.

inheritance of property,[200] presumably to fit within the common law mould. In contrast, living customary law involves the distribution of property to individuals but these rights over property are not absolute and are subject to the decision-making process of a family council. In this framework, a customary estate has a duty to provide for all members of the family, particularly the 'most vulnerable'. The assignment of absolute property rights and the equal division of an intestate estate among the deceased's children (where there is no surviving spouse) according to common law principles can jeopardise the equilibrium reached by the arrangements made under living customary law.[201]

As an advocate of women's rights and customary law, Himonga is equivocal about *Bhe*. On the one hand it is a victory for women in that the official customary law recognises women's constitutional right to succeed a deceased, while on the other hand she is dismissive of the decision and labels it 'tragic' because it has little impact on women who live under and practise living customary law.[202] Her point is that many black women have minimal contact with official customary law and other state law because they live in townships, informal settlements and rural communities where the state exerts negligible influence largely due to its lack of capacity. They inhabit a sphere of deep legal pluralism: in these areas, there is little implementation or enforcement of state law, either in the form of common law, official customary law or constitutional law. In this equation, 'the national (public, official) legal system is often the secondary rather than a primary locus of regulation'.[203] The primary locus of regulation is living customary law, which plays a significant role in women's lives as it sets social norms that are used to resolve disputes within and between families, covering matters that the common law rarely ventures to regulate.[204] In this context, deep legal pluralism is simply a fact in the lives of the 'most vulnerable groups' in South African society.

200 Rautenbach, 'Law of Succession', 107.

201 Ibid. See also Armstrong, 'Rethinking Women's Law', 124–5; Donzwa et al., 'Which Law?', 73–4.

202 Himonga, 'African Customary Law', 171. See also Himonga, 'Constitutional Rights of Women', 325–6.

203 Galanter, 'Justice in Many Rooms', 20, writing more generally about modern society.

204 One example is the promotion of compulsory virginity testing by customary courts: Open Society Foundation for South Africa, *South Africa: Justice Sector*, 121; but see the Northern Province, *Circumcision Act*.

Himonga observes that the lives of the majority of black women in South Africa straddle both the state sphere and the non-state sphere and hence she suggests that women can often improve their lives by negotiating and manipulating both living law and state law to their advantage. She relates that in some instances women have been able to 'secure resources outside of the "real rights culture of the general law" paradigm by negotiating their spaces within customary law frameworks'.[205] She gives scant detail as to how this negotiation can take place if women hold little power and status within their community. Various studies show that women's power to negotiate in this informal sphere depends on their shifting status in the social order of kinship networks, which relates to factors such as wealth, age, marriage, procreation and education.[206] Thus, unlike their white counterparts, black women do not experience the theoretical separation of the law from society; in accessing law they must negotiate a more complicated range of social factors which obscure the supposedly autonomous and central role of the law as promised by the rule of law model.

Himonga argues that the 'dynamism of the living law is a potential force for the improvement of women'.[207] Overall, she implies that living customary law serves 'the most vulnerable groups in society' better than either official customary law or the common law because it is the law that is most accessible and thus most easy to negotiate. Oomen addresses this same question when she examines how different versions of customary law advantage different groups within a community. On the one hand, Oomen is critical of official customary law and those magistrates, anthropologists and state officials who are reluctant to accept the changeable nature of custom. In her view, this approach hinders the coexistence of customary law and human rights[208] and suppresses the process of democratisation.[209] On the other hand, she acknowledges that 'the relatively powerless benefit from codification'[210] because when rules are set down and treated as determinative rather than open to negotiation, the outcome depends less on the status of the person in the community. She argues that uncertainty benefits those in power[211] and explains:

> The unclarity of norms is beneficial to those in power, who can draw from a whole pool of vague rules, notions, ideas, and state, biblical and other sources to support their position. To those who rule, there is a logic to the disorder.[212]

205 Himonga and Manjoo, 'What's in a Name?', 339.
206 See, e.g., Griffiths, *In the Shadow of Marriage*, Ch. 4; Oomen, *Chiefs in South Africa*, 214–16.
207 Himonga et al., 'Uncovering Reality', 363. 208 Oomen, *Chiefs in South Africa*, 250.
209 Ibid., 234, 210 Ibid., 204. 211 Ibid. 212 Ibid., 233.

That customary law is vulnerable to abuse and manipulation is confirmed by other studies.[213] This analysis juxtaposes legal flexibility and legal certainty and arguably aligns them with legal pluralism and the rule of law. In this equation it appears that the rule of law benefits the most vulnerable groups in society because it is based on the value of legal certainty achieved through rules and minimal discretion of the decision maker. Through fixing rules and procedures, the rule of law aims to eliminate the relational and negotiated aspects of law because it attempts to set down the ground rules for societies where *ubuntu* cannot be assumed to be operating. Theoretically, the horizontality rule entrenched in the Final Constitution's Bill of Rights means that constitutional protections extend to regulate the interactions between private citizens and thus protect vulnerable groups in everyday dealings.

However, as the 2011 UN Women Report noted,[214] the reality is that at a practical level the rule of *state* law protects vulnerable groups only in their interaction with the state. Its protection is very limited for women who live and work in the private sphere. The rule of law guarantees legal certainty in a formal sphere that most women are unable to access largely due to their lack of resources, status and care responsibilities. Thus, Himonga may be correct in arguing that, for many women, they are better off seeking to influence the development of living customary law which operates largely within the private sphere than relying on the rule of law, which for them is practically no more than a myth. However, the problem with this path is that women often experience bias and discrimination in participating in customary forums such as customary courts,[215] although this reputation for bias and discrimination is equally shared by state courts due to the legacy of apartheid.

In the customary law arena the invocation of relevant state law, such as equality guarantees, does not automatically empower a party negotiating

[213] See, e.g., the studies undertaken by the Women and Law in Southern Africa Project: Dow and Kidd, *Women, Marriage and Inheritance*, Ch. 7; Donzwa et al., 'Which Law', 96–7. The latter study argues that instances of abuse are rare while the former argues that customary law is highly open to manipulation by parties.

[214] See Chapter 3, section 2.1.

[215] According to research conducted by Oomen in the region of Sekhukhune, 42 per cent of women surveyed believed that they had suffered discrimination and bias at the hands of customary courts: Oomen, *Chiefs in South Africa*, 188. Note that s. 9(2)(a) of the Traditional Courts Bill 2012 stipulates that women be afforded 'full and equal participation' in the proceedings of customary courts and special consideration be given to 'vulnerable persons'.

the resolution of a dispute.[216] The usefulness of state law depends on the status of the person invoking it and whether they can rally sufficient support for their position.[217] In other words, the dynamics operating at the local and community level determine the extent to which state law can be empowering.[218] While dispute resolution in the customary law arena emphasises harmony and reconciliation, Oomen argues that it is deeply embedded in unequal power relations: 'Behind harmonious decisions there often lurches, explicitly or implicitly, the threat of force … bewitchment, expulsion from the community [and] the wrath of the ancestors.'[219] Nevertheless, she puts forward access to information about the common law system as a form of empowerment,[220] so that legal pluralism provides a real choice of systems and the protections offered by the rule of law are an option.

The problem is that traditional leaders are often the first and only contact that people have with the law. Many traditional leaders are hampering their community's access to information about forms of state law, apart from customary law, in order to retain their domain of power.[221] Magistrates are also to blame: where a party attempts to avoid a traditional leader by taking their matter straight to the Magistrates' Court, they are frequently redirected back to the customary court.[222] In this way, both forms of judicial officers who preside over the state's lowest courts are effectively obstructing legal pluralism and the path it potentially offers towards the empowerment of vulnerable groups in society.

The Traditional Courts Bill 2012 is likely to further entrench some of these problems given that, contrary to customary practice, it centralises the power of traditional leaders in the role of the court's presiding officer. The Bill distorts living customary law because the process prescribed by the Bill is neither consensual nor democratic in the sense that the ordinary community is unable to participate either in the decision-making process or in the appointment of their leader. The Bill excludes the active involvement of women in the development of living customary law and it proposes to do little to remove the bias and discrimination that

[216] Stewart, 'Juridifying Gender Justice', 48. Stewart elsewhere notes that when women in Africa resort to state law they are often perceived as 'anti-African, [and] as imperialists': Stewart, 'Should Women Give Up on the State?', 38.

[217] Griffiths, *In the Shadow of Marriage*, Ch. 4; Oomen, *Chiefs in South Africa*, 214.

[218] Stewart, 'Juridifying Gender Justice', 50.

[219] Oomen, *Chiefs in South Africa*, 210.

[220] Ibid., 252.

[221] Ibid., 234.

[222] Ibid., 205.

women experience in customary courts. In this sense the Bill may entrench structures of social inequality rather than transform them. At the same time its failure to provide for community involvement appears to reduce the social and democratic legitimacy of this form of law and to encourage the community to avoid state customary courts where possible, thus pushing communities back toward deep legal pluralism and 'self-help'. Through the National House of Traditional Leaders as well as CONTRALESA, traditional leaders have fought against an 'opt out' system in the belief that it would undermine their legitimacy but this argument gives insufficient consideration to the basis of this legitimacy which is related to the ability of people to choose their forum and leader and to participate.

Himonga's work indicates that a decentralised model of customary courts may be more conducive to women's negotiation of law in that such a model enables them to wield greater influence in the development of living customary law. A choice of forums is essential given that most customary systems do not allow women to represent themselves. Only occasionally do women and other vulnerable groups manage to use legal pluralism to their advantage because they experience the choice of law offered by legal pluralism differently and in a more limited fashion. For these groups, a first step is to ensure that they can experience legal pluralism as an empirical 'fact' so that they are able to exercise a real choice between legal systems. The Traditional Courts Bill 2012 prevents this choice and it does little to transform the traditional justice system into a system that respects gender equality.

4. Conclusion

It is uncontroversial to conclude that, as a result of its approach to legal pluralism, South Africa has a patchwork rule of law. For most rural South Africans, approximately 20 million, the rule of state law is largely a myth because the state struggles to make contact with their lives. State law pluralism is an attempt to extend the reach of the state but the Traditional Courts Bill 2012 offers a compromised version of the rule of law. Moreover, the Bill fails to transform the traditional justice system into a system that respects gender equality in line with South Africa's other courts.

While the rule of law is a dominant norm in the international arena, it has come to play an ambivalent role in South Africa's legal transformation. On the one hand it performs its function of assisting the new order to achieve international legitimacy: in the eyes of the international community, South Africa is a transitional country with strong state institutions that continue to uphold the Constitution. On the other hand, we have seen that the rule of law is readily compromised in the context of the new order's attempt to respect its constitutional commitment to legal pluralism. With the strong support of the state's main legal institutions, South Africa's Parliament is actively insulating the world of customary law and customary courts from the rule of law, a founding value of the Constitution, in order to establish a court system that is fast and cheap. This is creating double standards which operate on a socio-economic fault line as those South Africans living in poor rural communities do not enjoy many of the protections promised by the rule of law. The phrase 'One Law for One Nation' is currently proving to be an empty and unfulfilled slogan.

Thus we see that as post-apartheid South Africa undergoes a transition to a new legal order based on equality and human dignity, the relationship between the rule of law and legal pluralism is tense and complex. For the Constitutional Court, this transformation is guided by constitutional values and hence the Court's approach transforms the rule of law by paring it back to one of its core goals identified in Chapter 3, equality. Unlike with other rule-of-law principles, the Constitutional Court is vigilant in upholding the principle of equality as a means of improving access to justice for women and other vulnerable groups. However, the Constitutional Court shows that it is reluctant to directly invoke the rule of law given its close connection with the common law.

The Government's Traditional Courts Bill 2012 is an example of the ongoing political compromises in post-apartheid South Africa and the successful lobbying of those traditional leaders sitting in the National House of Traditional Leaders. The views of this House are not necessarily shared by all traditional leaders: the President of CONTRALESA, Chief Holomisa, has complained that 'the people who drafted this bill have no understanding of African law and are yet again imposing a Western perspective on how traditional courts function'.[223] In his view, 'constitutional democracy has undermined the authority and power of chiefs'.[224] The Government is weighing the views of such lobby groups against the Constitution and its guarantees of equality, democracy and the rule of law. Judging by the Bill, the result leans toward the

[223] Quoted in Pearlie Joubert, 'Traditional Courts Bill "Inadequate"', *City Press*, 19 February 2012.
[224] Ibid.

Government's interest in appeasing traditional leaders rather than upholding constitutional values. At the same time the Bill reflects the Government's desire to enhance access to justice in rural areas through establishing alternative dispute resolution mechanisms and for this reason the Bill emphasises the concept of restorative justice. The result is clearly a hybrid system which lacks some essential features of a system of customary living law; it also lacks Western accountability mechanisms related to the rule of law such as judicial independence and separation of powers, and, in its inclusion of coercive and punitive measures, it shows minimal connection to an internationally accepted process of restorative justice. The Bill shields traditional leaders from most of the customary and Western accountability mechanisms and in this way it opens up the potential for the abuse of power. It is debatable whether the Bill enhances access to justice for rural women, as they are excluded from participating in the decision-making process and may continue to be represented by male relatives in resolving disputes. Indeed, Nhlapo's words (quoted earlier in the context of the Constitutional Court's judgment in *Gumede*) appear to be apt to describe the position of rural women under the Bill in that it deprives African women 'of the opportunity to manipulate the rules to their advantage through the subtle interplay of social norms, and at the same time, [they are] denied the protection of the formal legal order' because there is no 'opt out' from this system.[225] In this sense, it is arguable that the Bill forces rural women in particular to become 'outlaws'.[226] For rural inhabitants the Government's attempt to transform customary courts is entrenching a second-class court system where constitutional guarantees are sidelined.

Almost two decades after the end of apartheid, South Africa continues to struggle to transform the concepts of the rule of law and legal pluralism. South Africa's experience shows that state law pluralism and 'linkage laws' such as the Traditional Courts Bill are very complex and can never be understood as a quick fix in regard to enhancing access to justice. This experience should be instructive to the international community, particularly the UN, World Bank and IDAs such as USAID, which are currently attempting to assist other post-conflict states such as Timor-Leste and Afghanistan, to establish such programmes and laws.

The next Part of this book presents a case study on Timor-Leste, which contrasts strongly with that on South Africa because Timor-Leste's

[225] Nhlapo, 'African Customary Law', 162. [226] Ibid.

Constitution does not make a commitment to state law pluralism. With the assistance of the international community, Timor-Leste is preparing to adopt state law pluralism through enacting a linkage law and hence it will benefit from South Africa's experience in understanding the myriad of challenges involved in establishing such legislation. Like in South Africa, many of the fault lines around the rule of law and legal pluralism in Timor-Leste relate to women and their position within customary systems of law. Unlike South Africa, however, Timor-Leste is one of many post-conflict states that have no mature state institutions to deliberate on the dynamics of the relationship between the rule of law and legal pluralism and hence, in this nascent state, it is possible to discern only a very fragmented and opaque approach to reconciling these two concepts.

PART III

6

Founding a legal system in post-conflict Timor-Leste

On 20 May 2002 Timor-Leste became an independent state with a Constitution that declares it to be "a democratic, sovereign, independent and unitary State based on the rule of law". Like South Africa, Timor-Leste has been subjected to waves of imposed foreign legal systems, starting with that of Portugal in the sixteenth century, of Indonesia in 1975 and the United Nations in 1999 following the UN ballot for independence. Unlike South Africa, efforts to found a legal system and to establish and promote the rule of law in post-conflict Timor-Leste have been heavily influenced by the international community. The extent and complexity of this international influence renders Timor-Leste another pertinent example of the dynamics involved in promoting the rule of law in post-conflict states.

International norms abound in Timor-Leste's Constitution while local norms are scarce. Timor-Leste's Constitution was not drafted through a participatory process unlike the South African Constitution: there was little public participation and the drafting process did not involve ongoing negotiations and compromises between leading actors. While international influence can be seen in Timor-Leste's negotiation of the rule of law and legal pluralism in its Constitution, such influence did not necessarily emanate directly from the UN administration of Timor-Leste during the period of constitutional drafting, but largely arose from various corners of the lusophone world and their particular political dynamics.

This chapter begins by sketching the extent of deep legal pluralism in Timor-Leste and the broader differences between state law and local customary law. It then traces the relationship between the rule of law and legal pluralism during three formative periods of Timor's history, Portuguese colonisation, Indonesian occupation and UN administration. It shows that state law has historically been weak and shown little respect for the rule of law, while local customary law has been tenacious in continuing through the centuries and periods of conflict to provide communities with mechanisms to resolve disputes. In regard to the UN administration the chapter argues that it provided a poor model of the rule of law for Timor's independence leaders. This is followed by an exploration of the drafting of Timor-Leste's 'mother law', its Constitution, and an analysis of the factors that led to both the invocation of the rule of law and the sidestepping of local customary law. The chapter argues that Timor-Leste's Constitution has not enjoyed broad social and political legitimacy because it is not a product of political compromise and public participation but a document drafted by a lusophone elite that was out of touch with the lived experience of most Timorese whose world is shaped by customary law. This failure to register legal pluralism as a critical factor in Timorese life has hampered broader efforts to establish a legal system and promote the rule of law.

1. Local customary law and its sources of legitimacy

When the UN arrived in 1999, there were few anthropological or sociological studies on Timor-Leste because of the territory's isolation during Portuguese colonisation and Indonesian occupation.[1] Since 1999, mainly Western anthropologists and NGOs have attempted to fill this gap. Using these studies, this section briefly explains some of the main norms of local customary law in order to show that these norms derive from a separate paradigm, and draw on a different source of legitimacy, to those of state and international law.

To refer to local customary law, the Indonesian word *adat* and the Tetum word *lisan* are often used.[2] Anthropologists emphasise that these terms refer to more than a system of legal principles governing crime, property, land and marriage: they relate to a whole system of social relationships.[3] On a broad level, law is considered part of a larger sociocosmic order in which there is a flow of goods and persons and in this scheme there is little conceptual separation of individuals from this larger order and flow of values.[4] This means that crimes are committed not just against a particular individual and their community but also against one's own ancestors.[5] Hence, it is considered essential that harmony also be

[1] See, e.g., van Wouden, *Types of Social Structure*; Fox (ed.), *The Flow of Life*; Traube, *Cosmology and Social Life*; Therik, *Wehali: The Four Corners Land*. Earlier studies, including lusophone studies, are discussed in Nixon, *Integrating Indigenous Approaches*, Ch. 7.

[2] *Adat* is the Indonesian word for the sacred laws or belief systems on which local law is based. In Tetum the word is *lisan*.

[3] See Hohe and Nixon, *Reconciling Justice*; Hohe, 'Justice Without Judiciary', 335.

[4] Hohe and Nixon, *Reconciling Justice*, 63. [5] Ibid., 23.

reached with the world of the ancestors, as it is the ancestors who legitimate, and set the principles of, the entire local customary order.[6] However, the central position of the ancestors in this order means that local leadership is based on descent and hierarchy. Ospina and Hohe explain: 'These traditional political concepts form a system in which traditional society can work without a proper state body.'[7]

There are numerous local systems of law across all regions of Timor-Leste but some underlying norms are shared. The main example is the process, sometimes described as arbitration or mediation, used by local legal systems to deal with disputes, where leaders such as a local spiritual leader (*lia nain*) or village chief (*chefe*) listen to the parties before a consensus is reached as to the required means of compensation. In 2002 anthropologist David Mearns explained the central role of compensation in Timorese systems of law thus:

> [J]ustice is never simply a matter of punishment but rather of compensation for the victim and the victim's family whose honour had been damaged by the crime or offence. Moreover, the acts of individuals as perpetrators have consequences not just for them alone, but also for their families whose shame and dishonour result from any member's crime or misbehaviour.[8]

From this observation it is apparent that justice and punishment are understood in a collective sense. The debt payment owed by the perpetrator for a crime committed is made in the name of the family as a whole and can be paid by the perpetrator's family. For example, the crime of arson may involve reimbursing the victim's family to the extent that the victim's family is offered the perpetrator's family belongings.[9] Similarly, sexual assault may be resolved through compensation paid by the perpetrator to the victim's family.[10] In this framework, individual rights, such as that of rape victims, are not given priority. Committing a crime is seen as more than an individual act of transgression: it is seen as a community problem.[11] The debt created by the act must be settled before social relations can return to normal.[12] In small and remote communities where the state

[6] Ibid., 17; Babo-Soares, 'Role of Customary Law', 3.

[7] Ospina and Hohe, *Traditional Power Structures*, 66.

[8] Mearns, *Looking Both Ways*, 43.

[9] Swaine, *Traditional Justice*, 21.

[10] The crime of rape is conceptualised differently: there is little distinction between rape and adultery. Local legal systems often require the perpetrator to marry the victim or to pay compensation. The case of a man reneging on his promise to marry a woman after consensual sexual intercourse is considered by local authorities to be more serious than that of a violent rape. See Hohe and Nixon, *Reconciling Justice*, 60. See also Swaine, ibid., 47.

[11] See Hohe and Nixon, *Reconciling Justice*, 22.

[12] See Mearns, *Looking Both Ways*, 43.

has little reach, this process of discussion, agreement and compensation is an important aspect of justice and social harmony. This process of reconciliation between the two parties is understood to be 'conducted under the eyes of the ancestors'.[13] Taking a matter to the state legal system may risk jeopardising eventual harmony between the parties and with the ancestors.[14] This can lead to the instigation of new crimes as the parties settle the matter in their own way and, in the worst-case scenario, it can spiral into generations of conflict, known as the '"blood-feud" phenomenon'.[15]

Anthropologists have pointed out that some of the distinctions employed by the state legal system are considered alien to local systems of law in Timor-Leste. One example is the distinction in the state legal system between civil and criminal law. Hohe and Nixon explain that in local legal systems non-violent crimes such as theft may be considered to be more serious than violent crimes while matters such as adultery and divorce are also considered to be very serious because they affect the social fabric.[16] At the same time, the Western legal system does not understand some of the basic tenets of local systems of law. One example is the belief in witchcraft in many districts in Timor-Leste which is contrary to streams of liberal rationalism found in the Western legal system.[17]

Thus, while state law and customary law are often in contact with each other and indeed influence each other,[18] they operate in distant paradigms. On the one hand, state law promotes legal mechanisms as the main means of resolving disputes, while, on the other hand, local customary law prioritises harmony and the kinship group and invokes the supernatural rather than the rule of law as its main source of legitimacy. According to Ugo Mattei's taxonomy of world legal systems, set out in Chapter 3, the two systems in Timor-Leste fall into different legal families. Like 'living law' in South Africa, local customary law in Timor-Leste is less legocentric than state law in its approach to resolving disputes. Interestingly, while these local systems of law show some elements of restorative justice in that they involve compensation and reconciliation, the leading researchers have not labelled them restorative justice systems *per se*. The next section considers the evolution of the

[13] Hohe and Nixon, *Reconciling Justice*, 23. [14] Ibid., 59.

[15] Babo-Soares, 'Role of Customary Law', 11–12.

[16] Hohe and Nixon, *Reconciling Justice*, 19, 63.

[17] Mearns, *Looking Both Ways*, 45. See Australian Broadcasting Corporation, '"Witches" Murdered in E Timor', 9 January 2008.

[18] Chopra et al., 'Lessons from East Timor', 130–1.

formal legal system in Timor-Leste and the tenacity of local customary law in the lives of the local population. It also traces the limited adherence to the concept of the rule of law in the state legal systems that operated prior to independence in 2002.

2. The Portuguese state and the Indonesian state

According to historians and anthropologists, successive formal legal systems never held great sway in Timor-Leste. The state legal system was weak during the periods of both Portuguese colonisation and Indonesian occupation, which has meant that local customary law has continued in operation until today.[19]

During their four centuries of colonial rule beginning in 1556[20] the Portuguese were more interested in tax collection and trade[21] than developing broader state administration and hence colonial rule did not have a significant impact on local power structures and systems of law.[22] The Portuguese ruled through a system that bestowed military power on local chiefs who were expected to provide strong loyalty to Portugal and maintain law and order, a form of indirect rule.[23] This was often accomplished through using the local custom of entering into blood oaths (*juramentu*) in order to make political connections and achieve peace. The use and manipulation of such local customs gave Portuguese rule a sense of local legitimacy.[24]

Jean Berlie states that until the twentieth century 'the local native authorities had considerable judicial power' but it is not apparent that a separate system of native courts was recognised by Portugal.[25] In 1910 the Republic of Portugal was founded and Portuguese rule became more

[19] See Hohe and Nixon, *Reconciling Justice*, 27; Berlie, 'A Concise Legal History', 138.

[20] This is the date of the first Portuguese settlement at Lifau (in the present day Oecusse). It was not until the beginning of the eighteenth century that a Portuguese Governor was appointed in East Timor. For a history of East Timor, see Taylor, *Indonesia's Forgotten War*; Dunn, *Timor: A People Betrayed*, Ch. 2.

[21] See Hohe and Nixon, *Reconciling Justice*, 27.

[22] Ibid., 27. More generally, Taylor states 'the salient features of East Timorese society remained in the mid-twentieth century much as they had been at the time of the Portuguese arrival': *Indonesia's Forgotten War*, 15.

[23] See Berlie, 'A Concise Legal History', 145.

[24] Ospina and Hohe, *Traditional Power Structures*, 46; Trindade, 'Reconciling the Conflicting Paradigms', 165.

[25] Berlie, 'A Concise Legal History', 147.

direct.[26] During Portuguese colonial rule, Timor-Leste was divided into nine administrative districts[27] and it is reported that four courts of justice existed in Dili, Bacau, Suai and Oecusse, presumably to hear serious crimes committed by locals and to resolve disputes relating to non-locals.[28] Contrary to Governor Da Silva's advice in 1897 that Portugal promulgate special laws for Timor-Leste that reflected the territory's social conditions and customs,[29] few such laws were made over the centuries.[30] However, this minimal outside interference allowed local legal systems to continue operating.[31] It would be difficult to argue that there was any semblance of the rule of law at work in colonial East Timor. There is no evidence of either due process being observed in the justice meted out under state law to locals and non-locals or of any avenues to check and restrain the abuse of state power by state officials.

A greater impact was felt by the imposition of the Indonesian legal system during the occupation (1976–1999). East Timor was annexed as the twenty-seventh province of Indonesia in 1976. As a province, it became subject to laws adopted by Indonesia's national legislative council and only civil matters were left to the local level to deal with.[32] According to one report, during the occupation, Indonesia passed a law that 'permitted no local traditional institution to exist apart from those adopted by the national legislative body'.[33] Due to widespread perceptions of its corruption, the local population viewed the Indonesian legal system with deep distrust.[34]

[26] After World War II, Portugal recognised East Timor as one of its 'overseas provinces', rather than a colony. See Berlie, 'A Concise Legal History', 148, who says that a 'politico-administrative statute for Timor was published in the Organic Law of the Portuguese Overseas (no 2066)' in June 1953. This was during the dictatorship of António de Oliveira Salazar (1932–68). It is possible that this issue was formalised earlier by the Portuguese Constitution in 1951. However, see Dunn, *East Timor: Rough Passage to Independence,* 32, who says that this status was declared in 1963.

[27] The nine districts were Dili, Lautem, Viqueque, Bacau, Manatuto, Suro, Ermera, Bobonaro and Oecusse.

[28] See Berlie, 'A Concise Legal History', 150.

[29] Da Silva, *Relatorio das Operações*, 291–2.

[30] Berlie, 'A Concise Legal History', 149.

[31] Hohe and Nixon, *Reconciling Justice*, 27.

[32] See ibid.

[33] Quast, *Report on East Timor,* 22. Babo-Soares explains that this law (UU No 5 Tahun 1974 tentang Pokok Pemerintahan di Daerah), adopted in 1974, 'permits no local traditional institution to exist apart from those adopted by the national legislative body': 'Role of Customary Law', 10.

[34] See Hohe and Nixon, *Reconciling Justice*, 7; see also 26–7. Babo-Soares writes that 'the degradation of public credibility on the judicial system' during the period 'prompted people to rely on traditional ways of solving disputes rather than on state courts': 'Role of Customary Law', 12.

People saw state law as the tool of the oppressor or as 'simply irrelevant'[35] and considered state courts to be partial and political, condoning impunity for perpetrators of serious crimes against the local population.[36] Amnesty International asserted in 2001:

> Under Indonesia the judiciary was independent in law, but in practice the courts were an arm of government used to detain and imprison political opponents – especially supporters of political independence. The Indonesian judiciary was, and still is, widely recognised as suffering from deeply rooted corruption.[37]

There was no separation of powers as the Indonesian executive controlled the actions of the judiciary.[38] It is fair to say that during this time there may have been rule *by* law but not rule *of* law in the sense that there were no effective mechanisms for constraining and disciplining the abuses of public power. Sarah Pritchard states:

> under Portuguese colonial administration and repressive Indonesian occupation, there was little opportunity for the East Timorese people to develop an understanding of and commitment to concepts such as the rule of law and the independence of the judiciary.[39]

Given these circumstances, there was minimal public confidence in state law: local people preferred to use the path of customary law wherever possible in order to avoid contact with the state.[40] Locals would rarely access the formal legal system, except when it came to report serious cases such as murder.[41] The formal legal system was seen as a last resort. In short, the rule of law was absent and the distrust of the state legal system meant deep legal pluralism flourished, with local customary law operating alongside state law.[42]

3. The UNTAET Administration

It is uncontroversial that the concept of the rule of law was not respected by the Indonesian state in East Timor during colonisation and occupation. The first concerted effort to establish the rule of law took place

[35] See *Chega!, Report of the Commission for Reception, Truth and Reconciliation*, Part 9, [143].

[36] Amnesty International, *East Timor: Justice Past, Present and Future*, 13. [37] Ibid.

[38] International Commission of Jurists and the Netherlands Institute of Human Rights, *Indonesia and the Rule of Law*, 61ff; International Commission of Jurists, *Ruler's Law*, 42–50.

[39] Pritchard, 'United Nations Involvement', 190.

[40] Hohe and Nixon, *Reconciling Justice*, 26–7. [41] Ibid., 19, 26.

[42] Berlie, 'A Concise Legal History', 149; Taylor, *Indonesia's Forgotten War*, 12.

during the UN administration from the arrival of the UN Transitional Administration in East Timor (UNTAET) in October 1999 to independence in May 2002. This period represents the first phase of the formation of East Timor's legal system. This section examines this formative period in Timor-Leste's history in order to determine: (1) the nature of the model of the rule of law that was bequeathed by UNTAET to the independence governments; and (2) UNTAET's approach to the question of legal pluralism.

Under UN Security Council Resolution 1272, the Transitional Administrator (TA) was given a mandate to exercise all legislative, executive and judicial power on behalf of the Security Council. The duty of establishing the rule of law was not included in the mandate although the Resolution does endorse the UN Secretary-General's report of 4 October 1999, which states that one of the mission's objectives was 'to ensure the establishment and maintenance of the rule of law and to promote and protect human rights'.[43] The wide scope of the TA's powers arguably placed his position in tension with the rule of law: in a candid reflection, the TA, Sergio Vieira de Mello, labelled his position as one of 'benevolent despotism', and compared his 'quasi-dictatorial powers' with the powers exercised by colonial regimes.[44] Pointing out the obvious democratic deficit, in that the UN Secretary-General appointed him with little or no consultation with the local population, he added: 'There is no separation of the legislative or judicial from the executive authority. There are no positive models on how to exercise such broad powers.'[45]

During his mandate the TA made efforts to mitigate this problem by appointing a consultative body of local leaders, the National Council,[46] and setting up bodies such as the Office of the Inspector General to provide a means of scrutinising the efficiency of the administration. But in the absence of elections and strong powers of scrutiny, it proved difficult to boost the local perception of legitimacy in his administration.

[43] UN Doc S/1999/1024 (4 October 1999) *Report of the Secretary-General on the Situation in East Timor*, [29(h)].

[44] De Mello, 'How Not to Run a Country', 4, 7. [45] Ibid., 4.

[46] The 'National Consultative Council' was set up by UNTAET Regulation 1999/2 (2 December 1999) to bolster the democratic local legitimacy of the TA's mandate to make and execute laws. This body was reformed in mid 2000 so as to make the body more broadly representative. The 'National Council' was formed by UNTAET Regulation 2000/24 (14 July 2000). See also UNTAET Regulation 2000/33 (26 October 2000). The body comprised thirty-six members from sectors of the East Timorese community including ten politicians and a representative from each of the thirteen districts.

At the end of UNTAET's mandate, one respected Timorese NGO, La'o Hamutuk, commented on UNTAET's legacy in relation to its governance model. It stated:

> Although UNTAET preached good governance, transparency, accountability, democracy and the rule of law to the East Timorese, it showed little of these in itself. UNTAET is a government without a constitution, with all power residing in one man, the Transitional Administrator Sergio Vieira de Mello.[47]

This comment singles out a constitution as a mechanism that would have enabled the overly broad powers of the administration to be properly limited and regulated by the law in line with the concept of the rule of law. Although the idea of a constitution at this point of time is somewhat fanciful, such a mechanism would have ideally given guidance to both UN administrators and the local population as to the applicable laws.

3.1 *The rule of law and the* Alves *case*

A case in the newly established Timorese courts that highlighted the absence of such a constitutional mechanism was that of Viktor Alves.[48] Alves had been arrested by the UN's International Force for East Timor and held in detention beyond the legal limit of 110 days permitted by the Indonesian Code of Criminal Procedure. Twelve days after his lawyers filed an application challenging his prolonged detention and a day before his hearing, UNTAET enacted Regulation 2000/14, which came into immediate effect. The Regulation included a provision that replaced the time limits imposed by Indonesian law with provisions allowing a panel of judges to extend detention periods beyond six months in particular circumstances.[49] At the hearing regarding Alves' prolonged detention, Judge Rui Perreira dos Santos, sitting alone, ruled that Regulation 2000/14 was invalid partly on the basis that it was inconsistent with s. 3 of UNTAET Regulation 1999/1, which provided that the 'applicable law in East Timor' was subject to international human rights law. While the

[47] La'o Hamutuk, 'Post UNTAET Challenges', 9.

[48] Unreported, District Court of Dili, Judge Perreira dos Santos, 17 May 2000; Putusan Nomor: 01/Pen.Pra/2000/PD.DIL. For an excellent discussion and analysis of this case, see Linton, 'Rising from the Ashes', 140ff. See also Trenkov-Wermuth, *United Nations Justice*, 121–2.

[49] Linton, 'Rising from the Ashes', 141.

judge may have been correct in this particular respect, he failed to understand that s. 3 was not intended to guide or constrain the enactment of all future law, such as the regulations passed by UNTAET. Instead, it was intended to act as a filter for all *past* legislation, namely Indonesian legislation that applied during the occupation. This meant that, strictly speaking, law enacted by UNTAET did not need to comply with international human rights law. As a consequence the judgment was ignored. The *Alves* case underlined the poor model provided by the UN administration in regard to the rule of law: here UNTAET was attempting to use retroactive legislation to validate a period of detention that was unlawful under the Indonesian Code and that appeared to violate Articles 9 and 14 of the *International Covenant on Civil and Political Rights* which set out the right to liberty and fair trial. This model was arguably dangerous in light of the fact that most Timorese leaders were part of the military resistance to Indonesian rule, a culture which, broadly speaking, does not generate respect for the idea of dispersing and limiting power according to a superior law. The focus of resistance culture is on subverting state structures of power and law rather than on upholding them.

One commentator asserts that following the *Alves* case, the executive attempted to interfere with the judiciary. Citing a personal communication with the presiding judge, Dionisio Babo-Soares claims:

> Days later, the head of the Justice Department intervened and warned the presiding judge to comply with UNTAET's rules of the game and not to repeat the same mistake in the future.[50]

If true, this precedent perverted the concept of the rule of law and the separation of powers because it constituted interference with the manner in which the courts interpret and apply the law. More broadly, it created a very weak model for Timor's future independent governments.

3.2 UNTAET and local customary law

UNTAET was caught unprepared in regard to the issue of local customary law which did not register on UNTAET's radar until well into its mission. Under the mandate given by Security Council Resolution 1272,

[50] Babo-Soares, *Law and Order*, 14.

UNTAET began the process of rebuilding Timor-Leste's formal legal system with its first regulation in late November 1999, setting out that the 'applicable law in East Timor' was the Indonesian law that operated prior to 25 October 1999, subject to its own regulations and international human rights law.[51] A few days later a third regulation set out the powers of the TA to appoint judges.[52] In March 2000 the TA issued Regulation 2000/11 for the organisation of courts in Timor-Leste, stating in s. 1 that: 'judicial authority in East Timor shall be *exclusively* vested in courts that are established by law and composed of judges who are appointed to these courts in accordance with UNTAET Regulation No 1999/3'.[53] Subsequently UNTAET established four district courts in Dili, Bacau, Suai and Oecusse, an arrangement mirroring pre-UNTAET administration,[54] with a Court of Appeal at the apex.[55] These initiatives attracted admiration from commentators at the time. For example, in 2001 Babo-Soares praised 'the success of UNTAET in laying the foundation of a legal infrastructure which has attracted the confidence of the population' and he called the justice sector a 'prestigious asset for East Timor'.[56]

[51] This was the date of UNTAET's establishment. Indonesian law was to apply in so far as it did not conflict with standards set out in the *Universal Declaration on Human Rights* and the six core UN human rights treaties: see ss. 2 and 3 of UNTAET Regulation No 1999/1, On the Authority of the Transitional Administration in East Timor. The six core treaties are: the 1966 International Covenant on Civil and Political Rights and its Protocols; 1966 International Covenant on Economic, Social and Cultural Rights; 1965 International Convention for the Elimination of All Forms of Racial Discrimination; 1979 Convention on the Elimination of Discrimination Against Women; 1984 Convention Against Torture and Other Cruel, Inhuman or Degrading Treatment; 1989 Convention on the Rights of the Child. In addition, six Indonesian statutes were declared inapplicable and capital punishment was abolished.

[52] UNTAET Regulation No 1999/3, On the Establishment of a Transitional Judicial Service Commission. For analysis of the establishment of East Timor's formal criminal legal system, see Linton, 'Rising from the Ashes'.

[53] Emphasis added. UNTAET subsequently established District Administrations in the thirteen districts established by Indonesia and created sub-district offices numbering sixty, each of which contain about eight villages.

[54] UNTAET Regulation No 2000/11 initially stipulated the establishment of eight district courts (s. 7) but this was later amended to four courts by UNTAET Regulation No 2000/14 (s. 2).

[55] East Timor's highest court is the Supreme Court of Justice but under Art. 164 of the Constitution, the Court of Appeal can exercise its functions until such time as it is established.

[56] Babo-Soares, *Law and Order*, 19.

Despite the manifold demands on its resources, UNTAET clearly gave some thought to the establishment of Timor-Leste's formal legal system. However, the Administration believed it was building the justice system from scratch. UNTAET's Acting Principal Legal Advisor from this period, Hans-jörg Strohmeyer, writes that the 'empty shell' metaphor was often used in UNTAET's early days in Timor-Leste.[57] While there was awareness that some areas, such as education, only needed 'resuscitation', there was the belief that a new legal framework had to be built in order to 'avoid a law vacuum'.[58] Despite this, Strohmeyer recognised that the viability of the new state legal system depended on 'the integration of customary law and traditional forms of dispute resolution'.[59] Overall, however, such beliefs were not transformed into policy and there is no evidence of any UNTAET regulation or policy regarding the role of local customary law and how it could assist in maintaining law and order.[60] Possibly this was due to the initial dearth of detailed knowledge of the local justice systems and how they function.[61]

On the ground, the result of this initial UN policy vacuum in regard to the role of local customary law was that a range of approaches was used in relation to local law by various UN staff. For example, some UN Civilian Police officers used local law, while others refused to do so.[62]

57 Strohmeyer, 'Making Multilateral Interventions', 109. Other reports use similar language that is potentially misleading and could be misread as suggesting a *terra nullius* doctrine. For example, the description 'complete legal vacuum' is used in the report by King's College, London. However, only a few paragraphs later there is discussion of 'the continued widespread reliance on traditional or customary justice mechanisms': King's College London, *A Review of Peace Operations*, [217, 219].

58 Strohmeyer, 'Making Multilateral Interventions', 109, 111. It is more correct to say that a legal vacuum existed in regard to the treatment of serious crimes.

59 Strohmeyer, 'Building a New Judiciary', 271.

60 There is some evidence that by the end of 2000, UNTAET had developed a proposal for using local customary law in resolving land disputes. Fitzpatrick, who spent three months with UNTAET's Land and Property Unit, states: 'In general terms, a three-tier system is proposed: traditional processes, then mediation and, failing that, judicial determination': 'Re-establishing Land Titles', 158.

61 The first detailed report on local law came out in 2001. See Mearns, *Variations on a Theme*. See also Mearns, *Looking Both Ways*; Hohe and Nixon, *Reconciling Justice*, 40. Presumably this initial policy vacuum resulted from a combination of a lack of resources and poor communication channels between the local community and the UN administration. See also Zaum, *The Sovereignty Paradox*, 202–5.

62 See Hohe and Nixon, *Reconciling Justice*, 40. Note that from early 2000 onwards, UNTAET showed interest in traditional mechanisms of conflict resolution in its approach to policing: see UN Doc S/2000/738 (26 July 2000) *Report of the Secretary-General on the United Nations Transitional Administration in East Timor (for the period 27 January–26 July 2000)*, [46].

This led to confusion: while locals were uncertain as to which law was applicable, UN personnel were unable either to distinguish local customary law from other structures or to identify customary law leaders on a consistent basis.[63] In January 2001, UNTAET's Language and Training Unit issued a booklet entitled *Working in East Timor: Culture, Customs and Capacity Building* in which a detailed account was given of local customary law.[64] According to Hohe and Nixon, this emergence of interest in local customary law related not simply to law and order but was largely due to pressure relating to land disputes.[65]

In the remote enclave of Oecusse, an initiative was developed by the UN district administration to divert minor crimes from the state legal system to a modified form of local customary law.[66] UNTAET headquarters apparently gave the Oecusse Diversionary Justice Programme 'conditional and partial' approval to operate a model that strove for consistency with human rights norms and emphasised community service in the place of exchange of livestock and other material wealth, which is the norm of local customary law.[67] This hybrid programme operated until early 2002 when a guideline was passed discouraging the diversion of matters from the state legal system.[68]

In regard to land disputes, UNTAET organised for a system of mediation on an interim basis. It encouraged local officials to assist parties to reach interim agreements on principles such as non-resort to violence, and to negotiate 'temporary use agreements'.[69] This system of mediation operated on an informal basis and presumably it worked to aid the maintenance of law and order and to divert cases from the courts.

On a technical level, Strohmeyer observed the difficulty in many regions of distinguishing 'customary law from other, more recent, structures for resolving disputes outside the formal court system (including

[63] Strohmeyer, 'Building a New Judiciary', 277.

[64] In September 2001, almost two years into UNTAET's mission, a workshop was held to discuss the manner in which local customary law could be used to complement the formal justice system: UN Doc S/2001/983 (22 October 2001) *Report of the Secretary General on the United Nations Transitional Administration in East Timor (for the period from 25 July to 15 October 2001)*, [18].

[65] Hohe and Nixon, *Reconciling Justice*, 41. In the drafting of the Constitution, this question of land ownership and management appears to have been one of the main drivers for the inclusion of the recognition of customary 'norms' in Art. 2(4).

[66] Hohe and Nixon describe this programme: *Reconciling Justice*, 47–9. See also Nixon, *Justice and Governance*, 188–9.

[67] Ibid. [68] Ibid. [69] Fitzpatrick, *Land Claims*, 177.

Indonesian, CNRT, or Falintil structures)'.[70] For Strohmeyer, a further complication was 'the possible bias of traditional justice against "marginalised" groups such as women, children or minorities'.[71] Such bias ran counter to the guarantees of non-discrimination found in international human rights law which UNTAET introduced in its first regulation.

From a broad perspective, UNTAET may not have been in a position to give state recognition to aspects of local customary law given that it was a foreign and transitional administrator. Its focus necessarily lay with setting up structures that would assist Timor reach independence and assist the state to function in the short term; it was envisaged that Timor's elected leaders would enjoy the legitimacy to pass legislation for the medium-to-long-term functioning of the state.

3.3 UNTAET and international law

UNTAET's ostensible concern regarding the legitimacy of enacting laws with long-term consequences did not prevent it from introducing two strands of international law, largely for the purpose of assisting the state in establishing the rule of law. The first strand, international human rights law, was brought in so as to erase the discriminatory and substandard aspects of Indonesian law and to herald a new era. The UN wanted the people of East Timor to 'embrace a national political culture based on respect for human rights and accountability'.[72] For example, Strohmeyer declared in 2001:

> UNTAET is ... attempting to mark a radical departure from the culture of the judiciary which existed under Indonesian rule by committing the new judiciary to international human rights standards.[73]

UNTAET aimed 'to establish a credible system of justice in which fundamental human rights are respected'.[74] International human rights

[70] Strohmeyer, 'Building a New Judiciary', 277. The National Council of Timorese Resistance (CNRT) was established in early 1999 as an umbrella organisation for the different nationalistic political parties in order to assist East Timor in its transition to a democratically elected government. Falintil was the armed wing of Fretilin, the main resistance party.

[71] Ibid.

[72] UN Doc S/2000/1105 (21 November 2000) *Report of the Security Council Mission to East Timor and Indonesia (9–17 November 2000)*, [29].

[73] Strohmeyer, 'Building a New Judiciary', 267.

[74] UN Doc S/2000/738 (26 July 2000) *Report of the Secretary General on the United Nations Transitional Administration in East Timor (for the period 27 January – 26 July 2000)*, [68].

standards were thus being held up as central to the project of building the rule of law in East Timor. The second strand was international criminal law, which was introduced through the establishment of the Special Panels for Serious Crimes (SPSC), an arm of the Dili District Court empowered by UNTAET Regulation 2000/15 to hear a list of crimes similar to that found in the *Statute for the International Criminal Court.*[75]

One challenge in introducing international law in the post-conflict context is the fact that international standards are likely to invoke values that are considered alien by many people. A local lawyer interviewed during the UNTAET period expresses this latter concern thus:

> The UN have a mandate to provide stability, but they should not just impose these human rights laws from New York and Geneva. People felt strange having these laws imposed. The UN should have consulted with the communities to ask the leaders what ideas they had about implementing UN laws.[76]

This comment questions the legitimacy of UNTAET's introduction of international human rights standards on the basis of the lack of consultation with the community.[77]

3.4 UNTAET's legacy

At the end of UNTAET's period of administration, a report by King's College London stated that: 'it is widely acknowledged that the fragility of the rule of law remains one of the greatest challenges for East Timor after UNTAET's departure'.[78] It further observed that:

> access to and awareness of the transitional court system remain minimal for many in East Timor, raising real questions about the relevance of the processes that were put in place by UNTAET. … As a result, many people still have no contact with the formal justice system and rely on customary law structures.[79]

[75] Established in June 2000, the Special Panels for Serious Crimes exercised jurisdiction over genocide, war crimes, crimes against humanity and torture. In addition, it had jurisdiction over the 'serious crimes' of murder and sexual offences committed between 1 January 1999 and 25 October 1999.

[76] Quoted by Hohe and Nixon, *Reconciling Justice*, 57.

[77] On the ground UNTAET may have had little opportunity to consult with communities before issuing Regulation 1999/1 but the point remains that the UN simply assumed that these international legal norms would contribute to the building of the rule of law in East Timor and hence be acceptable to the population.

[78] King's College London, *A Review of Peace Operations*, [214].

[79] Ibid., [252].

The impact of UNTAET's attempt to build a state legal system and establish the rule of law can also be partly measured by the comment of some local village heads in 2002 to the effect that they believed there was 'no law at present'.[80] Thus the first phase of the formation of Timor-Leste's legal system was marked by three things: failure to penetrate much beyond the capital Dili, little consideration of the complexities of legal pluralism and an inconsistent and weak model of the rule of law.

At the end of 2000, Xanana Gusmão, when speaking to a local audience, expressed concern regarding the 'critical acculturation to standards that hundreds of international experts try to convey to the East Timorese'.[81] After discussing the values of democracy and gender equality, Gusmão said:

> what seems absurd is that *we absorb standards just to pretend we look like a democratic society and please our masters of independence*. What concerns me is that *non-critical absorption of (universal) standards* … [and] that the East Timorese may become detached from their reality and, above all, *try to copy something* which is not yet clearly understood by them.[82]

Gusmão uses a different tune less than two years later, while speaking as the President of Timor-Leste at an international conference, when he declared:

> We were lucky to become independent in an environment in which the entire world, the people, and above all the government, are able to use a common language: democracy, human rights, civil society, good governance, anti-corruption policy, social justice … *in summary, the rule of law*.[83]

He then went on to explain that the Timor-Leste Constitution proclaims a 'sovereign and independent state, based on the rule of law'. These two speeches reveal the ambivalence of Gusmão and other Timorese leaders regarding the 'universal standards' promoted by UNTAET and their understanding that it is necessary to pay lip service to these standards within the international community. A sceptic might say that they provide evidence that UNTAET's legacy was that Timor's independence leaders learnt to 'copy' the 'common language' of the rule of law in order

[80] Mearns, *Looking Both Ways*, 38.
[81] 2000 New Year's Speech quoted in Charlesworth and Woods, 'Women and Human Rights', 335.
[82] Ibid. (emphasis added).
[83] 8 November 2002, Bangkok, quoted in Gusmão, *Timor Lives!*, 93 (emphasis added).

to legitimise the state and 'please [its] masters of independence', the international community.

4. The 'mother law' and its sources of legitimacy

Dubbed the 'mother law', Timor-Leste's Constitution was formally drafted within the very short timeframe of six months.[84] Before this six-month period, the Fretilin party had drafted a constitution, the final version of which differs little from this Fretilin draft because Fretilin won a majority of the seats in the drafting body, the Constituent Assembly.[85] This majority meant that unlike the ANC, Fretilin 'did not need to build consensus or compromise for the constitution to be adopted'.[86] Nevertheless, some semblance of public consultation was conducted, albeit possibly as a 'public relations' event.[87] Prior to the election of the Constituent Assembly in August 2001, the UN conducted the first set of public consultations in July 2001. In late February 2002, the Constituent Assembly also conducted public consultations in relation to its penultimate draft, publicly rejecting the UN consultations on the basis that they were not conducted by a body with democratic legitimacy.[88] In early March 2002, the limited consultation and the lack of a feeling of local ownership over the process drew the attention of the UN High Commissioner for Human Rights, who commented:

> [I]n emphasising the 'representative democratic' model of government, the work of the Assembly itself seems to minimise the right of individuals in East Timor to participate in political life by contributing to political debate

[84] See Regan, 'Constitution-Making in East Timor', 39; Baltazar, 'Constitution Drafting Process', 1.

[85] The Carter Center reports: 'Observers suspected that the Assembly did not intend to make any significant changes to the constitutional draft, and ultimately they did not': *The East Timor Political and Election Observation Project Final Report*, 45. Note that four other parties also submitted draft constitutions when the assembly began its process but that Fretilin's draft was chosen as a result of its majority.

[86] Aucoin and Brandt, 'East Timor's Constitutional Passage', 258.

[87] Brandt writes that some members of the Constituent Assembly privately maintained that the consultation process was an exercise in public relations only: Brandt, *Constitutional Assistance*, 17.

[88] Aucoin and Brandt, 'East Timor's Constitutional Passage', 262–3. Baltazar comments that the members of the Constitutional Commissions were concerned that the Constituent Assembly would not read their reports and hence requested to participate in the sessions so as to brief the Assembly: Baltazar, 'Constitution Drafting Process', 5. The Assembly never made the results of the second local consultations available to the public.

> surrounding the Constitution. … [T]here is a popular perception that, to a larger extent, the drafting process has focussed on the prepared drafts of political parties, rather than incorporating comments or suggestions from ongoing consultations or the public hearings. As a result, there appears to be a limited sense of ownership of the process amongst civil society and already a questioning of the responsiveness of the Assembly to its constituents.[89]

While local consultation was not considered a priority, the Constitution shows levels of influence emanating from the international sphere, specifically the United Nations, the Constitutions of Timor's lusophone kin, Portugal and Mozambique, and the resistance and diaspora politics of the Fretilin party, which relates to the Cold War divide. Little influence from local norms and traditions is apparent.

The Timor-Leste Constitution invokes the rule of law three times, twice in a mirror image of the Mozambican Constitution, which in turn draws on the Portuguese Constitution. The rule of law is first stated in Timor's constitutional preamble, which provides:

> Fully conscious of the need to build a democratic and institutional culture proper of *a State based on the rule of law* where respect for the Constitution [própria de um Estado de Direito onde o respeito pela Constituição], for the laws and for democratically elected institutions constitute its unquestionable foundation;[90]

Second, it is articulated as a foundational concept in Article 1:[91]

> The Democratic Republic of East Timor is a democratic, sovereign, independent and unitary *State based on the rule of law* [é um Estado de

[89] UN Doc E/CN.4/2002/39 (1 March 2002) *Situation of Human Rights – Report of the High Commissioner*, [46]. The report continues: 'there were serious concerns regarding the extent to which the Assembly members were receptive to the submissions of those outside the political party members'.

[90] Emphasis added. All three lusophone preambles show the influence of socialist constitutional models exemplified in the constitutions of China and the Soviet Union. However, they differ from these two models of China and the Soviet Union in that they are narratives of a new beginning based on the modern political values of democracy, equality and the rule of law. Mozambique is one of a number of African countries (such as Angola and Guinea-Bissau) to pursue the Soviet model of constitutionalism: see Serapaio and El Khawas, *Mozambique in the Twentieth Century*.

[91] Emphasis added. Article 2 of the Portuguese Constitution provides: 'The Portuguese Republic is a democratic *State based on the rule of law* [A República Portuguesa é um Estado de direito democrático], the sovereignty of the people, plurality of both democratic expression and democratic political organization as well as respect for and the safeguarding of fundamental rights and freedoms; its aim is to achieve economic, social, and cultural democracy and to push participatory democracy further' (emphasis added).

> direito democrático, soberano, independente e unitário], the will of the people and the respect for the dignity of the human person.[92]

The principle of constitutionalism is set out in Art. 2,[93] which is textually very close to Art. 3 of Portugal's Constitution.[94] Third, the rule of law is articulated as a state objective in Art. 6. While the list of state objectives in Art. 6 is, on the whole, fairly similar to those set out in the Portuguese and Mozambican Constitutions,[95] the Timorese list is extended to reiterate the rule of law.[96] This divergence from the two lusophone models can perhaps be explained by the influence of other actors such as the United Nations or the World Bank and the strong desire of the newly independent state to affirm its legitimacy and sovereignty at the international level. Overall, however, most of the machinery provisions of Timor-Leste's Constitution have been 'cut and pasted' from the constitutions of its lusophone friends with few modifications.

4.1 *International norms and local norms*

Overall, international norms are strongly articulated in the Constitution. In entrenching a Bill of Rights, Timor-Leste's Constitution incorporates most parts of the *UDHR*[97] and its Bill of Rights is extensive, including a number of provisions protecting due process.[98] Timor's leaders, particularly its then Foreign Minister,[99] José Ramos-Horta, were eager

92 Emphasis added.

93 Article 2, entitled 'Sovereignty and constitutionality', provides: '1. Sovereignty rests with the people, who shall exercise it in the manner and form laid down in the Constitution. 2. The State shall be subject to the Constitution and to the law. 3. The validity of the laws and other actions of the State and local Government depends upon their compliance with the Constitution.'

94 This is with the exception of Art. 2(4).

95 Generally Art. 6 mirrors provisions in Portugal's Constitution (Art. 9) and Mozambique's Constitution (Art. 6). Note that the listing of a state's goals is a feature of socialist constitutions. See Go, 'Modelling the State', 558.

96 Article 6 provides: 'The fundamental objectives of the State shall be: ... b) To guarantee and promote fundamental rights and freedoms of the citizens and the respect for the principles of the democratic State based on the rule of law'.

97 For a detailed analysis of this Bill of Rights in relation to the international bill of rights, see Charlesworth, 'The Constitution of East Timor', 325.

98 See Arts. 31–4, 136.

99 At this time, Ramos-Horta was the East Timor Transitional Administration Cabinet Member for Foreign Affairs.

for Timor's Constitution to be considered 'very progressive' on the world stage.[100] Ramos-Horta and other community leaders such as Bishop Belo were proud in announcing that the Constitution's Bill of Rights was to be interpreted in accordance with the *UDHR*.[101] Bishop Belo stated: 'It is our dream to build a society founded on the values enshrined in the *UDHR*. These are the values that guided and inspired our struggle for independence.'[102] At this time Ramos-Horta added that on independence, Timor-Leste intended to accede to 'the greatest possible number of international human rights treaties', a promise that was fulfilled shortly after independence.[103]

In addition to the extensive Bill of Rights, Article 9 of the Constitution elevates international law, as a source of law, to a position that is superior to the laws made by Timor-Leste's own Parliament. Article 9(1) provides: 'The legal system of East Timor shall adopt the general or customary principles of international law.' Article 9(3) states that the rules of international treaties approved by the state are empowered to trump internal state laws. The provision leaves the relationship between customary international law and state law vague but it appears that this mechanism may in some cases enable the executive to bypass the Parliament in introducing new law. This constitutional embrace of international law appears to be connected not only to the desire for Timor-Leste to be part of the international community but also to the belief that the standards set out by international law can assist the state in establishing the rule of law. However, a closer look at the UNTAET experience of introducing and implementing international law would have dispelled this belief.

Local norms are less visible in the Constitution; it makes minimal attempt to reach out and connect with local traditions. Section 2(4) states: 'The State shall recognise and value the norms and customs of

[100] Ministry of Foreign Affairs and Cooperation, 'Ramos-Horta Addresses the UN Security Council' (30 January 2002).

[101] Art. 23. In this it echoes Article 16 of the Portuguese Constitution.

[102] 'To Forge a Future, Timor Needs Justice for the Past', *Sydney Morning Herald*, 28 August 2001. According to the Executive Summary of the Constitutional Commissions, 'it was widely felt that these should be based on the universal principles of the declaration of the United Nations Charter of 1948' (i.e. the *UDHR*): Constitutional Affairs Branch, Office of Political Affairs, UNTAET, *Executive Summary of the Constitutional Commission Public Hearings*, 8.

[103] Ministry of Foreign Affairs and Cooperation, 'Ramos Horta Addresses the UN Security Council' (30 January 2002).

East Timor that are not contrary to the Constitution and to any legislation dealing specifically with customary law.'[104] From examining the drafts of the Constitution it appears that the recognition of local customary 'norms' in Article 2(4) was an afterthought and the provision is an enabling clause that fails to give unambiguous recognition to local customary *law* as part of the state's applicable law. The ambiguity arises from the drafters' use of the expression 'customary law' at the end of the provision although 'law' is not used in the first part of the provision in relation to the state's recognition.

This minimal attention to local customary law is noteworthy given that the first set of popular consultations indicated that there was strong local support for aspects of local customary law to be included in the Constitution.[105] The Executive Summary of the UN consultations states:

> There was wide support for the continued use of traditional forms of law making and law-enforcement to complement conventional laws. The role of the 'Adat' (unwritten customary law) in relation to the state justice system was a common topic. The people, in general, emphasised that the preservation of 'Adat' should be reflected in the future constitution.[106]

The drafters of the Constitution appear to have made a conscious choice when entrenching international norms and ignoring local norms. International norms such as social and gender equality, as well as the rule of law, have been given primacy over local *adat* norms, which, amongst other things, favour authority based on descent, gender and age.[107] The following section offers some explanations for why these latter norms were not considered relevant to the constitution of a modern state.

104 The Portuguese version reads: '4. O Estado reconhece e valoriza as normas e os usos costumeiros de Timor-Leste que não contrariem a Constituição e a legislação que trate especialmente do direito costumeiro.'

105 Aucoin and Brandt, 'East Timor's Constitutional Passage', 262.

106 See Constitutional Affairs Branch, Office of Political Affairs, UNTAET, *Executive Summary of the Constitutional Commission Public Hearings*. The Executive Summary sets out sixteen issues that were clearly a concern at the local level such as the flag, the name of the country as well as more substantive issues such as language, defence and security, the structure and system of government, and human rights. The Constitutional Assembly ignored the results of this consultation on the ground it was conducted by unelected members of the UN.

107 Hicks, 'Community and Nation-State in East Timor', 14.

4.2 Political dynamics of the resistance and the diaspora

The sidestepping of local customary law in the Timor-Leste Constitution can perhaps be traced to the political dynamics of the Fretilin party, which operated in resistance mode for a quarter of a century, was motivated during the Cold War mainly by Marxist-Leninist ideology and was financed by Marxist regimes. As the main resistance party, Fretilin looked to the international sphere for condemnation of Indonesia's invasion and continuing occupation. In this sphere it sought to establish, partly through legal argument, that Indonesia's invasion lacked legitimacy and that its occupation government failed to respect the rights of the Timorese population and the rule of law broadly.[108] In regard to the rule of law during the occupation, the International Commission of Jurists repeatedly investigated and publicised the absence of the rule of law in Indonesia at this time.[109] During this period, many of Timor's leaders spent years in exile in Portugal and Mozambique, when both countries were ruled by Marxist governments. One consequence of this exile was that these Timorese leaders lost a degree of connection with local values back in their homeland.

For example, Fretilin party leader Mari Alkitiri spent his exile in Mozambique at the time that it gained its independence. During these early years of independence, Mozambique's ruling party, Frelimo, took an antitraditionalist stance, seeing modernisation as crucial to ending all forms of discrimination, whether colonial or traditional.[110] The Government attempted to delegitimise traditional authorities by stripping them of their power and replacing them and customary law with popular tribunals.[111] Another Fretilin Minister, Ana Pessoa, who also spent exile in Mozambique and later became the Justice Minister in the East Timor Transitional Administration, reportedly dismissed customary law in 2004 by saying 'we're not savages and we won't use customary law'.[112] Overall, Frelimo is considered to have been Fretilin's 'mentor', so it is unsurprising that these attitudes toward traditional authorities and customary law were

[108] See for example the annual resolutions on East Timor adopted by the UN General Assembly between 1975 and 1982 and the resolutions adopted by the UN Commission on Human Rights in 1993 and 1997. See Budiardjo and Liong, *The War Against East Timor*, 150–3; International Commission of Jurists, *Ruler's Law*.

[109] Ibid. [110] Hall and Young, *Confronting Leviathan* 65

[111] Lubkemann et al., 'Dilemmas of Articulation', 20.

[112] Interview quoted in Nixon, *Justice and Governance*, 192.

echoed by Fretilin leaders. Indeed, these views on traditional authorities are similar to those of the ANC before it was forced to compromise and readjust its stance as a result of complex power dynamics during South Africa's constitutional dispensation discussed in Chapter 4.

After East Timor's first democratic election in August 2001, Timor's resistance leaders were able to draw on an additional source of power apart from their role in the resistance, namely, democracy. This democratic legitimacy effectively allowed Timor's leaders to bypass a more traditional source of leadership in Timor: local customary law relating to ancestry.[113] Given that Timor's leaders did not derive their power from the path set out by local customary law, and they foresaw that such law could have the potential to undermine their democratic role, it is hardly surprising that the drafters chose to sidestep the question of giving local customary law formal recognition. Instead they made a vague gesture towards recognising local 'norms and customs' in Article 2(4), which has no impact on the existing sources of applicable law. Indeed, there is some anecdotal evidence that on the opening day of the constitutional drafting process, Fretilin leader Alkitiri objected to the performance of a ceremony by local customary leaders to hand the keys of the capital to the elected Constituent Assembly. Alkitiri, who was to become Timor's first Prime Minister, possibly objected to the ceremony on the grounds that it would imply parallel power structures where in his view there was only one legitimate power structure, the democratically elected Constituent Assembly.[114] Alkitiri's objection is interesting in light of the fact that the resistance movement itself previously operated as a parallel authority structure that aimed to subvert the state. In its new life as the governing body, the former resistance movement, in particular the Fretilin party, has tended towards strong centralisation of power. However, in contrast to the aim of the resistance movement, it is not apparent that Timor's customary power structures were attempting to do more than complement the power of the state through performing the key ceremony.

This is not to say that Fretilin has lacked interest in tradition altogether. To the contrary, Hohe argues that Fretilin played upon tradition in its election campaign leading up to the August 2001 election.

113 Hohe, 'Totem Polls', 81.

114 Personal communication from Annemarie Devereux, August 2007. In 2001 Devereux was a legal adviser in UNTAET's Human Rights Unit.

She claims that it manipulated indigenous values and symbols, as well as the history of the resistance fight, to gain election.[115]

Overall it is curious that some former resistance leaders such as Alkitiri failed to acknowledge that parallel structures of authority do not disappear or lose their local legitimacy simply because the state refuses to give them recognition. As the resistance movement itself proved, this refusal by the state can often work to strengthen these parallel structures and allow deep legal pluralism to flourish.

4.3 Tension between local norms and constitutional human rights

Another possible reason why Timor's leaders have been reluctant to recognise local customary law is that such law may come into conflict with the human rights standards entrenched in the Constitution, which may in turn undermine efforts to establish the rule of law. It is worth noting that around the time of the constitutional drafting process in 2001, Amnesty International issued a report expressing disquiet over the use of 'non-judicial mechanisms of justice' in various districts and the impact of these mechanisms on the human rights of the vulnerable, particularly women and children. Amnesty International was concerned that such mechanisms would undermine law and order and the development of the state's legal institutions.[116] It is possible that this negative report influenced the decision not to recognise local customary law.

In 2001 the Constituent Assembly was alerted to the potential conflict between local customary law and human rights standards by a network of women's groups who attempted to influence the drafting process through submitting a petition entitled *The Women's Charter*, which set out a list of rights deemed important for women's equality.[117] Through the petition the women's groups requested that the Constitution regulate systems of local customary law and its impact on women. Article Eight of *The Women's Charter*, which carried 8,000 signatures, stated:

> The Constitution must guarantee equal rights to inheritance, and regulate the dowry system to prevent violence against women. Women must be guaranteed participation in traditional decision-making processes.

[115] Hohe, 'Totem Polls', 70. [116] Amnesty International, *East Timor*, 41.

[117] The Charter was prepared by the Gender and Constitutional Working Group. It appears in (2001) 2 *La'o Hamutuk Bulletin* 2. Note that versions of some of these Charter rights were incorporated into the Constitution but many have weak enforcement mechanisms.

This concern appears to have been ignored by the Constituent Assembly. Possibly the view was that it was unnecessary for the state to regulate local customary law given that such law had no formal state recognition and human rights guarantees were to be entrenched in the Constitution. According to Babo-Soares, all parties in the Constituent Assembly unanimously approved provisions dealing with human rights 'despite fears that traditional groups might refuse to back them, since women and children have a unique place in traditional customary law'.[118] Nevertheless, the failure of the Constituent Assembly to address the concern of *The Women's Charter* in relation to women's participation in local customary law ignores the concrete impact that such law can have on women's lives.

There was some pressure from within the Constituent Assembly itself in regard to the future role of local customary leaders. Some of the minor parties involved in the drafting process, such as KOTA, the traditionalist party with two seats, suggested the Constitution set up an Upper House of traditional leaders (called *liurais*),[119] possibly in a similar vein to South Africa's advisory upper house called the National House of Traditional Leaders. The form in which this body was proposed is uncertain,[120] but it appears to have been dismissed with little, if any, debate. Timor-Leste's local customary leaders were unable to mobilise much pressure to bear on this proposal, partly because, unlike their South African counterparts, they had neither a history of institutional standing nor an organised and vocal lobby group.[121]

The decision of the Constituent Assembly not to include state recognition of local customary law in Timor-Leste's Constitution is surprising given that most of the recently drafted constitutions in the Asia-Pacific region do incorporate some form of recognition of local customary

[118] Babo-Soares, 'Drafting a Constitution', 27.

[119] Nixon, 'Indonesia West Timor', 177. KOTA stands for Klibur Oan Timor Asuwain (Association of Timorese Heroes).

[120] It is not clear whether the proposed body would function along the lines of the pre-1958 House of Lords in the United Kingdom, or be of a more limited nature like a Council of Traditional Leaders in South Africa.

[121] While the Indonesian Government conscripted many traditional leaders to assist in governing local districts, this did not take place on the same uniform institutional basis as in South Africa under apartheid.

law.[122] The drafting of Timor-Leste's Constitution was guided partly by the Constitution of Mozambique which does not include such recognition despite the fact that such law exists in this African state.

However, the drafters did not reject outright the possibility of future legislation recognising and monitoring local customary law: Article 2(4) of the Constitution mentions 'any legislation dealing specifically with customary law'. In addition, there is a curious provision in the part of the Constitution that deals with the structure of the state legal system, which sets a path by which local customary mechanisms can be incorporated. Article 123 provides:

Article 123 Categories of courts

1. There shall be the following categories of courts in the Democratic Republic of East Timor:
   a) The Supreme Court of Justice and other courts of law;
   b) The High Administrative, Tax and Audit Court ...;
   c) Military Courts. ...

5. The law may institutionalise means and ways for the non-jurisdictional resolution of disputes. (emphasis added)

One interpretation of para. 5 is that it is an opening for legislation to allow a formal engagement with local systems of dispute resolution, which are clearly beyond the present jurisdiction of the formal court system. 'Non-jurisdictional' appears to refer to non-state law and thus this opaque provision allows for a degree of state law pluralism.

[122] Constitutional recognition of customary law has been chosen by most Pacific Island states. While some have chosen to assign customary law a rank in the hierarchy of laws, others have left this question somewhat vague. Only the *Tongan Constitution of 1875* makes no express mention of custom. In all other Pacific states, the written law expressly provides for customary law to be used in relation to land disputes. In the Solomon Islands, Samoa, Tuvalu, Kiribati, Nauru and Vanuatu, written law provides for the broader application of customary law. See, e.g., the *Constitution of the Solomon Islands*, s. 76 and sch. 3, [3(1)] which states 'subject to this paragraph, customary law shall have effect as part of the law of Solomon Islands'. Paragraph 3(2) states that [3(1)] 'shall not apply in respect of any customary law that is, and to the extent that it is, inconsistent with the Constitution or an Act of Parliament'. In the *1975 Papua New Guinea Constitution*, customary law is recognised as part of the underlying law by Sched. 2 in conjunction with s. 20 of the Constitution and the *Underlying Law Act 2000*. See New Zealand Law Commission, *Converging Currents*, App. 4; Corrin and Paterson, *South Pacific Law*, Ch. 3; Jessep and Regan, 'Developing a Coherent Underlying Law', Chs 9 and 10.

4.4 *Questioned legitimacy*

The process of drafting a constitution is in large part about establishing a state's legitimacy, particularly when the state is newly founded. It is thus essential that the constitution itself be widely considered to be legitimate. In the case of Timor-Leste's Constitution, it appears that the emphasis lay on establishing the state's *external* legitimacy, its legitimacy as a sovereign state in the international community. The large-scale importation of international norms into the Constitution shows that the process was weighted heavily towards establishing this external legitimacy. The Constitution's preamble shows the continuing power of this preoccupation in that it is a narrative of the past resistance movement rather than a map for the country's future. Both this recent past and the international norms invoked by the Constitution constitute the main sources of legitimacy for the country's new leaders. Little consideration was given to the Constitution's *internal*, local legitimacy in the second public consultation, this time conducted by the Constituent Assembly, or in the drafting process. This was simply assumed. Hence the side-stepping of local customary law was not considered controversial amongst Timor's national leaders. It is also possible that many of the drafters of the Constitution did not understand the extent of legal pluralism.

Following the enactment of the Constitution in May 2002, a few surveys were conducted in order to gauge the degree to which the population understands and uses state law and local customary law. The first large-scale survey was conducted six months after independence, in late 2002, by the Asia Foundation and involved more than 1,000 citizens across all the districts.[123] It found that *adat* rated much higher than state courts in terms of confidence in the institution and comfort in dealing with it, with language difficulties, cost and inaccessibility being cited as relevant factors militating against use of the courts.[124] A third of the interviewees said that they would avoid using the state court system if possible.[125] A fifth believed that there were times when it would be reasonable to take the law into their own hands.[126] The second study,

[123] Asia Foundation, *Law and Justice in East Timor*. The survey results partly reflect local perception of the manner in which UNTAET administered the legal system.

[124] Those most comfortable with the *adat* system are the older generation, are less educated and live in the more remote regions. In contrast, those less comfortable are the more educated, younger and tend to live in or near the capital. Ibid., 49.

[125] Ibid., 43. [126] Ibid.

conducted by Avocats Sans Frontières about two years later, was smaller, more limited in regional scope and focused on access to legal aid.[127] It found that although most interviewees recognised that only state courts have the formal power to hear cases,[128] almost half generally sought help from local authorities, such as the village head and council of elders, rather than the assistance of a lawyer or the state courts to resolve a dispute.[129] Of this group, a third had used local authorities to resolve disputes while only 12 per cent had had any contact with the state court system.[130] Interviewees believed state courts were not functioning well, citing delay, cost and inaccessibility as factors that made them reluctant to use the state court system. However, the survey showed that preference for one system over another depended on whether the matter was considered serious or minor, with the courts being the preferred forum for the former and the *adat* system preferred for the latter.[131]

These two surveys indicate that Timorese people negotiate and value both forms of law, state law and local customary law, although it is clear that the latter is used more widely, is better understood and is generally the preferred form of law for most matters. The surveys indicate that the population generally approaches the two systems of law in a complementary manner. The first survey stated:

> The East Timorese concept of justice clearly includes a *continuum* that encompasses both the adat system and the formal legal system. For more 'minor' offences, people are most likely to seek justice from the traditional *adat* system, while for more 'serious' crimes, the formal system seems appropriate.[132]

[127] Avocats Sans Frontières, *Access to Legal Aid in Timor-Leste*. The survey involved a total of 163 interviewees living in five different districts. The two surveys posed different questions and used different methodology and hence a direct comparison is not possible.

[128] Ibid., 10, fn 22. [129] Ibid., 5. [130] Ibid., 11, 8.

[131] Ibid., 10. Note, however, that local Timorese laws draw different distinctions as to what is serious. Hohe and Nixon explain that while theft is considered a serious crime, violence is not unless it leads to homicide: *Reconciling Justice*, 63, and Hohe, 'Justice Without Judiciary in East Timor', 346. According to Amnesty International, rape is frequently referred to local customary law for 'resolution': *Amnesty International Report 2004 – Timor Leste*. This is supported by the study of Grenfell et al., *Understanding Community*, 110–17. On the crime of rape, see Hohe and Nixon, *Reconciling Justice*, 27.

[132] Asia Foundation, *Law and Justice in East Timor*, 36 (emphasis added). More specifically, citizens prefer the state legal system for cases of assault involving family members, sexual assault, motor vehicle accidents, incidents of extended incarceration and conflicts involving outsiders, business or government. This continuum approach appears to have developed since first contact with the Portuguese colonial administration and flowed on during the Indonesian occupation and UNTAET period to the present.

The surveys attest that the rule of customary law remains an important part of the lives of most East Timorese. In 2003 Aisling Swaine conducted interviews with locals in three districts that indicated there was a strong feeling that 'if local justice was abolished as a method for resolving community disputes, they would lose a way of life and culture – and would have nothing to pass on to future generations'.[133] This implies that local customary law is important to an overall sense of identity, which is generated at the local level rather than the national level. Thus the rule of customary law is still more integral to local identity than the rule of state law.

Timorese consultant Josh Trindade argues that many Timorese view the Constitution 'as illegitimate'.[134] He states: 'The constitution is too foreign for a common East Timorese person to understand. It is a tool of alienation for most East Timorese and does not reflect the needs of the people.'[135] To some degree, this comment is supported by the findings of the Asia Foundation survey where a third of participants stated that they did not know what the Constitution meant.[136] Less than a third understood that it was the source of law or the country's basic law.[137] In regard to public participation in the constitutional drafting process, a large number of young Timorese, particularly women, felt there was insufficient genuine public participation,[138] presumably on the basis that it does not reflect their needs.

Trindade reports that a *lia nain* (traditional elder) from Viqueque commented that: 'our constitution is not strong here, it must be accepted by all and be blessed by elders – converted into a sacred object (*sasan lulik*) and be part of our culture'.[139] Trindade supports this suggestion that the Constitution be transformed through ritual into a national sacred object.[140] He also recommends the establishment of a council of *luirai* (elders) to ritualise and inaugurate the elected national leaders because, he argues, 'in the eyes of the Timorese [the *luirai*] are still the legitimate leaders'.[141] Such a ceremony would legitimate the power of the elected leaders as the temporary trustees of power and assist in showing respect to the 'Timorese worldview'.[142] Trindade reasons that this reconciliation between the two paradigms would

[133] Swaine, *Traditional Justice*, 63–4.
[134] Trindade, 'Reconciling the Conflicting Paradigms', 167.
[135] Open letter from Josh Trindade to the Prime Minister of Timor-Leste, 10 August 2006.
[136] Asia Foundation, *Law and Justice in East Timor*, 32. [137] Ibid., 32–3.
[138] Ibid., 33–4. [139] Trindade, 'Reconciling the Conflicting Paradigms', 167.
[140] Ibid., 181–2. [141] Ibid., 181.
[142] Trindade makes frequent reference to 'the Timorese worldview': e.g. ibid.

mean that leaders would exercise their power subject to both the rule of law *and* the prohibition of the ancestors (*bandu*). He asserts:

> if the national leaders abuse or misuse their political power and legitimacy, they will fear ancestral sanction as in Timorese traditions as well as consequences from the modern formal justice system. The first one will worry the Timorese leaders more than the later one.[143]

This lack of respect for the state justice system amongst Timor's national leaders is examined in the following chapter. Trindade sharply contrasts this disregard with the reverence shown towards the power of ancestral sanctions and ancestral legitimacy that drives local orders (and local legal systems). However, this authority does not fit with the Weberian conception of legitimate and rational legal authority: ancestral sanctions are connected to the spiritual world and lack any semblance to legal rationality, the basis of the rule of law. Hence there is tension between the rule of law on the one hand, and legal pluralism's acceptance of these local orders based on ancestral sanctions on the other. However, in this relationship, the rule of law is an aspiration and ideal to which Timor's leaders have committed the state while legal pluralism is a fact, which many of Timor's leaders have tried to ignore, possibly in the hope that it will wither and die.

Trindade's challenge to the Constitution's legitimacy is a sociological and moral challenge that questions whether Timorese actively believe that constitutional claims to authority deserve either respect or obedience. He effectively argues that the paradigm of the traditional draws a greater level of respect and obedience. According to anthropologist Maj Nygaard-Christensen, Trindade's views are an indication that a political diarchy (a system of double government) is operating in Timor-Leste which 'sees ritual or sacred authorities as necessary in the establishment of secular legitimacy'.[144] This diarchy is also evidenced by the frequent participation by state officials, such as parliamentarians and district administrators, in the enactment of sacred taboo laws, known as *taru bandu,* by ritual leaders. These laws are discussed in the following chapter.

The above discussion of Timor-Leste's Constitution illustrates that the internal, social legitimacy of a constitution will be undermined in the eyes of the population where the drafters ignore or sideline non-state structures or authorities who hold sway and thus fail to connect the concept of the state with large parts of the population. As Trindade points out, the consequence of the Timorese drafters' deliberate strategy

[143] Ibid., 182. [144] Nygaard-Christensen, 'The Rebel and the Diplomat', 225.

of ignoring local customary law and traditional leaders is that it has undermined both the legitimacy of the Constitution and a sense of identity valued by many Timorese.

5. Conclusion

Legitimacy is a prime concern for the state and state law in Timor-Leste. This chapter shows that while the international legitimacy of the newly independent state was given some attention in the drafting of the Constitution, little consideration was given to shoring up the internal, social legitimacy of the new state, so that its legal institutions and constitutional norms would have traction and resonance with local norms and the population, large portions of which continue to live predominantly under the influence of the local paradigm of customary law. The Constitution fails to take into account the lived experience of most Timorese in the post-conflict context.

While it is apparent that Timor-Leste is undergoing a transition from a period of foreign colonisation and occupation, conflict and international administration, the nature of the legal order to which it is transitioning is not clear. In passing, Mearns has referred to Timor-Leste's 'transition to an international standard of law'[145] by which he presumably means a liberal democratic system that upholds the rule of law. Through its Constitution, Timor-Leste has arguably committed to such an 'international standard of law' entailing Western-style state institutions, but its transition to this standard is doubtful given its severely limited capacity to ever deliver such a standard to its expectant population. More importantly, this constitutional aspiration places Timor-Leste's legal framework at odds with the state's post-conflict context where legal pluralism is strong. The Constitution's detachment from the lived experience of most Timorese casts doubt on the value of it as a founding document that sets down the rules of governance.

The following chapter analyses Timor-Leste's transition in its first decade of independence. In particular it traces the divergent policies of the two governments during this decade in regard to the development of the legal framework and its relationship with government priorities such as national reconciliation, as well as the realm of local custom and authority. It sets out the various initiatives aimed at strengthening the rule of law, enhancing access to justice and linking local systems of law to the formal legal system.

[145] Mearns, *Looking Both Ways*, 50.

7

Timor-Leste's first decade of independence

After a decade of independence, there is consensus among international organisations and independent assessors that Timor-Leste's constitutional aspiration to establish the rule of law remains one of the state's 'most serious challenges'.[1] In 2011 the Government of Timor-Leste acknowledged that the rule of law is a distant goal and that 'substantial efforts' will need to be made to realise this aspiration.[2] Its *Strategic Development Plan 2011–2030* states that the Timorese justice system is 'still too underdeveloped to serve our entire population'.[3] The Plan also acknowledges the role of legal pluralism in that it concedes that 'a substantial proportion of conflicts are addressed through traditional justice mechanisms'.[4] In other words, for most people in Timor-Leste, deep legal pluralism is still strong while the concept of the rule of (state) law is difficult to discern.

Unlike in South Africa, state law pluralism is absent in Timor-Leste because local customary law is not explicitly recognised in the Constitution or in any state law as a part of the applicable state law. The absence of state law pluralism means that Timor-Leste's Constitution does not directly influence or regulate the interaction between these two paradigms. Timor-Leste's transition also differs from South Africa's: as an embryonic state with nascent state institutions, Timor-Leste has been the subject of extensive, direct and continuing international intervention and assistance.

Timor-Leste's first decade as a state, beginning from 20 May 2002, the day the Constitution came into force, was mostly peaceful: it saw Timor-Leste make a rapid transition to liberal democracy under the guidance of the international community, culminating in

[1] USAID, *Fostering Justice*, 3; Independent Comprehensive Needs Assessment, *The Justice System of Timor-Leste*, 24.
[2] Democratic Republic of Timor-Leste, *Strategic Development Plan 2011–2030*, 178.
[3] Ibid. [4] Ibid.

Timor-Leste showing leadership on the international stage through its co-chairing of the G7+ international forum on fragile states. At the same time, the decade saw a resurgence of customary ceremonies within Timor-Leste.[5]

This chapter focuses on the relationship between the rule of law and legal pluralism in the first decade. It starts by analysing the operation and the role of Timor-Leste's rule-of-law institutions in relation to four events that rocked the peace during this time: the 2006 crisis, the attempt to apprehend Major Alfredo Reinado in 2007–2008, the 2009 release of Maternus Bere who had been indicted for crimes against humanity and, finally, the widespread granting of presidential pardons. It argues that these events have helped to marginalise Timor-Leste's Constitution as well as its strained formal rule-of-law institutions. The latter three of these events show that two of Timor-Leste's leaders, Gusmão and Horta, have been instrumental in sidelining the courts in their effort to promote national reconciliation and the national interest.

The state legal system was beset by other problems during its first decade. Foremost was the fact that the formal legal system continued to import a confusing patchwork of foreign norms without sufficient consideration of the Timorese context. This chapter argues that little consideration was given to the interaction between such international norms and local norms. It then maps how various state and non-state actors negotiate the relationship between the rule of law and legal pluralism. It shows that confusion racks the courts and the police force in determining and applying the 'applicable state law'. Equally the local population is facing serious challenges in attempting to access state justice. The chapter focuses particularly on the lived experience of some of the most vulnerable sections of society attempting to access the state legal system, namely victims of domestic violence.

Timor-Leste's first decade was marked by divergent policies towards the rule of law and legal pluralism. In the second half of the decade, the Alliance of the Parliamentary Majority (AMP) Government has been upfront about the operation of legal pluralism. It has sought international assistance to build linkages between the two systems. This is in strong contrast to the previous Fretilin-led Government which was strongly centralised and focused almost exclusively on the development of the formal court system.

[5] Brown and Freitas, 'Peacebuilding and Political Hybridity', 66. See section 4.1 of this chapter.

This approach in the first half of the decade led the state to overlook the positive and useful aspects of local customary law. Despite this approach, a number of local NGOs, mostly in conjunction with international organisations, developed programmes to establish links between the two legal systems. These initiatives aimed to give state law greater resonance with the population by linking it to customary legal mechanisms and norms. One example of such initiatives is the temporary mechanism of the Commission for Reception, Truth and Reconciliation ('the CAVR').

The result of the divergent policies of the Fretilin and AMP Governments towards the rule of law and legal pluralism is that a fragmented and sometimes inconsistent approach has been taken to the contextualisation of Timor-Leste's legal system. While the process of reconciling the rule of law and legal pluralism was initially driven by the NGO community and funded mostly by IDAs and IFIs, it has since been taken up by the AMP Government with direct assistance from the international community. The change of policy toward accepting legal pluralism as potentially strengthening the rule of law mirrors the shift taking place in the international community. This chapter argues that in Timor-Leste this shift cannot be entirely attributed to the influence of international actors as it was in part home-grown.

1. The decade's definitive events for the rule of law in Timor-Leste

Timor-Leste's Constitution sets out a raft of formal rule-of-law institutions comprising the state's courts, the Provedor for Human Rights and Justice ('the Provedor'), as well as the Parliament, the President and the Executive. In addition, there is the Office of the Inspector General (OIG) and the Anti-Corruption Commission. Informal rule-of-law institutions include the independent media and civil society which scrutinise government actions, and local leaders involved in dispute resolution at the community level. The Constitution entrenches important principles such as the separation of powers and the independence of the judiciary.[6] Before the 2006 crisis there was concern among some international organisations, such as the World Bank, that on the ground the Executive was too strong, and that if a proper balance was to be achieved, the other formal rule-of-law institutions needed strengthening.[7]

[6] Arts. 69 and 121.

[7] World Bank, *Strengthening the Institutions of Governance in Timor-Leste*, 6; World Bank Group and Asian Development Bank, *Economic and Social Development Brief*, 28.

Timor-Leste's first decade of independence was governed by two different parties: from 2002 to 2007 Fretilin was the elected Government and in 2007 a coalition Government, known as the AMP, was elected and headed by Xanana Gusmão who had served as President during the previous government. This section argues that the 2006 crisis, the failure to apprehend Major Alfredo Reinado, the 2009 release of former militia leader Maternus Bere and the extensive issuing of presidential pardons highlight the marginal role that the Constitution and the courts play in Timor's governance and crisis-resolution. These non-violent, legal mechanisms were sidelined, sometimes actively, during these events. It then sets out the various approaches to the rule of law among Timor's leaders by sketching the dispute regarding the apprehension of Reinado following the 2006 crisis when the courts were undermined by parts of the Executive and the international community. It argues that the lack of respect shown by all these actors for the state legal system may be encouraging ordinary Timorese to follow suit and place even greater reliance on non-state mechanisms for resolving disputes.

1.1 The 2006 crisis

Timor-Leste's formal rule-of-law institutions were tested when law and order collapsed in the crisis of April–May 2006 and the security forces, namely the police and the army, opened fire on each other. The crisis began in February 2006 when a group of almost 600 members of the Defence Force went on strike, asserting that the Government was ignoring their claims of discrimination with respect to promotion and accommodation. This led to a series of demonstrations in late April 2006 where it was apparent that the police force was unable to control the protestors. The Prime Minister, Mari Alkitiri, then called out the Defence Force to back up the police force, arguably breaching various legal procedures,[8] and the Minister for the Interior, Rogerio Lobato, illegally distributed weapons to the civilian population. In late May 2006, a confrontation took place between the Defence Force and the police, which had differing allegiances to members of the Executive,[9] leaving eight members of the police force dead.

[8] *Report of the UN Independent Special Commission of Inquiry* (2 October 2006) [164–8].

[9] Kingsbury and Leach, 'Introduction', 5.

During the crisis, Timorese leaders frequently invoked the rule of law as a guiding value.[10] Furthermore, it is also noteworthy that during the crisis the major players such as the Prime Minister and the President consistently upheld the Constitution, despite the call from one Member of Parliament for the President to suspend the Constitution's operation.[11] However, no attempt was made to involve the courts in providing a legal, non-violent resolution to the crisis. On the other hand, the newly opened Provedor's office was able to play a slightly greater role by monitoring the human rights violations that took place, which assisted the subsequent inquiry conducted by the UN.[12]

The assessment of the crisis by the UN Independent Special Commission of Inquiry for Timor-Leste predictably found that the crisis could be explained largely by the weak nature of state institutions and the rule of law.[13] It stated: 'Governance structures and existing chains of command broke down or were bypassed; roles and responsibilities became blurred; *solutions were sought outside the existing legal framework.*'[14] The UN's assessment identified weak accountability mechanisms as undermining the efficacy of Timor's security forces.[15] However, the assessment is short on detail as to how the existing legal framework could have been better used to resolve the soldiers' grievances and to prevent the escalation of violence.

In contrast to the UN assessment, Josh Trindade takes a non-state-centric approach to explaining the 2006 crisis, an approach he claims is more in line with 'traditional' Timorese perspectives.[16] Trindade argues that the confrontation between the police and the Defence Force illustrates the weak hold that the concept of the state has on Timor's main institutional actors.[17] He asserts that the crisis was precipitated by the failure of Timor's leaders to connect with local spiritual values. Arguing that the problem lies with the fact that Timor's leaders derive their

[10] See, e.g., Gusmão's comment quoted in AAP, 'E Timor President Vows', *Independent Weekly*, 14 June 2006; comment of Ana Pessoa (then Minister for State) quoted in Fitzpatrick, 'Ramos Horta Resigns'.

[11] See 'East Timor's President to Address Parliament on Crisis', *AFP*, 13 June 2006; Australian Broadcasting Commission News, 'Officials Welcome Gusmão's Parliamentary Address' (15 June 2006); New York Times, 'UN Prepares to Start New Peacekeeping Mission in East Timor', 14 June 2006; AAP, 'E Timor President Vows'.

[12] Nicolau, 'Ombudsman for Human Rights', 3.

[13] *Report of the UN Independent Special Commission of Inquiry* (2 October 2006), [136].

[14] Ibid., 2 (emphasis added). [15] Ibid., [142, 151].

[16] Trindade, 'Reconciling the Conflicting Paradigms', 172. [17] Ibid., 161.

ostensible legitimacy from elections rather than their connection to ancestors and sacred objects (*sasan lulik*), Trindade writes:

> Arguably, the 2006 crisis may be resulted from the fact that, wrong leaders were installed at national level from 2002–2006 without proper local legitimacy. There is little trust towards leaders that are not connected to sacred items and ancestral legitimacy.[18]

Trindade's logic is that the introduction of 'the imported new values of human rights and democracy' has undermined the common values and traditions of Timor as well as the 'cultural identity' of the Timorese.[19] Many in the international community may dismiss this approach as 'backward or uncivilised'[20] because the explanation is starkly at odds with that of the international community, which appears to have redoubled its efforts to promote the rule of law and strengthen state institutions after the 2006 crisis. The two explanations of the 2006 crisis illustrate the construction of 'conflicting paradigms' of the international and the local in Timor-Leste.[21]

1.2 The Reinado Affair and various approaches to the rule of law

One of the key recommendations made by the UN Independent Special Commission of Inquiry was that Major Alfredo Reinado, the former Commander of the Military Police, be prosecuted for his role in one of the events of the 2006 crisis which involved an armed confrontation in which five people were killed and ten injured.[22] At this time, Reinado opposed the Fretilin Government and attempted to align himself with President Gusmão. The events leading to Reinado's death in early 2008 provide a window into the competing approaches to the rule of law among some of the main actors in Timor-Leste, including the UN, Fretilin, the Prime Minister and the President.

18 Ibid., 172. See also Trindade and Castro, *Rethinking Timorese Identity*, 17–18, 22.

19 Trindade, 'Reconciling Conflicting Paradigms', 173. It seems that Trindade is attempting to use the customary sphere as the focal point for national self-definition. This inevitably involves a reinterpretation of the customary sphere and the assumption that culture is pure and homogeneous. This arguably shows little recognition that the customary sphere has been in the process of hybridisation since at least the beginning of colonisation and the importation of a human rights culture is simply one more step in this process.

20 Trindade and Castro, *Rethinking Timorese Identity*, 26 quoting an interview with a 'political leader'. See also Grenfell, 'Making Modernity', 9.

21 Trindade uses this terminology of 'conflicting paradigms', drawing on the work of Hohe.

22 *Report of the UN Independent Special Commission of Inquiry* (2 October 2006), [117, 64–6].

The basic facts of the case are as follows: after a failed attempt by the Australian-led International Stabilisation Force (ISF) to apprehend Reinado resulted in the death of five of his followers in March 2007, the ensuing months of 2007 saw a protracted battle between two state institutions to determine the best path to bring Reinado to justice.

The main tension regarding Reinado lay between the Presidency, held by Ramos-Horta, and the courts, specifically Ivo Rosa, a Judge of the Dili District Court who arrived in mid 2006 from Portugal and occupied a UN-funded position. After some negotiations with Reinado wherein he gave written indication of his readiness to face justice, Ramos-Horta suspended Rosa's court warrant for the arrest of Reinado and his men on the grounds that the group would surrender voluntarily and he issued them with a letter allowing them freedom of movement. The President further requested that all international and national institutions in Timor-Leste 'fully respect, comply with and implement the present order'.[23] Judge Rosa challenged this order as unconstitutional and questioned the power of the President to suspend a court order for arrest. On 9 October 2007, Judge Rosa issued a written notice of a ruling to the effect that the actions of the President were violating the guarantee of separation of powers entrenched in the Constitution. Moreover, he stated that the actions to waive the arrest warrant were undermining the courts and the rule of law. Judge Rosa ordered that the ISF and the UN, which was legally the head of enforcement in the country, comply with the court order and arrest Reinado. This ruling was made in the face of some possible intimidation: a few days before, the Minister of Justice reportedly stated that those foreign judges who were not performing well would have their contracts terminated.[24] In addition, a few days after the ruling, the President reportedly advised foreign judges in Timor-Leste to show more respect for the country's democratically-elected leaders.[25] Reinado's trial was set for late January 2008 but by this time neither the ISF nor the police, for which the UN had responsibility, had apprehended Reinado. From one angle, what would appear to be a reluctance to comply with a court order on the

[23] Order 'Freedom of Movement for Major Alfredo Reinado and his Group' quoted in UN Mission in Timor-Leste Report, *UNMIT Internal Review Panel, Conducted From 1 April to 24 April 2008*, 7. This report can be accessed through wikileaks. See the International Crisis Group, *Timor-Leste*, 2.

[24] Fretilin media release, 'Minister Threatens to Sack Foreign Judges' (5 October 2007).

[25] This is reported in Fretilin's media release dated 23 November 2007 and entitled 'Australian Military Commander Under Fire in East Timor'.

part of the relevant actors could be interpreted as indicating some disregard for Timor's 'Mother Law', its Constitution.

The failure to arrest Reinado symbolised a major problem of impunity. Reports of the UN Mission in Timor-Leste (UNMIT) give little detail as to the internal wrangling between the President and the courts. In August 2007 the UN Secretary-General's report on UNMIT's operation broadly stated that there is 'a public perception that the entire rule of law system is not functioning well'.[26] Four months later a mission of the UN Security Council conducted its first visit to the country, and its report also brushed over the rift developing between the state's institutions. The Reinado case takes up half of the report's short entry on 'Justice and the Rule of Law' but it focused mainly on the President's views on the case and it glosses over the internal problems – the constitutional problems – that the case raises. For example, the report states:

> The resolution of these issues … would also demonstrate that justice is being done and seen to be done, *reinforce the primacy of the rule of law in the country* and thus counter the perception of impunity.[27]

This sentence illustrates that, as an external actor, the UN understands the rule of law in relation to perceptions of impunity. Arguably in these circumstances the UN's approach to the rule of law is restricted, as it has no mandate as such to monitor the constitutional complexities of Timor-Leste; hence it must understand the rule of law in an accountability and impunity framework. The UN reasons that it must take its cue from the country's leaders and hence the constitutionality of various orders is not for international actors to determine. It is possible to detect some tension in this position in the following statement of the Security Council's mission Report: '[T]he mission was concerned that UN and international assistance *should be seen to be encouraging the strengthening of democratic institutions, the rule of law* and self-reliance in Timor-Leste.'[28] This

[26] UN Doc S/2007/513 (28 August 2007) *Report of the Secretary-General on the United Nations Integrated Mission in Timor-Leste (for the period from 27 January to 20 August 2007)* [22].

[27] UN Doc S/2007/711 (6 December 2007) *Report of the Security Council Mission to Timor-Leste, 24 to 30 November 2007*, [24] (emphasis added). Note that at [22] it refers obliquely to internal matters: 'Central to the crisis were issues of governance, the separation of powers and the building of sustainable institutions.' This refers to the 2006 crisis.

[28] UN Doc S/2007/711 (6 December 2007) *Report of the Security Council Mission to Timor-Leste, 24 to 30 November 2007*, [27]; emphasis added.

sentence implies that the UN was aware that international actors might not be seen by the local population to be strengthening the rule of law.

The Fretilin party, which was now in opposition, presents an alternative approach to the rule of law: this approach is internally focused and is based closely on adherence to the text of the Constitution. For example, in its media release dated 13 November 2007, Fretilin cites Article 118 of the Constitution, which states, in part, that: 'The decisions of the courts are to be compulsorily obeyed and prevail over the decisions of all other constitutional state institutions.' In a later media release, it invokes the concept five times, almost always in relation to the Constitution, even though its main target is the ISF and its 'decision to ignore' Reinado's arrest warrant.[29] For example, the media release states:

> Fretilin's position is … to uphold the rule of law and ensure no constitutional entity, be it the president, the government or the parliament, is permitted to interfere with the independent administration of justice. … the rule of law has almost been lost in Timor Leste. Justice is no longer functioning in accordance with the constitution.

In this media release, Fretilin does not mention any concern regarding impunity; its interest lies in scrutinising whether the Constitution is being upheld in all its detail and that the law be enforced in an impartial and non-political manner. Fretilin's concern, shared in part by the courts, is that external actors, such as the UN and the ISF, and state institutions such as the Presidency are not giving full respect to the checks on power entrenched into the Constitution. Fretilin's approach of formally invoking the rule of law as a constitutional value can also be found in legislation introduced during its time of government.[30]

President Ramos-Horta's approach to the rule of law can only be surmised in this instance. His actions in attempting to arrange for Reinado's voluntary surrender to justice appear to favour reconciliation and stability of the state over strict adherence to the constitutional text. Around the time that Judge Rosa issued his notice of ruling, Reinado held one of a number of rallies that attracted hundreds of supporters, showing that the Timorese culture of supporting clandestine and resistance actors did not disappear upon independence. Reinado's continuing refusal to face the ordinary justice system attracted a large number of unemployed

[29] Fretilin's media release dated 23 November 2007, 'Australian Military Commander Under Fire in East Timor' (on file with author).

[30] See s. 1 of the 2004 *Decree on Community Authorities* and Art. 7 of the 2005 *Criminal Procedure Code*, both discussed below.

and disaffected male youths in particular. In March 2007 one Timorese national newspaper reported that at one of Reindao's rallies, 'all the traditional leaders of Manufahi who possess cosmological magic assembled [and] ... bestowed cosmological power' on him; this was a ritual that was apparently also attended by the Manufahi District Administrator, a government appointee, as well as some members of parliament.[31] According to an unconfirmed report, at the time that Reinado was set to be tried, President Ramos-Horta negotiated a secret deal with Reinado, offering him a Presidential decree of amnesty if he surrendered and faced justice.[32] Ramos-Horta's approach to the rule of law gives primacy to peace and reconciliation, values more commonly characterised as pertaining to informal justice. Arguably, Ramos-Horta understood the significance of this customary ritual in the eyes of the population for whom the legitimacy conferred by cosmological ancestral power is equal to democratic legitimacy.[33]

This tension between President Ramos-Horta and the courts surfaced again in November 2008 when President Ramos-Horta was initially openly critical of the role of international judges sitting on the Court of Appeal, including Judge Rosa, after that Court held the AMP Government's allocation of $240 million to the Petroleum Fund to be unconstitutional.[34] The President of the National Parliament requested the reversal of the decision and also, according to Fretilin, publicly announced that it was 'time the government brought the Court of Appeal into line'.[35] On the same day that the Court of Appeal notified the Parliament of its decision, the contract of Judge Rosa was not renewed. The decision not to renew Rosa's contract was made by the Superior Council for the Judiciary (SCJ), which at the time was presided over by Dionisio Babo-Soares, the Secretary General of Prime Minister Gusmão's political party. The timing of the decision gave the

[31] Quoted and translated from the *Suara Timor Lorosa'e*, 12 March 2007, by Nygaard-Christensen, 'The Rebel and the Diplomat', 220–1.

[32] Toohey, 'Timor Rebel was to be Pardoned'; Murdoch, 'Ramos Horta and Reinado'. Dodd, reporting for *The Australian* newspaper, has claimed that the President offered Reinado a Presidential decree of amnesty in mid 2007: Dodd, 'Judge Revokes Reinado Amnesty'.

[33] Nygaard-Christensen, 'The Rebel and the Diplomat'.

[34] UN Doc S/2009/72 (4 February 2009) *Report of the Secretary-General on the UN Integrated Mission in Timor-Leste (for the period from July 2008 to 20 January 2009)* [5]. This report states that President Ramos-Horta later 'made an unequivocal public statement that the decision of the Court must be respected'.

[35] See Fretilin media releases dated 13 November 2008, 16 November 2008 and 2 December 2008. The Government's media release in response is dated 14 November 2008.

appearance of political interference with the principles of judicial independence and security of judicial tenure.[36]

Ramos-Horta's approach to the rule of law is in line with that of Xanana Gusmão: after the 2006 crisis Gusmão placed more emphasis on reconciliation rather than on justice and accountability,[37] which is consistent with his approach to the crimes committed during the occupation and the post-ballot period.[38] Gusmão describes reconciliation as 'a very positive trait in traditional justice' as it prevents problems being 'dragged on into the future by the parties'.[39] Speaking before the UN Security Council in 2006 Gusmão explained his preference for reconciliation and 'restorative justice' over punitive justice, by drawing on South Africa's experience, which he read as illustrating the notion that reconciliation is not antithetical to a democratic society.[40] Like Ramos-Horta, Gusmão appears to understand reconciliation as compatible with the rule of law. This diverges from common understandings of the rule of law in the West, which equate the concept with legal predictability, due process, accountability and individual rights. More critically, the approach of Ramos-Horta and Gusmão is incompatible with that of the UN, which

[36] The SCJ's decision was appealed to the Court of Appeal which found that although Rosa's contract was periodically renewable, in the context that there was a continuing need for him to remain in the Timorese judiciary, he had a legitimate expectation that it would be renewed. The Court of Appeal held that the SCJ's decision was not motivated by public interest and was an arbitrary one. It found that the SCJ's interpretation of the relevant law meant that international judges were vulnerable to pressures of a political nature. Furthermore, the Court expressed concern that the circumstances and manner of the SCJ's decision affected the SCJ's image in light of its function which is to protect the independence and impartiality of the judiciary.

[37] In an Asia Foundation survey, most East Timorese respondents appear to have understood the term 'justice' as connoting the state legal system encapsulating law enforcement and human rights. A noteworthy 22 per cent responded that they did not know what 'justice' means. In contrast, there was a very high understanding of the term 'reconciliation': Asia Foundation, *Law and Justice in East Timor*, 30–1.

[38] UN Doc S/2006/628 (8 August 2006) *Report of the Secretary-General on Timor-Leste pursuant to Security Council Resolution 1690* [22, 49]. This emphasis is consistent with the support of most of Timor's leadership for the Commission on Truth and Friendship between Timor-Leste and Indonesia. See also Xanana Gusmão's First Speech to the National Parliament: Considering a Policy of National Reconciliation (21 October 2002) printed in *Timor Lives!*, 97–138. The priority given to reconciliation at the expense of justice and accountability appears to have discomforted the UN: see UN Doc S/2007/50 (1 February 2007) *Report of the Secretary-General on the United Nations Integrated Mission in Timor-Leste (for the period from 9 August 2006 to 26 January 2007)*, [24].

[39] Quoted in *Timor Lives!*, 219.

[40] See Gusmão's speech to the UN Security Council: UN Doc S/PV.5351 (23 January 2005) UNSCOR, provisional session, 5351st meeting, 6–7.

resolutely rejects the use of amnesty in respect of serious crimes and considers such mechanisms to be contrary to international law, and, by implication, the international rule of law.[41]

In February 2008 the European Parliament expressed 'its concern at the message of impunity and *disrespect for the rule of law which may have been conveyed, in an effort to promote national reconciliation, by the ambiguous attitude of the authorities of Timor-Leste*, UNMIT and international security forces towards people who are summoned to face justice'.[42] This resolution diplomatically questions Ramos-Horta's and Gusmão's approach to the rule of law and the willingness of international actors to follow their lead. From some angles it may appear that there is tension between the versions of the rule of law extolled by Western and international organisations and those embraced by Timor's leaders. However, the Reinado affair shows that both Timor's leaders and the international community may be inadvertently undermining state courts as a major rule-of-law institution.

In regard to the Reinado affair, the international community appears to be sending mixed messages about the rule of law, its meaning and its implications, which may be encouraging Timorese leaders to skew the concept for their own political ends. Both Gusmão and Ramos-Horta understand the need to invoke the rule of law in order to appease the international community but at the same time they have been determined to follow their chosen direction for Timor, which is one of reconciliation. Thus their position has been to insist that the two concepts, reconciliation and the rule of law, can sit comfortably together. In this context, it would be unsurprising if disaffection with state institutions as well as international organisations led the population to embrace non-state institutions.

1.3 The 2009 release of Maternus Bere

The 2009 arrest and subsequent release of former militia subcommander Maternus Bere is another illumination of how the actions of the

[41] This principled approach was spelt out in mid 2006 by the UN Secretary General in relation to the terms of reference of the Joint Commission on Truth and Friendship that allowed for amnesty for some crimes. The report states that such amnesty is inconsistent with the bar in international law on amnesties for serious violations of international law, crimes against humanity, war crimes and other serious crimes. See UN Doc S/2006/580 (26 July 2006) *Report of the Secretary-General on Justice and Reconciliation for Timor-Leste*, [30].

[42] European Parliament, *Resolution on Timor-Leste* (21 February 2008) [N4].

Executive Government are undermining the state's attempt to establish the rule of law. Bere was indicted for crimes against humanity by the UN Serious Crimes Unit for his role in the Suai massacre in 1999. A decade after the massacre and living as a provincial official in West Timor, Bere returned to his hometown of Suai and was, according to some reports, recognised and severely beaten by locals. The police then stepped in and arrested him and after a court appearance he was ordered to be detained in Becora Prison before being tried in the Dili District Court. Before he could stand trial, he was released to Indonesian authorities. This took place on the order of Prime Minister Gusmão, acting at the request of Indonesia's Foreign Affairs Minister. No judicial order was issued for his release.

This event was a blow to Timor-Leste's constitutional aspiration to establish the rule of law because it showed a number of actors acting outside the state's legal framework. For example, the Suai locals' decision to take the law into their own hands showed little faith in the state legal system. According to a 2008 survey, this avenue of self-help is widespread in Timor-Leste, with more than 50 per cent of those surveyed saying that people in their area take justice into their own hands if a serious problem is not resolved by the state.[43] More critical are the actions of the state's leaders, whose role is to uphold the rule of law: Gusmão's order was not only contrary to Article 245(1) of the *Penal Code* but also a breach of the constitutional separation of powers, as Articles 118 and 119 of the Constitution give the courts exclusive competence in relation to the administration of justice and stipulate that all court decisions are binding. According to the 2009 Independent Comprehensive Needs Assessment (ICNA) of Timor-Leste's Justice System, '[t]his disregard for a judicial order and direct interference with the judicial system was a grave violation of judicial independence and the separation of powers'.[44] Arguably Gusmão's actions also contravened international (customary) law by effectively giving Bere an amnesty: Gusmão hindered and prevented Bere's prosecution for crimes against humanity with the knowledge that Indonesia is highly unlikely to prosecute. In addition, the executive

[43] Asia Foundation, *Law and Justice in Timor-Leste*, 16.

[44] Independent Comprehensive Needs Assessment, *The Justice System of Timor-Leste*, 16. Following the 2006 crisis the UN Secretary-General, in conjunction with UNMIT, set in train an independent assessment mission with a mandate to undertake an assessment of Timor's justice system. The four-person team comprised: Justice Phillip Rapoza (US), Judge Helena Bolieiro (Portugal), and two lawyers – Roza Salibekova (Kazakhstan) and John Stompor (US). UNMIT prepared the Terms of Reference.

actions went against a series of UN Security Council resolutions that emphasise the need to bring to justice perpetrators of crimes against humanity and serious crimes committed in Timor-Leste in 1999.[45]

Gusmão's actions drew criticism from many quarters including Timor-Leste's Parliament, the UN's High Commissioner for Human Rights and from international NGOs such as Amnesty International.[46] When summoned by Parliament to explain his actions, Gusmão cited some medical reasons relating to Bere's case but he emphasised that the national interest required that he override both the rule of law and the Constitution.[47] His lengthy address pointed to some legalities which he presumably believed legitimated his actions but at the same time he openly derided 'legalistic' justice.[48]

1.4 Presidential pardons

The fourth event comprises a series of events which began in 2008 when Timorese President Ramos-Horta granted pardons and commutations of sentence to ninety-four prisoners including nine prisoners convicted for crimes against humanity and three for gender-based violence.[49] International concern began mounting in late 2009 and then in August 2010 when pardons and commutations were given to twenty-six persons convicted in the courts for their involvement in the 2006 killings of the police force and the 2008 attacks against the Prime Minister and President. A number of those pardoned were FDTL members who have subsequently returned to active duty.

This series of events drew concern among various national and international NGOs as well as UN bodies. For example, in February 2010 the UN Security Council's Technical Assessment Mission commented that Ramos-Horta's actions have 'further contributed to perceptions of impunity'.[50]

[45] SC Res. 1271 (22 October 1999); SC Res 1338 (31 January 2001); SC Res 1410 (17 May 2002). See JSMP, *Impact of the Maternus Bere Case.*

[46] Amnesty International, *Indonesia Shelters Indicted Timorese Suspect*; Letter of Navanethem Pillay, UN High Commissioner for Human Rights, dated 2 September 2009.

[47] Gusmão, *Intervention – Response by His Excellency.* [48] Ibid., 13.

[49] JSMP, *Presidential Pardons.*

[50] The Report of this Mission is part of UN Doc S/2010/85 (12 February 2010) *Report of the Secretary-General on the UN Integrated Mission in Timor-Leste (for the period from 24 September 2009 to 20 January 2010)*, [24].

Ramos-Horta's response to this international criticism came one month later in a high profile UN forum:

> On the justice sector, we have been unfairly criticized by some fringe elements in this amorphous international community, an 'international community' that is invoked time and again whenever some people want to bestow on themselves a measure of world authority in regurgitating ready-made clichés or academic jargon on justice.
>
> One charge against me, is that I have some flaws in my heart as I issue too many pardons for individuals convicted of serious crimes.
>
> The same fringe foreign society criticized us when in August 2009 the sovereign national authorities of my country decided, upon medical recommendation, to hand-over to the authorities of the neighbouring country, one of their citizens who had been indicted for serious crimes in 1999 in my country.[51]

In this speech Ramos-Horta questioned the right of some parts of the 'international community', presumably NGOs, to criticise sovereign acts of his Government. It is difficult to forget that only little more than a decade ago he was actively involved in mobilising the international community, including international human rights NGOs such as Amnesty International, to recognise the illegality of Indonesia's occupation of East Timor at international law. This open criticism of the international community was not new: Ramos-Horta's opposition to an international tribunal for Timor-Leste, along the lines of the *ad hoc* international tribunals for Rwanda and the Former Yugoslavia, has been loud and clear. While he prefers social justice and reconciliation, he, like Gusmão, has publicly derided what he calls 'prosecutorial justice',[52] thus undermining a central tenet of the rule of law as understood in the West.

In October 2010 the UN Secretary-General commented that Horta's actions are causing the perception that individuals involved in high-profile cases are being given favourable treatment and that this could adversely impact on the state's efforts to establish the rule of law.[53] This is an instance of some friction between Timorese leaders and the UN. However, these events, particularly the Bere affair and the pardons, have highlighted that there are divisions within the international community itself. This

[51] Ramos-Horta, 'Timor-Leste: The Decade of Peace and Prosperity'.

[52] Ramos-Horta, 'The Dreams', 5.

[53] UN Doc S/2010/522 (13 October 2010) *Report of the Secretary-General on the UN Integrated Mission in Timor-Leste (for the period from 21 January 2010 to 20 September 2010)* [64].

problem is flagged by a UN report which states that: 'The divisions over the issue of accountability and impunity pose a challenge to the country and the United Nations.'[54] Debates in the UN Security Council show that only some of the permanent five members are willing to express concern about the implications for impunity flowing from these events while other Western states that champion the rule of law, such as Australia, are unwilling to comment because their regional proximity to Indonesia means that they too prioritise the national interest over the rule of law.

Ramos-Horta and Gusmão believe they are acting in the national interest, for the enduring stability of Timor-Leste. Arguably Timor-Leste's long-term aspiration of establishing the rule-of-law state does not appear to be at the forefront of their minds as they endeavour to achieve reconciliation and good neighbourly relations. However, their actions can be seen to be undermining the state legal system and the constitutional order. The ICNA report observes: 'The policy of choosing forgiveness and reconciliation over prosecution has long been the preferred approach on the part of the leadership of Timor-Leste.'[55] It then rebukes Timor-Leste's leaders: 'That position, however, even when expressed as a policy of the national government does not trump the Constitution and laws of Timor-Leste.'[56]

It must be remembered that at the time the 2002 Constitution was drafted, neither Ramos-Horta nor Gusmão were members of Fretilin and they were not directly involved in the constitution-drafting process. They do not appear to share Fretilin's drive for modern, Western-style legal institutions that sideline reconciliation and customary law. Their understanding of the rule of law differs from the version often advocated by Western states and IFIs. Arguably they advocate a contextualised, compromised version of the rule of law which places emphasis on reconciliation. This is consistent with their attempts to bridge the two paradigms of the state and the local. For example, upon becoming Prime Minister in mid-2006, Ramos-Horta acknowledged that the government must work with institutions like the Catholic Church and customary authorities given the nascent nature of the state's institutions. He stated his intention to meet with 'heads of villages [so as] to mobilise the society towards the development process'.[57] Commentators Damien Kingsbury and Michael Leach argue that for Timor-Leste, this 'indicated a major change of

[54] Ibid., 50, 81. [55] Ibid.

[56] Independent Comprehensive Needs Assessment, *The Justice System of Timor-Leste*, 58.

[57] *Suara Timor Lorosae* Newspaper 2006, quoted in Niner, 'A Reassertion of Customary Practices in Timor Leste', 46.

direction' and a possible step away from the centralisation of power in Dili that was a feature of the previous Fretilin Government headed by Alkitiri.[58] Unlike Fretilin's pro-courts approach, Gusmão has consistently shown interest in the possibility of reconciling the positive aspects of local customary law and the state legal system.[59]

These four events show that Timor-Leste's Constitution is not widely considered by the state's leaders to be a useful mechanism for the non-violent resolution of disputes. While President Gusmão did not accept calls to suspend the Constitution during the 2006 crisis, later, when Prime Minister, he did effectively suspend it when ordering Bere's release. Under this weak constitutional framework, the courts are currently unable to provide a check on state power, in particular the actions of the Executive: when the courts attempt to assert their independence, as Judge Rosa did in ordering Reinado's arrest, they are overpowered, and sometimes intimidated and openly derided, by the Executive. Efforts to end a culture of impunity in Timor-Leste have been repeatedly undermined by Ramos-Horta's actions such as suspending Reinado's court warrant and giving pardons to those convicted of crimes against humanity. All these actions show that Timor-Leste's Constitution and legal framework have failed to provide the ground rules for its post-conflict government.

The next section looks at how other problems have beset and undermined Timor-Leste's formal rule-of-law institutions and legal framework. It argues that these institutions and framework were established with insufficient consideration to the post-conflict context where the concept of the state is nascent and has little traction outside the capital.

2. Timor-Leste's rule-of-law institutions

2.1 The formal legal system

It is fair to say that Timor-Leste's courts have been far from the Western style rule-of-law institutions to which the Constitution aspires. By the time of the 2006 crisis, it was apparent that Fretilin's dream of modern state institutions was doomed to failure. Despite this, Fretilin did not revise its policy of ignoring local customary law.

[58] Kingsbury and Leach, 'Introduction', 9.

[59] See, e.g., Gusmão, *Timor Lives!*, 217–22.

Since its establishment, Timor-Leste's formal court system has been plagued by a huge backlog of cases and chronic delay,[60] a lack of qualified local personnel and ordinary resources, with only the Dili District Court consistently functioning.[61] One year into independence, in April 2003, the UN noted that these problems were 'favour[ing] an increased reliance on the traditional dispute settlement mechanisms, even when they may not provide adequate protection for the rights of minorities, vulnerable groups and women'.[62] For example, in 2003 there was evidence that delay encouraged many victims, such as victims of domestic violence, to withdraw their cases from the state legal system and seek a resolution from local customary law.[63] Before Fretilin lost the 2007 election there were also reports that the serious backlog of criminal cases was encouraging some courts to 'disregard due process in the interests of fast-tracking cases'.[64] At this time the President of the Court of Appeal conceded that the state court system would not cope if all matters were brought to it for resolution.[65]

During this time, the state legal system was unable to offer one of the central tenets of the rule of law, legal certainty. This is partly because of the vagueness of the Constitution in regard to the applicable law and the need to prop up the Timorese judiciary with foreign judges, most of whom came from Portugal with little understanding of Timor-Leste's legal framework or context. This was illuminated in the *Dos Santos case*,[66] where the majority of the Court of Appeal, comprising two judges from Portugal, decided that contrary to popular belief, the Indonesian Penal Code did not apply to crimes committed during the 1999 ballot for independence because Indonesian law has never been validly in force in East Timor as a result of Indonesia's occupation being illegal under international law. The majority then

[60] According to UNMIT, in mid 2007 the case-load of the Dili district Prosecution Office was 2413 cases: *Report on Human Rights Developments in Timor-Leste (August 2006-August 2007)* (2007), 21.

[61] See reports of the JSMP, *Overview of the Courts in East Timor in 2004*, 6; JSMP, *Overview of the Justice Sector: March 2005*. See also reports of UNDP, *Strengthening the Justice System in Timor-Leste* (2007) 23.

[62] UN Doc S/2003/449 (21 April 2003) Report of the Secretary-General on the United Nations Mission of Support in East Timor, [18].

[63] The JSMP reports that in 2003, out of 148 domestic violence cases reported, 104 of the complaints were withdrawn, partly due to the lengthy delays. See JSMP, *Women in the Formal Justice Sector*, 16; JSMP, *Access to Justice for Women Victims*, 21.

[64] USAID, *The Rule of Law*, 24. [65] Ibid., 40.

[66] Court of Appeal Decision, *Prosecutor* v. *Armando dos Santos* (unpublished, 15 July 2003).

proceeded to decide that Portuguese law was applicable, a decision that was met with a strenuous dissent from the sitting Timorese judge. The practical implications of this majority judgment on the applicable law were vast: all legal transactions conducted from 1976 to 2003 would be potentially invalid and all people already convicted by the Special Panels for Serious Crimes[67] under Indonesian Law and UNTAET Regulation 2000/15 in the previous three years would need to be released.[68] Uncertainty as to the applicable state law reigned for two and a half months before the Parliament enacted legislation countering this majority judgment.[69] This decision underlined Timor-Leste's confusing patchwork of different foreign laws and ruptured public confidence in the predictability of state law.

During the Fretilin Government, little legislation was enacted to replace Indonesian law and there was little community knowledge of new law, partly because it was written in Portuguese, an official language spoken by a small percentage of the population.[70] The Government's approach to legislation showed minimal sensitivity to context or to making law accessible. In the drafting of laws, foreign models were used by foreign drafters with little consideration of the Timorese context. The World Bank described much of it as 'more or less "off the shelf" of laws that prevail in countries with very different challenges from those present in Timor-Leste'.[71] Only a handful of statutes were translated into Tetum, the other official language with which a majority of Timorese are conversant. The result is an incomplete statute book that is a 'patchwork of competing legal influences (both historical carryovers and more recent donor imports)'.[72]

Opportunities for community consultation on legislation were thus curtailed with the result that the community has little knowledge of

[67] In regard to the SPSC, this part of the state legal system closed before it tried 75 per cent of indicted suspects, particularly those 'big fish' that were beyond the SPSC's jurisdiction. According to various NGOs, this process has seriously undermined public confidence in the state legal system and the concept of the rule of law: JSMP, *The JSMP's Submission to the UN Commission of Experts*, 6; The International Center for Transitional Justice (Reiger and Wierda), *The Serious Crimes Process in Timor-Leste*, 41.

[68] JSMP, *Report on the Court of Appeal Decision*, 4.

[69] JSMP, 'East Timorese Parliament Passes New Legislation'.

[70] Timor-Leste's 2004 Census estimates 13.6 per cent of the population speak Portuguese while the Asia Foundation estimates less than 7 per cent: Asia Foundation, *Law and Justice in East Timor*, 3.

[71] World Bank, *Strengthening the Institutions*, 8.

[72] Marriott, 'Justice Sector Dynamics', 55.

the existence and operation of some of these laws. In 2004 the Asia Foundation argued that:

> East Timorese have limited knowledge of the substance of the law and the procedures for accessing legal services. … For most of the population the Constitution and the laws enacted by the government are remote. This is reflected by the East Timorese expression … [the mother of law (constitution) is there, but we have not yet seen the children (organic law)].[73]

Outside the capital, this lack of awareness extended to state officials and members of civil society. For example, according to a 2007 report, a district administration chief in Suai was unaware that the Suai District Court had been functioning since 1999.[74] As a whole, the state legal system risked looking irrelevant to the lives of ordinary people.

Despite these problems, the Fretilin Government maintained its policy of ignoring legal pluralism although in November 2005 it exacerbated the courts' workload by introducing the *Criminal Procedure Code*, Article 7 of which provides that the formal courts have exclusive jurisdiction over criminal justice, thus effectively delegitimising the work of local customary mechanisms in administering criminal justice even in minor cases. It states:

1. Only the courts provided in the law on judicial organisation are competent to administer criminal justice.
2. In the exercise of this function, the courts owe obedience only to the law and the rule of law.

However, in line with the international trend for alternative dispute resolution, mentioned in Chapter 2, Article 262 of the Code empowers the courts to offer conciliation in relation to 'semi-public crimes' where the victim has the right to file or withdraw a complaint. It was only shortly before the 2007 election, which it lost, that Fretilin looked likely to revise this policy on legal pluralism in order to include a mediation programme aimed at diverting various general civil cases to mediation by local leaders.[75]

Overall, in the first half of Timor-Leste's first decade of independence, foreign legal norms and institutions continued to be imported with little consideration of how they would fit into the Timorese context and sit

[73] Asia Foundation, *Law and Justice in East Timor*, 11.
[74] UNDP, *Strengthening the Justice System in Timor-Leste Programme* (September 2007) [4.2.9].
[75] Nixon, *Justice and Governance*, 196.

with prevailing local norms and institutions. The importation of Western-modelled institutions into Timor-Leste's post-conflict context led to some paralysis in the formal legal system.

Some of the responsibility for the failure of Timor-Leste's institutions has been accepted by the World Bank Group (WBG) which, in 2011, published an evaluation of its decade of programmes in Timor-Leste, including its Governance programmes which assisted in developing the state's legal framework. In this report the WBG rated its own support for governance as 'moderately unsatisfactory'.[76] It describes some of Timor-Leste's new rule-of-law institutions, the OIG and Provedor, as 'mostly ineffective'.[77] It explains that the WBG's contribution has been unsuccessful and limited partly because it did not have a 'realistic' strategy.[78] In regard to the legal framework it states:

> Timor-Leste still has a long road ahead in the development of the legislative framework. A central challenge is to harmonize the different pieces of legislation that come from separate legal traditions, so that they are congruent and adapted to the uses and mores of the country.[79]

This evaluation acknowledges the disconnection between the state's legal framework and the legal mechanisms used by the majority of the population. It implies that Timor-Leste's new legal framework needs to establish a connection with the population by showing sensitivity to the local context and traditions.

Since being elected in 2007, the AMP Government has put more effort into ensuring the public have greater access to legal and judicial information and in ensuring that there is more consultation on draft laws. In 2009 the AMP Government introduced the *Penal Code* which integrates some important aspects of local customary law, thus making the law more socially relevant. For example, under the 2009 *Penal Code*, courts have the power to order the payment of civil compensation for damage arising from the commission of a criminal offence.[80] While the aim of a criminal trial is not one of achieving reconciliation, under Article 55 of the *Penal Code* the courts may consider evidence of reconciliation between the victim and perpetrator as a mitigating circumstance in sentencing. In 2011, Timor-Leste's Civil Code, based largely on Portugal's Civil Code, was approved and promulgated. While section 2

[76] World Bank Group, *Timor-Leste*, xvii.
[77] Ibid., xi, referring to the OIG and the Provedor. [78] Ibid., xvi. [79] Ibid., 68.
[80] Penal Code, Art. 104.

provides that 'local customs are judicially applicable when the law so determines', there is no evidence that the Government or Parliament conducted consultations either with communities and authorities in the districts or civil society to determine the nature of local customs relating to family responsibility or inheritance. This has meant that common customary practices, such as *barlake* (dowry), are not specifically mentioned in the Civil Code, leading to questions as to whether the Code is sufficiently adapted to Timorese culture.[81]

The AMP Government's 2011–2013 *Justice Sector Strategic Plan* argues that the current justice system is 'too small' to serve the entire Timorese population and 'to fulfil its constitutional mandate of applying the law and ensuring the respect for the Rule of Law'.[82] It acknowledges the need to ensure that Timor-Leste's legal framework is adequately adapted for 'the Timorese context'.[83] The Plan candidly recognises that, like other post-conflict states, most people access justice through customary justice mechanisms whose lack of state regulation 'presents a great risk because these practices can clash with the law and human rights, especially women's and children's rights'.[84] It mentions that the Government has undertaken consultation processes to address this problem and it highlights the need for 'the recognition of the local customs and norm/traditional justice systems, *through proper legislation*, in order to increase their conformity with the Constitution, human rights and law'.[85] In addition to this draft Linkage Law, the Plan mentions a draft Mediation Law which is also designed to alleviate some of the burden of the courts in regard to civil matters by diverting some matters out of the formal court system. This is timely given that the 2012 World Bank statistics for Timor-Leste indicate that it is the hardest country in the world in which to enforce a contract using state law or to register property.[86] On the other hand, as a result of serious pressure from the international community as well as some local NGOs,[87] the AMP Government introduced the *2010 Domestic Violence Law* which diverts

[81] JSMP, *Proposal for the Draft Civil Code 5.* [82] Ibid., 10.

[83] Democratic Government of Timor-Leste, *Justice Sector Strategic Plan*, 27.

[84] Ibid., 32. [85] Ibid., 33 (emphasis added).

[86] World Bank, *Doing Business Report for 2012.*

[87] UN Doc CEDAW/C/TLS/CO/1 (7 August 2009) Concluding Observations of CEDAW – Timor-Leste, [30]; Timor-Leste NGOs Alternative Report, 58. The 2010 Law was adopted with the support of the World Bank Group: see World Bank Group, *Timor-Leste*, 69. International interest in this law is ongoing: UN Doc A/HRC/19/17 (3 January 2012) *Report of the Working Group on the Universal Periodic Review – Timor-Leste.*

all domestic violence cases back to the state legal system despite the fact that a huge backlog of cases and chronic delay still plague the courts.[88]

Thus we see in the second policy approach taken during Timor-Leste's first decade of independence a shift toward embracing legal pluralism and recognising its relationship with the rule of law. While this policy shift largely mirrors the shift taking place in the international community, as shown in Chapter 2, the convergence is not necessarily internationally driven but is arguably home-grown to a certain degree. Both as President and then as Prime Minister leading the AMP Government, Gusmão has consistently shown an interest in local customary law: in 2003, for example, he made a speech as the President, setting out both the positive and negative aspects of local customary law. He concluded by considering the feasibility of linking the two systems and the challenges involved:

> It is essential to place modern laws within a context to counterbalance the confines of the interpretation of values by traditional justice, so as to clearly define the limits to which traditional justice must comply and thus avoid trampling on the spirit of the law of a country or stepping on human rights. Consequently, it will be possible to establish what levels of disputes in villages should be handled by traditional justice. For traditional justice to gain greater credibility, it is necessary to reorganize its components; this will enable these 'courts' to truly serve the communities and continue to be open and accessible to the general public at a greater level.[89]

Gusmão's optimism regarding the linking of the two systems did not manifest in any legislative action during his leadership of the AMP Government during its first term (2007–2012) as it did not succeed in enacting any linkage law to integrate the two systems in this period.

Despite the policy shift, persistent problems in the formal legal system are pushing people back toward continued reliance on customary law, thus marginalising the role of the Constitution and the courts and weakening public confidence in the concept of the rule of law. The next section looks at how various state actors are currently negotiating local customary law and it focuses on how vulnerable parts of the population experience the parallel legal systems.

[88] UN Doc S/2012/43 (18 January 2012) *Report of the Secretary-General on the United Nations Integrated Mission in Timor-Leste (for the period from 20 September 2011 to 6 January 2012)* [39].

[89] Gusmão, *Timor Lives!*, 220.

3. Local customary law

At the ground level, the question of whether local customary law is applicable in any shape or form has created much confusion for the local population. Article 2(4) of the Constitution states: 'The State shall recognise and value the norms and customs of East Timor that are not contrary to the Constitution and to any legislation dealing specifically with customary law.' This provision contemplates the possibility of the Parliament enacting legislation dealing with customary law but this has not yet taken place. The section gives recognition to 'norms and customs' rather than customary law, which has led to some uncertainty in the courts as to whether customary law is applicable to sentencing or to defences in criminal law.[90] State courts have been grappling in an *ad hoc* fashion with questions such as whether local law can be legitimately used as a criminal law defence, as a ground for dismissing a case, to mitigate a sentence, or in sentencing generally. This confusion clouds the work of the police force, who must straddle the divide between state institutions and local communities, and it particularly affects those vulnerable sections of the community seeking justice.

3.1 The courts and local customary law

One documented case of customary law being invoked in Timor's highest court was the 2003 case of Raimundo Soares who appealed to the Court of Appeal his conviction and one-year sentence for the maltreatment of his wife.[91] Amongst Soares' grounds of appeal was that the conduct of his adulterous pregnant wife violated local traditions and provoked his attack. The Court of Appeal completely failed to address this ground of appeal or to explain the relationship between local norms and customs and women's rights under the Constitution and international law.

In the lower courts, however, there is a trend in remote districts of Timor-Leste to take notice of out-of-court agreements reached through local customary law mechanisms. In 2005 the Timorese NGO the JSMP reported on three examples that took place in Suai and Oecusse,[92] where

[90] JSMP, *The Role, Practice and Procedure of the Court of Appeal*, 15; JSMP, *Overview of the Justice Sector 2005*, 14–15; JSMP, 'Judge Applies Customary Law'.

[91] Soares, Case 14a/2001, discussed in JSMP, *The Role, Practice and Procedure, of the Court of Appeal*, 14–15.

[92] JSMP, *The Interaction of Traditional Dispute Resolution*; JSMP, 'Judge Applies Customary Law'.

the district courts have operated only sporadically during the decade and there is less knowledge of state laws.[93] All three cases were criminal in nature: the first involved a large fight between rival martial arts gangs, the second involved the sexual assault of a minor by an adult relative and the third involved maltreatment of a woman by a minor. In the first case, the judge expressly acknowledged customary law as something the court could consider but she found it inapplicable in this case because of the serious implications that such fights pose to public security. In the second case the Oecusse District Court decided that the seriousness of the matter meant the case could not be dismissed but in the sentencing process the judge took into account the defendant's out-of-court agreement to pay compensation of livestock and buffalo to the victim's family. The third case was dismissed by the Oecusse District Court on the ground that it had already been resolved in accordance with local customary law as the offender had paid the victim compensation. In this last case the presiding judge was a foreign judge and, according to the JSMP, during the proceedings the judge made no reference to the applicable formal law, the Indonesian Penal Code.[94]

From a strictly technical point of view, the consideration of these extra-legal factors, particularly in the third case, undermines the rule of law. On the other hand, the courts' cautious use of customary law in the first two cases can be understood as assisting to build confidence in the state legal system: at a symbolic level the integration of customary law by state institutions such as the courts makes the state legal system more relevant to the local population. Many Timorese consider the processes used by the state legal system to be alien and remote to their understanding of law, which means that in some areas, decisions of the district courts are not necessarily considered to be legitimate at the local level. Legitimacy in local legal systems depends on who made the judgment, whether the punishment delivers the desired result, and whether

[93] According to the 2004 Asia Foundation survey, few people in Oecusse were aware of state legislation: Asia Foundation, *Law and Justice in East Timor*, 42. Note that mobile courts are now operating in a number of remote regions.

[94] What is interesting in the second Oecusse case discussed above is that the presiding judge was not local and yet was confident that he had sufficient understanding of the local legal system to be sure that the matter had been satisfactorily resolved according to local custom. Given the large number of foreign judges, this raises a number of questions relating to judges' source of understanding of local law. Ultimately this problem has proven to be controversial across the world where customary law operates.

compensation has been arranged.[95] Thus in these 2005 cases, some district courts were making an effort to take into account some of these factors, particularly the issue of compensation and reconciliation. The problem was that this process was *ad hoc*, unmonitored and outside of the existing legal framework.

In 2011 the JSMP undertook some monthly case summaries of the four district courts. These summaries show that the Oecusse District Court was prepared to openly validate 'amicable settlements' which involve the use of customary law.[96] Other courts such as the Suai District Court refer to the process of conciliation under the Criminal Procedure Code.[97] At present, judges do not have standard operating procedures to guide the courts' interaction with local authorities so as to provide a degree of consistency and accountability in this interaction.

3.2 *The police and local customary law*

The police force has been less cautious in interacting with local customary law than the courts. In an *ad hoc* fashion it has been actively promoting the use of non-state institutions to assist in dispute resolution, thus sending mixed messages about the state legal system. As the first point of contact with the state legal system, the police have frequently taken a pragmatic approach, possibly because they do not trust the formal legal system.[98] For example, the police have often encouraged victims of domestic violence to take their case to local leaders.[99] In 2005, in the first half of the decade, less than a quarter of cases of gender-based violence reported to the police were sent to prosecution in the court system.[100] According to a 2006 report of Human Rights Watch, some members of the police force even referred complaints of police mistreatment to local customary mechanisms.[101] Of concern in these particular cases is the lack of parity between the parties to the dispute. Such practice could be read as an indication that the police did not have faith in the

95 Hohe and Nixon, *Reconciling Justice*, 64.

96 JSMP, *Summary of cases dealt with by the Oecusse District Court in September 2011.*

97 JSMP, *Summary of cases tried at the Suai District Court during August 2011.*

98 USAID, *The Rule of Law*, 22.

99 Swaine, *Traditional Justice*, 22. See also UN Doc S/2006/628 (8 August 2006) *Report of the Secretary-General on Timor-Leste pursuant to Security Council Resolution 1690*, [103].

100 UN Doc S/2006/628 (8 August 2006) *Report of the Secretary-General on Timor-Leste pursuant to Security Council Resolution 1690*, [103].

101 Human Rights Watch, *Tortured Beginnings*, 45.

courts, thus undermining the state's rule-of-law institutions. Swaine argues that the effect of this informal interaction between state and non-state institutions 'has caused much confusion for women users who are caught in the interface between the two systems'.[102]

While the parallel systems of justice are creating some disorder, it has also been the case that this situation has allowed victims of domestic violence a choice between systems, sometimes called forum shopping. Domestic violence is a very serious problem in Timor-Leste with at least one in three women having experienced physical violence since the age of 15.[103] In some circumstances this choice between systems can be beneficial to women where one of the two systems fails to address the serious nature of domestic violence. Indeed, a report on customary law produced by the Law Commission of one of Timor-Leste's neighbours, New Zealand, recommends that women, who comprise the majority of domestic violence victims, be given a genuine choice as to which system they will use or both.[104]

Generally Timorese women initially approach the police or local leaders for assistance in resolving the problem. A 2008 survey shows that domestic violence is the single most common grievance brought to the police and mediated by the police.[105] For social and economic reasons women have avoided the state legal system: for example, if the action goes ahead in the formal legal system there is a high risk that it will lead to divorce which, in this strongly Catholic country, carries a serious social stigma or, alternatively, lead to imprisonment for the perpetrator or a fine which would economically imperil the whole family. However, the decision to use local customary mechanisms is not always a voluntary one for a number of reasons. First, a victim may be pressured by her family or the perpetrator to resolve the matter through traditional means.[106] Second, local leaders often believe that using the formal legal system is a sign of disrespect: reporting a matter to the police can be considered as an affront by local leaders. In addition, 'appealing a decision of a traditional leader is not culturally acceptable' because the decision is 'sacred and not to be challenged'.[107] The risk of angering

[102] Swaine, *Traditional Justice*, 4.
[103] National Statistics Directorate et al., *Timor-Leste*, 228, 236.
[104] *Converging Currents*, 240, 163.
[105] Chinn and Everett, *A Survey of Community-Police Perceptions*, 49.
[106] Democratic Republic of Timor-Leste, *Initial Report – CEDAW* (2007) 14.
[107] Ibid., 64.

the decision-maker effectively prevents both men and women from appealing such decisions from local leaders.[108] Traditional leaders thus act as 'gate keepers' between the two systems and sometimes impose fines on those who dare to report directly to the police.[109]

There appears to be tension between local leaders and the formal legal system in regard to the traditional position of women. According to the Government's report to CEDAW, traditional leaders openly state that 'formal justice processes have had a bad impact on women' and that reporting matters to the police 'gives a woman the power to destroy a family'.[110] For many women, reporting domestic violence to the police is a strategy used in the hope of deterring further violence. Most victims consider the state legal system to be the last resort. Reporting domestic violence to the police can be a gamble for victims as it appears that a significant proportion of the police force feel able to openly assert that they have a right to beat their wives and they connect this right to customary law.[111] It is clear that for domestic violence victims, both the state legal system and local customary systems have serious weaknesses.

In 2003 Swaine observed that Timorese women interviewed for her research expressed strong support for a combination of the two systems.[112] Presumably this support for a hybrid model of law results from the fact that women face bias in engaging with local law; local biases and cultural beliefs regarding women's status in society frequently inform rulings at the local level. For example, the local legal systems are seen 'to often blame women for the cases of [domestic] violence presented'.[113] Generally women victims and offenders feel that their needs and input into the process are ignored.[114] This is partly because women are not

[108] Ibid. [109] USAID, *Fostering Justice*, 25. [110] Ibid.

[111] Ibid., 43. This accords with the results of a 2009 government survey that found 86 per cent of women and 80 per cent of men believe that a husband is justified in beating his wife where she neglects her duties, for example by burning the food: National Statistics Directorate et al., *Timor-Leste*, 213.

[112] Swaine, *Traditional Justice*, 4. This research only surveyed three districts of Timor-Leste in 2003. In 2011 UNDP's Justice System Programme in Timor-Leste conducted a more comprehensive survey, covering twelve sub-districts. At the time of writing, the results had not been released.

[113] Ibid. For examples, see ibid., 27–33. Swaine states: 'The systems are inherently biased towards women's status, decision making capabilities and their roles within their communities': 3.

[114] Interview with Manuela Leong Pereira, the Director of Fokupers, Dili, 17 June 2005. The potential for bias also lies in the fact that most disputes are dealt with initially in the family sphere.

permitted to speak at customary ceremonies in patrilineal communities (which comprise the majority of areas in Timor-Leste). According to a 2008 survey, less than 40 per cent of those surveyed approved of women being allowed to speak in local justice processes.[115] Furthermore, the local system of resolving domestic violence by paying compensation may effectively encourage and condone such crimes in the cases where men have the economic power to pay such compensation.[116]

In 2011 the JSMP reported a domestic violence case heard by the Oecusse District Court in 2010 involving the customary payment of *barlake* (dowry) by the husband to his wife's family.[117] The desire for the Constitution to regulate the customary dowry system was articulated by women's NGOs in 2001 when they submitted *The Women's Charter* to the constitutional drafters.[118] This request was ignored but women's NGOs continue to lobby the Government 'to draft an anti-dowry law in order to regularize dowry'.[119] In the 2010 Oecusse case the wife was the victim of ongoing domestic violence but because of the dowry payment her family understood this as a private matter between the couple and believed that they were unable to intervene or to take the matter to the formal legal system. Although the wife suffered serious injuries and the husband was convicted, the Court imposed a relatively low fine as a punishment. Nevertheless, this was one of the few reported domestic violence cases in which a conviction in the formal legal system was successful as the victim was prepared to give evidence against her husband.[120]

Overall, victims of domestic violence are more likely to show interest in hybrid models of law that bring together the best elements of customary law and state law: the speed and social enforcement of the local system combined with the promise of unbiased decision making offered by the formal legal system. This is a tall order, as I will explain below.

3.3 Sucos *and local customary law*

The role of maintaining security at the local level is considered by the public to be the primary responsibility of community leaders rather than

[115] Asia Foundation, *Law and Justice in Timor-Leste* 44. This approval rate has declined since the 2004 survey.

[116] NGOs Alternative Report, *Implementation of CEDAW – Timor-Leste*, 18.

[117] JSMP, *Overview of the Justice Sector in Timor-Leste 2010*, 17–18.

[118] See Chapter 6, section 4.3.

[119] NGOs Alternative Report, *Implementation of CEDAW – Timor-Leste*, 17.

[120] JSMP, *Provisions of Article 125*.

the police.[121] This means that people are continuing to depend on non-state institutions to address their daily problems.[122] At this village and *Suco* (village administrative unit) level, the rule of *customary law*, and not the rule of law, remains for most disputes. Adding to this is the fact that some *Suco* chiefs give out misinformation about the formal legal system and its cost, which discourages its use.

In some respects the Fretilin Government condoned this state of affairs when it decreed in 2004 that elected *Suco* chiefs and village heads 'should provide for the creation of grassroots structures for the settlement and resolution of minor disputes' at the *Suco* and village level.[123] The Decree also assigned these elected local leaders the function of facilitating mechanisms to *prevent* domestic violence and to *punish* perpetrators.[124] The 2004 Decree did not clarify whether 'grassroots structures' meant customary law although this would seem the logical source of law for such community leaders to apply given that they are unlikely to be either trained in state law or even fully literate. However, section one of the 2004 Decree, ambitiously entitled 'Community authorities and the rule of law', stated that these functions must be performed 'with due respect for the Constitution and laws regarding State property'.[125]

The 2004 Decree fell under the purview of the Ministry of State Administration, but according to USAID, the Ministry provides 'limited oversight' of these local justice mechanisms, which 'represents a significant risk to the legitimacy and effectiveness of dispute resolution at the *Suco* level'.[126] In response to this, NGOs, mostly funded by the international community, have been assisting community authorities by engaging with these local justice mechanisms and in setting up services for legal aid and mediation in Timor's thirteen

[121] Chinn and Everett, *A Survey of Community-Police Perceptions* 8. See also Asia Foundation, *Law and Justice in East Timor*, 5, 39.

[122] These problems generally do not include serious crimes such as murder or business matters but see Chapter 6, section 1. See the study of four aldeias conducted by Grenfell et al., *Understanding Community*.

[123] *Decree Law No 5/2004 of April 2004*, subss. 3(2)(c) and 8(a). Note that *suco* refers to a group of villages. For a brief analysis of this decree, see Butt et al., *Looking Forward*, 70–1. On the status of decree laws, see JSMP, *Overview of the Justice Sector 2005* (January 2006), 5–6.

[124] Subss. 3(2)(d), 3(2)(e), 8(f), 8(g). Subsection 8(g) states that this must be performed 'for the protection of the domestic violence victims and for the condemnation and repression of domestic violence perpetrators'.

[125] Ibid., s. 1(2).

[126] USAID, *The Rule of Law*, 27.

districts.[127] For example, the women's NGO, Fokupers, has been involved in mediating domestic violence matters alongside community leaders for a number of years.[128]

A 2009 Law passed by Parliament under the AMP Government replaced the 2004 Decree but the responsibilities of elected local leaders in relation to domestic violence are almost identical.[129] One distinction is that the 2009 Law does not mention the rule of law or the Constitution and it clarifies the role of local leaders in relation to the government and the state legal system as follows: 'The community leaders are not included in the Public Administration and their decisions are not binding upon the State.'[130] Under the 2009 Law the *Suco* Council must 'promote the respect for the principle of equality' while village leaders must 'promote the respect for the law'.[131] Another distinction is that the 2009 Law gives responsibility for the 'creation of base structures for the settlement and resolution of minor disputes' only to village leaders, while *Suco* leaders should 'favor the settlement of minor disputes involving two or more of the Suco's Villages'.[132] Presumably minor disputes do not encompass crimes as *Suco* leaders must 'request the intervention of the security forces … whenever crimes are committed or disturbances occur'.[133] Furthermore, Article 7 of the *Criminal Procedure Code* requires that the formal legal system exclusively deal with criminal cases. Thus the 2009 Law appears to be giving some limited state recognition to legal pluralism without explicitly addressing the need for these local dispute resolution mechanisms to abide by human rights standards set out in the Constitution, with the exception of the right to equality. Possibly Parliament was more concerned about the gender bias shown by these mechanisms and less concerned about protecting due process rights, much like the South African Parliament in the Traditional Courts Bill 2012.

[127] Ibid. E.g. the Asia Foundation, which is funded largely by international organisations such as USAID, has been supporting a number of legal aid organisations across Timor-Leste. See also Soares and Laakso, 'Mediation in Timor-Leste', 363, 367.

[128] Despite these initiatives involving local leaders and NGOs, a 2008 Asia Foundation survey found there has been a dramatic change in attitude to domestic violence for the worse: in 2004 75 per cent of those surveyed thought domestic violence to be wrong whereas in 2008 only 34 per cent believed that a man has no right to hit his wife – Asia Foundation, *Law and Justice in Timor-Leste*, 14.

[129] *Law No 3/2009 of 8 July 2009, Community Leaderships and Their Election*, Arts. 11(2)(c) and (d).

[130] Art. 2(3). [131] Arts. 12(e) and 14(e). [132] Art. 14 (d); Art. 11(2)(b).

[133] Art. 11(2)(e).

In regard to the constitution of *Suco* Councils, the 2009 Law differs from its predecessor by making these bodies hybrid political institutions: the 2009 Law allows the elected Council to appoint a non-elected local spiritual leader (*lia nain*) to the Council.[134] Local leaders are increasingly functioning as a bridge between the two worlds of the state and local practice. In this, the government is not facing much resistance from local leaders, who, according to M. Anne Brown, have an 'explicit desire' to make their work consistent with national guidelines and legislation.[135] Despite this, there is evidence that local leaders are drawing a line in relation to the state policy of empowering the active participation of women and youth representatives on these Councils.[136]

Overall these laws are a pragmatic approach to addressing the absence of the rule of state law at the local level as they effectively confer a degree of state legitimacy on elected (and unelected) local leaders at the *Suco* and village level. In terms of domestic violence, there is an emphasis on local leaders creating mechanisms to prevent domestic violence although the 2009 Law does not in itself set out that domestic violence is a crime.

3.4 Dealing with domestic violence

In 2010 Parliament passed the *Law on Domestic Violence*, which requires all cases of domestic violence to be taken to the state legal system and in this it reinforces Article 7 of the 2005 Criminal Procedure Code. The 2010 Law labels domestic violence a 'public crime' and enumerates certain crimes found in the Penal Code to be 'public crimes' if they take place within the context of 'the family' which is broadly defined.[137] The 2010 Law means that if the police are aware of an act of domestic violence, they are required to refer it to the formal legal system regardless of whether the victim makes a complaint. It is not permissible to

134 Art. 5(2)(d). On the hybridity of *suco* councils, see Cummins and Leach, 'Democracy Old and New'.

135 Brown, 'The Nation-Building Agenda', 34.

136 Cummins, 'The Problem of Gender Quotas'; Cummins and Leach, 'Democracy Old and New', 94; see also Trembath et al., *Impacts of National NGO Gender Programming.*

137 *Law No. 7/2010* (3 May 2010), Arts. 35 and 36. Art. 35 identifies certain crimes and types of unlawful conduct found in the Penal Code as crimes of domestic violence. Art. 106(2) of the 2009 Penal Code provides that 'public crimes are those the criminal prosecution of which does not depend on a complaint being filed'. Art. 286 states that persons can be punished if they are aware of the commission of a public crime, and have the obligation to report it and fail to do so.

circumvent the state legal system by resolving the matter informally through traditional justice or via mediation by local police. Where the victim and perpetrator come to an informal agreement, the courts must still issue a decision and impose a punishment, although in some circumstances imprisonment can be replaced with a fine.[138] Previously domestic violence was a 'semi-public crime' whereby victims had to ask for charges to be made against the perpetrator but the 2010 Law means that a victim cannot ask for the charge to be withdrawn on the grounds that the dispute has been dealt with informally between the parties. The victim's lack of consent regarding the charge cannot terminate a case; however, the victim can choose whether or not to give evidence in the hearing, as Article 125 of the *Criminal Procedure Code* means victims cannot be compelled to give evidence. Effectively the 2010 Law takes away the agency of victims to choose between legal systems and to directly withdraw their complaint.

The 2010 Law is a result of seven years of drafting and consultations. Labelling domestic violence a 'public crime' is intended to signal to the population, including state institutions and officials, that such violence is not acceptable. It also indicates that local customary mechanisms as well as the police are not suitable for addressing such violence but it does not clarify whether *Suco* leaders are required to assist in the police investigation of such cases once they have requested police intervention. Nor does it directly address the problem of double jeopardy given that the 2009 Law appears to give *Suco* leaders the responsibility of punishing perpetrators of domestic violence.

On the one hand this domestic violence law is a positive development: it means that the state legal system is no longer condoning mediation for this type of crime or encouraging victims to use customary law. It recognises that mediation is not appropriate where vulnerable groups are involved. The law attempts to address the problem of women's economic dependence on their husbands by setting out that the Ministry of Social Solidarity will offer provisional alimony to victims.[139] The 2010 Law does not mention the issue of compensation but presumably, under Article 104 of the Penal Code, in certain circumstances the courts can order perpetrators of domestic violence to pay compensation to victims, thereby addressing the issue of restitution which is important in local customary systems. In 2011

[138] Art. 38(1). [139] Arts. 29–32.

the Provedor reported an increase in the number of domestic violence cases reported to the police since 2010 and observed that half of these cases had been taken before the courts, although only very few had been processed.[140] This may point to a surge of confidence in the formal legal system.

The 2010 Law faces some serious institutional and cultural barriers. The problem is that the legislation may be no more than a piece of paper in rural and remote regions because the state is still very weak and has little capacity to reach these parts of the population despite the recent introduction of mobile courts. The 2010 Law effectively diverts all cases to the embryonic formal legal system which is unable to offer either speedy resolution of cases or forensic investigation.[141] The likely reality is that some key actors will find ways to circumvent the 2010 Law and the formal legal system. For example, the police are likely to turn a blind eye to the 2010 Law by continuing to mediate such disputes or by deciding to classify the crime as a simple assault which is a 'semi-public crime', thus enabling the victim to withdraw the complaint. For their part, victims may stop resorting to the police and simply use customary law under pressure from community leaders.[142] These possibilities could operate to undermine the formal legal system and Timor-Leste's aspiration to establish the rule of law.

Overall it is difficult to say that the 2010 Law brings together the best aspects of both systems given that the state legal system cannot offer speedy resolutions. The problem of addressing domestic violence shows the palpable tensions between the two systems, with the state legal system attempting to assert itself on this matter. The police force effectively acts as a grey zone between the two systems, thus blurring the two systems together. While the 2010 Law diverts cases from local customary systems, there have been a number of initiatives that have focused on linking the two systems.

140 Office of the Provedor, *Joint Submission*, 4.

141 Independent Comprehensive Needs Assessment, *The Justice System of Timor-Leste*, 38. The problem of pushing women's issues into a dysfunctional formal legal system in the post-conflict context is discussed at a global level by Chopra and Isser, 'Women's Access to Justice', 26.

142 A study of those US laws requiring mandatory reporting of domestic violence where victims cannot withdraw complaints indicates that 'arrests deter victim reporting rather than perpetrator abuse' and may lead to an increase in intimate partner homicide: Iyengar, 'Does the Certainty', 97. See also World Bank, *World Development Report 2012*, 312.

4. Initiatives to link the state and customary legal systems

The idea of a hybrid model of justice based on legal pluralism, driven by the dual problems of perceived gender bias in local customary law and chronic delay in the state legal system, has inspired a number of internationally-funded NGO initiatives, sometimes in conjunction with local leaders and the government, to initiate programmes to link the two systems. This section examines the relationship between the rule of law and legal pluralism in these models. The tension apparent in these models is the need to modify local customary law so as to be consistent with international human rights norms while retaining sufficient of the local and spiritual legitimacy that is important to a sense of East Timorese identity.

4.1 Tara bandu

One example of a grassroots initiative devised by local leaders and NGOs has been the enactment of ritual prohibition laws, known as *tara bandu*, as a form of customary law. In 2007, researcher Lisa Palmer reported on a *tara bandu* which took place in a village in the Ermera district on the instigation of local leaders in collaboration with a Timorese student-based NGO, HaKDea. In this case, the laws decreased the amount of goods and offerings that are required to be exchanged during ritual ceremonies and for dowries, prohibited pre-marital sex (whether or not it is consensual), the burning of land and cutting of young trees and imposed obligations to seek permission before taking another's crops. The aim of this *tara bandu* was to alleviate poverty and conserve natural resources so as to ensure a more reliable food supply and to maintain law and order. HaKDea was responsible for transforming the *tara bandu* into a signed formal agreement, a first, according to Palmer.[143] She relates that government officials such as the Secretary of State for Youth and Culture were present as the law was sung, danced and then signed. While the Secretary of State was not willing to sign the agreement on the pretext of lacking authority, another government appointee, the local sub-district administrator, signed it while indicating that the onus lay with the community to implement the agreement.[144]

[143] Palmer, 'Developing Timor-Leste', 35–40.
[144] Ibid., 38.

This event illustrates six points. First, it illustrates that local customary law has continued to be a dynamic form of law in Timor: it is an example of living customary law. Second, it shows that living customary law regulates aspects of life, such as consensual adult sex, that are generally avoided by the modern legal state. Third, when disputes are being resolved, these *tara bandu* laws become mixed and matched by local leaders with other customary laws as well as non-customary laws such as state regulations and possibly the Constitution. This means that, much like communities in South Africa,[145] Timorese communities subject to these *tara bandu* laws experience customary law and non-customary law as something of a blur. Fourth, the process of building legitimacy is understood to be a two-way process: both local state representatives and local customary leaders saw something beneficial in their mutual participation in this event. Fifth, it highlights the operation of a political diarchy in Timorese culture, mentioned in Chapter 6, as well as the local desire for, and continuing adaptation to, a degree of hybridity in political culture and legal institutions. Finally, it raises the problem of who makes the law: the *tara bandu* cannot be considered the product of a liberal democratic process and yet, as an agreement made by local leaders with community participation, it arguably enjoys considerable local legitimacy.[146] This raises the question as to whether it would be legitimate in local eyes for a state judge sitting in the Dili District Court, the closest court to this village, to uphold and enforce the agreement in the process of resolving a connected dispute.

Since 2007 there are reports of a resurgence of such customary ceremonies.[147] For example, in 2011 the Remexio Sub District of Aileu presented a formal petition to the President to provide a $15,000 budget for its series of *tara bandu* ceremonies. The petition sets out the *tara bandu* as a charter of the rights and responsibilities of the community relating to care for state property and the environment, 'respect for each other according to East Timorese tradition' and taking responsibilities for the family. Under 'respect for each other according to East Timorese tradition' the document stipulates that citizens must 'not accuse each

[145] See Oomen's view of living customary law in Chapter 5, section 3.2.

[146] Cummins and Leach observe that *lisan/adat* is understood as displaying many characteristics that Timorese people consider to be democratic largely because of the opportunity for community participation in decision-making and the emphasis on consensus: 'Democracy Old and New', 93. Similarly, in South Africa living customary law is sometimes understood as a democratic form of law: see Chapter 6, section 3.2.

[147] Brown and Freitas, 'Peacebuilding and Political Hybridity', 66.

other as witch … not to assault a woman in any part' and imposes a penalty of community service in the form of 'clean[ing] the herbs' for two months in the local administrator's office. In other *tara bandu* documents, monetary penalties are imposed and these penalties increase incrementally for a multiple offender. The resurgence of these ceremonies was met by the 2010 establishment of a government department, the Department of Peacebuilding and Social Cohesion, to assist local leaders with this form of social regulation, thus replacing the role of local NGOs. This UNDP-sponsored Department offers mediation training to local leaders and Government intervention where violence is intense. With UNDP support, the Department has facilitated another customary ceremony, known as *simu malu*, which is more focused on dialogue to arbitrate conflict between clashing groups. Thus, through this Department, the AMP Government is openly embracing customary ceremonies for dispute resolution and acknowledging the inability of the formal legal system to effectively resolve certain disputes. Furthermore, the Government is endorsing hybrid models of dispute resolution that combine modern mediation methods with informal and traditional methods of resolving disputes.

4.2 Initiatives relating to land law disputes

Many key NGO initiatives on non-state justice have focused on civil rather than criminal matters because, as the World Bank statistics show,[148] these matters have been largely neglected by the struggling state court system. To reduce the burden on the state legal system, NGOs are proposing the formal use of mediation so as to divert these matters from the long waiting lists in the courts. This is part of a broader global trend to encourage the use of alternative dispute resolution in post-conflict states. Mediation is favoured in Timor-Leste because it is seen as a vehicle that focuses on the similarities in procedure in the diverse local customary law systems. Such initiatives are also useful in highlighting some of the compromises to the rule of law that international and state actors deem to be acceptable.

One particularly pressing area of civil disputes involves land law: land disputes are numerous and pose considerable potential to fuel conflict. This problem of land law is exacerbated by the legacy of a complex

[148] World Bank, *Doing Business Report for 2012.*

framework of laws from the country's history of colonisation, occupations and administration.[149] The majority of land disputes are resolved outside the state legal system using a process of arbitration or mediation.[150] These disputes comprise a significant proportion of all disputes addressed at the local level.[151] The importance of legal pluralism to land law is confirmed by research conducted by USAID funded Associates in Rural Development (ARD) into local forms of mediation and alternative dispute resolution in relation to land law. This research found that local forums are overwhelmingly preferred to formal state courts for settling land tenure disputes because the former are faster, cheaper, easier to access and more sensitive to local norms. In its final report the ARD describes these systems of customary mediation and arbitration as 'sophisticated and effective'.[152]

State law has a role to play, particularly in relation to land tenure of non-residents in rural areas. The ARD report argues that in this area there is 'a surprising and encouraging appreciation for rule of law throughout the country'. It explains:

> The research indicated that Timorese by and large recognised land ownership claims based on laws even when those laws were promulgated and applied by former regimes. Those same respondents by contrast roundly criticised land claims based on expropriation by force, demonstrating their clear grasp of the distinction betwen the rule of law and rule of men (force). Their willingness to apply rule of law principles even-handedly to non-national claimants reveals a strong desire to live consistently by those principles.[153]

Despite the predominance of local customary law in the determination of land disputes, this study asserts that state law is nevertheless respected in relation to land parcels subject to claim by non-residents and that law generally is a respected concept amongst East Timorese. Presumably this aspect of the research was driven by the prior concern of international financial institutions regarding the possibility that the predominance of customary tenure may discourage foreign investment.

149 See Fitzpatrick, *Land Claims*.

150 JSMP, *Land Law Report*, 11. Mediation is used in approximately one third of all disputes with the assistance of community leaders and officers of the government's Directorate of Land and Property (DNTP). The involvement of the DNTP appears to have no legislative backing.

151 Urresta and Nixon, *Legal Framework for Land Dispute Mediation*.

152 ARD Inc, *USAID Land Law Program II Timor-Leste – Final Report*, 5.

153 Ibid., 5.

The ARD has proposed that the state give legal recognition to state-assisted local mediation by requiring that it be the first option for land dispute resolution, followed by the court system in the case that mediation is unsuccessful or impossible. This programme of state-assisted mediation was initiated during the UNTAET period and is currently operating without formal state sanction. To give this process formal state endorsement, the ARD has drafted a number of pieces of legislation for the Government to consider, including a decree law, which has been placed on the agenda of the Council of Ministers.[154]

The World Bank has praised the ARD land project as an 'excellent' example in consultation.[155] One of the sidelined policy concerns of the ARD project has been the inheritance rights of women. This issue highlights the tension between international norms and local value systems. Most societies in Timor-Leste are patrilineal, which affects and limits the inheritance rights to land of unmarried women and women upon marriage.[156] On this problem, the ARD report comments:

> Policymakers may be tempted to consider the loss of a woman's inheritance rights at marriage an injustice, yet to ignore existential components of Timorese life ... could be counterproductive in terms of the overall well-being of the population of Timor-Leste and could compromise popular support for state-formulated policies, laws and rules.[157]

This comment implies that the rights of individual Timorese women should be compromised and sacrificed for the stability and cohesion of Timorese society. In its readiness to embrace a seemingly uncontested version of the 'existential components of Timorese life', the ARD fails to mention the constitutional guarantees of the rule of law and the right to equality or Timor-Leste's ratification of various international human rights treaties relating to equality and women's rights.[158] The project also glosses over the tension between individual rights, generally promoted by the international community, and collective rights, seemingly prioritised by the Timorese worldview. The ARD seems to rely on the

[154] The draft Decree is entitled *Official Mediation Process of Land Conflicts*.

[155] World Bank, *Strengthening the Institutions of Governance in Timor-Leste*, 8.

[156] Note that these rights relate to access and use to land rather than ownership. The customary land tenure system holds that land belongs to lineages (i.e. collectives) and hence cannot be privately owned by individuals: Babo-Soares, 'Customary Law in East Timor', 6.

[157] Urresta and Nixon, *Report on Research Findings*, 36.

[158] See Convention on the Elimination of Discrimination Against Women, Arts. 15–16; International Covenant on Civil and Political Rights, Art. 26.

government and courts taking a pragmatic approach in the application and enforcement of constitutional and international norms that promote equality. Furthermore, the support of USAID and the World Bank for this project indicates that they condone this compromising of formal equality, which is a key component of the rule of law.

In 2011 Timor-Leste's Government showed a high level of defensiveness and intractability in relation to the issue of gender equality and land rights during the peer review process of its human rights record at the UN Human Rights Council, known as the Universal Periodic Review (UPR). Timor-Leste was receptive to the majority of the 125 recommendations made during the UPR but outright rejected the specific recommendation that it 'repeal provisions in its legislation which are discriminatory towards women, including in respect of inheritance, and ownership and legal capacity'.[159]

4.3 A mediation model for general civil disputes

One early mediation initiative for general civil disputes was spearheaded by the Peace and Democracy Foundation (PDF), a NGO founded by the then Minister for Foreign Affairs, Ramos-Horta. The 2004 initiative aimed to establish and formalise a mediation model for civil cases generally,[160] so as to improve local dispute resolution and 'correct the problems with the customary practice'.[161] The idea was that a mediation model could become the 'one common model to be used in all communities'.[162] The initiative recognised the negative aspects of local customary law and sought to remedy them while retaining the core of the customary process. Thus the model sought to implement an alternative mechanism that makes decision-making 'more transparent' and 'can reduce discrimination' suffered by women and young people who are traditionally excluded from dispute resolution in the local legal sphere.[163]

The model used mediation instead of the system of arbitration most commonly used at the local customary level because mediation would allow parties to a conflict to find a solution to their problem with the assistance of a mediation team made up of customary leaders, as well as

[159] UN Doc A/HRC/19/17 (3 January 2012), *Report of the Working Group on the Universal Periodic Review – Timor-Leste*, [81].

[160] Peace and Democracy Foundation, *Proposed Mediation Model.*

[161] Ibid., 5. [162] Ibid., 9. [163] Ibid.

representatives of women, youth and religion. If the parties could reach an agreement, it was then to be put in writing and signed by the parties and the mediation panel as the witnesses. Copies of the agreement were to be given to the parties as well as the *Suco* chief and sub-district administrator and it could be registered with the state court. Under this model the *Suco* chief had the responsibility of submitting to the court a monthly report regarding the number of cases mediated, the number of cases resolved by other means and the agreements. If the parties could not reach an agreement, they could opt to proceed to court. In other words, there would be an official alternative option; this does not exist in the current framework of local customary law where people generally accept unfair or excessive fines 'because they are afraid to defy the sacred traditional house and sacred word'.[164] The pioneers of this model presumably counted on the participation of local customary leaders as giving sufficient spiritual legitimacy to this process. Overall, it is unclear as to how such mediation services can be accessed if the 'gatekeeper', the traditional leader, does not give sanction to it. Furthermore, the model did not address the ability of the overburdened courts to deal with *Suco* chiefs' reports and to provide proper insight and monitoring.

It is noteworthy that the PDF's report did not make any grandiose claims that the mediation model would help build the rule of law. It merely stated that state recognition would reduce confusion within the community and constitute 'ways to follow the constitution and uphold the law'.[165] While the pilot for this project was completed in 2005, there is no evidence of any specific follow-up by the Fretilin Government.

In 2008–2009, the German development agency, GTZ (now known as GIZ), in conjunction with Avocats Sans Frontières and The Asia Foundation (sponsored by USAID), operated a similar programme to train almost 600 mediators in selected districts, setting up 284 mediation panels as well as 77 mediation centres, which are strategically located in each *Suco* so as to be separate from the traditional realm. In the view of GTZ, the mediation concept strengthens access to justice particularly for those 'groups of people who have until now been excluded from the traditional legal system'.[166] Its mediation training focused particularly on local leaders and included information on the state legal framework. In addition, GTZ assisted the AMP Government in drafting a mediation bill

[164] Ibid., 9. [165] Peace and Democracy Foundation, *Proposed Mediation Model*, 4.
[166] Website project description for GTZ's 'Supporting Alternative Concepts for Conflict Resolution'.

which aims to formalise mediation services at the national level by introducing a system of registering mediators as well as mediation training facilities and courses. This system would be overseen by a committee made up of the Minister of Justice, the Prosecutor-General, a judge, a lawyer, a mediator and a NGO representative.

Rod Nixon believes that a national mediation programme is viable as long as the Government tenders it out to outside agencies.[167] In his view this would ensure continued funding while allaying concerns as to whether the Ministry of Justice is presently capable of implementing and administering such a programme itself.

It is uncertain as to whether this mediation programme will proceed. For a hybrid mechanism of this kind, the Government would need to give serious consideration to how it would interact with existing power structures. For example, where local leaders are not involved as mediators, there may be problems of social enforcement.[168] Where they are involved, the entrenched power imbalances within local communities would affect the voluntary nature of the mediation process. It is important to recognise that in communal societies such as in Timor-Leste, mediation is more coercive than in non-communal societies where individual rights are prioritised. Given this coercive element, it is difficult to see whether this hybrid mechanism offers any easy path to strengthening access to justice for vulnerable groups as GTZ claims. This could only be ascertained if regular surveys of its users were conducted to determine whether this mechanism does indeed add anything to existing avenues of dispute resolution for vulnerable groups.

4.4 The CAVR

The largest-scale initiative that has drawn together legal pluralism and the rule of law is the Commission for Reception, Truth and Reconciliation, known by its Portuguese acronym CAVR, which began formally in mid 2001.[169] CAVR was a temporary transitional justice mechanism that aimed to assist in the reintegration of perpetrators of minor crimes back into the community through the process of truth telling and reconciliation. It was designed to work hand in hand with the Serious Crimes Process (SCP), which was set up to prosecute

[167] Nixon, *Justice and Governance*, 196. [168] USAID, *Fostering the Rule of Law*, 16–17.

[169] For a history of its inception, see CAVR, *Chega!*, Part 1.

perpetrators of serious crimes before the Special Panel for Serious Crimes. CAVR was largely the initiative of local leaders after consultation with the districts and support from international experts and UNTAET. While the SCP was intended to achieve 'justice' for serious crimes including murder and rape that took place in 1999 up until UNTAET's arrival, the CAVR aimed to bring about 'reconciliation' within communities and between individuals for minor crimes such as arson and assault committed during the Indonesian occupation and the post-UN ballot period.

The central feature of the CAVR was the Community Reconciliation Process (CRP) programme, which operated in each of the thirteen districts from mid 2002 to early 2004. The CRP was a hybrid legal process that fused together elements of the state legal system and local systems of customary law. The CRP programme heard confessions from 1371 perpetrators and, in all, approximately 40,000 people, roughly 5 per cent of the population, attended and participated in the CRP hearings, making it at the time the most visible face of state-endorsed justice for the local population since at least 1999.

The legitimacy of the CRP programme drew on two sources. The first was the state in the form of UNTAET Regulation 2001/10. However, the CAVR styled itself as an independent body that did not rely on the state for funding.[170] The second source of legitimacy was local *lisan* practices. *Lisan* is a term that covers traditional practices; it encompasses local customary law but it is broader than it. The incorporation of *lisan* was achieved in two ways: through the inclusion of local ceremonial practices to begin each CRP hearing and through the integration of some aspects of local customary law into the design of the process.[171] The ceremonial practices generally involved the elders (known as the *lia nain*) rolling out a large mat on which the parties were seated. This symbolic process is known as *nahe biti*. In addition, the *lia nain* began the hearings by summoning the community's ancestors to be witnesses to the ceremony so as to validate the proceedings. An example of the inclusion of aspects of local law is that perpetrators were required to admit their actions

[170] For an analysis of the CAVR's funding, see La'o Hamutuk, 'Reviewing the East Timor Commission for Reception, Truth and Reconciliation', 6–7. See the final list of foreign donors at CAVR, *Chega!*, Annex 4, 3.

[171] According to Burgess, who was the CAVR's Principal Legal Counsel, the importance of local customary law developed during the CRP programme to a degree not anticipated during the design of the CAVR: Burgess, 'A New Approach to Restorative Justice', 189.

publicly[172] and the community was able to offer its points of view.[173] The hearings gave victims an opportunity to participate in the hearing.[174] These aspects were uniformly carried out in the CRP programme but the use of local ceremonial practices varied from district to district[175] and depended on whether the reconciliation was an intra-community matter. None of these *lisan* practices were detailed or even referred to in the Regulation.[176]

While the Regulation gave much leeway to the process, it set out aspects of due process to be satisfied as the base line of the programme. For example, the process worked whereby a CRP hearing would only take place if a perpetrator made a full and voluntary confession of their crime.[177] Once an oral confession was given in front of the community and the CRP panel had determined an act of reconciliation to be carried out by the perpetrator,[178] then the agreement was registered at the district court but only if the form of reconciliation was proportionate to the crime and there was no violation of international human rights standards.[179] If the agreement was fulfilled, then the perpetrator had

172 The process was that a confession took place before the community and a three to five person panel comprising Regional Commissioner, community and *lisan* leaders (the *lia nain*), and one or two women. Each panel had to have 'appropriate gender representation' (s. 26.1). This provision was necessary given that in most districts, political and spiritual leaders are male.

173 CAVR, *Chega!*, Part 9, [92].

174 Ibid., [159–61].

175 For example, in some hearings public apologies were made in front of sacred objects that symbolised links with the ancestors. In other hearings palm wine mixed with animal blood was used to symbolise the sincerity of the person's apology: ibid., [96–8].

176 The procedure for CRPs was left to the discretion of the CAVR by s. 27(2) of the Regulation: CAVR, *Chega!*, Part 9, [37]. See generally Part IV of the Regulation. For a description of this hybrid procedure, see CAVR, *Chega!*, Part 9.1.1, [2].

177 Note that perpetrators could not be compelled to participate in the process. This confession was initially set out in writing and referred to the Office of the General Prosecutor (OGP) to check that it dealt only with minor offences. Where there was evidence of a serious crime, the matter had to be adjourned and referred to the OGP.

178 One conflict between the two systems of law occurred in relation to the participation of victims in the agreement reached by the panel. According to local customary law, the victim must consent to the settlement and has the power to veto it. Given the practical problem that some crimes such as arson involved numerous victims, s. 27.7 of the Regulation did not follow local customary law in requiring this consent. This caused tension in a few cases where the consent was refused: according to Burgess, the local rule was observed here and the matters were then forwarded to the OGP for resolution: Burgess, 'A New Approach to Restorative Justice', 190–1.

179 UNTAET Regulation 2001/10, s. 28 (On the Establishment of a Commission for Reception, Truth and Reconciliation in East Timor, UNTAET Regulation No 2001/10) stipulated judicial consideration of agreements. See also ss. 30–2. According to section 1

immunity from prosecution in the state legal system.[180] Thus the CRP programme brought together aspects of local customary law and practice with core safeguards of the state legal system.

In regard to the dual legitimacy of the CAVR, some participants emphasised the importance of 'the fact that CAVR comes to communities as an outsider'.[181] Researcher Sandra Scheeringa relates that in the village of Mouris Dame, the CAVR was understood as an authority sent by the Government and hence it was entitled to solve the community's problems.[182] However, the use of *lisan* practices made the CRP accessible in that participants were encouraged to speak in their local language and were able to use a familiar process.

The decision to fuse aspects of the two systems appears to have been a largely pragmatic one. At the time of the CAVR's creation, it was clear that the state legal system would struggle to prosecute all the serious crimes and would not be able to deal with the minor crimes. The alternative was 'complete impunity' and immunity for perpetrators of minor offences and the possibility of vigilante justice and revenge attacks. Local customary law, on the other hand, was not designed to deal with such a massive scale of harmful acts. Instead it 'evolved to address isolated cases at the community level'.[183] The effect was the bridging of an individualised approach to justice with a more collective understanding of justice based on reconciliation at the community level.

The CRP has been criticised for its failure to accord full due process to perpetrators and its failure to consider fully the needs of victims. For example, Patrick Burgess points out that perpetrators were not given legal advice before making voluntary confessions despite the possibility that these confessions could have been used in later prosecutions.[184] Another factor is that a perpetrator's non-compliance with an agreement could lead to one-year imprisonment.[185] The 2005 CAVR report, *Chega!*, acknowledged these weaknesses by stating: 'the CRP was not able to offer the same depth of investigation, legal certainty or uniformity of application and guarantees of due process and fairness that the courts can provide'.[186] Another criticism is that the CRP programme failed to pay

of the Regulation, international human rights standards means the six core human rights treaties listed in section 2 of UNTAET Regulation No 1999/1.

180 UNTAET Regulation 2001/10, ss. 30–2.

181 Scheeringa, 'Enhancing the Local Legitimacy', 137.

182 Ibid. 183 Part 9, [52].

184 See Burgess, 'A New Approach to Restorative Justice', 155.

185 UNTAET Regulation 2001/10, s. 30. 186 Part 9, [157].

sufficient attention to the needs of victims; some victims felt that the CRP was overly focused on the community and complained that their needs had been sacrificed for the collective good.[187] These complaints show some contestation as to whether such sacrifice is necessarily part of the Timorese 'worldview'.[188]

Overall, *Chega!* claimed that the CRP mechanism was a success and it attributed this success to its mixing of the two legal systems and its inclusion of a range of stakeholders.[189] Furthermore, it asserted that 'the success of the CRP was an example for the new nation of the value of the rule of law'.[190] Indeed, it argued that the CRP programme 'reinforced the value of the rule of law'.[191] Paradoxically, at the same time, the use of *lisan* practices in the CRP reportedly helped to reinvigorate local customary law.[192] During the Indonesian occupation, Indonesian security forces had manipulated many customary procedures for their own purposes but some of this damage was washed away by the CRP's incorporation of *lisan* practices and by the ceremonial and mediation role played by *lisan* leaders. *Chega!* stated that some of the participants in the programme said 'that the prominence given to *lisan* within the CRP, including the element of official recognition, had helped to restore its place as a unifying force within communities'.[193] Thus the report appears to be claiming that the CRP programme managed to simultaneously strengthen both the rule of law and legal pluralism. According to the logic of *Chega!*, legal pluralism can be used as a tool for the establishment of the rule of law.

Overall the CAVR approach exemplified 'sustainable justice': through a temporary form of state law pluralism the state was able to enjoy a stake in the process of reconciliation at the grass-roots level and was able to offer participants a measure of the rule of law, albeit compromised. The CRP's compromises to due process and the rule of law are similar to those found in South Africa's Traditional Courts Bill 2012 except that procedures in South Africa's customary courts cannot lead to a term of imprisonment. The feasibility of providing a raft of procedural safeguards such as legal advice to defendants is perceived as unrealistic in the post-conflict context where the modern state paradigm is weak and the customary law paradigm is strong. This means that international norms relating to individual rights are being

[187] JSMP, *Unfulfilled Expectations*, 33, 45. [188] Ibid., 45.
[189] CAVR, *Chega!*, Part 9, [50–1]. [190] Ibid., [143]. [191] Ibid., [164].
[192] CAVR, *Chega!*, Part 9, [52]. [193] Ibid., [9].

compromised in order to achieve broader state aims, such as reconciliation, which are more in tune with local norms. As we saw above in the area of land law, this balancing of individual and collective rights as well as international norms and local norms can have serious economic consequences for some groups in society. In this balancing process the involvement of the international community can be both beneficial and problematic.

4.5 *Linkage law*

Two months after being elected, in October 2007, Timor-Leste's AMP Government officially embraced legal pluralism by publicly announcing a policy of justice that is no longer centred on the exclusiveness of the courts.[194] The Government then formally approached the UN for assistance in drafting a linkage law to integrate the state and non-state systems of dispute resolution.[195] This decision to give formal recognition to legal pluralism followed on from considerable pressure applied by local NGOs and the international community, in particular the World Bank, USAID and the UN.[196] This linkage law presumably seeks to realise the Constitution's ambiguous aspiration, articulated in Article 2(4), to recognise the 'norms and customs' of Timor-Leste.

According to the Government's 2010 *Justice Sector Strategic Plan* (JSSP), this linkage law has a number of goals: to regulate the interaction between the two systems; to enable the systematic monitoring of customary systems so as to ensure their conformity with the Constitution, human rights and laws; to guarantee that serious public crimes such as sexual assault and domestic violence are referred to the formal justice system; to set out formal avenues of appeal for those who are not satisfied with a decision obtained in the traditional justice system; and to clarify the role of customary rules and norms.[197] The introduction of the law would involve the training of local leaders in human rights, customary law and fundamental legal principles while judicial actors would receive

[194] Democratic Republic of Timor-Leste, Presidency of the Ministers' Office, *IV Constitutional Government Program, 2007–2012*, 71.

[195] UN Mission in Timor-Leste, *Report on Human Rights Developments*, [36].

[196] World Bank, *Strengthening the Institutions*, [60]; USAID, *The Crisis in Timor-Leste*, 30; UN Mission in Timor-Leste, *Report on Human Rights Developments*, 29, 15, 17, 23; UNDP, *Strengthening the Justice System in Timor-Leste Programme, September 2007*, 31, 36, 71.

[197] Democratic Republic of Timor-Leste, *Justice Sector Strategic Plan*, 33, 39, 93.

training in customary law.[198] The Plan indicates that the Government aims to draw on comparative studies in drafting and implementing the law.[199] Given the frequency with which Timorese leaders refer to South Africa,[200] it is safe to assume that the Government will consider the South African experience of state law pluralism.

These goals indicate that the proposed law has realistic jurisdictional aims: it appears that it may not intend to divert *all* criminal cases to the formal legal system but instead focus on particular crimes such as domestic violence and sexual assault where local customary law shows some overt gender bias. Furthermore, there is no indication that the linkage law will impose any precise distinctions between criminal and civil law which, as mentioned in Chapter 6, are foreign to local customary systems in Timor-Leste. Overall it appears the draft linkage law recognises customary norms without formalising any single avenue to how decisions are made so long as they are consensual and consistent with the state's legal framework. The JSSP is short on detail: it mentions both the draft linkage law and the draft law on mediation as part of the AMP's strategic plan for the justice sector, but it gives no insight as to how it is envisaged that the hybrid programme of mediation, if it goes ahead, will interact with the state regulation of local customary law.

The draft linkage law was prepared with UNDP assistance in 2009 but as at September 2012 the Ministry of Justice had not released it for public consultation even though the JSSP's proposed timeframe for the law's introduction and implementation are respectively set at 2013 and 2015. One possible reason for the delay was the holding of elections in mid 2012 and the Government's fear that vigorous debate could imperil its re-election. In these elections the Government retained power and it appointed as Minister of Justice Dionisio Babo-Soares, who is considered an expert on customary law in Timor-Leste. No doubt Babo-Soares understands that the law deals with sensitive power relations between the Government and local leaders. One legal commentator, Andrew Marriott, believes that such a linkage law would be 'replacing the locally-derived credibility of local leaders' and that this 'risks undermining the validity of their decisions'.[201] This concern echoes a more general view that manufactured links such as these can potentially harm the legitimacy of both the informal system as

[198] Ibid., 93. [199] Ibid.
[200] See, for example, quotations from Ramos-Horta's 2010 speech in Chapter 1 and Gusmão's 2006 speech in this chapter, section 1.2.
[201] Marriott, 'Leaders, Lawyers, and *Lia Nains*', 162.

well as the formal system. Drawing on the experience of South Africa, it is clear that state law pluralism entails compromises to both the rule of law and customary law. South Africa's example demonstrates that state recognition of customary law can potentially destroy its local legitimacy by reducing its perceived fairness within the community. On the other hand, state law pluralism may harm the state legal system as it may dilute the state's guarantees of procedural rights such as due process which are not embedded in customary mechanisms. For example, like South Africa's Constitution, Timor-Leste's Constitution includes a due process guarantee, found in section 34(2), which ensures that an accused person has the right to be assisted by a lawyer at all stages of criminal proceedings. It is not clear whether this constitutional guarantee will be reconciled with the continued exercise of some criminal jurisdiction by customary forums. At the same time it is difficult for a state to guarantee any level of human rights standards unless those customary law and informal mechanisms that serve a significant part of the population are recognised and regulated by the state. Compromise is inevitable on this path.

The linkage law will inevitably lead to transformation of the customary sphere: for this process to enjoy a degree of legitimacy with the population the transformation needs to be incremental and organic and involve ongoing education and training of all the relevant actors. It remains to be seen whether Timor-Leste's Government will follow the approach taken by South Africa in allowing its linkage law to insulate and thus protect the sphere of customary law from various rule-of-law values such as due process and the separation of powers entrenched in its Constitution. Timor-Leste's transition obviously differs from that of South Africa in a number of respects: first, there is much less emphasis on equality; second, customary law is not accorded the same constitutional status; and third, Timor-Leste is focused on establishing a formal legal system rather than transforming an existing formal legal system. Thus it is unclear whether its Government and courts would draw the same line at compromising on equality when implementing the linkage law. The position of Timor-Leste's Government on equality may be surmised from its 2011 engagement with the international community at the UN's UPR when it openly rejected recommendations that it repeal provisions in its legislation which are discriminatory towards women, including in respect of inheritance, and ownership and legal capacity. This stance may indicate that the Timorese Government will not implement and enforce measures to ensure that women have proper access to customary mechanisms as both litigants and as participants in the making of decisions.

5. Conclusion

Timor-Leste's first decade as an independent state indicates the considerable challenges that post-conflict states face in their aspiration to establish and promote the rule of law. The Constitution's aspiration for modern state institutions failed to ease this transition as it did not give sufficient consideration to the state's post-conflict context and the challenges it poses: the feasibility of building such institutions in a short timeframe; the need to ensure that such state institutions enjoy social legitimacy through adapting to the local context; the need to address the interaction between these institutions and non-state institutions; and the complex array of hurdles faced by vulnerable groups in accessing these state institutions.

The four events that marked this decade of transition show that Timor-Leste's state institutions are still very embryonic. They also demonstrate that the rule of law is often compromised by government policies which prioritise the national interest and national reconciliation, priorities that are common to most post-conflict states. In general this compromise should not necessarily be considered the death knell for the rule of law but as one step in the process of contextualising the rule of law as a useful concept for Timor-Leste as a state. At the same time, this compromise should not go so far as to undermine the main goal of the rule of law which is to check abuse of power. Indeed, Timorese leaders risk setting themselves up as 'above the law'.

During Timor-Leste's rapid transition to liberal democracy, strong legal pluralism has provided the state with relative peace and stability as local customary law has been able to maintain a laudable level of law and order. This has also been achieved through the contribution of NGO initiatives which have been largely funded by the international community.

For its part, the international community's primary interest in promoting the rule of law in post-conflict states lies in the belief that the rule of law is an important means of maintaining regional stability. Behind the scenes, international actors such as the World Bank have played a role in shaping Timor-Leste's legal framework and institutions, but not always with sufficient concern for the Timorese context. As the *World Development Report 2011* shows, only recently has the international community come to the view that legal pluralism may assist in achieving stability at the state and regional level. In line with this shift the *WDR 2011* effectively encourages post-conflict states to adopt a policy of recognising legal pluralism.

In the first half of Timor-Leste's first decade, the Government's policy did not recognise local customary systems. This policy ignored the contribution of legal pluralism and focused exclusively on building Western-style legal institutions, thus giving insufficient consideration to the local context. This approach has led to paralysis in the formal court system and a confusing patchwork of foreign laws which struggle to have social traction. The 2006 crisis showed that this approach of ignoring local norms in the post-conflict was not sustainable.

In the absence of a state approach during this time, NGOs drove the agenda through various programmes which opened opportunities for some grass-roots initiatives to arise. In some cases these initiatives mirrored international developments because of the sponsorship of international donors while in others it is arguable that Timorese experiences have helped to shape the current policy of international organisations such as the World Bank. For Timor-Leste, NGO-driven initiatives have produced a fragmented approach to reconciling the rule of law and legal pluralism. Despite this, through their initiatives, these NGOs such as the JSMP, The Asia Foundation and Fokupers, have created spaces in which tensions regarding access to justice between the state and local paradigms are being debated and filtered.

The change of government in 2007 led to a policy of state recognition of legal pluralism. This policy is in line with international thinking but during its first five years of government the AMP Government was unable to translate this policy into legislation by setting in place the linkage law by which to formalise the state's relationship with local customary systems. Furthermore, it failed to legislate for a hybrid mechanism to resolve civil disputes through mediation which would alleviate the present paralysis in the civil jurisdiction of the state's courts.

For those vulnerable sections of Timorese society caught in the interface between the two systems, neither system offers sufficient protection at present, regardless of whether they are linked in the near future. In the long term, for victims of domestic violence the answer lies more in economic empowerment hand in hand with a broader shift in cultural attitudes than in law and legal institutions. This predicament is similar to that faced by vulnerable sections of other post-conflict states, even in economically-robust South Africa. Neither the rule of law nor legal pluralism offers any simple solution for these problems in post-conflict states.

8

Conclusion

A. V. Dicey would have been surprised that in the twenty-first century governments in every corner of the world invoke the concept of the rule of law, largely in an attempt to establish the legitimacy of their legal order within the international community. This book has highlighted how the rule-of-law enterprise has become the dominant paradigm, spreading across the world in the name of advancing development, legal empowerment of the poor, investment and human rights. Despite the apparently extensive reach of the rule of law, the concept has retained a parochial edge as little consideration has been given to how it fits within those post-conflict situations where customary law prevails and legal pluralism has a strong presence. In the past the approaches taken by those promoting the rule of law did not recognise the strength of the rule of customary law in post-conflict states in Africa and the Asia–Pacific region. These approaches failed to see or fully comprehend the operation of legal pluralism and its benefits.

The rule-of-law enterprise has viewed legal pluralism as something of a distraction and has failed to recognise its full implications. Legal pluralism has been ignored because the rule-of-law enterprise is shaped and driven largely by Western states which have had interests in sidelining the fact of legal pluralism. One reason is that legal pluralism points to the contested nature of sovereignty in many regions of the world: it highlights the fact that states, including many in the West, rarely enjoy a monopoly over law within their territory. Legal pluralism has also been sidelined because Western states have believed that regional stability would be best served if post-conflict states modelled themselves on modern, democratic Western states which rely on a range of modern institutions and where there is an emphasis on the predictability of the law.

Legal pluralism cannot be so easily dismissed by leaders in post-conflict states such as South Africa and Timor-Leste. In these post-conflict states large parts of the population live under the rule of customary law and have only limited access to state legal institutions. For many people, the rule of state law is remote and justice (at least its promise) lies in many rooms. For this reason there is an urgency to recognise the fact of legal pluralism and to engage with customary law. This urgency was understood during South Africa's constitutional dispensation, which led to state law pluralism being constitutionally entrenched in a bid to strengthen the legitimacy of both the state and the Constitution in rural areas. Since this time the Government has struggled to practically transform state law pluralism in line with constitutional values. In Timor-Leste it was to its cost that Fretilin attempted to ignore legal pluralism during its time of government. Fretilin drafted a Constitution which sidelines customary law and aspires to establish Western, modern institutions. In 2006 Fretilin paid a political price when the state rapidly lost its reputation as a model post-conflict state and became characterised as a failed state. The 2006 crisis led Fretilin to rethink its approach to building the state's legitimacy, but before it was able to revise its policy on legal pluralism, it lost power.

It is apparent that in the international arena a significant shift is taking place. There is no longer an assumption among international institutions that it is beneficial for post-conflict states to import state institutions and legal frameworks based on Western models in order to strengthen the rule of law. Rather than seeking to impose foreign models, rule-of-law actors are now taking up the recommendation made by Stromseth, Wippman and Brooks in 2006 to design rule-of-law programmes that 'build on pre-existing informal dispute resolution mechanisms'.[1]

Legal pluralism is now understood as 'an empirical reality'.[2] In 2011 the UN's Secretary-General's Report on the rule of law in post-conflict societies stated that 'the Organization has increased its understanding of informal justice systems'.[3] In particular it has gradually recognised that these systems are 'justice institutions' with the potential to 'strengthen the rule of law'.[4] The UN has been assisting post-conflict states in building linkages between informal and formal systems. Linkage laws enable international institutions and development agencies to work more directly with non-state actors who provide dispute resolution mechanisms to large parts of the populations in post-conflict states. This can strengthen the rule of law where the linkage laws are 'grounded in human

[1] Stromseth et al., *Can Might Make Rights?*, 315.

[2] UN Women/UNICEF/UNDP, *Informal Justice Systems* 7.

[3] UN Doc S/2011/634 (12 October 2011) *Report of the Secretary General on the Rule of Law and Transitional Justice in Conflict and Post-Conflict Societies*, [39].

[4] Ibid.

rights standards' and designed to 'enhance participation, accountability, and empowerment' and 'increase the protection of the most vulnerable groups'.[5] However, the success of such laws depends on mutual acceptance of core human rights principles by non-state actors and a willingness to adapt.[6]

The World Bank's *WDR 2011* echoes this shift, signalling that at least on paper the international community is no longer taking a purely state-based approach to the rule of law. Alongside development agencies, the World Bank is now looking to engage non-state actors in rule-of-law programmes aimed at improving the quality of justice offered by customary mechanisms. Indeed the *WDR 2011* encourages post-conflict states to adopt a policy of state law pluralism in a bid to boost national and regional stability.

State-building is no longer narrowly modelled, or funded, on the Westphalian state but it is increasingly based on a broader understanding of the post-conflict state as one of hybrid political orders which combine both customary and Western forms of political order and justice. In these hybrid orders, building links between the state and non-state actors is the norm;[7] one advantage of this is that it reflects the way in which ordinary people experience law as a blurred negotiation of customary and non-customary law. For those actors involved in the rule-of-law enterprise in post-conflict states, this means they must engage with the dynamics and tensions of plurality and hybridity.

Both South Africa and Timor-Leste are in the process of connecting customary mechanisms to the state legal system by introducing linkage laws that aim to uphold constitutional values. In South Africa, which aims to transform the apartheid programme of state law pluralism into a programme that respects and upholds constitutional rights and democracy, this process of introducing a linkage law has been a serious challenge. In 2003 the Law Commission submitted its recommendations and draft bill, and from this time there has been ongoing and vigorous debate. Since 2008 the Government has been attempting to introduce its Traditional Courts Bill in the hope that it will simultaneously provide accessible justice to rural South Africans, appease traditional leaders, and pass muster with the Constitutional Court. The fact that South Africa has a Constitution which gives explicit recognition to the plurality and hybridity in its legal and political order and that it has mature legal and political institutions eases this complex process of incrementally

[5] UN Women/UNICEF/UNDP, *Informal Justice Systems*, 141.
[6] Ibid., 138. [7] Baker, 'Linking State'.

balancing and filtering the tensions between these often-conflicting interests. Notwithstanding, the process has been slow and divisive.

Timor-Leste began its trajectory to state law pluralism in 2007. It has neither a Constitution that enables such balancing nor mature state institutions that can assist in reconciling state and customary paradigms. Efforts to reconcile these paradigms have been driven by an array of NGOs outside of the constitutional framework which has meant that constitutional values have played little role in guiding the process of adapting Timor-Leste's legal framework.

For those drafting constitutions in post-conflict countries, this book advises that careful consideration and attention be given to two issues: the nature and scale of legal pluralism operating in the state; and whether the rule of law is a concept that enjoys sufficient legitimacy and understanding with the population and is thus a potentially useful constitutional norm. Ideally, rather than articulating elite aspirations, a constitution should identify, through the process of public participation and political compromise, key values that enjoy widespread legitimacy within the state and map the state's relationship with non-state actors, particularly non-state authorities, in order for tensions between these actors to be incrementally reconciled within a non-violent space. In this regard, South Africa's Constitution, while by no means perfect, demonstrates a useful model.

This book argues it is important that, in a post-conflict context, the relationship between the rule of law and legal pluralism is understood as a process of balance and compromise which transforms both concepts. Krygier points out that where the rule of law is balanced with other values, 'there is no reason *a priori* to imagine compromise on either or both is impossible or unattractive'.[8] Through showing the dynamics in South Africa and Timor-Leste this book contends that in those post-conflict contexts where legal pluralism is strong, 'compromise' is an unavoidable part of the relationship between the rule of law and legal pluralism and in efforts to promote the rule of law. Ideally this compromise takes place within the constitutional framework, as in South Africa, because constitutions set out the ground rules by which a state should be governed.

In South Africa, the rule of law may be compromised by the state's proposed linkage law, the Traditional Courts Bill 2012, which allows for due process rights to be sidelined in customary courts. The lower courts

[8] Krygier, 'The Rule of Law', 151.

in South Africa are also taking this compromise approach, as seen in their generous delimitation of the powers of customary courts which allows certain principles such as a separation of powers to be muted in the context of customary law and customary courts. The rationale behind this compromise is the safeguarding of customary law from the imposition of, and destruction by, Western values. In a trilogy of cases, the Constitutional Court similarly shows certain reluctance to invoke openly the constitutional founding value of the rule of law in the context of legal pluralism, and in particular customary law. This is because, despite efforts to transform the concept of the rule of law in the new legal order, the concept continues to be widely viewed as a Western, common law value that was 'tragically ineffectual' in protecting the rights of the majority of South Africans during apartheid. At the same time, the trilogy of cases shows that in the context of legal pluralism, the Constitutional Court draws the line at any compromise on equality, one value connected to the rule of law which lies at the core of South Africa's transformation. Thus the historical context and present dynamics of legal pluralism in South Africa are producing a constitutional jurisprudence where some values of the rule of law, such as due process and the separation of powers, are muted while other values, such as equality, are illuminated. To some commentators this may represent an 'unattractive' compromise of the rule of law while to others it may illustrate the maturity of South Africa's Constitutional Court in articulating its own sense of the rule of law which is particular to South Africa's transition and transformation from apartheid.

In Timor-Leste, Gusmão and Ramos-Horta are part of a group of non-Fretilin leaders who view the concept of the rule of law as relating to the need for national reconciliation. This position does not draw on an understanding of the Constitution and it stands in strong contrast to the approach taken by most international actors involved in the rule-of-law enterprise who understand the concept as requiring accountability and adherence to the Constitution. For some international actors this divergence may be a cause for concern and represent an 'unattractive' or even 'impossible' compromise to the rule of law. Presumably the stance of such leaders would be that in Timor-Leste the rule of law is being transformed into a concept that may be more useful and attuned to national interests as well as to the local situation. While the goals of promoting the rule of law in a post-conflict context may need to be reconsidered where the state and its legal system are very weak and have little reach, it is still important that the rule of law is understood as a concept that is concerned with limiting the abuse of power, regardless of whether the power is exercised by the state or through customary systems. In this sense the approach of both Gusmão and Ramos-Horta may be stretching the rule of law to the point of impossible compromise.

Gusmão and Ramos-Horta understand state law pluralism as part of the national interest and have been attempting to guide Timor-Leste toward a legal framework which recognises that local systems of law can be harnessed and regulated by the state so as to strengthen the rule of law. As Chapter 7 observed, this policy is in line with the current approach of the international community. However, it cannot be said that these Timorese leaders have necessarily been working under the influence of international organisations such as the World Bank in that in many respects the convergence appears to be more home-grown than globally orchestrated.

Timor-Leste and South Africa, even with the latter's strong economy and long-standing institutions, show the complex nature of improving access to justice for vulnerable groups in post-conflict states. The post-apartheid South African state has realised that in order to enhance access to justice for people in rural areas, it needs to continue a policy of state law pluralism that respects customary law and customary courts. Thus it is attempting to reach a pragmatic compromise between legal pluralism and the rule of law that does not threaten the fundamental principle of equality upon which the constitutional transformation of the state is based. At the same time the Government is attempting to mollify traditional leaders who have been mobilising in order to ensure that the new linkage law entrenches their position of power in rural areas. The dynamics between state and non-state actors in Timor-Leste are different to those in South Africa: Timorese traditional leaders do not have the same strongly-organised political voice but they do play a significant role in administering justice in a state where formal institutions are so weak.

By examining South Africa and Timor-Leste it is apparent that, partly as a result of legal pluralism, each post-conflict state is producing its own sense of the rule of law that differs from versions espoused by dominant Western states and global institutions. While this is not surprising, it is rarely acknowledged or understood by policy makers and practitioners working to promote the rule of law across the world. The idea that there is a commonly-agreed, universal understanding of the rule of law must finally be put to rest as a myth. It is more useful and relevant to understand the rule of law as a cluster of values; from this cluster, communities choose, via their constitution or elected head of state, to elevate particular values according to the context. As this book shows, the choice of these values can be compatible with legal pluralism. South Africa's Constitutional Court has chosen to interpret the South African Constitution as singling out and elevating the value of equality, thus allowing the programme of legal pluralism involving customary courts to be insulated from most other rule-of-law values. In Timor-Leste the AMP Government has chosen to interpret the rule of law as requiring national reconciliation, a value more commonly associated with customary law. These choices mean that the rule of law does not conform to dominant understandings propounded by Hayek and Dicey. International debate on these choices must be embraced as useful and constructive as it ultimately forces some global rethinking of what the rule of law entails in different contexts. The idea of a *contextualised understanding of the rule of law* may spell danger in the minds of some scholars and practitioners, but the alternative to this understanding, at least in post-conflict states such as South Africa and Timor-Leste, is that the rule of law becomes completely empty and redundant.

A contextualised understanding of the rule of law should not be equated with a cultural relativist approach to the rule of law where it is anchored to a constitutional document that articulates international human rights standards. Like constitutions, the rule of law is a long-term project: both constitutions and the rule of law aim for long-term cultural resonance which cannot be achieved between electoral cycles. The cluster of values that inform the context of the rule of law should be drawn from a state's constitution where that constitution enjoys strong social legitimacy. In South Africa, the constitutional value of equality is central to this cluster. In most cases it can be argued that this constitutional anchoring means that a contextualised understanding of the rule of law is not open to easy manipulation by a state leader. Such is not the case in Timor-Leste where the current understanding of the rule of law is not drawn from the Constitution although it does take account of the state's socio-economic and institutional challenges.

For those actors involved in the rule-of-law enterprise in post-conflict states with strong legal pluralism, a contextualised understanding of the rule of law requires some refinement in their thinking in order to have a more informed approach to understanding how their populations experience law. For example, vulnerable sections of society such as women are most in need of the protection theoretically provided by the rule of law and yet they are least able to access these protections because neither the state legal system nor the customary legal system is able or willing to offer them. This means that in the long term it is prudent for rule-of-law actors to be involved in building up state institutions so as to develop the reach, capacity and quality of the state legal system. However, at the same time, efforts should continue to be made to strengthen the quality of avenues of accessible justice and dispute resolution that serve the most vulnerable sections of society. In this sense the rule of law needs to be balanced with the need for accessible dispute resolution; in other words, legal pluralism.

South Africa's long struggle to introduce a new linkage law in line with its constitutional values shows the nature and scale of the difficulties inherent in reaching this balance. It underlines that rule-of-law actors in post-conflict states should never consider state law pluralism as a quick fix for enhancing access to justice. It also illustrates that linkage laws have the potential to entrench structures of social inequality rather than transform them. Thus, in its efforts to assist post-conflict states such as Timor-Leste to promote the rule of law by introducing linkage laws, the international community needs to have a deep understanding of the fragile nature of post-conflict states and their institutions as well as the complex role played by gender and customary law in such societies.

In contrast to E. P. Thompson, who famously praised the rule of law as 'an unqualified human good',[9] there are some who question the universal benefits promised by the rule of law. In regard to the imposition of the rule of law in societies where communal law is the ideal, Raz advises that we must consider whether it 'does more harm than good'.[10] H. P. Glenn goes further to describe the rule of law as 'a liability in much of the world' and argues that its drive for uniformity is 'one of the principal causes' of conflict in the world.[11] Certainly if states were to understand the rule of law as requiring complete uniformity in the law, the result would be alienating for large sections of the world's population and inevitably lead to tension and conflict within states. More concerning is the charge of the Report of the Center on International Cooperation that there is little, if any, empirical evidence underpinning and informing the rule-of-law strategies deployed by the international community, particularly the UN.[12] Indeed, there appears to be some foundation to this claim if one considers the minimal impact that the rule-of-law

[9] Thompson, *Whigs and Hunters*, 266. [10] Raz, *Ethics in the Public Domain*, 356.

[11] Glenn, 'Sustainable Diversity in Law', 56, 54.

[12] Kavanagh and Jones, *Shaky Foundations* [22]–[24].

enterprise has in relation to those women in post-conflict societies who live and work mostly in the private sphere.

The international community must take a holistic, contextualised and pragmatic approach to the promotion of the rule of law that takes into account the socio-economic and political realities of the post-conflict setting. The increasing acceptance of legal pluralism by the international community needs to be complemented by a profound understanding of its complexities. The dynamics of gender in post-conflict states is one such complexity. Failure by the international community to recast its understanding of legal pluralism in this way presents the real risk that the rule-of-law enterprise will cause harm in these societies and fail in its ultimate aim of checking the abuse of power.

BIBLIOGRAPHY

Abel, Richard L., *Politics by Other Means: Law in the Struggle Against Apartheid, 1980–1994* (New York, NY: Routledge, 1995)

The Politics of Informal Justice: Volume I, The American Experience (New York, NY: Academic Press, 1982)

Adelman, Sammy, 'Constitutionalism, Pluralism and Democracy in Africa' (1998) 42 *Journal of Legal Pluralism and Unofficial Law* 73

Afghanistan Human Development Report 2007, *Bridging Modernity and Tradition: Rule of Law and the Search for Modernity* (2007)

African Commission on Human and Peoples' Rights, *Principles and Guidelines on the Right to a Fair Trial and Legal Assistance in Africa* (2001)

African National Congress, 'Constitutional Guidelines for a Democratic South Africa' (1989) 5 *South African Journal on Human Rights* 129

'Mass Action for People's Power: Statement of the National Executive Committee of the ANC, 8 January 1989', [February 1989] *Sechaba* 2

Albertyn, Catherine, 'Women and the Transition to Democracy in South Africa' in Christina Murray (ed.), *Gender and the New South African Legal Order* (Cape Town: Juta, 1994) 39

Allan, Trevor R. S., *Constitutional Justice. A Liberal Theory of the Rule of Law* (Oxford University Press, 2001)

Allen, Tim, 'Ritual (Ab)Use? Problems with Traditional Justice in Northern Uganda' in Nicholas Waddell and Phil Clark (eds.), *Courting Conflict? Justice, Peace and the ICC in Africa* (London: Royal African Society, 2008), 47–54

Amnesty International, *Amnesty International Report 2004 – Timor Leste* (2004)

East Timor: Justice Past, Present and Future (July 2001)

Rwanda: Gacaca: A Question of Justice (December 2002)

'Rwanda: Gacaca – Gambling with Justice' (Press Release, 19 June 2002)

'Rwanda: Suspects must not be transferred to Rwandan courts for trial until it is demonstrated that trials will comply with international standards of justice' (Press Release, 2 November 2007)

Rwanda: The Troubled Course of Justice (April 2000)

Amnesty International and the JSMP, *Indonesia – Justice for Timor-Leste: The Way Forward* (April 2004)

Anderson, Gavin W., *Constitutional Rights After Globalization* (Oxford: Hart Publishing, 2005)

Andrews, Penelope, 'From Gender Apartheid to Non-Sexism: The Pursuit of Women's Rights in South Africa' (2001) 26 *North Carolina Journal of International Law and Commercial Regulation* 693

'The Stepchild of National Liberation: Women and Rights in the New South Africa' in Penelope Andrews and Stephen Ellmann (eds.), *Post-Apartheid Constitutions: Perspectives on South Africa's Basic Laws* (Ohio University Press, 2001) 326

'Women's Rights and Traditional Law: A Conflict' (1994–1995) 9 *Third World Studies* viii

Anghie, Antony, *Imperialism, Sovereignty and the Making of International Law* (Cambridge University Press, 2005)

'Time Present and Time Past: Globalisation, International Financial Institutions, and the Third World' (1999–2000) 32 *New York University Journal of International Law and Politics* 243

An-Na'im, Abdullahi Ahmed, 'Protecting Human Rights in Plural Legal Systems of Africa: A Comparative Overview' in An-Na'im (ed.), *Universal Rights, Local Remedies: Implementing Human Rights in the Legal Systems of Africa* (London: Interights, 1999) 39

Aolain, Fionnuala Ni and Michael Hamilton, 'Gender and the Rule of Law in Transitional Societies' (2009) 18 *Minnesota Journal of International Law* 380

ARD Inc, *USAID Land Law Program II Timor-Leste – Final Report* (30 April 2006)

Aristotle, *On Rhetoric* (George A. Kennedy trans., 1991 edn)

The Politics (George A. Kennedy trans., 1991 edn)

Armstrong, Alice, 'Rethinking Women's Law in Southern Africa' in Welshman Ncube and Julie Stewart (eds.), *Widowhood, Inheritance Laws, Customs and Practices in Southern Africa* (Harare: WLSA, 1995) 116

Arthurs, Harry W., *Without the Law: Administrative Justice and Legal Pluralism in Nineteenth Century England* (University of Toronto Press, 1985)

Asia Foundation, *Afghanistan in 2006: A Survey of the Afghan People* (2006)

Law and Justice in East Timor: A Survey of Citizen Awareness and Attitudes Regarding Law and Justice in East Timor (2004)

Law and Justice in Timor-Leste: A Survey of Citizen Awareness and Attitudes Regarding Law and Justice 2008 (2009)

Timor Lorosa'e National Survey of Citizen Knowledge (2002)

Atkinson, Doreen, 'Principle Born of Pragmatism? Central Government in the Constitution' in Steven Friedman and Doreen Atkinson (eds.), *South African Review 7: The Small Miracle, South Africa's Negotiated Settlement* (Johannesburg: Ravan Press, 1994) 92

Aucoin, Louis, 'The Role of International Experts in Constitution-Making: Myth and Reality' (2004) 5 *Georgetown Journal of International Affairs* 89

Aucoin, Louis and Michele Brandt, 'East Timor's Constitutional Passage to Independence' in Laurel E. Miller and Louis Aucoin (eds.), *Framing the State in Times of Transition* (Washington, DC: United States Institute of Peace Press, 2010) 245

Austin, John, *The Province of Jurisprudence Determined* (London: Weidenfeld and Nicolson, Reprint, 1954)

Australian Law Reform Commission, *The Recognition of Aboriginal Customary Laws,* Report No 31 (1986)

Avocats Sans Frontières, *Access to Legal Aid in Timor-Leste – Survey Report* (November 2006)

Babo-Soares, Dionisio, *A Brief Overview of the Role of Customary Law in East Timor* (paper presented at a symposium on East Timor, Indonesia and the Region organised by the Universidade Nova de Lisboa, July 1999) (on file with author)

Law and Order: Judiciary Development in East Timor (Conference paper, 2001) (on file with author)

'*Nahe Biti*: The Philosophy and Process of Grassroots Reconciliation (and Justice) in East Timor' (2004) 5 *The Asia and Pacific Journal of Anthropology* 15

'The Challenges of Drafting a Constitution' in Babo-Soares, Michael Maley, James J. Fox and Anthony J. Regan (eds.), *Elections and Constitution-Making in East Timor* (Canberra: Australian National University Press, 2003) 25

Baghramian, Maria and Attracta Ingram (eds.), *Pluralism: The Philosophy and Politics of Diversity* (London: Routledge, 2000)

Baker, Bruce, 'Linking State and Non-State Security and Justice' (2010) 28 *Development Policy Review* 597

Baker, Bruce and Eric Scheye, 'Multi-layered Justice and Security Delivery in Post-Conflict and Fragile States' (2007) 7 *Conflict, Security and Development* 503

Baltazar, Alipio, 'An Overview of the Constitution Drafting Process in East Timor' (2004) 9 *East Timor Law Journal* 1

Banda, Fareda, *Women, Law and Human Rights: An African Perspective* (Oxford: Hart Publishing, 2005)

Barfield, Thomas, Neamat Nojumi and J. Alexander Thier, *The Clash of Two Goods: State and Non-State Dispute Resolution in Afghanistan* (2006) (Report for the United States Institute of Peace) also published in Deborah Isser (ed.), *Customary Justice and the Rule of Law in War-Torn Societies* (Washington, DC: United States Institute of Peace Press, 2011) 159

Barkin, J. Samuel, 'The Evolution of the Constitution of Sovereignty and the Emergence of Human Rights Norms' (1998) 27 *Millennium* 229

Bassiouni, M. Cherif, *Post-Conflict Justice* (Ardsley, NY: Transnational Publishers, 2002)

Baxi, Upendra, 'Discipline, Repression and Legal Pluralism' in Peter Sack and Elizabeth Minchin (eds.), *Legal Pluralism: Proceedings of the Canberra Law Workshop VII* (Canberra: Australian National University Press, 1986) 51

Baylis, Elena A., 'Parallel Courts in Post-Conflict Kosovo' (2007) 32 *Yale Journal of International Law* 1

Beauvais, Joel, 'Benevolent Despotism: A Critique of UN State-Building in East Timor' (2001) 33 *New York Journal of International Law and Politics* 1101

Beinart, William, *Twentieth-Century South Africa* (Oxford University Press, 2001)

Bekker, J. C., 'Administration of Justice by Traditional Leaders in Post-Apartheid South Africa' (2002) 16 *Speculum Juris* 240

Bell, Christine and Catherine O'Rourke, 'Does Feminism Need a Theory of Transitional Justice? An Introductory Essay' (2007) 1 *The International Journal of Transitional Justice* 23

Bell, Christine, Colm Campbell and Fionnuala Ni Aoláin, 'Foreword – Transitional Justice: (Re)conceptualising the Field' (2007) 3 *International Journal of Law in Context* 81

'Justice Discourses in Transition' (2004) 13 *Social and Legal Studies* 305

Bellamy, Richard (ed.), *The Rule of Law and the Separation of Powers* (Aldershot, Hampshire: Ashgate Publishing, 2005)

Bennett, Tom W., 'Access to Justice and Human Rights in the Traditional Courts of Sub-Saharan Africa' in Bennett, Eva Brems, Giselle Corradi, Lia Nijzink and Martien Schotsmans (eds.), *African Perspectives on Tradition and Justice* (Cambridge: Intersentia, 2012)

A Sourcebook of African Customary Law for Southern Africa (Cape Town: Juta, 1991)

'Boundaries Between African Customary Law and the Constitution in South Africa' in Michael Rösler and Tobias Wendl (eds.), *Frontiers and Borderlands: Anthropological Perspectives* (New York, NY: Peter Lang, 1999) 187

'Customary Criminal Law in the South African Legal System' in Jeanmarie Fenrich, Paolo Galizzi and Tracy E. Higgins (eds.), *The Future of African Customary Law* (Cambridge University Press, 2011)

Customary Law in South Africa (Cape Town: Juta, 2004)

Human Rights and African Customary Law under the South African Constitution (Cape Town: Juta, 1995)

'Re-Introducing African Customary Law to the South African Legal System' (2009) 57 *American Journal of Comparative Law* 1

'The Compatibility of African Customary Law and Human Rights' [1991] *Acta Juridica* 18

'The Conflict of Laws' in J. C. Bekker, Christa Rautenbach and N. M. I. Goolam (eds.), *Introduction to Legal Pluralism* (Durban: LexisNexis Butterworths, 2nd edn, 2006) 15

'The Contribution of Legal Theory and Judicial Practice to the Future Development of Customary Law' in Graham Glover (ed.), *Essays in Honour of AJ Kerr* (Durban: LexisNexis Butterworths, 2006) 181

Bennett, Tom W. and Christina Murray, 'Traditional Leaders' in Stuart Woolman and Theunis Roux (eds.), *Constitutional Law of South Africa* (Cape Town: Juta, 2nd edn, 2002)

Bennett, Tom W. and T. Vermeulen, 'Codification of Customary Law' (1980) 24 *Journal of African Law* 206

Benton, Lauren, *Law and Colonial Cultures: Legal Regimes in World History, 1400–1900* (Cambridge University Press, 2002)

Bentzon, Agnete, Anne Hellum, Julie Stewart, Welshman Ncube and Rorben Agersnap, *Pursuing Grounded Theory in Law: South-North Experiences in Developing Women's Law* (Harare: Mond Books, 1998)

Berlie, Jean A., 'A Concise Legal History of East Timor' (2000) 3 *Studies in Languages and Cultures of East Timor* 138

Berman, Paul Schiff, 'Global Legal Pluralism' (2007) 80 *Southern California Law Review* 1155

Bhuta, Nehal, 'Great Expectations – East Timor and the Vicissitudes of Externalised Justice' (2001) XII *Finnish Yearbook of International Law* 165

Binchy, William, 'The Constitution of Timor Leste in Comparative Perspective' in William Binchy (ed.), *Timor-Leste: Challenges for Justice and Human Rights in the Shadow of the Past* (Dublin: Clarus Press, 2009)

Bingham, Lord, 'The Rule of Law' (2007) 66 *Cambridge Law Journal* 67

Blagg, Harry, *Crime, Aboriginality and the Decolonisation of Justice* (Annandale, NSW: Hawkins Press, 2008)

Blau, Loammi C., 'The *Rechtsstaat* Idea Compared with the Rule of Law as a Paradigm for Protecting Rights' (1990) 107 *South African Law Journal* 76

Bond, Patrick, *Against Global Apartheid: South Africa Meets the World Bank, IMF and International Finance* (London: Zed Books, 2nd edn, 2003)

Bongiorno, Carla, 'A Culture of Impunity: Applying International Human Rights Law to the United Nations in East Timor' (2002) 33 *Columbia Human Rights Law Review* 623

Bowles, Edith and Tanja Chopra, 'East Timor: State-Building Revisited' in Charles T. Call (ed.), *Building States to Build Peace* (Boulder, CO: Lynne Rienner Publishers, 2008)

Braithwaite, John, Hilary Charlesworth and Adérito Soares, *Networked Governance of Freedom and Tyranny: Peace in Timor-Leste* (Canberra: Australian National University E Press 2012)

Brandt, Michele, *Constitutional Assistance in Post-Conflict Countries. The UN Experience: Cambodia, East Timor and Afghanistan* (2005) (Report for UNDP)

Brandt, Michele, Jill Cottrell, Yash Ghai and Anthony Regan, *Constitution-Making and Reform: Options for the Process* (Geneva: Interpeace, 2011)

Bronstein, Victoria, 'Reconceptualizing the Customary Law Debate in South Africa' (1998) 14 *South African Journal on Human Rights* 388

Brooks, Rosa Ehrenreich, 'The New Imperialism: Violence, Norms and the Rule of Law' (2003) 101 *Michigan Law Review* 2275

Brown, M. Anne, 'The Nation-Building Agenda in Timor-Leste' in Vandra Harris and Andrew Goldsmith (eds.), *Security, Development and Nation-Building in Timor-Leste: A Cross-Sectoral Assessment* (New York, NY: Routledge, 2011) 17

Brown, M. Anne and Alex Gusmao Freitas, 'Peacebuilding and Political Hybridity in East Timor' (2009) 21 *Peace Review* 61

Budiardjo, Carmel and Liem Soei Liong, *The War Against East Timor* (London: Zed Books, 1984)

Bull, Carolyn, *No Entry Without Strategy: Building the Rule of Law under UN Transitional Administration* (New York, NY: United Nations University Press, 2008)

Burgess, Patrick, 'A New Approach to Restorative Justice – East Timor's Community Reconciliation Processes' in Naomi Roht Arriaza and Javier Mariezcurrena (eds.), *Transitional Justice in the Twenty-First Century – Beyond Truth Versus Justice* (Cambridge University Press, 2006) 176

'Justice and Reconciliation in East Timor – The Relationship Between the Commission for Reception, Truth and Reconciliation and the Courts' (2004) 15 *Criminal Law Forum* 135

Burman, Sandra and Wilfried Schärf, 'Creating People's Justice: Street Committees and People's Courts in a South African City' (1990) *Law and Society Review* 693

Burns, Yvonne, *Administrative Law under the 1996 Constitution* (Durban: LexisNexis Butterworths, 2nd edn, 2003)

Butt, Simon, Natalie David and Nathan Laws, *Looking Forward: Local Dispute Resolution Mechanisms in Timor-Leste* (2004) (Draft Report prepared for Australian Legal Resources International) (on file with author)

Caplan, Richard, *International Governance of War-Torn Territories: Rule and Reconstruction* (Oxford University Press, 2005)

Carothers, Thomas, *Aiding Democracy Abroad: The Learning Curve* (Washington, DC: Carnegie Endowment for International Peace, 1999)

'The Problem of Knowledge' in Carothers (ed.), *Promoting the Rule of Law Abroad: In Search of Knowledge* (Washington, DC: Carnegie Endowment for International Peace, 2006)

'The Rule of Law Revival' (1998) 77 *Foreign Affairs* 95

(ed.), *Promoting the Rule of Law Abroad: In Search of Knowledge* (Washington, DC: Carnegie Endowment for International Peace, 2006)

Carter Center, *The East Timor Political and Election Observation Project Final Report* (2004)

Chandler, David, *Empire in Denial: The Politics of State-Building* (London: Pluto Press, 2006)

'Imposing the "Rule of Law": The Lessons of BiH for Peacebuilding in Iraq' (2004) 11 *International Peacekeeping* 312

Chanock, Martin, 'Law, State and Culture: Thinking About "Customary Law" After Apartheid' [1991] *Acta Juridica* 52

'The Law Market: The Legal Encounter in British East and Central Africa' in W. J. Mommsen and J. A. De Moor (eds.), *European Expansion and Law: The Encounter of European and Indigenous Law in 19th- and 20th-Century Africa and Asia* (Oxford: BERG, 1992) 279

'The South African Native Administration Act of 1927: Reflections on a Pathological Case of Legal Pluralism' in Oliver Mendelsohn and Upendra Baxi (eds.), *The Rights of Subordinated Peoples* (Delhi: Oxford University Press, 1994) 295

Charlesworth, Hilary, 'Human Rights and the Rule of Law After Conflict' in Peter Cane (ed.), *The Hart-Fuller Debate in the Twenty-First Century* (Oxford: Hart Publishing, 2010) 43

'The Constitution of East Timor, May 20, 2002' (2003) 1 *International Journal of Constitutional Law* 325

Charlesworth, Hilary and Mary Wood, 'Women and Human Rights in the Rebuilding of East Timor' (2002) 71 *Nordic Journal of International Law* 325

Chesterman, Simon, 'An International Rule of Law?' (2008) 56 *American Journal of Comparative Law* 331

East Timor in Transition: From Conflict Prevention to State Building (New York, NY: International Peace Academy, 2001) (Report for the International Peace Academy)

'Imposed Constitutions, Imposed Constitutionalism and Ownership' (2005) 37 *Connecticut Law Review* 947

Justice under International Administration: Kosovo, East Timor and Afghanistan (New York, NY: International Peace Academy, 2002) (Report for the International Peace Academy)

'Rough Justice: Establishing the Rule of Law in Post-Conflict Territories' (2005) 20 *Ohio State Journal on Dispute Resolution* 69

'The Spy Who Came in From the Cold War: Intelligence and International Law' (2006) 27 *Michigan Journal of International Law* 1071

The UN Security Council and the Rule of Law: The Role of the Security Council in Strengthening a Rules-Based International System (Final Report and Recommendations from the Austrian Initiative, 2004–2008) (New York, NY: United Nations, 2008)

You, the People: The United Nations, Transitional Administration and State Building (New York, NY: Oxford University Press, 2004)

Chesterman, Simon, Michael Ignatieff and Ramesh Thakur (eds.), *Making States Work: State Failure and the Crisis of Governance* (New York, NY: United Nations University Press, 2005)

Chiba, Masaji, 'Introduction' in Chiba (ed.), *Asian Indigenous Law in Interaction with Received Law* (London: KPI, 1986) 1

'Other Phases of Legal Pluralism in the Contemporary World' (1998) 11 *Ratio Juris* 228

Chinn, Liam and Silas Everett, *A Survey of Community-Police Perceptions: Timor Leste in 2008* (Report for The Asia Foundation) (2008)

Chirayath, Leila, Caroline Sage and Michael Woolcock, *Customary Law and Policy Reform: Engaging with the Plurality of Justice Systems* (July 2005) (Report prepared as a background paper for the *World Development Report 2006: Equity and Development*)

Chopra, Jarat, 'Building State Failure in East Timor' (2002) 33 *Development and Change* 979

Chopra, Jarat and Tanja Hohe, 'Participatory Peacebuilding' in Tom Keating and W. Andy Knight (eds.), *Building Sustainable Peace* (New York, NY: United Nations University Press, 2004) 241

Chopra, Tanja, Christian Rannheim and Rod Nixon, 'Local-Level Justice under Transitional Administration: Lessons from East Timor' in Deborah Isser (ed.), *Customary Justice and the Rule of Law in War-Torn Societies* (Washington, DC: United States Institute of Peace Press, 2011)

Chopra, Tanja and Deborah Isser, 'Women's Access to Justice, Legal Pluralism and Fragile States' in Peter Albrecht, Helene Maria Kyed, Deborah Isser and Erica Harper (eds.), *Perspectives on Involving Non-State and Customary Actors in Justice and Security Reform* (Rome: International Development Law Organisation 2011)

Claassens, Aninka, 'Women, Customary Law and Discrimination: The Impact of the Communal Land Rights Act' [2005] *Acta Juridica* 42

Claassens, Aninka and Sizani Ngubane 'Women, Land and Power: The Impact of the Communal Land Rights Act' in Aninka Claassens and Ben Cousins (eds.), *Land, Power and Custom: Controversies Generated by South Africa's Communal Land Rights Act* (University of Cape Town Press, 2008) 154

Cockrell, Alfred, 'Rainbow Jurisprudence' (1996) 12 *South African Journal on Human Rights* 1

Comaroff, Jean and John Comaroff, 'The Struggle Between the Constitution and "Things African"' (2004) 1 *The Wiser Review* 6

Comaroff, John and Simon Roberts, *Rules and Process* (University of Chicago Press, 1981)

Commission on Legal Empowerment of the Poor and UNDP, *Making the Law Work for Everyone: Volume 1, Report of the Commission on Legal Empowerment of the Poor* (2008)

Conference on Security and Cooperation in Europe, *Document of the Copenhagen Meeting of the Conference on the Human Dimension* (29 June 1990) (1990) 29 *International Legal Materials* 1305

Constitutional Committee of the African National Congress, 'A Bill of Rights for a Democratic South Africa: Working Draft for Consultation' (reprinted) [1990] *Monitor* 64

Coomaraswamy, Radhika, 'Broken Glass: Women, Violence and the Rule of Law' in Cheryl Saunders and Katherine Le Roy (eds.), *The Rule of Law* (Leichhardt, NSW: Federation Press, 2003) 143

Corder, Hugh, 'Judicial Policy in a Transforming Constitution' in John Morison, Kieran McEvoy and Gordon Anthony (eds.), *Judges, Transition and Human Rights* (Oxford University Press, 2007) 91

'South Africa's Transitional Constitution: Its Design and Implementation' [1996] *Public Law* 291

'Towards a South African Constitution' (1994) 57 *Modern Law Review* 491

Corell, Hans, 'A Challenge to the United Nations and the World: Developing the Rule of Law' (2004) 18 *Temple International and Comparative Law Journal* 391

Cornell, Drucilla and Karin van Marle, 'Exploring *Ubuntu*: Tentative Reflections' (2005) 5 *African Human Rights Law Journal* 195

Corrin, Jennifer and Don Paterson, *Introduction to South Pacific Law* (London: Routledge-Cavendish, 2nd edn, 2007)

Costa, Anthony, 'The Myth of Customary Law' (1998) *South African Journal on Human Rights* 525

Craig, Paul, 'Constitutional Foundations, the Rule of Law and Supremacy' [2003] *Public Law* 92

'Formal and Substantive Conceptions of the Rule of Law: An Analytical Framework' [1997] *Public Law* 467

Cummins, Deborah, 'The Problem of Gender Quotas: Women's Representatives on Timor-Leste's Suku Councils' (2011) 21 *Development in Practice* 85

Cummins, Deborah and Michael Leach, 'Democracy Old and New: The Interaction of Modern and Traditional Authority in East Timorese Local Government' (2012) 4 *Asian Politics and Policy* 89

Curran, Ericka and Elsje Bonthuys, *Customary Law and Domestic Violence in Rural South African Communities* (Report for the Centre for the Study of Violence and Reconciliation, 2004)

Currie, Iain, 'The Future of Customary Law: Lessons from the Lobolo Debate' [1994] *Acta Juridica* 146

Currie, Iain and Johan De Waal, *The Bill of Rights Handbook* (Cape Town: Juta, 5th edn, 2005)

The New Constitutional and Administrative Law Vol 1 (Cape Town: Juta, 2002)

Czarnota, Adam, Martin Krygier and Wojciech Sadurski (eds), *Rethinking the Rule of Law After Communism* (Budapest: Central European University Share Co, 2005)

Da Silva, José Celestino, *Relatorio das Operações de Guerra no Districto Autónomo de Timor no Anno de 1896, Enviado ao Ministro e Secretario D'Estado dos Negocios da Marinha e Ultramar pelo Governador do Mesmo Districto* (Lisbon: Imprensa Nacional, 1897)

Daly, Erin, 'Between Punitive and Reconstructive Justice' (2002) 34 *New York University Journal of International Law and Politics* 355

Dam, Kenneth W., *The Law-Growth Nexus: The Rule of Law and Economic Development* (Washington, DC: Brookings Institution Press, 2006)

Daniels, Ron J. and Michael Trebilcock, 'The Political Economy of Rule of Law Reform in Developing Countries' (2005) 26 *Michigan Journal of International Law* 99

Danish Ministry for Foreign Affairs and Danida, *Evaluation: Danish Support to Promotion of Human Rights and Democratisation, Volume 2: Justice, Constitution and Legislation* (2000)

David, René and John E. C. Brierly, *Major Legal Systems in the World Today: An Introduction to the Comparative Study of Law* (London: Stevens, 2nd edn, 1978)

Davies, Margaret, 'The Ethos of Pluralism' (2005) 27 *Sydney Law Review* 87

Davis, D. M., 'Constitutional Borrowing: The Influence of Legal Culture and Local History in the Reconstitution of Comparative Influence: The South African Experience' (2003) 1 *International Journal of Constitutional Law* 181

Davis, Kevin E. 'What Can the Rule of Law Variable Tell Us About Rule of Law Reforms?' (2004–2005) 26 *Michigan Journal of International Law* 141

Davis, Kevin E. and Michael J. Trebilcock, 'Legal Reforms and Development' (2001) 22 *Third World Quarterly* 21

De Brito, Alexandra Barahona, Carmen González-Enríquez and Paloma Aguilar (eds.), *The Politics of Memory: Transitional Justice in Democratizing Societies* (Oxford University Press, 2001)

De Grieff, Pablo and Roger Duthie (eds.), *Transitional Justice and Development: Making Connections* (New York, NY: Social Science Research Council, 2009)

De Mello, Sergio Vieira, 'How Not to Run a Country: Lessons for the UN from Kosovo and East Timor' (2000) (on file with author)

De Villiers, François, *Selected South African Legislation on Customary Law and Traditional Authorities* (Johannesburg: Konrad-Adenauer-Stiftung, 1998)

Democratic Republic of Timor-Leste, *Initial Report – Committee on the Elimination of Discrimination Against Women* (2007)

Justice Sector Strategic Plan for Timor-Leste, 2011–2030 (2010)

Strategic Development Plan 2011–2030 (2010)

Democratic Republic of East-Timor, *Presidency of the Ministers' Office, IV Constitutional Government Program, 2007–2012* (October 2007)

Department of Foreign Affairs of the Republic of South Africa, *South Africa and the Rule of Law* (1968)

Department of Justice and Constitutional Development, *Policy Framework on the Traditional Justice System under the Constitution*

Devenish, G. E., *A Commentary on the South African Constitution* (Durban: LexisNexis Butterworths, 1998)

Devereux, Annemarie, 'Searching for Clarity: A Case Study of UNTAET's Application of International Human Rights Norms' in Nigel D. White and Dirk Klaasen (eds.), *The United Nations, Human Rights and Post-Conflict Situations* (Manchester University Press, 2005) 293

Dexter, Tracy and Philippe Ntahombaye, *The Role of Informal Justice Systems in Fostering the Rule of Law in Post-Conflict Situations: The Case of Burundi* (Geneva: Henry Dunant Centre for Humanitarian Dialogue, 2005)

Diamond, Stanley, 'The Rule of Law Versus the Order of Custom' (1971) 38 *Social Research* 42

Dicey, A. V., *An Introduction to the Study of the Law of the Constitution* (first published 1885, London: Macmillan Press, 10th edn, 1959)

Dixon, Rosalind, 'Constitutional Transitions: Lessons for East Timor from Namibia, Cambodia and South Africa' (2000) 3 *Constitutional Law and Policy* 50

Dlamini, C. R. M., *The Role of Chiefs in the Administration of Justice in Kwazulu* (DPhil Thesis, University of Pretoria 1983)

'The Role of Customary Law in Meeting Social Needs' [1991] *Acta Juridica* 71

Dodd, Mark, 'Judge Revokes Reinado Amnesty', *The Australian*, 24 July 2007

Donzwa, Beatrice, Welshman Ncube and Julie Stewart, 'Which Law? What Law? Playing with the Rules' in Welshman Ncube and Julie Stewart (eds), *Widowhood, Inheritance Laws, Customs and Practices in Southern Africa* (Harare: WLSA, 1995) 73

Dow, Unity and Puseletso Kidd, *Women, Marriage and Inheritance* (Women and Law in Southern Africa Trust, 1994) Ch 7

Drumbl, Mark, 'Law and Atrocity: Settling Accounts in Rwanda' (2005) 31 *Ohio Northern University Law Review* 41

Du Bois, François, 'The Influence of Foreign Law in South Africa' (2003) 13 *Transnational Law and Contemporary Problems* 593

'The Past and Present of South African Law' (2004) 32 *International Journal of Legal Information* 217

Du Plessis, Lourens and Hugh Corder, *South Africa's Transitional Bill of Rights* (Cape Town: Juta, 1994)

Dugard, John, *Human Rights and the South African Legal Order* (Princeton University Press, 1978)

'International Law and the South African Constitution' (1997) 8 *European Journal of International Law* 77

'Retrospective Justice: International Law and the South African Model' in A. James McAdams (ed.), *Transitional Justice and the Rule of Law in New Democracies* (University of Notre Dame Press, 1997)

'The South African Judiciary and International Law During the Apartheid Era' (1998) 14 *South African Journal on Human Rights* 110

Dunn, James, *East Timor: Rough Passage to Independence* (Sydney: Longueville Books, 3rd edn, 2003)

Timor: A People Betrayed (Sydney: ABC Books, 1996)

Dworkin, Ronald, 'Political Judges and the Rule of Law' (1978) 64 *Proceedings of the British Academy* 259

Dyzenhaus, David, 'Form and Substance in the Rule of Law: A Democratic Justification for Judicial Review?' in Christopher Forsyth (ed.), *Judicial Review and the Constitution* (Oxford: Hart Publishing, 2000) 141

'Judicial Independence, Transitional Justice and the Rule of Law' (2003) 10 *Otago Law Review* 345

Recrafting the Rule of Law: The Limits of Legal Order (Oxford: Hart Publishing, 1999)

'The Pasts and Future of the Rule of Law in South Africa' (2007) 124 *South African Law Journal* 734

'Transitional Justice: Review Essay' (2003) 1 *International Journal of Constitutional Law* 163

Ehrlich, Eugen, *Fundamental Principles of the Sociology of Law* (New York, NY: Arno Press, 1975)

Ellis, Stephen and Tsepo Sechaba, *Comrades Against Apartheid: The ANC and the South African Communist Party in Exile* (London: James Currey, 1992)

Elster, Jon, 'Forces and Mechanisms in the Constitution-Making Process' (1996) 45 *Duke Law Journal* 364

English, Rosalind, '*Ubuntu*: The Quest for an Indigenous Jurisprudence' (1996) 12 *South African Journal on Human Rights* 641

Fajardo, Raquel Yrigoyen, 'Legal Pluralism, Indigenous Law and the Special Jurisdiction in the Andean Countries' (2004) 10/27 *Beyond Law, Informal Justice and Legal Pluralism in the Global South* 32

Fallon, Richard H., '" The Rule of Law" as a Concept in Constitutional Discourse' (1997) 97 *Columbia Law Review* 1

Farrall, Jeremy, *United Nations Sanctions and the Rule of Law* (Cambridge University Press, 2008)

Faundez, Julio, 'Legal Pluralism and International Development Agencies: State Building or Legal Reform?' (2011) 3 *Hague Journal on the Rule of Law* 18

'Should Justice Reform Projects Take Non-State Justice Systems Seriously? Perspectives from Latin America' in Caroline Mary Sage and Michael Woolcock (eds.), *The World Bank Legal Review: Law, Equity and Development, Vol 2* (The Hague: Martinus Nijhoff, 2006) 113

'The Rule of Law Enterprise: Promoting a Dialogue Between Practitioners and Academics' (2005) 12 *Democratization* 567

Feldman, Noah, 'Imposed Constitutionalism' (2005) 37 *Connecticut Law Review* 857

Fierens, Jacques, '*Gacaca* Courts: Between Fantasy and Reality' (2005) 3 *Journal of International Criminal Justice* 896

Fitzpatrick, Daniel, *Land Claims in East Timor* (Canberra: Asia Pacific Press, 2002)

'Re-establishing Land Titles and Administration in East Timor' (2000) 15 *Pacific Economic Bulletin* 152

Fitzpatrick, Daniel, Andrew McWilliam and Susana Barnes, 'Policy Notes on Customary Land in Timor-Leste' (2008) 5 *East Timor Law Journal*

Fitzpatrick, Peter, 'Law and Societies' (1984) 22 *Osgoode Hall Law Journal* 115

Fitzpatrick, Stephen, 'Ramos Horta Resigns but PM Hangs On', *The Australian*, 26 June 2006

'UN Forces Sack Timor Advisor Roque Rodriguez', *The Australian*, 12 June 2008

Fletcher, Laurel and Harvey M. Weinstein, *Justice, Accountability and Social Reconstruction: An Interview Study of Bosnian Judges and Prosecutors* (Report, University of California, Berkeley; University of Sarajevo, 2000)

Fletcher, Laurel, Harvey M. Weinstein and Jamie Rowen, 'Context, Timing and the Dynamics of Transitional Justice: A Historical Perspective' (2009) 31 *Human Rights Quarterly* 163.

Forsyth, Miranda, *A Bird That Flies with Two Wings: The Kastom and State Justice Systems in Vanuatu* (Canberra: Australian National University E Press, 2009)

Fox, James J. (ed.), *The Flow of Life: Essays on Eastern Indonesia* (Cambridge, MA: Harvard University Press, 1980)

Frankenberg, Günter, 'Comparing Constitutions: Ideas, Ideals, and Ideology – Toward a Layered Narrative' (2006) 4 *International Journal of Constitutional Law* 439

Fretilin, 'Australian Military Commander Under Fire in East Timor' (Media Release, 23 November 2007)

'Minister Threatens to Sack Foreign Judges' (Media Release, 5 October 2007)

Fuller, Chris, 'Legal Anthropology, Legal Pluralism and Legal Thought' (1994) 10 *Anthropology Today* 9

Fuller, Lon, 'Positivism and Fidelity to Law – A Reply to Professor Hart' (1958) 71 *Harvard Law Review* 593

The Morality of Law (New Haven, CT: Yale University Press, 1967)

Gahima, Gerald, 'Alternatives to Prosecution: The Case of Rwanda' in Edel Hughes, William Schabas and Ramesh Thakur (eds.), *Atrocities and International Accountability: Beyond Transitional Justice* (New York, NY: United Nations University Press, 2007) 159

Galanter, Marc, 'Justice in Many Rooms: Courts, Private Ordering, and Indigenous Law' (1981) 19 *Journal of Legal Pluralism* 1

'The Modernization of Law' in Myron Weiner (ed.), *Modernization: The Dynamics of Growth* (Washington, DC: Voice of America, 1967)

Galanter, Marc and Jayanth K. Krishnan, 'Debased Informalism: *Lok Adalats* and Legal Rights in Modern India' in Erik G. Jensen and Thomas C. Heller (eds.), *Beyond Common Knowledge: Empirical Approaches to the Rule of Law* (Stanford University Press, 2003)

Gardner, James A., *Legal Imperialism and Foreign Aid in Latin America* (Madison: University of Wisconsin Press, 1980)

Garrison, Randall, *The Role of Constitution-Building in Democratization: Case Study – East Timor* (2005) (Report for the International Institute for Democracy and Electoral Assistance)

Gesellschaft für Technische Zusammenarbeit, *Local Perspectives: Foreign Aid to the Justice Sector* (2000)

Ghai, Yash, 'A Journey Around Constitutions: Reflections on Contemporary Constitutions' (2005) 122 *South African Law Journal* 804

Ghai, Yash and Guido Galli, *Constitution Building Processes and Democratization* (2006) (Report for the International Institute for Democracy and Electoral Assistance)

Ghai, Yash and Jill Cottrell, 'The Rule of Law and Access to Justice' in Ghai and Cottrell (eds.), *Marginalised Communities and Access to Justice* (Oxford: Routledge, 2010) 1

Ghani, Ashraf and Clare Lockhart, *Fixing Failed States: A Framework for Rebuilding a Fractured World* (Oxford University Press, 2008)

Gibson, James L. and Amanda Gouws, 'Support for the Rule of Law in the Emerging South African Democracy' (1997) 152 *International Social Science Journal* 173

Ginsburg, Tom, *Judicial Review in New Democracies: Constitutional Courts in Asian Cases* (New York, NY: Cambridge University Press, 2003)

Glenn, H. Patrick, 'Sustainable Diversity in Law' (2011) 3 *Hague Journal on the Rule of Law* 39.

Go, Julian, 'Modelling the State: Postcolonial Constitutions in Asia and Africa' (2002) 39/4 *Southeast Asian Studies* 558

Golding, Martin P., 'Transitional Regimes and the Rule of Law' (1996) 9 *Ratio Juris* 387

Golub, Stephen, 'A House Without a Foundation' in Thomas Carothers (ed.), *Promoting the Rule of Law Abroad: In Search of Knowledge* (Washington, DC: Carnegie Endowment for International Peace, 2006) 105

'The Rule of Law and the UN Peacebuilding Commission: A Social Development Approach' (2007) 20 *Cambridge Review of International Affairs* 47

Gopal, Mohan Gopalan, 'Law and Development: Toward a Pluralist Vision' (1996) 90 *American Society of International Law Proceedings* 231

Government of the Islamic Republic of Afghanistan, *Afghan National Development Strategy (ANDS). An Interim Strategy for Security, Governance, Economic Growth and Poverty Reduction* (2006)

Afghanistan National Development Strategy 2008–2013 (ANDS). A Strategy for Security, Governance, Economic Growth and Poverty Reduction (2008)

Government of the Islamic Republic of Afghanistan (Ministry of Justice), *Justice for All: A Comprehensive Needs Analysis for Justice in Afghanistan* (2005)

Grant, Evadne, 'Human Rights, Cultural Diversity and Customary Law in South Africa' (2006) 50 *Journal of African Law* 2

Graydon, Carolyn, 'Local Justice Systems in Timor-Leste: Washed Up, or Watch This Space?' (2005) 68 *Development Bulletin* 66

Grenfell, Damian, 'Making Modernity in Timor-Leste' (2007) 90 *Arena Magazine* 9

Grenfell, Damian, Mayra Walsh, Anna Trembath, Carmenesa Moniz Noronha and Kym Holthouse, *Understanding Community: Security and Sustainability in Four Aldeia in Timor-Leste* (Melbourne: RMIT University, 2009)

Grenfell, Laura, 'Harnessing Local Law in the Post-Conflict State: The Case of Timor-Leste' in William Binchy (ed.), *Timor-Leste: Challenges for Justice and Human Rights in the Shadow of the Past* (Dublin: Clarus Press, 2009)

'Legal Pluralism and the Challenge of Building the Rule of Law in Post-Conflict States: A Case-Study of Timor-Leste' in Brett Bowden, Hilary Charlesworth and Jeremy Farrall (eds.), *The Role of International Law in Rebuilding Societies after Conflict: Great Expectations* (Cambridge University Press, 2009)

'Legal Pluralism and the Rule of Law in Timor-Leste' (2006) 19 *Leiden Journal of International Law* 305

'Promoting the Rule of Law in Timor-Leste' (2009) 9 *Conflict, Security and Development* 213–38

Griffiths, Anne, *In the Shadow of Marriage: Gender and Justice in an African Community* (University of Chicago Press, 1997)

'Legal Pluralism' in Reza Banakar and Max Travers (eds.), *An Introduction to Law and Social Theory* (Oxford: Hart Publishing, 2002) 289

'Reconfiguring Law: An Ethnographic Perspective from Botswana' (1998) 23 *Law and Social Inquiry* 587

Griffiths, John, 'What is Legal Pluralism?' (1986) 24 *Journal of Legal Pluralism* 1

Gumede, William Mervin, *Thabo Mbeki and the Battle for the Soul of the ANC* (Cape Town: Zebra Press, 2005)

Gusmão, Xanana, *Intervention – Response by His Excellency the Prime Minister on the Occasion of the Motion of No Confidence* (Plenary Session of the National Parliament, 12 October 2009).

Timor Lives! Speeches of Freedom and Independence (Sydney: Longueville Media, 2005)

Gutteridge, William, 'South Africa: Apartheid's Endgame' in William Gutteridge (ed.), *South Africa: From Apartheid to National Unity, 1981 to 1994* (Aldershot: Dartmouth, 1995) 147

Hahlo, H. R. and Ellison Kahn, *The Union of South Africa: The Development of its Law and Constitution* (London: Stevens, 1960)

Hall, Margaret and Tom Young, *Confronting Leviathan: Mozambique since Independence* (Athens, OH: Ohio University Press, 1997)

Hamnett, Ian, *Chieftainship and Legitimacy: An Anthropological Study of Executive Law in Lesotho* (London: Routledge & Kegan Paul, 1975)

Harper, Erica, *Customary Justice: From Program Design to Impact Evaluation* (Rome: International Development Law Organization, 2011)

'Delivering Justice in the Wake of Mass Violence: New Approaches to Transitional Justice' (2005) 10 *Journal of Conflict and Security Law* 149

(Re)Constructing a Legal System in East Timor: Challenges to Introducing International Legal Norms and Principles into Post-Conflict States Under UN Administration (D Phil Thesis, University of Melbourne, 2007)

(ed.), *Working with Customary Justice Systems: Post-Conflict and Fragile States* (Rome: International Development Law Organization, 2011)

Harrington, Andrew, 'Institutions and the East Timorese Experience' (2006) 7 *East Timor Law Journal* 2

Harrington, Andrew and Tanja Chopra, *Arguing Traditions: Denying Kenya's Women Access to Land Rights* (Research Report of the World Bank's Justice for the Poor Programme, 2010)

Harris-Rimmer, Susan, *Gender and Transitional Justice: The Women of East Timor* (London: Routledge, 2010)

Hart, H. L. A., 'Positivism and the Separation of Law and Morals' (1958) 71 *Harvard Law Review* 593.

Harvey, William B., *Introduction to the Legal System in East Africa* (Kampala: East African Literature Bureau, 1975)

Hayek, Friedrich, *The Road to Serfdom* (University of Chicago Press, 1975)

The Constitution of Liberty (University of Chicago Press, 1960)

The Political Ideal of the Rule of Law (Cairo, 1955)

Henkin, Louis, 'A New Birth of Constitutionalism' (1992) 14 *Cardozo Law Review* 533

Hicks, David, 'Community and Nation-State in East Timor' (2007) 23 *Anthropology Today* 13

Himonga, Chuma, 'African Customary Law in South Africa – Many Faces of *Bhe* v. *Magistrate Khayelitsha*' [2005] *Recht in Afrika* 163

'Constitutional Rights of Women under Customary Law in Southern Africa: Dominant Interventions and "Old Pathways"' in Beverley Baines, Daphne Barak-Erez and Tvsi Kahana (eds.), *Feminist Constitutionalism: Global Perspectives* (Cambridge University Press, 2012)

'Law and Gender in Southern Africa: Human Rights and Family Law' in York Bradshaw and Stephen N. Ndegwa (eds.), *The Uncertain Promise of Southern Africa* (Bloomington, IN: Indiana University Press, 2000) 275

'Taking Stock of Changes to Customary Law in a New South Africa' in Graham Glover (ed.), *Essays in Honour of AJ Kerr* (Durban: LexisNexis Butterworths, 2006) 215

'The Advancement of African Women's Rights in the First Decade of Democracy in South Africa: The Reform of the Customary Law of Marriage and Succession' [2005] *Acta Juridica* 82

'The Future of Living Customary Law in African Legal Systems in the Twenty-First Century and Beyond with Special Reference to South Africa' in Jean-Marie Fenrich, Paolo Galizzi and Tracy E. Higgins (eds.), *The Future of African Customary Law* (Cambridge University Press, 2011)

Himonga, Chuma and Craig Bosch, 'The Application of African Customary Law under the Constitution of South Africa: Problems Solved or Just Beginning?' (2000) 117 *South African Law Journal* 306

Himonga, Chuma and Rashida Manjoo, 'The Challenges of Formalisation, Regulation, and Reform of Traditional Courts in South Africa' (209) 3 *Malawi Law Journal* 157

'What's in a Name? The Identity and Reform of Customary Law in South Africa's Constitutional Dispensation' in Manfred O. Hinz (ed.), *The Shade of New Leaves: Governance in Traditional Authority, A Southern African Perspective* (Berlin: Lit Verlag, 2006) 329

Himonga, Chuma, Alice Armstrong, Chaloka Beyani, Janet Kabeberi-Macharia, Athaliah Molokomme, Welshman Ncube, Thandabantu Nhlapo, Bart Rwezaura and Julie Stewart, 'Uncovering Reality: Excavating Women's Rights in African Family Law' (1993) 7 *International Journal of Law and the Family* 314

Hoexter, Cora, 'The Principle of Legality in South African Administrative Law' (2004) 4 *Macquarie Law Journal* 165

Hohe, Tanja, 'Delivering Feudal Democracy in East Timor' in Edward Newman and Roland Rich (eds.), *The UN Role in Promoting Democracy: Between Ideals and Reality* (Tokyo: United Nations University Press, 2004) 302

'Justice Without Judiciary in East Timor' (2003) 3/3 *Conflict, Security and Development* 335

'The Clash of Paradigms: International Administration and Local Political Legitimacy in East Timor' (2002) 24 *Contemporary South East Asia* 569

'Totem Polls: Indigenous Concepts and "Free and Fair" Elections in East Timor' (2002) 9 *International Peacekeeping* 69

Hohe, Tanja and Rod Nixon, *Reconciling Justice: 'Traditional' Law and State Justice in East Timor (Final Report)* (2003) (Report prepared for the United States Institute of Peace)

Honeyman, Catherine, Jens Meierhenrich, Leila Chirayath, Justina Hierta, Shakirah Hudani, Andrew Iliff and Alfa Tiruneh, *Gacaca Jurisdictions: Transitional Justice in Rwanda – Observations from 10 June to 8 August 2002* (Cambridge, MA: Harvard University Press, 2002)

Hooker, M. B., *Legal Pluralism: An Introduction to Colonial and Neo-Colonial Laws* (Oxford: Clarendon Press, 1975)

Human Rights Watch, 'Elections May Speed Genocide Trials' (Press Release, 2001)

Tortured Beginnings: Police Violence and the Beginnings of Impunity in East Timor Vol 18, No 2(c) (April 2006)

Hund, John, 'African Witchcraft and Western Law – Psychological and Cultural Issues' in John Hund (ed.), *Witchcraft Violence and the Law in South Africa* (Pretoria: Protea Book House, 2003) 1

Hurwitz, Agnès, 'Civil War and the Rule of Law: Towards Security, Development and Human Rights' in Agnès Hurwitz and Reyko Huang (eds.), *Civil War and the Rule of Law: Security, Development, Human Rights* (Boulder, CO: Lynne Rienner Publishers, 2008) 1

Huyse, Luc and Mark Salter (eds.), *Traditional Justice and Reconciliation after Violent Conflict: Learning from African Experiences* (Stockholm: International IDEA, 2008) (Report of the Institute for Democracy and Electoral Assistance)

Independent Comprehensive Needs Assessment, *The Justice System of Timor-Leste* (October 2009)

Independent Evaluation of SDC's Human Rights and Rule of Law Guidance Documents: Influence, Effectiveness and Relevance within SDC (March 2004)

Ingelaere, Bert, 'The Gacaca Courts in Rwanda' in Luc Huyse and Mark Salter (eds.), *Traditional Justice and Reconciliation after Violent Conflict: Learning from African Experiences* (Stockholm: International IDEA, 2008) 24 (Report of the Institute for Democracy and Electoral Assistance)

International Center for Transitional Justice (Caitlin Reiger and Marieke Wierda), *The Serious Crimes Process in Timor-Leste: In Retrospect* (March 2006)

International Center for Transitional Justice (Megan Hirst and Howard Varney), *Justice Abandoned? An Assessment of the Serious Crimes Process in East Timor* (June 2005)

International Commission of Jurists, *African Conference on the Rule of Law: A Report on the Proceedings of the Conference* (1961)

Erosion of the Rule of Law in South Africa (1968)

Ruler's Law: Mission to Indonesia (1999)

South Africa and the Rule of Law (1988)

International Commission of Jurists and the Netherlands Institute of Human Rights, *Indonesia and the Rule of Law: Twenty Years of 'New Order' Government* (1987)

International Council on Human Rights Policy, *Local Perspectives: Foreign Aid to the Justice Sector* (2000)

When Legal Worlds Overlap: Human Rights, State and Non-State Law (2009)

International Crisis Group, *Timor-Leste: No Time for Complacency* (9 February 2009)

Isser, Deborah (ed.), *Customary Justice and the Rule of Law in War-Torn Societies* (Washington, DC: United States Institute of Peace Press, 2011)

Iyengar, Radha, 'Does the Certainty of Arrest Reduce Domestic Violence? Evidence from Mandatory and Recommended Arrest Laws' (2009) 93 *Journal of Public Economics* 85

Jackson, Vicki C. and Mark Tushnet, *Comparative Constitutional Law* (New York, NY: Foundation Press, 1999)

Jagwanth, Saras and Christina Murray, '"No Nation Can be Freed When One Half of it is Enslaved": Constitutional Equality for Women in South Africa' in Beverley Baines and Ruth Rubio-Marin (eds.), *The Gender of Constitutional Jurisprudence* (New York, NY: Cambridge University Press, 2004)

Jenkins, Catherine, 'A Truth Commission for East Timor: Lessons from South Africa' (2002) 7 *Journal of Conflict and Security Law* 233

Jennings, William Ivor, *The Law and the Constitution* (University of London Press, 1933)

Jensen, Erik G., 'Justice and the Rule of Law' in Charles T. Call (ed.), *Building States to Build Peace* (Boulder, CO: Lynne Rienner Publishers, 2008)

Jensen, Erik G. and Tomas C. Heller, *Beyond Common Knowledge: Empirical Approaches to the Rule of Law* (Stanford University Press, 2003)

Jessep, Owen and Anthony Regan, 'Developing a Coherent Underlying Law – Integrating Custom and Common Law, Pts 1–2' in Anthony Regan and Owen Jessep (eds.), *Twenty Years of the Papua New Guinea Constitution* (Sydney: Lawbook, 2001) 114, 134

JSMP, *Access to Justice for Women Victims* (July 2004)

Analysis of Decisions Issued by the Baucau District Court in Cases Involving Female Victims: July 2007–December 2008 (December 2008)

Digest of the Jurisprudence of the Special Panels for Serious Crimes (April 2007)

'East Timorese Parliament Passes New Legislation on the Applicable Subsidiary Law' (Press Release, 1 October 2003)

Facing the Challenge of Domestic Violence in Timor-Leste: Can the New Law Deliver? (July 2011)

Impact of the Maternus Bere Case on the Justice System and the Rule of Law in Timor-Leste (September 2009)

'Judge Applies Customary Law in a Criminal Case' (Press Release, 19 May 2005)

Key Themes in Legal Development: A JSMP Retrospective, 27 April 2001–27 April 2008 (2008)
Land Law Report (27 September 2005)
New Players in Timor-Leste's Justice System (August 2006)
Oppressive Indonesian Law Applied by the Court of Appeal (30 June 2005)
Overview of the Courts in East Timor in 2004 (17 December 2004)
Overview of the Justice Sector 2005 (January 2006)
Overview of the Justice Sector 2006–2007 (2007)
Overview of the Justice Sector 2008 (January 2009)
Overview of the Justice Sector: March 2005 (2005)
Overview of the Justice Sector in Timor-Leste 2010 (March 2011)
Presidential Pardons and Commutation of Sentences: The Need for Regulation and Clarity (A Submission from JSMP to the Ministry of Justice) (October 2010)
Proposal for the Draft Civil Code to Reflect the Real Situation in Timor-Leste (Proposal for Committee A of the National Parliament) (23 September 2010)
Provisions of Article 125 of the Criminal Procedure Act are an Obstacle for Victims of Domestic Violence (June 2011)
Report on the Court of Appeal Decision in the Case of Armando dos Santos (August 2003)
Summary of Cases dealt with by the Oecusse District Court in September 2011 (2011)
Summary of Cases tried at the Suai District Court during August 2011 (2011)
The Interaction of Traditional Dispute Resolution with the Formal Justice Sector in Timor-Leste (November 2005)
The JSMP's Submission to the UN Commission of Experts (6 April 2005)
The Private Lawyers Statute: Overview and Analysis (18 September 2008)
The Role, Practice and Procedure of the Court of Appeal (28 June 2005)
Unfulfilled Expectations: Community Views on CAVR's Community Reconciliation Process (August 2004)
Women in the Formal Justice Sector: Report on the Dili District Court (April 2004)

Judicial Advisers' Conference, Makerere College, Kampala, Uganda 1953, *Native Courts and Native Customary Law in Africa.*

Kaganas, Felicity and Christina Murray, 'The Contest Between Culture and Gender Equality under South Africa's Interim Constitution' (1994) 21 *Journal of Law and Society* 409

Kairys, David, 'Searching for the Rule of Law' (2003) 36 *Suffolk University Law Review* 307

Katz, Stanley N., *Constitutionalism in East Central Europe: Some Negative Lessons from the American Experience* (Washington, DC: German Historical Institute, 1994)

Katzenstein, Suzanne, 'Hybrid Tribunals: Searching for Justice in East Timor' (2003) 16 *Harvard Human Rights Journal* 245

Kavanagh, Camino and Bruce Jones, *Shaky Foundations: An Assessment of the UN's Rule of Law Support Agenda* (Report of NYU's Center for International Cooperation, November 2011)

Kennedy, David, 'Laws and Developments' in John Hatchard and Amanda Perry-Kessaris (eds.), *Law and Development: Facing Complexity in the Twenty-First Century – Essays in Honour of Peter Slinn* (London: Cavendish, 2003) 17

'The International Human Rights Movement: Part of the Problem?' (2002) 15 *Harvard Human Rights Law Journal* 101

'The "Rule of Law", Political Choices, and Development Common Sense' in David Trubek and Alvaro Santos (eds.), *The New Law and Economic Development: A Critical Appraisal* (Cambridge University Press, 2006) 95

Kerr, A. J., 'Customary Law, Fundamental Rights and the Constitution' (1994) 111 *South African Law Journal* 720

'Inheritance in Customary Law under the Interim Constitution and under the Present Constitution' (1998) 115 *South African Law Journal* 262

'The Bill of Rights in the New Constitution and Customary Law' (1997) 114 *South African Law Journal* 346

King's College London, *A Review of Peace Operations – A Case for Change* (London: International Policy Institute, 2003)

Kingsbury, Damien and Michael Leach, 'Introduction' in Kingsbury and Leach (eds.), *East Timor: Beyond Independence* (Clayton, VIC: Monash University Press, 2007)

Kingson, Jeff, 'East Timor's Search for Justice, Reconciliation and Dignity' in Edel Hughes, William A. Schabas and Ramesh Thankur (eds.), *Atrocities and International Accountability: Beyond Transitional Justice* (New York, NY: United Nations University Press, 2007) 81

Klare, Karl, 'Legal Culture and Transformative Constitutionalism' (1998) 14 *South African Journal on Human Rights* 146

Kleinfeld, Rachel, 'Competing Definitions of the Rule of Law' in Thomas Carothers (ed.), *Promoting the Rule of Law Abroad: In Search of Knowledge* (Washington, DC: Carnegie Endowment for International Peace, 2006) 31

Kleinhaus, Martha-Marie and Roderick A. MacDonald, 'What is *Critical* Legal Pluralism?' (1997) 12 *Canadian Journal of Law and Society* 25

Klug, Heinz, *Constitutional Democracy: Law, Globalism and South Africa's Political Reconstruction* (Cambridge University Press, 2000)

'Hybrid(ity) Rules: Creating Local Law in a Globalized World' in Yves Dezalay and Bryant G. Garth (eds.), *Global Prescriptions: The Production, Exportation, and Importation of a New Legal Orthodoxy* (Ann Arbor, MI: University of Michigan Press, 2002) 276

'Participating in the Design: Constitution-making in South Africa' in Penelope Andrews and Stephen Ellmann (eds.), *Post-Apartheid Constitutions: Perspectives on South Africa's Basic Laws* (Johannesburg: Witwatersrand University Press, Ohio University Press, 2001) 128

'South Africa: From Constitutional Promise to Social Transformation' in Jeffrey Goldsworthy (ed.), *Interpreting Constitutions: A Comparative Study* (New York, NY: Oxford University Press, 2006) 266

Kondoch, Boris, 'Human Rights Law and UN Peace Operations in Post-Conflict Situations' in Nigel D. White and Dirk Klaasen (eds.), *The United Nations, Human Rights and Post-Conflict Situations* (New York, NY: Manchester University Press, 2005) Ch 2

Könz, Peider, 'Legal Development in Developing Countries' (1969) 63 *Proceedings of the American Society of International Law* 91

Koskenniemi, Martti, 'The Fate of Public International Law: Between Technique and Politics' (2007) 70 *Modern Law Review* 1

The Gentle Civilizer of Nations: The Rise and Fall of International Law 1870–1960 (New York, NY: Cambridge University Press, 2001)

Koyana, D. S., J. C. Bekker and R. B. Mqeke, 'Traditional Authority Courts' in J. C. Bekker, Christa Rautenbach and N. M. I. Goolam (eds.), *Introduction to Legal Pluralism* (Durban: LexisNexis Butterworths, 2nd edn, 2006) 131

Krastev, Ivan, 'Corruption, Anti-Corruption Sentiments, and the Rule of Law' in Adam Czarnota, Martin Krygier and Wojciech Sadurski (eds), *Rethinking the Rule of Law after Communism* (Budapest: Central European University Share Co, 2005) 323

Kritz, Neil, 'The Rule of Law in Conflict Management' in Chester A. Crocker, Fen Osler Hampson and Pamela Aall (eds.), *Leashing the Dogs of War: Conflict Management in a Divided World* (Washington, DC: United States Institute of Peace Press, 2007) 401

(ed.), *Transitional Justice: How Emerging Democracies Reckon with Former Regimes – Country Studies* (Washington, DC: United States Institute of Peace Press, 1995)

Krygier, Martin, 'False Dichotomies, True Perplexities, and the Rule of Law' in András Sajó (ed.), *Human Rights with Modesty: The Problem with Universalism* (Leiden: Martinus Nijhoff, 2004) 251

'Marxism and the Rule of Law: Reflections After the Collapse of Communism' (1990) 15 *Law and Social Inquiry* 633

'The Rule of Law' in Neil J. Smelser and Paul B. Baltes (eds.), *International Encyclopedia of the Social and Behavioural Sciences* (Oxford: Elsevier Science, 2001) 13404

'The Rule of Law: An Abuser's Guide' in András Sajó (ed.), *Abuse: The Dark Side of Fundamental Rights* (Utrecht: Eleven International Publishing, 2006) 129

'Transitional Questions about the Rule of Law: Why, What, and How?' (2001) 28 *East Central Europe-L'Europe du Centre Est. Eine Wissenschaftliche Zeitschrift* 1

Krygier, Martin and Adam Czarnota (eds.), *The Rule of Law After Communism: Problems and Prospects in East-Central Europe* (Aldershot: Ashgate, 1999)

Kuper, Adam, 'The Kgalagari and the Jural Consequences of Marriage' (1970) 5 *Man (New Series)* 466

La'o Hamutuk, 'East Timor Faces Post-UNTAET Challenges: What is To Be Done?' (2002) 3 *La'o Hamutuk Bulletin* 1

'Reviewing the East Timor Commission for Reception, Truth and Reconciliation (CAVR)' (2003) 4 *La'o Hamutuk Bulletin* 1

Lau, Martin, *Afghanistan's Legal System and its Compatibility with International Human Rights Standards, Final Report* (2003) (Report for the International Commission of Jurists)

Law, Race and Gender Research Unit, *Submission on the Traditional Courts Bill (B1–2012)* (15 February 2012)

Law Reform Commission of Western Australia, *Aboriginal Customary Laws – Final Report: The Interaction of WA Law with Aboriginal Law and Culture* (2006)

Lawrence, Peter, 'The State versus Stateless Society in Papua and New Guinea' in B. J. Brown (ed.), *Fashion of Law in New Guinea: Being an Account of the Past, Present and Developing Systems of Laws in Papua and New Guinea* (Sydney: Butterworths, 1969) 15

Legal Resources Centre, *Submissions to the Portfolio Committee on Justice and Constitutional Development* (2008)

Leggett, Ted, 'Just Another Miracle: A Decade of Crime and Justice in Democratic South Africa' (2005) 74 *Social Research* 581

Linton, Suzannah, 'Cambodia, East Timor and Sierra Leone: Experiments in International Justice' (2001) 12 *Criminal Law Forum* 185

'Prosecuting Atrocities at the District Court in Dili' (2001) 2 *Melbourne Journal of International Law* 414

'Rising from the Ashes: The Creation of a Viable Criminal Justice System in East Timor' (2001) 25 *Melbourne University Law Review* 122

Longman, Timothy, 'Justice at the Grassroots? Gacaca Trials in Rwanda' in Naomi Roht-Arriaza and Javier Mariezcurrena (eds.), *Transitional Justice in the Twenty-First Century: Beyond Truth versus Justice* (Cambridge University Press, 2007) 206

Longman, Timothy, Phuong Pham and Harvey M. Weinstein, 'Connecting Justice to Human Experience: Attitudes Toward Accountability and Reconciliation in Rwanda' in Harvey Weinstein and Eric Stover (eds.), *My Neighbor, My Enemy: Justice and Community in the Aftermath of Mass Atrocity* (New York, NY: University of Cambridge Press, 2004) 206

Lubkemann, Stephen C., Helene Maria Kyed and Jennifer Garvey, 'Dilemmas of Articulation in Mozambique: Customary Justice in Transition' in Isser (ed.), *Customary Justice and the Rule of Law* (Washington, DC: United States Institute of Peace Press, 2011)

Ludsin, Hallie, 'Cultural Denial: What South Africa's Treatment of Witchcraft Says for the Future of its Customary Law' (2003) 21 *Berkeley Journal of International Law* 62

Lugard, Frederick, *The Dual Mandate in British Tropical Africa* (first published 1922, London: Frank Cass, 5th edn, 1965)

Lutz, Ellen, 'Transitional Justice: Lessons Learned and the Road Ahead' in Naomi Roht-Arriaza and Javier Mariezcurrena (eds.), *Transitional Justice in the Twenty-First Century: Beyond Truth Versus Justice* (Cambridge University Press, 2007) 325

MacKinnon, Aran S., *The Making of South Africa: Culture and Politics* (Upper Saddle River, NJ: Prentice Hall, 2003)

Malinowski, Bronislaw, *Crime and Custom in Savage Society* (London: Kegan Paul, Trench, Trubner & Co, 1926)

Maloka, Tshidiso and David Gordon, 'Chieftainship, Civil Society, and the Political Transition in South Africa' (1996) 22 *Critical Sociology* 37

Malone, Ross L., 'The American Lawyer's Role in Promoting the Rule of Law' (1959–1960) 43 *Marquette Law Review* 3

Mamdani, Mahmood, *Citizen and Subject: Contemporary Africa and the Legacy of Late Colonialism* (Princeton University Press, 1996)

Manderson, Desmond, 'Beyond the Provincial: Space, Aesthetics, and Modernist Legal Theory' (1996) 20 *Melbourne University Law Review* 1048

Mani, Rama, *Beyond Retribution: Seeking Justice in the Shadows of War* (Cambridge: Polity Press, 2002)

'Exploring the Rule of Law in Theory and Practice' in Agnès Hurwitz and Reyko Huang (eds.), *Civil War and the Rule of Law: Security, Development, Human Rights* (Boulder, CO: Lynne Rienner Publishers, 2008) 23

Manji, Ambreena S., 'Imagining Women's "Legal World": Towards a Feminist Theory of Legal Pluralism in Africa' (1999) 8 *Social and Legal Studies* 435

Marriot, Andrew, 'Justice in the Community, Justice in the Courts: Bridging East Timor's Legal Divide' in David Mearns (ed.), *Democratic Governance in Timor-Leste: Reconciling the Local and the National* (Darwin: Charles Darwin University Press, 2008) 21

'Justice Sector Dynamics in Timor-Leste: Institutions and Individuals' (2012) 4 *Asian Politics and Policy* 53

'Leaders, Lawyers, and *Lia Nains*: Sources of Legal Authority in Timor-Leste' in Michael Leach, Nuno Canas Mendes, Antero B. da Silva, Alarico da Costa Ximenes and Bob Boughton (eds.), *Understanding Timor-Leste* (Dili: Timor-Leste Studies Association, 2010)

'The Legal Profession in Timor-Leste's Justice Sector Reconstruction: Opportunities and Constraints' in Vandra Harris and Andrew Goldsmith (eds.), *Security, Development and Nation-Building in Timor-Leste: A Cross-Sectoral Assessment* (London: Routledge, 2011)

Mathews, Anthony, *Freedom, State Security and the Rule of Law: Dilemmas of the Apartheid Society* (Cape Town: Juta, 1986)

Law, Order and Liberty in South Africa (Berkeley: University of California Press, 1972)

Mattei, Ugo, 'Three Patterns of Law: Taxonomy and Change in the World's Legal Systems' (1997) 45 *American Journal of Comparative Law* 5

McAuliffe, Pádraig, 'East Timor's Community Reconciliation Process as a Model for Legal Pluralism in Criminal Law' (2006) 2 *Law, Society and Global Development Journal* 1

McAuslan, Patrick, 'Law, Governance and the Development of the Market: Practical Problems and Possible Solutions' in Julio Faundez (ed.), *Good Government and Law: Legal and Institutional Reform in Developing Countries* (New York. NY: St Martin's Press, 1997) 25

McEvoy, Kieran, 'Letting Go of Legalism: Developing a "Thicker" Version of Transitional Justice' in McEvoy and Lorna McGregor (eds.), *Transitional Justice from Below: Grassroots Activism and the Struggle for Change* (Oxford: Hart Publishing, 2008) 15

McGregor, Lorna, 'International Law as a "Tiered Process": Transitional Justice at the Local, National and International Level' in Kieran McEvoy and McGregor (eds.), *Transitional Justice from Below: Grassroots Activism and the Struggle for Change* (Oxford: Hart Publishing, 2008) 47

McNamara, Luke, '"Equality Before the Law" in Polyethnic Societies: The Construction of Normative Criminal Law Sanctions' (2004) 11 *Murdoch University Electronic Journal of Law*

McWilliam, Andrew, 'Introduction: Restorative Custom: Ethnographic Perspectives on Conflict and Local Justice in Timor' (2007) 8 *The Asia Pacific Journal of Anthropology* 1

Mearns, David, *Looking Both Ways: Models for Justice in East Timor* (2002) (Report for Australian Legal Resources International)

Variations on a Theme: Coalitions of Authority in East Timor (2001) (Report for Australian Legal Resources International)

Mégret, Frédéric, 'Is There Ever a "Right to One's Own Law"? An Exploration of Possible Rights Foundations for Legal Pluralism' (2012) 45 *Israel Law Review* 3

Memorandum addressed to 'Members of the Theme Committee #5 of the Constitutional Assembly' from Fikile Kobese, Martin Monyela and Daniel Nina, Re Community Courts, 9 February 1995 (on file with author)

Menski, Werner, *Comparative Law in a Global Context: The Legal Systems of Asia and Africa* (Cambridge University Press, 2nd edn, 2006)

Merry, Sally Engle, *Human Rights and Gender Violence: Translating International Law into Local Justice* (University of Chicago Press, 2006)

'Legal Pluralism' (1988) 22 *Law and Society Review* 869

'Legal Pluralism and Transnational Culture: The *Ka Ho'okolokolonui Kanaka Maoli* Tribunal, Hawai'i, 1993' in Richard A. Wilson (ed.), *Human Rights, Culture and Context: Anthropological Perspectives* (London: Pluto Press, 1997) 28

Merryman, John Henry, 'Comparative Law and Social Change: On the Origins, Style, Decline and Revival of the Law and Development Movement' (1977) 25 *American Journal of Comparative Law* 457

Michelman, Frank I., 'The Rule of Law, Legality and the Supremacy of the Constitution' in Stuart Woolman and Theunis Roux (eds), *Constitutional Law of South Africa* (Cape Town: Juta, 2nd edn, 2002) 11–1

Middleton, A. J., 'When "Why?" is "Who?"' [1999] *Obiter* 176

Migdal, Joel S., *State in Society: Studying How States and Societies Transform and Constitute One Another* (Cambridge University Press, 2001)

Strong Societies and Weak States: State-Society Relations and State Capabilities in the Third World (Princeton University Press, 1988)

Mokgoro, Yvonne, 'The Customary Law Question in the South African Constitution' (1997) 41 *Saint Louis University Law Journal* 1279

'Traditional Authority and Democracy in the Interim South African Constitution' (1996) 3 *Review of Constitutional Studies* 60

Moore, Sally Folk, *Law as Process: An Anthropological Approach* (London: Routledge & Kegan Paul, 1978)

Moreira, Adriano, 'Portuguese Territories in Africa: Customary Law in the Portuguese Overseas' in Peter Idenburg (ed.), *The Future of Customary Law in Africa* (Leiden University Press, 1956) 229

Morris, H. F. and James S. Read, *Indirect Rule and the Search for Justice: Essays in East African Legal History* (Oxford: Clarendon Press, 1972).

Murdoch, Lindsay, 'Ramos Horta and Reinado had Amnesty Deal', *The Age*, 16 February 2008

Mureinik, Etienne, 'A Bridge to Where? Introducing the Interim Bill of Rights' (1994) 10 *South African Journal on Human Rights* 31

Murray, Christina, 'A Constitutional Beginning: Making South Africa's Final Constitution' (2001) 23 *University of Arkansas at Little Rock Law Review* 809

'Negotiating Beyond Deadlock: From the Constitutional Assembly to the Court' in Penelope Andrews and Stephen Ellmann (eds.), *Post-Apartheid Constitutions: Perspectives on South Africa's Basic Laws* (Johannesburg: Witwatersrand University Press, Ohio University Press, 2001) 103

'One Law for One Nation: South Africa's New Constitution' (1997) 8 *Public Law Review* 10

'South Africa's Troubled Royalty: Traditional Leaders after Democracy' (2004) 23 *Law and Policy Paper Series* (Centre for Public and International Law, Australian National University)

Mutua, Makau, 'Savages, Victims and Saviors: The Metaphor of Human Rights' (2001) 42 *Harvard International Law Journal* 201

Nagel, Thomas, 'Moral Conflicts and Political Legitimacy' (1987) 16 *Philosophy and Public Affairs* 215

National Statistics Directorate [Timor-Leste], Ministry of Finance [Timor-Leste] and ICF Macro, *Timor-Leste Demographic and Health Survey 2009–2010* (November 2010)

Neumann, Michael, *The Rule of Law: Politicizing Ethics* (Aldershot: Ashgate, 2002)

New Zealand Law Commission, *Converging Currents: Custom and Human Rights in the Pacific* (2006)

Nhlapo, Thandabantu, 'African Customary Law in the Interim Constitution' in Sandra Liebenberg (ed.), *The Constitution of South Africa from a Gender Perspective* (Capetown: University of the Western Cape, 1995) 157

'Indigenous Law and Gender in South Africa: Taking Human Rights and Cultural Diversity Seriously' (1994–1995) 9 *Third World Legal Studies* 49

'The African Family and Women's Rights: Friends or Foes?' [1991] *Acta Juridica* 135

Ni Aoláin, Fionnula, 'Political Violence and Gender During Times of Transition' (2006) 15 *Columbia Journal of Gender and the Law* 829

Nicolau, Guteriano, 'Ombudsman for Human Rights: The Case of Timor-Leste' (2007) 47 *Asia Pacific News* 3

Niner, Sara, 'A Reassertion of Customary Practices in Timor Leste' in Lisa Palmer, Sara Niner and Lia Kent (eds.), *Exploring the Tension of Nation-Building in Timor-Leste* (SSEE Research Paper No 1/2007) 41

Nixon, Rod, 'Indonesia West Timor: The Political-Economy of Emerging Ethno-Nationalism' (2004) 34 *Journal of Contemporary Asia* 163

Integrating Indigenous Approaches into a 'New Subsistence State': The Case of Justice and Conflict Resolution in East Timor (PhD Thesis, Charles Darwin University, 2008)

Justice and Governance in East Timor: Indigenous Approaches and the 'New Subsistence State' (London: Routledge, 2012)

'Non-State Actors as Agents of Order: *Suco* Justice and Dispute Resolution Systems in East Timor' in William Binchy (ed.), *Timor-Leste: Challenges for Justice and Human Rights in the Shadow of the Past* (Dublin: Clarus Press, 2009)

North, Douglass C., *Institutions, Institutional Change and Economic Performance* (Cambridge University Press, 1990)

Ntsebeza, Lungisile, *Democracy Compromised: Chiefs and the Politics of Land in South Africa* (Leiden: Brill, 2006)

Nyamu-Musembi, Celestine, 'Are Local Norms and Practices Fences or Pathways? The Example of Women's Property Rights', in Abdullahi Ahmed An-Na'im (ed.), *Cultural Transformation and Human Rights in Africa* (London: Zed Books, 2002) 126

'How Should Human Rights and Development Respond to Cultural Legitimization of Gender Hierarchy in Developing Countries?' (2000) 41 *Harvard International Law Journal* 381

'Ruling out Gender-Equality? The Post-Cold War Rule of Law Agenda in Sub-Saharan Africa' (2006) 27 *Third World Quarterly* 1193

Nygaard-Christensen, Maj, 'The Rebel and the Diplomat: Revolutionary Spirits, Sacred Legitimation and Democracy in Timor-Leste' in Nils Bubandt and Martijn van Beek (eds.), *Varieties of Secularism in Asia: Anthropological Explorations of Religion, Politics and the Spiritual* (London: Routledge, 2011)

O'Connor, Vivienne and Colette Rausch, *Model Codes for Post-Conflict Criminal Justice Volume I: Model Criminal Code* (Washington, DC: United States Institute of Peace Press, 2007)

Odinkalu, Chidi Anselm, 'Poor Justice for the Poor? A Policy Framework for Reform of Customary and Informal Justice Systems in Africa' in Caroline Mary Sage and Michael Woolcock (eds.), *The World Bank Legal Review: Law, Equity and Development, Vol 2* (Washington, DC: World Bank, 2006) 141

Office of the Provedor for Human Rights and Justice and Civil Society Organizations in Timor-Leste, *Joint Submission – UN Universal Periodic Review* (21 March 2011)

Okoye, Ada O., 'The Rule of Law and Sociopolitical Dynamics in Africa' in Paul Tiyambe Zeleza and Philip J. McConnaughay (eds.), *Human Rights, the Rule of Law, and Development in Africa* (Philadelphia, PA: University of Pennsylvania Press, 2004) 71

Ombudsman Institution in Kosovo, *Second Annual Report (2001–2002)* (10 July 2002)

Oomen, Barbara, *Chiefs in South Africa: Law, Power and Culture in the Post-Apartheid Era* (Oxford: James Currey; New York: Palgrave, 2005)

Open Society Foundation for South Africa, *South Africa: Justice Sector and the Rule of Law* (2005)

Orentlicher, Diane, '"Settling Accounts" Revisited: Reconciling Global Norms with Local Agency' (2007) 10 *International Journal of Transitional Justice* 1

Organisation of Economic Cooperation and Development, *Economic Assessment of South Africa 2008* (15 July 2008)

Enhancing the Delivery of Justice and Security: Governance, Peace and Security (2007)

Orth, John V., 'Exporting the Rule of Law' (1998) 24 *North Carolina Journal of International Law and Commercial Regulation* 71

Ospina, Sofi and Tanja Hohe, *Traditional Power Structures and Local Governance in East Timor: A Case Study of the Community Empowerment Project* (Geneva: Graduate Institute of Development Studies, 2002)

Pahuja, Sundhya, *Decolonising International Law: Development, Economic Growth and the Politics of Universality* (Cambridge University Press, 2011)

Palmer, Lisa, 'Developing Timor-Leste: The Role of Custom and Tradition' in Lisa Palmer, Sara Niner and Lia Kent (eds.), *Exploring the Tension of Nation-Building in Timor-Leste* (SSEE Research Paper No.1/2007) 35

Palmer, Lisa and Demetrio do Amaral de Carvalho, 'Nation Building and Resource Management: The Politics of "Nature" in Timor Leste' (2008) 39 *Geoforum* 1321

Paris, Roland, 'International Peacebuilding and the "Mission Civilisatrice"' (2002) 28 *Review of International Studies* 637

Paterson, D. E., 'South Pacific Customary Law and Common Law: Their Interrelationship' (1995) 21 *Commonwealth Law Bulletin* 660

Peace and Democracy Foundation, *Report about Research on Customary Dispute Resolution and Proposed Mediation Model for the Democratic Republic of Timor-Leste* (November 2004)

Peerenboom, Randall, 'Human Rights and the Rule of Law: What's the Relationship?' (2005) 36 *Georgetown Journal of International Law* 809

'Let One Hundred Flowers Bloom, One Hundred Schools Contend: Debating Rule of Law in China' (2002) 23 *Michigan Journal of International Law* 471

'Varieties of Rule of Law: An Introduction and Provisional Conclusion' in Randall Peerenboom (ed.), *Asian Discourses of Rule of Law: Theories and Implementation of Rule of Law in Twelve Asian Countries, France and the United States* (London: Routledge, 2004) 1

Penal Reform International, *Access to Justice in Sub-Saharan Africa: The Role of Traditional and Informal Justice Systems* (November 2000)

Pieterse, Marius, 'It's a Black Thing: Upholding Culture and Customary Law in a Society Founded on Non-Racialism' (2001) 17 *South African Journal on Human Rights* 364

'Killing it Softly: Customary Law in the New Constitutional Order' (2000) 33 *De Jure* 35

'The Promotion of Equality and Prevention of Unfair Discrimination Act 4 of 2000: Final Nail in the Customary Law Coffin?' (2000) 117 *South African Law Journal* 627

Pigou, Piers, *Crying Without Tears – In Pursuit of Justice and Reconciliation in Timor-Leste: Community Perspectives and Expectations* (2003) (Report for the International Center for Transitional Justice)

The Community Reconciliation Process of the Commission for Reception, Truth and Reconciliation (2004) (Report for UNDP Timor-Leste)

Piron, Laure-Hélène, 'Time to Learn, Time to Act in Africa' in Thomas Carothers (ed.), *Promoting the Rule of Law Abroad: In Search of Knowledge* (Washington, DC: Carnegie Endowment for International Peace, 2006) 275

Pistor, Katharina, 'The Standardisation of Law and its Effect on Developing Economies' (2002) 50 *American Journal of Comparative Law* 97

Plunkett, Mark, 'Re-establishing the Rule of Law' in Gerd Junne and Willemijn Verkoren (eds.), *Post Conflict Development: Meeting New Challenges* (Boulder, CO: Lynne Rienner Publishers, 2005) 78

Posner, Eric A. and Adrian Vermeule, 'Transitional Justice as Ordinary Justice' (2004) 117 *Harvard Law Review* 761

Potter, Antonia, *The Rule of Law as the Measure of Peace? Responsive Policy for Reconstructing Justice and the Rule of Law in Post-Conflict and Transitional Environments* (2004) (Report for the Centre for Humanitarian Dialogue)

Pritchard, Sarah, 'United Nations Involvement in Post-Conflict Reconstruction Efforts: New and Continuing Challenges in the Case of East Timor' (2001) 24 *University of New South Wales Law Journal* 183

Pritchett, Lant and Frauke de Weijer, *Fragile States: Stuck in a Capability Trap?* (Background Paper for the World Development Report 2011) (November 2010)

Progress Report of the Secretary-General on the United Nations Office in Timor Leste, UN Doc S/2005/533 (18 August 2005)

Quast, Shelley R., *Report on East Timor* (March 2002) (Report for the International Legal Assistance Consortium).

Rajagopal, Balakrishnan, 'Invoking the Rule of Law in Post-Conflict Rebuilding: A Critical Examination' (2007–2008) 49 *William and Mary Law Review* 1347

Rakate, Phenyo Keiseng, 'The Status of Traditional Courts under the Final Constitution' (1997) 30 *Comparative and International Law Journal of Southern Africa* 175

Ralushai Commission, *Report of the Commission of Inquiry into Witchcraft, Violence and Ritual Murders in the Northern Province of the Republic of South Africa* (1996)

Ramos-Horta, José, 'The Dreams shall Never Die, we must Keep the Faith, the Struggle must go on', *Speech*, 30 August 2009

'Timor-Leste: The Decade of Peace and Prosperity', *Speech given at the 13th Session of the UN Human Rights Council*, 11 March 2010.

Ranheim, Christian, *Legal Pluralism in East Timor: The Formal Judicial System and Community-Based Customary law* (2005) (Report prepared for the project, The Role of Non-State Justice Systems in Fostering the Rule of Law in Post-Conflict Societies, USIP)

Ratmapala, Suri, *Australian Constitutional Law: Foundations and Theory* (Melbourne: Oxford University Press, 2002)

Rautenbach, Christa, 'Law of Succession and Inheritance' in J. C. Bekker, Christa Rautenbach and N. M. I. Goolam (eds.), *Introduction to Legal Pluralism* (Durban: LexisNexis Butterworths, 2nd edn, 2006) 97

Raz, Joseph, *Ethics in the Public Domain: Essays in the Morality of Law and Politics* (Oxford: Clarendon Press, 1994)

'The Rule of Law and Its Virtue' in Raz, *The Authority of Law* (Oxford: Clarendon Press, 1979) 210

Regan, Anthony, 'Constitution-Making in East Timor: Missed Opportunities' in Dionisio Babo-Soares, Michael Maley, James J. Fox and Anthony J. Regan (eds.), *Elections and Constitution-Making in East Timor* (Canberra: Australian National University Press, 2003) 39

Rei, Naldo, 'Where Now for East Timor?' *The Advertiser*, 23 February 2008

Reilly, Niamh, 'Seeking Gender Justice in Post-Conflict Transitions: Towards a Transformative Women's Human Rights Approach' (2007) 3 *International Journal of Law in Context* 155

Report of the Secretary-General on Justice and Reconciliation for Timor-Leste, UN Doc S/2006/580 (26 July 2006)

Report of the Secretary-General on the Situation in East Timor, UN Doc S/1999/1024 (4 October 1999)

Report of the Secretary-General on Timor-Leste pursuant to Security Council Resolution 1690, UN Doc S/2006/628 (8 August 2006)

Report of the Secretary-General on the United Nations Integrated Mission in Timor-Leste (for the period from 9 August 2006 to 26 January 2007), UN Doc S/2007/50 (1 February 2007)

Report of the Secretary-General on the United Nations Integrated Mission in Timor-Leste (for the period from 27 January to 20 August 2007), UN Doc S/2007/513 (28 August 2007)

Report of the Secretary-General on the United Nations Integrated Mission in Timor-Leste (for the period from 21 August 2007 to 7 January 2008), UN Doc S/2008/26 (17 January 2008)

Report of the Secretary-General on the United Nations Integrated Mission in Timor-Leste (for the period from 8 January to 8 July 2008), UN Doc S/2008/501 (29 July 2008)

Report of the Secretary-General on the United Nations Integrated Mission in Timor-Leste (for the period from July 2008 to 20 January 2009), UN Doc S/2009/72 (4 February 2009)

Report of the Secretary-General on the United Nations Integrated Mission in Timor-Leste (for the period from 24 September 2009 to 20 January 2010), UN Doc S/2010/85 (12 February 2010)

Report of the Secretary-General on the United Nations Integrated Mission in Timor-Leste (for the period from 21 January 2010 to 20 September 2010), UN Doc S/2010/522 (13 October 2010)

Report of the Secretary-General on the United Nations Integrated Mission in Timor-Leste (for the period from 20 September 2011 to 6 January 2012), UN Doc S/2012/43 (18 January 2012)

Report of the Secretary-General on the United Nations Mission of Support in East Timor, UN Doc S/2003/449 (21 April 2003)

Report of the Secretary-General on the United Nations Transitional Administration in East Timor (for the period 27 January - 26 July 2000), UN Doc S/2000/738 (26 July 2000)

Report of the Secretary-General on the United Nations Transitional Administration in East Timor (for the period from 25 July to 15 October 2001), UN Doc S/2001/983 (18 October 2001)

Report of the Security Council Mission to East Timor and Indonesia (9–17 November 2000), UN Doc S/2000/1105 (21 November 2000)

Report of the Security Council Mission to Timor-Leste, 24 to 30 November 2007, UN Doc S/2007/711 (6 December 2007)

Report of the UN Special Rapporteur on the Situation of Human Rights and Fundamental Freedoms of Indigenous People, Mr Rodolfo Stavenhagen, UN Doc E/CN.4/2006/78 (16 February 2006)

République du Rwanda, Cour Suprême, *Mise au Point au Sujet du Rapport et Différentes Correspondances d'Amnesty International* (2003)

Richmond, Oliver and Jason Franks, 'Liberal Peacebuilding in Timor-Leste: The Emperor's New Clothes?' (2008) 15 *International Peacekeeping* 185

Rickard, Carmel, 'Equality for Women? No Thanks', *Sunday Times*, 8 August 1993

Rittich, Kerry, 'The Future of Law and Development: Second Generation Reforms and the Incorporation of the Social' (2004–2005) 26 *Michigan Journal of International Law* 199

Roberts, Simon, 'After Government? On Representing Law Without the State' (2005) 68 *Modern Law Review* 1

'Law and the Study of Social Control in Small-Scale Societies' (1976) 39 *Modern Law Review* 663

Order and Dispute: An Introduction to Legal Anthropology (New York, NY: St Martin's Press, 1979)

Robson, William, *Justice and Administrative Law* (London: Stevens, 2nd edn, 1947)

Rosenfeld, Michel, 'The Rule of Law and the Legitimacy of Constitutional Democracy' (2001) 74 *Southern California Law Review* 1307

(ed.), *Constitutionalism, Identity, Difference and Legitimacy: Theoretical Perspectives* (Durham, NC: Duke University Press, 1994)

Sachs, Albie, 'South Africa's Unconstitutional Constitution: The Transition from Power to Lawful Power' (1997) 41 *Saint Louis University Law Journal* 1249

'The Creation of South Africa's Constitution' (1997) 41 *New York Law School Law Review* 669

Sadurski, Wojciech, 'Transitional Constitutionalism: Simplistic and Fancy Theories' in Adam Czarnota, Martin Krygier and Sadurski (eds.), *Rethinking the Rule of Law After Communism* (Budapest: Central European University Share Co, 2005) 9

Sage, Caroline, Brian Z. Tamanaha and Michael Woolcock (eds.), *Legal Pluralism and Development: Dialogues for Success* (Cambridge University Press, 2012)

Samuels, Kirsti, *Rule of Law Reform in Post-Conflict Countries: Operational Initiatives and Lessons Learnt*, World Bank Social Development Papers, Paper No 37 (October 2006)

Santos, Alvaro, 'The World Bank's Uses of the "Rule of Law" Promise in Economic Development' in David Trubek and Santos (eds.), *The New Law and Economic Development: A Critical Appraisal* (Cambridge University Press, 2006) 253

Santos, Boaventura de Sousa, *Toward a New Common Sense: Law, Science and Politics in the Paradigmatic Transition* (New York, NY: Routledge, 1995)

Toward a New Legal Common Sense: Law, Globalization and Emancipation (London: LexisNexis Butterworths, 2nd edn, 2002)

Sarkin, Jeremy, 'The Drafting of South Africa's Final Constitution From a Human Rights Perspective' (1999) 47 *American Journal of Comparative Law* 67

'The Effect of Constitutional Borrowings on the Drafting of South Africa's Bill of Rights and Interpretation of Human Rights Provisions' (1998) 1 *University of Pennsylvania Journal of Constitutional Law* 176

Sarkin, Jeremy and Erin Daly, 'Too Many Questions, Too Few Answers: Reconciliation in Transitional Societies' (2004) 35 *Columbia Human Rights Law Review* 661

Schapera, Isaac, *A Handbook of Tswana Law and Custom* (London: Oxford University Press, 2nd edn, 1955)

Scharf, Wilfried and Daniel Nina (eds.), *The Other Law: Non-State Ordering in South Africa* (Cape Town: Juta, 2001)

Scheeringa, Sandra, 'Enhancing the Local Legitimacy of Transnational Justice Institutions: Local Embeddedness and Customary Law in CAVR' in Damien Kingsbury and Michael Leach (eds.), *East Timor: Beyond Independence* (Melbourne: Monash University Press, 2007) 137

Schlicher, Monika, *East Timor Faces Up to its Past: The Work of the Commission for Reception, Truth and Reconciliation* (Aachen: Missio, 2005) (Report for Watch Indonesia!)

Schreiner, Oliver, *The Contribution of English Law to South Africa; and the Rule of Law in South Africa* (London: Stevens, 1967)

Schreuder, Deryck, 'The Commonwealth and Peacemaking in South Africa' in Norman Etherington (ed.), *Peace, Politics and Violence in the New South Africa* (London: Hans Zell Publishing, 1992) 73

Security Council Report, *Cross-Cutting Report on the Rule of Law 2011 No 3* (28 October 2011)

Seekings, Jeremy, 'Social Ordering and Control in the African Townships of South Africa: An Historical Overview of Extra-State Initiatives from the 1940s to the 1990s' in Wilfried Schärf and Daniel Nina (eds.), *The Other Law: Non-State Ordering in South Africa* (Cape Town: Juta, 2001) Ch 4

Seider, Rachel, 'Rethinking Democratisation and Citizenship: Legal Pluralism and Institutional Reform in Guatemala' (1999) 3 *Citizenship Studies* 103

Selznick, Philip, *The Moral Commonwealth: Social Theory and the Promise of Community* (Berkeley, CA: University of California Press, 1992)

Sen, Amartya, *Development as Freedom* (New York, NY: Knopf, 1999)

Inequality Re-examined (New York, NY: Russell Sage Foundation, 1992)

Senier, Amy, 'Rebuilding the Judicial Sector in Afghanistan: The Role of Customary Law' (2006) *Al Nakhlah* 1

Serapaio, Luis B. and Mohamed A. El Khawas, *Mozambique in the Twentieth Century: From Colonialism to Independence* (Washington, DC: University Press of America, 1979)

Shaw, Rosalind, Lars Waldorf and Pierre Hazan, *Localizing Transitional Justice: Interventions and Priorities after Mass Violence* (Stanford University Press, 2010)

Shihata, Ibrahim, *The World Bank in a Changing World: Selected Essays, compiled and edited by Franziska Tschofen* (Dordrecht: Martinus Nijhoff, 1991)

Shklar, Judith N., 'Political Theory and the Rule of Law' in Allan Hutchinson and Patrick Monahan (eds.), *The Rule of Law: Ideal or Ideology* (Toronto: Carswell, 1987) 1

Shoesmith, Dennis, 'Divided Leadership in a Semi-Presidential System' (2003) XLIII *Asian Survey* 231

Sieder, Rachel and Maria Teresa Sierra, *Indigenous Women's Access to Justice in Latin America* (CMI Working Paper, 2010)

Siegel, Richard Lewis, 'Transitional Justice: A Decade of Debate and Experience' (1998) 20 *Human Rights Quarterly* 431

Snyder, Francis G., 'Colonialism and Legal Form: The Creation of "Customary Law" in Senegal' (1981) 19 *Journal of Legal Pluralism* 49

Snyman, Johannes Henrik, *South Africa and the Rule of Law: Testimony of a Supreme Court Judge* (1970)

Soares, Santina and Jennifer Laakso, 'Mediation in Timor-Leste: Opportunities and Challenges' (2007) 1 *World Arbitration and Mediation Review* 361

South African Law Commission, *Alternative Dispute Resolution*, Issue Paper 8, Project 94 (1997)

Community Dispute Resolution Structures, Discussion Paper 87, Project 94 (1999)

Customary Law: Succession, Discussion Paper 93, Project 90 (2000)

Harmonisation – Conflicts of Law, Discussion Paper 76, Project 90 (1998)

Report on Conflicts of Law, Project 90 (1999)

Report on Traditional Courts and the Judicial Function of Traditional Leaders, Project 90 (2003)

Simplification of Criminal Procedure (Access to the Criminal Justice System), Issue Paper 6, Project 73 (1997)

Traditional Courts and the Judicial Function of Traditional Leaders, Discussion Paper 82, Project 90 (1999)

South African Truth and Reconciliation Commission, *Final Report of the South African Truth and Reconciliation Commission* (1998)

Spitz, Richard and Matthew Chaskalson, *The Politics of Transition: A Hidden History of South Africa's Negotiated Settlement* (Oxford: Hart Publishing, 2000)

Stahn, Carsten, 'Justice Under Transitional Administration: Contours and Critique of a Paradigm' (2005) *Houston Journal of International Law* 311

'The Geometry of Transitional Justice: Choices of Institutional Design' (2005) 18 *Leiden Journal of International Law* 425

Stewart, Ann, 'Juridifying Gender Justice: From Global Rights to Local Justice' in John Hatchard and Amanda Perry-Kessaris (eds.), *Law and Development: Facing Complexity in the 21st Century* (London: Cavendish, 2003) 36

'Should Women Give Up on the State? – The African Experience' in Shirin M. Rai and Geraldine Lievesley (eds.), *Women and the State: International Perspectives* (London: Taylor & Francis, 1996) 23

Stover, Eric, Hanny Megally and Hania Mufti, 'Bremer's "Gordian Knot": Transitional Justice and the US Occupation of Iraq' (2005) 27 *Human Rights Quarterly* 830.

Strohmeyer, Hansjörg, 'Building a New Judiciary for East Timor: Challenges of a Fledgling Nation' (2001) 11 *Criminal Law Forum* 259

'Collapse and Reconstruction of a Judicial System: The United Nations in Kosovo and East Timor' (2001) 95 *American Journal of International Law* 46

'Making Multilateral Interventions Work: The UN and the Creation of Transitional Justice Systems in Kosovo and East Timor' (2001) 25 *Fletcher Forum of World Affairs* 107

'Policing the Peace: Post-Conflict Judicial System Reconstruction in East Timor' (2001) 24 *University of New South Wales Law Review* 171

Stromseth, Jane, David Wippman and Rosa Brooks, *Can Might Make Rights? Building the Rule of Law after Military Interventions* (Cambridge University Press, 2006)

Sukhre, Astri and Kaja Borchgrevink, 'Negotiating Justice Sector Reform in Afghanistan' (2009) 51 *Crime, Law and Social Change* 211

Sunder, Madhavi, 'Enlightened Constitutionalism' (2005) 37 *Connecticut Law Review* 891

Swaine, Aisling, *Traditional Justice and Gender Based Violence* (August 2003) (Report for the International Rescue Society)

Sweet, Alec Stone, 'Constitutionalism, Legal Pluralism, and International Regimes' (2009) 16.2 *Indiana Journal of Global Legal Studies* 621

Tamale, Sylvia, 'The Right to Culture and the Culture of Rights: A Critical Perspective of Women's Sexual Rights in Africa' (2008) 16 *Feminist Legal Studies* 47

Tamanaha, Brian, *A General Jurisprudence of Law and Society* (Oxford University Press, 2001)

On the Rule of Law: History, Politics, Theory (Cambridge University Press, 2004)

'Rule of Law in the United States' in Randall Peerenboom (ed.), *Asian Discourses of Rule of Law: Theories and Implementation of Rule of Law in Twelve Asian Countries, France and the United States* (London: Routledge, 2004) 56

'The Folly of the "Social-Scientific" Concept of Legal Pluralism' (1993) 20 *Journal of Law and Society* 192

'The Lessons of Law-and-Development Studies' (1995) 89 *American Journal of International Law* 470

'Understanding Legal Pluralism: Past to Present, Local to Global' (2008) 30 *Sydney Law Review* 375

Tan, Poh-Ling (ed.), *Asian Legal Systems: Law, Society and Pluralism in East Asia* (Sydney: Butterworths, 1997)

Taylor, Ian, *Stuck in Middle GEAR: South Africa's Post-Apartheid Foreign Relations* (Westport, CT: Praeger, 2001)

Taylor, John G., *Indonesia's Forgotten War: The Hidden History of East Timor* (London: Zed Books, 1991)

Teitel, Ruti, 'Transitional Jurisprudence: The Role of Law in Political Transformation' (1997) 106 *Yale Law Journal* 2009

Transitional Justice (Oxford University Press, 2000)

'Transitional Justice Genealogy' (2003) 16 *Harvard Human Rights Journal* 69

'Transitional Justice in a New Era' (2003) 26 *Fordham International Law Journal* 893

Teubner, Gunther, 'The Two Faces of Janus: Rethinking Legal Pluralism' (1991) 13 *Cardozo Law Review* 1443

The Government of Rwanda, *Genocide and Justice*

Therik, Gerzon, *Wehali: The Four Corners Land: The Cosmology and Traditions of a Timorese Ritual Centre* (DPhil Thesis, The Australian National University, 1995)

Thomas, Ph. J. and D. D. Tladi, 'Legal Pluralism or a New Repugnancy Clause' (1999) 32 *Comparative and International Law Journal of Southern Africa* 354

Thompson, Edward Palmer, *Whigs and Hunters: The Origin of the Black Act* (London: Allen Lane, 1975)

Thompson, Leonard, *A History of South Africa* (New Haven, CT: Yale University Press, rev edn, 1995)

Thorne, Kristina, *Rule of Law through Imperfect Bodies? The Informal Justice Systems of Burundi and Somalia* (HD Centre 2005)

Timor-Leste Commission for Reception, Truth and Reconciliation, *Chega!, Report of the Commission for Reception, Truth and Reconciliation* (2005)

Timor-Leste NGOs Alternative Report, *Implementation of CEDAW – Timor-Leste* (March 2009)

Tolbert, David and Andrew Solomon, 'United Nations Reform and Supporting the Rule of Law in Post-Conflict Societies' (2006) 19 *Harvard Human Rights Journal* 29

Tondini, Matteo, 'From Neocolonialism to a "Light-Footprint Approach": Restoring Justice Systems' (2008) 15 *International Peacekeeping* 237

Statebuilding and Justice Reform: Post-Conflict Reconstruction in Afghanistan (London: Routledge, 2010)

'The Role of Italy in Rebuilding the Judicial System in Afghanistan' (2006) 45 *Revue de Droit Militaire et de Droit de la Guerre* 79

Toohey, Paul, 'Timor Rebel was to be Pardoned', *The Australian*, 1 March 2008

Toomey, Leigh T., 'A Delicate Balance: Building Complementary Customary and State Legal Systems' (2010) 3/1 *The Law and Development Review* Article 6

Traube, Elizabeth, *Cosmology and Social Life* (University of Chicago Press, 1986)

Trebilcock, Michael J. and Ronald J. Daniels, *Rule of Law Reform and Development: Charting the Fragile Path of Progress* (Cheltenham: Edward Elgar, 2008)

Trembath, Anna, Damian Grenfell and Carmenesa Moniz Noronha, *Impacts of National NGO Gender Programming in Local Communities in Timor-Leste* (Melbourne: RMIT University, 2010)

Trenkov-Wermuth, Calin, *United Nations Justice: Legal and Judicial Reform in Governance Operations* (Tokyo: United Nations University Press, 2010)

Trindade, Josh, *Open Letter to the Prime Minister of Timor-Leste*, 10 August 2006 (on file with author)

'Reconciling the Conflicting Paradigms: An East Timorese Vision of the Ideal State' in David Mearns (ed.), *Democratic Governance in Timor-Leste: Reconciling the Local and the National* (Darwin: Charles Darwin University Press, 2008) 160

Trindade, Josh and Bryant Castro, *Rethinking Timorese Identity as a Peacebuilding Strategy: The Lorosa'e-Loromu Conflict from a Traditional Perspective* (2007) (Report for the EU Rapid Reaction Mechanism Programme)

Trubek, David, 'Law and Development' in Neil J. Smelser and Paul B. Baltes (eds.), *2001 International Encyclopedia of the Social and Behavioural Sciences* (Oxford: Elsevier Science, 2001) 8443

'Law and Development: Then and Now' (1996) 90 *American Society of International Law Proceedings* 223

'Max Weber on Law and the Rise of Capitalism' [1972] *Wisconsin Law Review* 720

'The Rule of Law in Development Assistance' in David Trubek and Alvaro Santos (eds.), *The New Law and Economic Development: A Critical Appraisal* (Cambridge University Press, 2006) 74

'Toward a Theory of Law: An Essay on the Study of Law and Development' (1972) 82 *Yale Law Journal* 1

Trubek, David and Alvaro Santos, 'Introduction: The Third Moment in Law and Development Theory and the Emergence of a New Critical Approach' in David Trubek and Alvaro Santos (eds.), *The New Law and Economic Development: A Critical Appraisal* (Cambridge University Press, 2006) 1

Trubek, David and Marc Galanter, 'Scholars in Self-Estrangement: Some Reflections on the Crisis in Law and Development Studies in the United States' [1974] *Wisconsin Law Review* 1062

Tshela, Boyane, *Traditional Justice in Practice: A Limpopo Case Study* (Pretoria: Institute for Security Studies, 2005)

Tully, James, *Strange Multiplicity: Constitutionalism in an Age of Diversity* (Cambridge University Press, 1995)

Twining, William, *Globalisation and Legal Theory* (London: Butterworths, 2000)

Ubink, Janine and Thomas McInerney (eds.), *Customary Justice: Perspectives on Legal Empowerment* (Rome: International Development Law Organization, 2011)

UK Department for International Development, *Justice and Poverty Reduction*, DFID Issues Paper (2000)

Non-State Justice and Security Systems, DFID Briefing (May 2004)

Safety, Security and Accessible Justice: Putting Policy into Practice (July 2002)

UN Committee on the Elimination of Discrimination Against Women, *Concluding Observations of the Committee on the Elimination of Discrimination against Women – South Africa*, UN Doc CEDAW/C/ZAF/CO/4 (4 February 2011)

UN Department of Peacekeeping Operations, *United Nations Primer for Justice Components in Multidimensional Peace Operations: Strengthening the Rule of Law* (December 2006)

UN Development Programme, *Access to Justice – Practice Note* (2004)

Programming for Justice: Justice For All: A Practitioner's Guide to a Human Rights-Based Approach to Access to Justice (2005)

Strengthening the Justice System in Timor-Leste Programme – Independent/External Mid-Term Evaluation Report (September 2007)

Strengthening the Justice System in Timor-Leste – Semi-Annual Progress Report, 1 January 2007–31 July 2007 (August 2007)

Strengthening the Rule of Law in Conflict and Post-Conflict Situations: A Global UNDP Programme for Justice and Security 2008–2011

UN High Commissioner for Human Rights, *Rule of Law Tools for Post-Conflict States: Mapping the Justice Sector* (2006)

Situation of Human Rights – Report of the High Commissioner, UN Doc E/CN.4/2002/39 (1 March 2002)

UN Human Rights Council, *Report of the Working Group on the Universal Periodic Review – Timor-Leste*, UN Doc A/HRC/19/17 (3 January 2012)

UN Independent Special Commission of Inquiry, *Report of the UN Independent Special Commission of Inquiry* (Geneva 2 October 2006)

UN Mission in Timor-Leste, *Report on Human Rights Developments in Timor-Leste (August 2006-August 2007)* (2007)

UNMIT Internal Review Panel, Conducted from 1 April to 24 April 2008 (2008)

UN News Service, 'TL: UN Envoy Decries Political Attacks, Hails Government Response' (12 February 2008)

UN Population Fund, *Gender-Based Violence in Timor-Leste* (2005)

UN Secretary-General, *Guidance Note of the Secretary-General: United Nations Approach to Rule of Law Assistance* (April 2008)

Guidance Note of the Secretary-General: United Nations Assistance to Constitution-Making Processes (April 2009)

In Larger Freedom: Towards Development, Security and Human Rights For All, Report of the Secretary General, UN Doc A/59/2005 (2005)

Report of the Secretary General on the Rule of Law and Transitional Justice in Conflict and Post-Conflict Societies, UN Doc S/2004/616 (23 August 2004)

Report of the Secretary General on the Rule of Law and Transitional Justice in Conflict and Post-Conflict Societies, UN Doc S/2011/634 (12 October 2011)

Report of the Secretary General – Strengthening and Coordinating United Nations Rule of Law Activities, UN Doc A/66/133 (8 August 2011)

Uniting our Strengths: Enhancing United Nations Support for the Rule of Law, Report of the UN Secretary-General, UN Doc A/61/636-S/2006/980 (14 December 2006)

UN Transitional Administration in East Timor, Constitutional Affairs Branch, Office of Political Affairs, *Executive Summary of the Constitutional Commission Public Hearings* (September 2001)

UN Women, *Progress of the World's Women 2011–2012: In Pursuit of Justice* (2011)

UN Women/UNICEF/UNDP, *Informal Justice Systems: Charting a Course for Human Rights-Based Engagement* (September 2012)

United Nations, *Report of the Panel on United Nations Peace Operations*, UN Doc A/55/305-S/2000/809 (21 August 2000)

United Nations and Boutros Boutros-Ghali, *The United Nations and Apartheid, 1948–1994* (1994)

Upham, Frank, 'Mythmaking in the Rule-of-Law Orthodoxy' in Thomas Carothers (ed.), *Promoting the Rule of Law Abroad: In Search of Knowledge* (Washington, DC: Carnegie Endowment for International Peace, 2006) 75

Urresta, Edwin and Rod Nixon, *Report on Research Findings and Policy Recommendations for a Legal Framework for Land Dispute Mediation* (Timor-Leste Land Law Program, 2004)

USAID, *Afghanistan Rule of Law Project: Field Study of Informal and Customary Justice in Afghanistan and Recommendations on Improving Access to Justice and Relations Between Formal Court and Informal Bodies* (2005)

Afghanistan Rule of Law Stabilization (Informal Component) Assessment (2011)

Alternative Dispute Resolution: Practitioners' Guide (March 1998)

At Freedom's Frontiers: A Democracy and Governance Strategic Framework (2005)

Fostering Justice in Timor-Leste: Rule of Law Program Evaluation (January 2009)

Guide to Rule of Law Country Analysis: The Rule of Law Strategic Framework – A Guide for USAID Democracy and Governance Officers (January 2010)

Legal Empowerment and Access of Women to Justice Assessment (2008)

The Crisis in Timor-Leste: Causes, Consequences and Options for Conflict Management and Mitigation (12 November 2006)

Freedom House and American Bar Association Rule of Law Initiative, *The Rule of Law in Timor-Leste* (June 2007)

USAID and US Department of State, *Strategic Plan: Fiscal Years 2007–2012 – Transformational Diplomacy* (2007)

US Department of State, *Afghanistan and Pakistan Regional Stabilization Strategy* (January 2010)

Van Binsbergen, Wim (ed.), *The Dynamics of Power and the Rule of Law: Essays on Africa and Beyond* (Munster: Lit Verlag, 2003)

Van der Vyer, J. D., 'Human Rights Aspects of the Dual System Applying to Blacks in South Africa' (1982) XV *Comparative and International Law Journal of Southern Africa* 306

van Niekerk, Gardiol J., 'Indigenous Law and Narrative: Rethinking Methodology' (1999) XXXII *Comparative and International Law Journal of Southern Africa* 208

'Indigenous Law, Public Policy and Narrative in the Courts' (2000) *Tydskrif vir Hedendaagse Romeins-Hollandse Reg* 403

'Legal Pluralism' in J. C. Bekker, Christa Rautenbach and N. M. I. Goolam (eds.), *Introduction to Legal Pluralism* (Durban: LexisNexis Butterworths, 2nd edn, 2006) 3

'Succession, Living Indigenous Law and *Ubuntu* in the Constitutional Court' (2005) 26 *Obiter* 474

Van Wouden, F. A. E., *Types of Social Structure in Eastern Indonesia* (The Hague: Nijhoff, Rodney Needham trans., 1968 edn)

Van Wyck, John Dugard, Bertus de Villiers and Dennis Davis (eds.), *Rights and Constitutionalism: The New South African Legal Order* (Oxford: Clarendon, 1996)

Venter, Francois, 'The Withering of the "Rule of Law"' (1973) 8 *Speculum Juris* 69

Verhelst, Thierry, *Safeguarding African Customary Law: Judicial and Legislative Processes for Its Adaptation and Integration*, Occasional Paper, No 7 (1968)

Villa-Vicencio, Charles, 'Whither South Africa? Constitutionalism and Law-Making' (1991) 40 *Emory Law Journal* 141

Von Bogdandy, Armin, Stefan Häußler, Felix Hanschmann and Raphael Utz, 'State-Building, Nation-Building, and Constitutional Politics in Post-Conflict Situations: Conceptual Clarifications and an Appraisal of Different Approaches' (2005) 9 *Max Planck Yearbook of United Nations Law* 579

Waldorf, Lars, '"Like Jews waiting for Jesus": Posthumous Justice in Post-Genocide Rwanda' in Rosalind Shaw, Lars Waldorf and Pierre Hazan, *Localizing Transitional Justice* (Stanford University Press, 2010) 183

Waldron, Jeremy, 'Is the Rule of Law an Essentially Contested Concept (in Florida)?' (2002) 21 *Law and Philosophy* 137

'The Rule of Law in Contemporary Liberal Theory' (1989) 2 *Ratio Juris* 79

Walker, Neil, 'The Idea of Constitutional Pluralism' (2002) 65 *Modern Law Review* 317

Wardak, Ali, 'Building a Post-War Justice System in Afghanistan' (2004) 41 *Crime, Law and Social Change* 319

Waylen, Georgina, 'Constitutional Engineering: What Opportunities for the Enhancement of Gender Rights?' (2006) 27 *Third World Quarterly* 1209

Weber, M., *The Theory of Social and Economic Organization* (New York, NY: Free Press, 1947)

Wesley-Smith, Peter, 'Cultural Diversity and the Law in East Timor' in Marie-Claire Foblets, Jean-François Gaudreault-DesBiens and Alison Dundes Renteln (eds.), *Cultural Diversity and the Law: State Responses from Around the World* (Brussels: Bruylant, 2010)

West, Robin, *Re-Imagining Justice: Progressive Interpretations of Formal Equality, Rights and the Rule of Law* (Aldershot: Ashgate, 2003)

Wet, Ronald A., 'Lawyers, Guns and Money: Justice and Security Reform in East Timor' in Charles T. Gall (ed.), *Constructing Justice and Security After War* (Washington, DC: United States Institute of Peace, 2007) 313

White, Nigel D., 'Towards a Strategy for Human Rights Protection in Post-Conflict Situations' in Nigel White and Dirk Klaasen (eds.), *The United Nations, Human Rights and Post-Conflict Situations* (Manchester University Press, 2005) 463

Whitson, Sarah Leah, 'Neither Fish, nor Flesh, Nor Good Red Herring. *Lok Adalats*: An Experiment in Informal Dispute Resolution in India' (1992) 15 *Hastings International and Comparative Law Review* 391

Widner, Jennifer, *Building the Rule of Law* (New York: W. W. Norton, 2001)

'Courts and Democracy in Post-Conflict Transitions: A Social Scientist's Perspective on the African Case' (2001) 95 *American Journal of International Law* 64

Wilde, Ralph, *International Territorial Administration: How Trusteeship and the Civilizing Mission Never Went Away* (Oxford University Press, 2008)

Williams, George and Devika Hovell, 'A Tale of Two Systems: International Law in Constitutional Interpretation in Australia and South Africa' (2005) 29 *Melbourne University Law Review* 95

Wilson, Richard A., *The Politics of Truth and Reconciliation in South Africa: Legitimizing the Post-Apartheid State* (Cambridge University Press, 2001)

Wojkowska, Ewa, *Doing Justice: How Informal Justice Systems Can Contribute* (December 2006) (Report for UNDP and the Oslo Governance Centre)

Wolfensohn, James, *A Proposal for a Comprehensive Development Framework* (May 1999)

Women's Legal Centre, *Recognition of Customary Marriages* (Cape Town: Women's Legal Centre, 2011)

Woodman, Gordon R., 'Legal Pluralism and the Search for Justice' (1996) 40 *Journal of African Law* 152

World Bank, *Doing Business Report for 2012* (2012)

Land Policies for Growth and Poverty Reduction, World Bank Policy Research Report (2003)

Land Reform: Sector Policy Paper (1975)

Legal Vice Presidency, Legal and Judicial Reform Observations, Experiences and Approach of the Legal Vice Presidency (2002)

Strengthening the Institutions of Governance in Timor-Leste (April 2006)

Sub-Saharan Africa: From Crisis to Sustainable Growth – A Longterm Perspective Study (1989)

World Development Report 2011: Conflict, Security and Development (2011)

World Development Report 2012: Gender Equality and Development (2012)

World Bank Group, *Timor-Leste Country Program Evaluation 2000–2010* (May 2011)

World Bank Group and Asian Development Bank, *Economic and Social Development Brief* (August 2007)

Wright, Jesse, 'Freedom to Kill in East Timor', *Asia Times*, 25 June 2008

Yasuaki, Onuma, 'In Quest of Intercivilizational Human Rights: "Universal" vs "Relative" Human Rights Viewed from an Asian Perspective' (2000) 1 *Asia-Pacific Journal on Human Rights* 53

Yoder, Laura Meitzner, *Custom, Codification, Collaboration: Integrating the Legacies of land and Forest Authorities in Oecusse Enclave, East Timor* (DPhil Thesis, Yale University, 2005)

Zaum, Dominik, *The Sovereignty Paradox: The Norms and Politics of International Statebuilding* (Oxford University Press, 2007)

Zifcak, Spencer, 'Combining Community Reconciliation and Local Justice: A Modest Proposal for Reform' in William Binchy (ed.), *Timor-Leste: Challenges for Justice and Human Rights in the Shadow of the Past* (Dublin: Clarus Press, 2009)

(ed.), *Globalisation and the Rule of Law* (New York, NY: Routledge, 2005)

INDEX